Petroleum and Progress in Iran

From the 1940s to 1960s, Iran developed into the world's first "petro-state," where oil represented the bulk of state revenue and supported an industrializing economy, expanding middle class, and powerful administrative and military apparatus. Drawing on both American and Iranian sources, Gregory Brew explores how the Pahlavi petro-state emerged from a confluence of forces – some global, some local. He shows how the shah's particular form of oil-based authoritarianism evolved from interactions with American developmentalists, Pahlavi technocrats, and major oil companies, all against the looming backdrop of the United States' Cold War policy and the coup d'état of August 1953. By placing oil at the center of the Cold War narrative, Brew contextualizes Iran's slide into petrolic authoritarianism within its relationship to international oil, the global development movement, and the United States. Synthesizing a wide range of sources and research methods, this book demonstrates that the Pahlavi petro-state was not born but made, and not solely by the Pahlavi shah.

Gregory Brew is a Kissinger Visiting Fellow at the Jackson School of Global Affairs at Yale University. He is a historian of modern Iran, the Cold War, and international oil. He has written extensively on contemporary issues of energy and geopolitics, and his work has appeared in *Iranian Studies*, the *International History Review*, and the *Texas National Security Review*.

Petroleum and Progress in Iran

Oil, Development, and the Cold War

Gregory Brew
Yale University

CAMBRIDGE UNIVERSITY PRESS

CAMBRIDGE
UNIVERSITY PRESS

Shaftesbury Road, Cambridge CB2 8EA, United Kingdom

One Liberty Plaza, 20th Floor, New York, NY 10006, USA

477 Williamstown Road, Port Melbourne, VIC 3207, Australia

314–321, 3rd Floor, Plot 3, Splendor Forum, Jasola District Centre, New Delhi – 110025, India

103 Penang Road, #05-06/07, Visioncrest Commercial, Singapore 238467

Cambridge University Press is part of Cambridge University Press & Assessment, a department of the University of Cambridge.

We share the University's mission to contribute to society through the pursuit of education, learning and research at the highest international levels of excellence.

www.cambridge.org
Information on this title: www.cambridge.org/9781009206341

DOI: 10.1017/9781009206327

© Gregory Brew 2022

This publication is in copyright. Subject to statutory exception and to the provisions of relevant collective licensing agreements, no reproduction of any part may take place without the written permission of Cambridge University Press & Assessment.

First published 2022

A catalogue record for this publication is available from the British Library.

ISBN 978-1-009-20634-1 Hardback

Cambridge University Press & Assessment has no responsibility for the persistence or accuracy of URLs for external or third-party internet websites referred to in this publication and does not guarantee that any content on such websites is, or will remain, accurate or appropriate.

To Megan and Margot

Contents

List of Figures	*page* ix
Acknowledgments	x
Note on Transliteration	xii
List of Abbreviations	xiii

Introduction		1
0.1	"A Modern Major General"	1
0.2	The Dual Integration of Oil	5
0.3	Themes and Structure	10

Part I

1	**Iran, Global Oil, and the United States, 1901–1947**	21
1.1	Oil Imperialism and Petro-Nationalism	23
1.2	"A Bird That Lost Its Feathers": Oil and Pahlavi Iran, 1921–1941	29
1.3	Occupation, "Incapacity," and Expertise: American Advisors in Iran, 1941–1945	33
1.4	Oil, Iran, and the Cold War	41
1.5	The Dual Integration of Iranian Oil	48
1.6	Conclusion	51
2	**"We Have Done Nothing": The Seven-Year Plan and the Failure of Dual Integration in Iran, 1947–1951**	53
2.1	Development in Iran	55
2.2	"Know-How": The World Bank, Max Thornburg, and the Plan, 1947–1949	61
2.3	Paying for the Plan: AIOC and Iran, 1946–1949	68
2.4	The Collapse of Dual Integration, July 1949–March 1951	77
2.5	Conclusion	82
3	**The Mosaddeq Challenge: Nationalization and the Isolation of Iranian Oil, 1951–1952**	86
3.1	Mosaddeq and "Nationalization"	88
3.2	Defining Nationalization: Negotiations, June 1951–March 1952	97

Contents

    3.3 Embargo: Iran's De-integration and the Myth of Iranian Incapacity ... 107
    3.4 Conclusion ... 116

4 The Collapse Narrative: The Coup and the Reintegration of Iranian Oil, 1952–1954 ... 118
    4.1 "Oil-Less" Economics ... 120
    4.2 Judging Collapse: Analyzing the Oil-Less Economy ... 128
    4.3 Making the Coup Decision, August 1952–March 1953 ... 135
    4.4 Settling Accounts ... 141
    4.5 Conclusion ... 147

Part II

5 The Petrochemical Paradise: Oil-Driven Development and the Second Plan, 1954–1963 ... 151
    5.1 After AJAX: Pahlavi Power Post-coup ... 153
    5.2 Modernization Theory, Ebtehaj, and the Second Plan ... 157
    5.3 "A Pioneering Kind of Pattern": Lilienthal, Clapp, and the KDS ... 162
    5.4 Scapegoat: The Shah Turns on the Second Plan, 1958–1962 ... 172
    5.5 Conclusion ... 178

6 The Golden Goose: Iran, the Consortium, and the First OPEC Crisis, 1954–1965 ... 182
    6.1 The Golden Age: The Mechanics of the Oligopoly, 1954–1960 ... 184
    6.2 Iran, the Consortium, and Performative Petro-Nationalism, 1954–1960 ... 191
    6.3 The Scholar and the "Wild Men" ... 197
    6.4 Conciliation or Conflict: Oil Negotiations, 1962–1963 ... 200
    6.5 Sabotage: Fallah's Intervention ... 206
    6.6 Conclusion ... 211

7 Controlled Revolution: Expertise, Economics, and the American View of Iran, 1960–1965 ... 214
    7.1 "The Harvard Boys": The Economic Bureau and the Financial Crisis of 1960 ... 216
    7.2 The Kennedy Administration and the Amini Experiment ... 222
    7.3 "A Revolutionary Monarch" ... 232
    7.4 The End of Development? ... 240

Epilogue ... 246
    E.1 Unthinkable ... 246
    E.2 Tragedy ... 249

Bibliography ... 253
Index ... 270

Figures

0.1	Mohammed Reza Pahlavi, the shah of Iran	*page* 2
0.2	Map of Iran's petroleum resources, 1956	3
1.1	Pipelines running through Khuzestan, Iran's oil province, 1950	25
2.1	The First Plan: expenditures and funding (billion rials)	60
2.2	Aerial view of Abadan, the world's largest refinery, 1950	69
2.3	Share of Middle East production, 1950 (barrels per day)	70
2.4	Iran oil production, British taxes, and royalty payments, 1932–1950	73
3.1	Mohammed Mosaddeq (middle) with Ambassador Henry F. Grady (left), 1951	89
3.2	Middle East production, 1945–1952	114
4.1	AIOC contribution, 1951–1952 (estimated)	130
5.1	US aid to Iran and total Iran government spending (million $)	153
5.2	Iran's expenditures and revenues (billion rials), 1955–1961	159
5.3	Gordon R. Clapp (first on left) at a build site, 1953	165
5.4	Artist's rendition of the Dez Dam, 1958	167
5.5	Total Second Plan spending (million $)	180
6.1	European oil consumption (thousand bpd)	185
6.2	Revenues from oil (million $), 1948–1960	187
6.3	Royalty expense compromise, 1964	210
7.1	The shah with President John F. Kennedy (middle) and Secretary of Defense Robert S. McNamara (right), 1962	223
7.2	Comparison of Second and Third Plans (billion rials)	227

Acknowledgments

This book began in 2014 as a dissertation at Georgetown University on the international history of Iranian oil. It then evolved over the course of seven years and two separate postdoctoral appointments. I would be remiss if I did not thank the community at Georgetown – where I began as a wide-eyed master's student in 2011 – for all their help and support. This includes my dissertation committee members Aviel Roshwald and Joseph Sassoon, and my friends and colleagues Ben Feldman, Abby Holekamp, Cory Young, Tom Foley, Paul K. Adler, Eric Gettig, Oliver Horn, Graham Pitts, Nick Danforth, Alex Finn MacArtney, and Chad Frazier. A special thanks is owed to Nathan J. Citino, who served as outside reader on my dissertation committee, and to my friend, collaborator, and mentor David S. Painter, who first encouraged me to pursue a PhD in history and has been a source of guidance and inspiration throughout my career.

Two years at Southern Methodist University granted me the time and resources necessary to revise the dissertation into a book. Additional work on the manuscript occurred while I served as deputy managing editor of *Texas National Security Review*, and final changes were made shortly after I began a postdoctoral fellowship at the Jackson School of Global Affairs at Yale University in 2021. I benefited from the advice and support of Jeffrey Engel, director of the Center for Presidential History. Special thanks to Hervey Priddy, Brian Franklin, Ronna Spitz, LaiYee Leong, Sabri Ates, and Thomas J. Knock, and to postdoctoral fellows Elizabeth Ingleson, Lindsay Chervinsky, Blake Earle, Kaete O'Connell, Sharron Conrad, and Amanda Regan for their friendship and support. A manuscript workshop in late 2019 benefited from comments and suggestions from Christopher Dietrich and Mark J. Gasiorowski. I would also like to thank Ryan Evans and Doyle Hodges for teaching me how to be a better writer (and editor), and Ted Wittenstein, Mike Brenes, and Odd Arne Westad at Yale University.

Some of the key ideas and concepts in this book were presented at the conferences of the Society for Historians of American Foreign Relations,

Acknowledgments

the Middle East Studies Association, and the Association of Iranian Studies. I'd like to thank colleagues, friends, and countless others who offered feedback, comments, and suggestions, particularly Roham Alvandi, Mattin Biglari, Touraj Atabaki, Rasmus Christian Elling, Nelida Fuccaro, Arash Azizi, Mary Ann Heiss, Malcolm Byrne, Anand Toprani, Victor McFarland, Brandon Wolfe-Hunnicutt, Karine Walther, Siavush Randjbar-Daemi, and Eskandar Sadeghi-Boroujerdi. Special thanks go to Peter Housego and Joanne Burman of the BP Archive, Patricia Rosenfield of the Rockefeller Archive Center, as well as the staff of the US National Archives at College Park, Maryland, and the National Archives of the United Kingdom at Kew Gardens, London. Thanks to Varsha Venkatasubramanian for drafting the Index. A particular debt is owed to Atifa Jiwa, Maria Marsh, and Rachel Imbrie at Cambridge University Press, and my two peer reviewers. Finally, I must thank my family – my parents, Peter and Maura, and my wife, Megan – for years of patient support and friendship.

Note on Transliteration

Persian names are transliterated into English according to the system used by the Library of Congress. For ease of reading, diacritical marks have been removed and spellings rendered in the form most frequently used in English-language publications: "Khudādād Farmānfarmā'iyān" becomes "Khodadad Farmanfarmaian," for example.

Abbreviations

AIOC/ APOC	Anglo-Iranian Oil Company Anglo-Persian Oil Company
BP	British Petroleum (BP Archives) Coventry, UK
DDEPL	Dwight D. Eisenhower Presidential Library
DELP	David E. Lilienthal Papers
DRCR	Development and Resources Corporation Records
FDRPL	Franklin D. Roosevelt Presidential Library, Poughkeepsie, New York
FIS	Foundation for Iranian Studies
FISDS	Foundation for Iranian Studies, Development Series
FO	Records of the Foreign Office
FPSC	Foreign Petroleum Supply Committee
FRUS	Foreign Relations of the United States
HAG	Harvard Advisory Group
HIOHP	Harvard Iranian Oral History Project
HSTPL	Harry S. Truman Presidential Library, Independence, Missouri
JFKPL	John F. Kennedy Presidential Library, Boston, Massachusetts
KDS	Khuzestan Development Service
LBJPL	Lyndon B. Johnson Presidential Library, Austin, Texas
MKI	Morrison & Knudsen Inc.
NIOC	National Iranian Oil Company
OCI	Overseas Consultants Inc.
OPEC	Organization of the Petroleum Exporting Countries
PAD	Petroleum Administration for Defense
RAC	Rockefeller Archive Center, Tarrytown, New York
RG	Record Group (National Archives and Records Administration)

RUSFAA	Records of US Foreign Assistance Agencies
SGMML	Seeley G. Mudd Manuscript Library, Princeton University
UKNA	United Kingdom National Archives, Kew Gardens, London, UK
USLETCGR	US Legation and Embassy, Tehran, Classified General Records
USNA	US National Archives, College Park, Maryland
WBGA	World Bank Group Archives

Introduction

0.1 "A Modern Major General"

It was May 1964 and Hossein Mahdavy had run out of patience. The Iranian economist, known by his colleagues as a brilliant though hot-headed nationalist, held a high-ranking position in Iran's esteemed Economic Bureau. He worked alongside economists, budget analysts, and statisticians – Iran's best and brightest – to prepare a development program, the Third Plan, budgeted at $1 billion. The plan would tap Iran's oil revenues, a stream of wealth worth $400 million per year, to kick-start the economy and stabilize the regime of Iran's shah, Mohammed Reza Pahlavi (Figure 0.1). The bureau received help from a team of American advisors, sent to Iran with the backing of the Kennedy administration, which worried about the shah's shaky grip on power. Mahdavy and his colleagues toiled away at the Third Plan under the watchful eye of American developmentalists who regarded the final plan outline as "the best drafted piece of legislation" in Iran's modern history.[1] The plan was a blueprint for Iran's future, and like many educated Iranians, Mahdavy hoped that future would include a transition away from authoritarianism toward liberal secular democracy. In May 1961, under US pressure, the shah appointed a reformer prime minister. In January 1962, he approved the Third Plan.

But within months, to Mahdavy's dismay, Iran's monarch changed course. In July 1962, the shah pushed out his prime minister and marginalized the Economic Bureau. Instead of the Third Plan, he launched the "White Revolution," a campaign centered on land distribution for Iran's peasants. A political maneuver disguised as a reform movement, the White Revolution destroyed or co-opted what was left of Iran's traditional elite and middle-class opposition, cementing the shah's status as Iran's unquestioned ruler.[2]

---

[1] McLeod to Mason, February 17, 1962, FFR R-0813, RAC.
[2] Ali M. Ansari, "The Myth of the White Revolution: Mohammed Reza Shah, 'Modernization' and the Consolidation of Power," *Middle East Studies* 37 (2001): 1–24.

Figure 0.1 Mohammed Reza Pahlavi, the shah of Iran.
Photo from 1962. US News & World Report magazine photograph collection, Library of Congress

The United States, though skeptical of the White Revolution's economic potential, regarded the shah's political consolidation as a smashing success. In August 1953, the Central Intelligence Agency (CIA) had helped put the shah in power through a covert coup d'état. Ten years later, the move seemed to have paid off. "We created a modern revolutionary monarch," noted Kennedy administration official Robert Komer in October 1964, "from the very model of a modern major general."[3] In the wake of the White Revolution, the shah emerged as a poster child for US-backed modernization, where human rights' violations and political repression were papered over by high GDP growth, rising literacy, and a booming middle class. By the end of the decade, the shah was arguably the most important US ally between Bonn and Tokyo.[4]

[3] Robert W. Komer Oral History Interview, JFK #4, October 31, 1964, Papers of John F. Kennedy, Presidential Papers, NSF, JFKPL.
[4] Roham Alvandi, *Nixon, Kissinger and the Shah: The United States and Iran in the Cold War* (New York: Oxford University Press, 2014), 28–64.

0.1 "A Modern Major General"

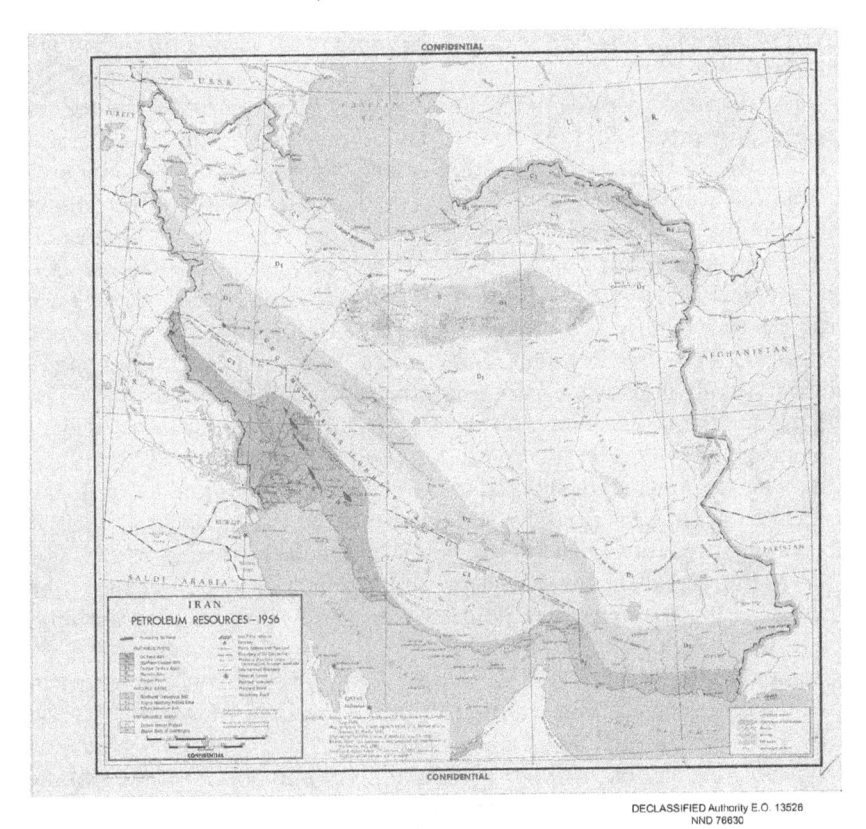

Figure 0.2 Map of Iran's petroleum resources, 1956.
RG 263, Records of the Central Intelligence Agency, NARA

As with the Third Plan, the secret to the shah's success could be summed up in one word: oil. Between 1960 and 1970, Iranian production rose from 1.05 million barrels per day (bpd) to 3.82 million bpd (Figure 0.2). Revenues from the production of Iranian oil rose steadily after the coup of 1953 and reached $1 billion by 1970.[5] For US policymakers, it did not matter that the shah's economic reform program was defined by "hazy, inconclusive gesture[s]," or that he had tossed aside his experts in the Economic Bureau.[6] What mattered was that

---

[5] Degolyer and MacNaughton, *Twentieth Century Petroleum Statistics* (Dallas, TX: 1984), 9; *FRUS 1964–1968, XXII*: 28–29.
[6] Memo for Komer, May 7, 1963, Robert W. Komer Papers, Box 424, JFKPL.

Iran's future appeared secure, so long as oil (and oil wealth) continued to flow.

The Economic Bureau, meanwhile, was forgotten. Most chose to resign, frustrated with the course of the country's development program, "as it was turned into a political tool of the shah."[7] The bureau's American allies were equally disheartened. While the White Revolution secured the shah's power and ostensibly liberated the peasant population from the tyranny of feudal landlords, without planned and organized development the future of the shah's government looked grim, since his reforms had yet to deliver any substantive improvements to most Iranians. "Pressures from the rural element," wrote one Ford Foundation officer, "will ultimately ... force a basic change in government."[8] The shah's program, according to Kennedy advisor Kenneth Hansen, "[failed] to engage directly with the crucial problems of economic development ... the basis for political stability." If the United States supported the shah and sidelined the more progressive and democratic forces within Iran, it risked becoming irrevocably tied "to a regime whose policies are characterized by short-term expediency and neglect of ... the increased well-being of the people."[9] In the euphoric response to the shah's reforms, these warnings went unnoticed.

Mahdavy left government service in 1964 and spent the remainder of the decade working for the anti-shah Iranian student movement. Yet he never fully abandoned his former vocation. In 1970, the economist penned a chapter for an obscure volume on the economic history of the Middle East. Amid the charts and figures, Mahdavy dropped a bombshell. The shah's policies, he argued, were unsustainable. And oil was the problem. Financially independent, the Pahlavi state had no need for a popular mandate, as it could rule through the financial power conferred by oil. If the flow ever slowed, the state's basis in legitimacy would weaken and the forces working to destabilize his government – rural poverty, urban dissatisfaction, the suppression of democracy, the dominance of a corrupt minority, and the centralization of power around a single, fallible ruler – would return. In time, Iran would collapse into social and economic upheaval, possibly even revolution. Mahdavy coined a new term to describe his nation: Iran had now become a "rentier state."[10]

---

[7] HIOHP, Muqaddam, Tape No. 3, 1–2
[8] "Final Report on Iran: A Possible Basis for Re-Entry," July 11, 1964, FFR R-0814, RAC.
[9] Memo for Komer, May 7, 1963, Robert W. Komer Papers, Box 424, JFKPL.
[10] Hossein Mahdavy, "The Patterns and Problems of Economic Development in Rentier States: the Case of Iran," in *Studies in the Economic History of the Middle East: From the Rise of Islam to the Present Day*, ed. M.A. Cook (London: U.P., 1970), 443–467.

His prediction was proven true in 1979. The shah's outwardly imposing regime collapsed amid economic crisis, social upheaval, and revolution. Oil laid the foundation for the success of the Pahlavi state. Oil also proved fundamental to that state's end. Yet the mere existence of oil did not render such an outcome inevitable. The shah's petro-state, a creation credited to his own breathless ambition, did not spring fully formed into being. Nor was it conjured through the machinations of Western oil companies or the imperial interference of the shah's superpower benefactor, the United States of America. Rather, the Pahlavi petro-state emerged from a confluence of global and local forces, driven by foreign and domestic actors, that came together in the twenty-five years before the White Revolution and the shah's consolidation of political power. The formation of the shah's government was inextricably linked to the birth of the global fossil fuel economy, the Cold War policies of the United States, and the international development movement. Its birth marked the creation of a new political formation, one characterized by fossil fuel extraction and authoritarian militarism that would come to dominate the oil-producing world and link the global movement of oil to the local application of oil wealth. To understand the nature of the original rentier state, it is necessary to explore the history of the dual integration of Iranian oil.

0.2 The Dual Integration of Oil

"Don't talk to me about barrels of oil," Henry Kissinger allegedly told his staff, "they might as well be bottles of Coca-Cola."[11] His frustration is understandable: Oil is not always the easiest thing to grasp. The most valuable traded commodity on earth, in terms of sheer volume, oil's consumption forms the foundation for modern industrial society. Machines are lubricated, engines powered, homes heated, and crops nourished by products derived from oil and natural gas. In popular discourse, oil is synonymous with wealth and the struggle for power. It is, to paraphrase Sir Winston Churchill, "a prize from fairyland," which once discovered guarantees prosperity.[12] The promise of riches then produces conflict. Nations, it is believed, go to war over oil.[13]

---

[11] Quoted in Daniel Yergin, *The Prize: The Epic Quest for Oil, Money and Power* (New York: Simon and Schuster, 1991), 595.

[12] Timothy Mitchell, *Carbon Democracy: Political Power in the Age of Oil* (New York: Verso, 2011), 60.

[13] Emily Meierding, *The Oil Wars Myth: Petroleum and the Causes of International Conflict* (Ithaca, NY: Cornell University Press, 2020); Toby Jones, "America, Oil and War in the Middle East," *Journal of American History* 99, no. 1 (June 2012): 208–218.

The production and consumption of fossil fuels has made modern life possible while planting the seeds of calamitous alterations in global climate that threaten to displace millions and radically restructure social, geographic, economic, and political boundaries.[14] Oil conjures ideas of freedom and images of excess, of life and death. It is both a blessing and a curse.[15]

Drawing on Mahdavy's rentier state thesis, the study of oil has generated a school of thought centered on the concept of the resource curse. Once capital investment is recouped, oil can be produced cheaply, resulting in large profits. States that enjoy high returns from oil sales can govern without resorting to taxation, freeing them from popular pressures while leaving them vulnerable to oil's volatile boom-and-bust cycle.[16] This produces a contradiction, "the paradox of plenty," in social scientist Terry Lynn Karl's formulation, where the runaway success of the energy export sector depresses economic growth, resulting in uneven development or the so-called Dutch Disease.[17] Petro-states – nations which depend upon oil's production and sale for a disproportionate share of government revenue, export value, and GDP – are susceptible to corruption, repression, and political instability.[18] One line of reasoning contends that oil produces the conditions for authoritarian government while suppressing democracy, though this ignores those states – including the United States of America, far and away the most prolific petroleum producer in history – which have not (yet) devolved into centralized autocracies.[19]

---

[14] Bryan Lovell, *Challenged by Carbon: The Oil Industry and Climate Change* (Cambridge: Cambridge University Press, 2011), 67–90.

[15] Mitchell, *Carbon Democracy*, 1–7, Matthew Huber, *Lifeblood: Oil, Freedom and the Forces of Capital* (Minneapolis, MN: Minnesota University Press, 2013), xv–xviii.

[16] A sample of the resource curse literature includes Alan Gelb, *Oil Windfalls: Blessing or Curse?* (New York: Oxford University Press, 1989), Michael Ross, *The Oil Curse: How Petroleum Shapes the Development of Nations* (Princeton, NJ: Princeton University Press, 2013), Hossein Askari, *Middle East Oil Exporters: What Happened to Economic Development?* (Cheltenham, UK: Edward Elgar Publishing, 2006).

[17] Terry Lynn Karl, *Paradox of Plenty: Oil Booms and Petro States* (Berkeley, CA: University of California Press, 1997).

[18] Ross, *The Oil Curse*, 1–26, Askari, *Middle East Oil Exporters*, 5; Hazem Beblawi and Giacomo Luciani, eds., *The Rentier State* (New York: Croon Helm, 1987), Daron Acemoglu and James A. Robinson, *Why Nations Fail: the Origins of Power, Prosperity and Poverty* (New York: Crown Publishers, 2012), Kiren Aziz Chaudhry, "Economic Liberalization and the Lineages of the Rentier State," *Comparative Politics* 27, no. 1 (Oct. 1994): 1–25.

[19] The political scientist Samuel Huntington famously deployed this argument while explaining the failure of democracy to spread in the Middle East. See Huntington, *The Third Wave: Democratisation in the Late Twentieth Century* (Norman, OK: University of Oklahoma Press, 1991), 65.

0.2 The Dual Integration of Oil

The argument that oil is "cursed" tends to fixate on local circumstances, finding blame for the misappropriation of oil wealth "in the decision-making organs of the individual producer states," according to social scientist Timothy Mitchell.[20] This framing elides or ignores the global history of oil, particularly the origins of the international oil industry and the efforts undertaken by a small group of Western oil corporations to extend private control over oil deposits in the Global South during the first three-quarters of the twentieth century.[21] These companies, known as the "Seven Sisters," were important actors during the global Cold War, assisting the British and US governments and facilitating the flow of oil in service of Western strategic objectives.[22] Yet the impact of oil capital's activities range far beyond the Cold War frame. Taking cues from the work of political scientist Robert Vitalis, scholars have drawn on company records to explore how international forces helped shape local oil-producing communities.[23] Recent scholarship emphasizes a broad swathe of ecological, social, cultural, and political impacts derived from the development of oil.[24] Foreign-owned oil

---

[20] Mitchell, *Carbon Democracy*, 5.
[21] Peter F. Cowhey, *The Problems of Plenty: Energy Policy and International Politics* (Berkeley, CA: University of California Press, 1985), Edith Penrose, *The Large International Firm in Developing Countries: The International Petroleum Industry* (London: Allen and Unwin, 1968), John Blair, *The Control of Oil* (New York: Pantheon Books, 1976), Neil H. Jacoby, *Multinational Oil: A Study in Industrial Dynamics* (New York: Macmillan, 1974), Anthony Sampson, *The Seven Sisters: The Great Oil Companies and the World They Shaped* (New York: Viking Press, 1975); for Latin America, see George Philip, *Oil and Politics in Latin America: Nationalist Movements and State Companies* (New York: Cambridge University Press, 1982); for Middle East oil, see Wayne A. Leeman, *The Price of Middle East Oil: An Essay in Political Economy* (Ithaca, NY: Cornell University Press, 1962), Benjamin Shwadran, *The Middle East, Oil and the Great Powers* (New York: Wiley, 1974), George W. Stocking, *Middle East Oil: A Study in Political and Economic Controversy* (Nashville, TN: Vanderbilt University Press, 1970).
[22] David S. Painter, *Oil and the American Century: The Political Economy of U.S. Foreign Oil Policy, 1941–1954* (Baltimore MD: Johns Hopkins University Press, 1986), Aaron David Miller, *Search for Security: Saudi Arabian Oil and American Foreign Policy, 1939–1949* (Chapel Hill, NC: University of North Carolina Press, 1980), Nathan J. Citino, *From Arab Nationalism to OPEC: Eisenhower, King Saud and the Making of U.S.-Saudi Relations*, 2nd Edition (Bloomington, IN: Indiana University Press, 2005).
[23] Robert Vitalis, *America's Kingdom: Mythmaking on the Saudi Oil Frontier* (New York: Verso, 2009), Arbella Bet-Shlimon, *City of Black Gold: Oil, Ethnicity and the Making of Modern Kirkuk* (Stanford, CA: Stanford University Press, 2019), Nelida Fuccaro, "Structural and Physical Violence in Saudi Arabian Oil Towns, 1953–1956," in *Urban Violence in the Middle East: Changing Cityscapes in the Transformation from Empire to Nation-State*, eds. Ulrike Freitag, Nelida Fuccaro, Claudia Ghrawi and Nora Lafi (New York: Berghahn Books, 2015), 243–266.
[24] Fernando Coronil, *The Magical State: Nature, Money and Modernity in Venezuela* (Chicago: University of Chicago Press, 1997), Toby Jones, *Desert Kingdom: How Oil and Water Forged Modern Saudi Arabia* (Cambridge, MA: Harvard University Press, 2010), Martin Melosi and Joseph A. Pratt, *Energy Metropolis: An Environmental History*

industries were grounds upon which states could contest terms of sovereignty, challenging the models of dependence that bound the Global South to the Global North during the Cold War era.[25]

In other words, what occurs *locally* – the ways in which oil's wealth is deployed to shape a state, form a society, or develop a national economy – is addressed separately from oil's movement *globally*, where its flow is managed by private corporations and factors into international politics through so-called oil diplomacy and the struggle of oil-producing states against superpower influence and the dominance of fossil fuel capital. This separation obscures the ways in which the local integration of oil wealth depends upon oil's integration into a global network.

Michael Tanzer observed that "the mere fact of foreign ownership automatically involves a country in the complex relationship," which he calls "the political economy of international oil."[26] Viewed through a broader lens, oil loses its simplicity as a "prize" and instead emerges, argues historian Toby Craig Jones, as the foundation for "a set of relations among politics, big business, global capital, labor and scientific expertise."[27] Oil represents more than mere wealth. Its production and movement conveys a promise of material and even spiritual progress, as the inert crude is somehow magically transformed into a vessel for modernity.[28] "Everywhere oil was found," writes historian Darren Dochuk, "people believed it could move them ... into a higher state of civilization."[29] Oil is global, but also local, an expression of international relations and multinational capitalism that has profound effects on the

---

of Houston and the Gulf Coast (Pittsburgh, PA: University of Pittsburgh Press, 2007), Laurie E. Adkin, ed., *First World Petro-Politics: The Political Ecology and Governance of Alberta* (Toronto: University of Toronto Press, 2016), Miguel Tinker Salas, *The Enduring Legacy: Oil, Culture and Society in Venezuela* (Durham: Duke University Press, 2009), David E. Nye, *Consuming Power: A Social History of American Energy* (Cambridge, MA: Harvard University Press, 1998).

[25] Christopher Dietrich, *Oil Revolution: Anticolonial Elites, Sovereign Rights, and the Economic Culture of Decolonization* (Cambridge: Cambridge University Press, 2017), Victor McFarland, *Oil Powers: A History of the U.S.-Saudi Alliance* (New York: Columbia University Press, 2020), Giuliano Garavini, *The Rise and Fall of OPEC in the Twentieth Century* (New York: Oxford University Press, 2019), David M. Wight, *Oil Money: Middle East Petrodollars and the Transformation of US Empire, 1967–1988* (Ithaca, NY: Cornell University Press, 2021).

[26] Michael Tanzer, *The Political Economy of International Oil and the Underdeveloped Countries* (Boston, MA: Beacon Press, 1969), 6.

[27] Jones, *Desert Kingdom*, 13.

[28] Alison Fleig Frank, *Oil Empire: Visions of Prosperity in Austrian Galicia* (Cambridge, MA: Harvard University Press, 2005).

[29] Darren Dochuk, *Anointed with Oil: How Christianity and Crude Made Modern America* (New York: Basic Books, 2019), 82.

landscapes, communities, and polities wherever it is exploited, consumed, or integrated into strategies of economic development.

Petroleum and Progress in Iran merges the local with the global. The chosen context is Iran between 1941 and 1965, years which marked a period of substantive interaction between the Pahlavi government, the major oil companies, and development groups aligned with the United States. Understanding how the Pahlavi regime came to depend on oil, and how oil fits within Iran's complicated relationship with the United States, American NGOs, and private oil companies, requires an approach combining oil's global and local characters: The dual integration of oil, an idea that provides the spine of this book.

The dual integration of oil is the process by which a global oil economy produced oil wealth which was then utilized by oil-producing states for purposes of economic development and state formation. Global and local integration relied on one another. The companies created a global energy network premised on limiting competition and maximizing profits. They did this to enrich themselves, but also to provide stability to a tumultuous energy market that, if left unchecked, would threaten long-term profitability. Operating concessions in the colonial or quasi-colonial states of the Global South, the companies split their oligopoly profits with producing governments, in the hope that it might ameliorate "petro-nationalism," ensuring continued access for the companies and security for Western consumers.[30] Utilizing this wealth, in turn, allowed governments to manage internal unrest, ward off social revolution, and maintain internal cohesion, thereby providing a cushion from which to manage the transitional challenges posed by decolonization.

Both local and global integration served the Cold War strategic interests of the US government. A profitable global oil industry controlled by Western capital ensured access to cheap oil for Western consumers, while the provision of revenues to oil-producing states protected those states from pressures tied (sometimes in reality, more usually in the minds of American officials) to the influence of the Soviet Union. Dual integration was conceived as a Cold War project and occurred in various oil-producing countries between the 1940s and the 1970s. It was not always fully articulated, nor was it ever labeled "dual integration," yet the idea that a nation's place in the global fossil fuel economy provided tools for furthering economic development and thus internal political

---

[30] I use the term "petro-nationalism" to describe the unique form of indigenous nationalist opposition that arises in reaction to the presence of a foreign-owned oil industry. See Garavini, *The Rise and Fall of OPEC*, 39–52.

stability was a salient one throughout the period (1941–1965) under discussion here.

Petroleum and Progress in Iran examines the dual integration of oil in Iran. Its central contention is that Iran's dependence on oil emerged from interactions between American developmentalists, Pahlavi technocrats, and an oligopoly of major oil companies under the aegis of the Cold War policies of the United States. The Pahlavi petro-state was not born. It was made, and not solely by the Pahlavi shah. The global Cold War, together with the modernizing presumptions of American developmentalists and the oligopolistic practices of the major oil companies, produced the context for Iran's slide into the petrolic authoritarianism of the Pahlavi shah.

0.3 Themes and Structure

This book emphasizes three themes. The first concerns US-Iranian relations during the Cold War. For the United States, Iran was a country of strategic importance. It shared a long border with the Soviet Union and straddled the oil-producing regions of the Persian Gulf. After World War II, American policy focused on strengthening the government of Mohammed Reza Pahlavi in the hope of preventing Iran's fall to communism. Successive administrations pursued this goal by encouraging economic development, steering the shah's government toward reforms that would produce lasting political stability, while simultaneously backing the monarchy through financial and military assistance.[31]

Though it has received relatively little attention in the Iranian context, the study of development has experienced a scholarly renaissance since 2000.[32] Practiced within the European empires before 1945,

---

[31] For US relations with Pahlavi Iran, see Mark J. Gasiorowski, *U.S. Foreign Policy and the Shah: Building a Client State in Iran* (Ithaca: Cornell University Press, 1991), James A. Bill, *The Eagle and the Lion: The Tragedy of American-Iranian Relations* (New Haven: Yale University Press, 1988), James F. Goode, *The United States and Iran, 1946–51: the Diplomacy of Neglect* (New York: St. Martin's Press, 1989), and *The United States and Iran: in the Shadow of Musaddiq* (New York: St. Martin's Press, 1997), Richard Cottam, *Iran and the United States: A Cold War Case Study* (Pittsburgh: University of Pittsburgh Press, 1989).

[32] Nick Cullather, "Development? It's History," *Diplomatic History* 24, no. 4 (Fall 2000): 641-653, Sara Lorenzini, *Global Development: A Cold War History* (Princeton, NJ: Princeton University Press, 2019), Odd Arne Westad, *The Global Cold War: Third World Interventions and the Making of Our Times* (New York: Cambridge University Press, 2007), David C. Engerman, Mark H. Haefele, Michael E. Latham, Nils Gilman, eds., *Staging Growth: Modernization, Development and the Global Cold War* (Amherst, MA: University of Massachusetts Press, 2003), Nils Gilman, *Mandarins of the Future: Modernization Theory in Cold War America* (Baltimore, MD: Johns Hopkins

0.3 Themes and Structure

development served to construct, strengthen, or preserve an existing imperial order. In the postwar period, development was a strategy for pushing back against the "alternative modernity" represented by the Soviet Union.[33] Development was also a sphere where local concerns complicated the bipolar frame of the superpower struggle, revealing a geopolitical landscape defined by conflicts beyond the showdown between Washington and Moscow.[34] Though encouraged and occasionally directed by the US or Soviet governments, development processes in the Global South engaged a host of non-state actors. It was a "new style of diplomacy," in the words of historian Nick Cullather, which acted through "the panoply of private and multilateral funding networks … [pitting] transnational coalitions of experts against one another."[35] Examining the American development mission in Iran therefore requires a view encompassing not just the US government but also nongovernment organizations (NGOs) that worked within a Cold War ideological milieu while possessing their own agendas and approaches.

Throughout the 1941–1965 period, American officials and NGOs viewed Iran as an unstable, immature country perpetually teetering on the brink of collapse. This view represented a distinct ideology formed within the context of the American engagement with the Global South during the Cold War. Throughout the developing world, but particularly in the Middle East, American developmentalists deployed racial

---

University Press, 2003), Irene Gendzier, *Managing Political Change: Social Scientists and the Third World* (Boulder, CO: Westview Press, 1985), David Ekbladh, *The Great American Mission: Modernization and the Construction of an American World Order* (Princeton, NJ: Princeton University Press, 2010), Michael E. Latham, *The Right Kind of Revolution: Modernization, Development, and U.S. Foreign Policy from the Cold War to the Present* (Ithaca, NY: Cornell University Press, 2011), Nathan J. Citino, *Envisioning the Arab Future: Modernization in U.S.-Arab Relations, 1945–1967* (Cambridge: Cambridge University Press, 2017). For development in the Iranian context, see Gregory Brew, "'What They Need Is Management:' American NGOs, the Second Seven Year Plan and Economic Development in Iran, 1954–1963," *The International History Review* 44, no. 1 (2019): 1–22, Richard Garlitz, *A Mission for Development: Utah Universities and the Point Four Program in Iran* (Logan, UT: Utah State University Press, 2018); Matthew K. Shannon, *Losing Hearts and Minds: American-Iranian Relations and International Education During the Cold War* (Ithaca, NY: Cornell University Press, 2017).

[33] Westad, *The Global Cold War*, 17; Lorenzini, *Global Development*, 9–21; Cyrus Schayegh, "Imperial and Transnational Developmentalisms: Middle East Interplays, 1880s–1960s," in *The Development Century: A Global History*, eds. Stephen J. Macekura and Erez Manela (New York: Cambridge University Press, 2018), 61–82.

[34] Lorenz Luthi, *Cold Wars: Asia, the Middle East, Europe* (New York: Cambridge University Press, 2020), 2–3; Timothy Nunan, *Humanitarian Invasion: Global Development in Cold War Afghanistan* (New York: Cambridge University Press, 2015).

[35] Nick Cullather, *The Hungry World: America's Cold War Battle against Poverty in Asia* (Cambridge, MA: Harvard University Press, 2011), 5, 6–7.

hierarchies and perceptions of indigenous backwardness.[36] Racially, Iran did not fit neatly into predetermined categories, as Iranians did not consider themselves non-White. Americans nevertheless regarded Iran as part of the Orient and deployed a form of cultural othering that distinguished Iranians from White Anglo-Saxons.[37]

American officials and developmentalists adopted a view that emphasized Iranian incapacity and the need for foreign assistance. "Incapacity" here refers to an inability to manage development processes – a deficit of administrative, operational, and material skill – and assumed the country's oil wealth could not be properly applied, and US Cold War objectives achieved, without American expertise. This view reflects a commitment to what Melani McAlister has termed the US "imperial stewardship" and Megan Black calls "resource primitivism," which contended that US control of oil resources was necessary to ensure they were adequately integrated into the global economy.[38]

Foreign oil companies used arguments of local incapacity to justify their control of oil resources. Similarly, American developmentalists believed that Iran needed oil and could not achieve stability without the financial potential it provided. Developmentalists and their allies in the American embassy in Tehran and in Washington borrowed from the legacy of American missionaries who worked in Iran from the nineteenth century onward: The country appeared in need of salvation, chiefly from the mismanagement of its own leadership class.[39]

Perceptions of Iranian incapacity influenced official US policy and drove a series of interventions into Iranian politics between 1941 and 1965. Historians have noted the US tendency to back authoritarian

---

[36] Michael H. Hunt, *Ideology and U.S. Foreign Policy* (New Haven, CT: Yale University Press, 1987), 1–19, 160, 9–42, Melani McAlister, *Epic Encounters: Culture, Media, & U.S. Interests in the Middle East, 2nd Edition* (Berkeley, CA: University of California Press, 2005), 1–39, Matthew Jacobs, *Imagining the Middle East: the Building of an American Foreign Policy, 1918–1967* (Chapel Hill, NC: The University of North Carolina Press, 2011), 1–22; Zachary Lockman, *Contending Visions of the Middle East: the History and Politics of Orientalism* (New York: Cambridge University Press, 2004), 136.

[37] For a discussion of this racial coding, see Neda Maghbouleh, *The Limits of Whiteness: Iranian Americans and the Everyday Politics of Race* (Stanford, CA: Stanford University Press, 2017), Kelly J. Shannon, "Approaching the Islamic World," *Diplomatic History* 44, no. 3 (June 2020): 387–408.

[38] McAlister, *Epic Encounters*, 154–155; Megan Black, *The Global Interior: Mineral Frontiers and American Power* (Cambridge, MA: Harvard University Press, 2018).

[39] John H. Lorentz, "Educational Development in Iran: The Pivotal Role of the Mission Schools and Alborz College," *Iranian Studies* 44, no. 5 (Sept., 2011): 647–55, Michael P. Zirinsky, "A Panacea for the Ills of the Country: American Presbyterian Education in Interwar Iran," *American Presbyterians*, 72 no. 3 (Fall, 1994): 187–201.

governments during the Cold War.[40] This was the case in Iran. While US officials frequently expressed rhetorical support for democracy, as early as 1946 the unofficial stance of the US government was to support a political order with ties to the military rather than Iran's nascent democratic institutions, which were seen as corrupt, incompetent, unreliable, and vulnerable to communist pressure.[41] Framed as a choice driven by expediency, the decision to back authoritarianism was also guided by American skepticism of Iran's capacity for self-rule. Economic growth and social stability were imagined as preludes to political reform: Development was best directed by a powerful state unimpeded by democratic opposition.

Mohammed Reza Pahlavi was the usual beneficiary of US support. But the period of 1941–1965 found Americans frequently looking for alternatives to the mercurial monarch. The United States and its developmentalist allies were in Iran by invitation, and their agency was constricted by Iran's domestic politics. The shah, his technocratic allies, and other right-wing politicians desired help from the United States, first to bolster Iran against the pressure of other Great Powers and later to support their own state-building projects. While US officials and American developmentalists found willing collaborators among Pahlavi technocrats, they were frequently at odds with their Iranian counterparts over how best to manage the country's oil wealth.

The origins and evolution of the global energy economy forms the second major theme. Oil played a pivotal role in the formation of the US-led postwar international order. However, imagining the companies as proxies or even willing partners of the US government obscures the nature of their relations with one another and with oil-producing states. Before World War II, the companies united to manage the global oil market. By 1946 they had formed an oligopoly, or union of colluding producers. Their operations depended on securing a degree of support from oil-producing states which could, in theory, impose sovereign control over subsoil rights and bar the companies from exploiting oil reserves by nationalizing their oil industries. Exploitation formed a part of this dynamic, but so did cooperation, as the governments accepted revenue in exchange for allowing companies to manage production

---

[40] Westad, *Global Cold War*, 36; Bradley R. Simpson, *Economists with Guns: Authoritarian Development and U.S.-Indonesian Relations, 1960–1968* (Stanford, CA: Stanford University Press, 2008), 3–4.

[41] Habib J. Ladjevardi, "The Origins of US Support for an Autocratic Iran," *International Journal of Middle Eastern Studies* 15, no. 2 (May, 1983): 225–239; David Collier, *Democracy and the Nature of American Influence in Iran, 1941–1979* (Syracuse, NY: Syracuse University Press, 2017).

through agreements, or concessions, that delineated the companies' obligations. Ties of dependence bound elites in oil-producing states and the oligopoly together.[42]

While equitability was important, market power gave the oligopoly the upper hand and served to maintain the imbalance between Western capital and indigenous petro-nationalism throughout the postwar period, until the price revolution and nationalizations of the 1970s.[43] Despite the bonds formed through dual integration, the postwar petroleum order was ultimately coercive and bound to collapse once petro-nationalist pressure grew too great, a state of fragility that was apparent to oil executives as early as the 1930s. Though Iran chafed under the yolk of the oligopoly, the companies' market power proved useful to the Pahlavi government – it is what made the rentier state possible. It was only through the oligopoly's methods of boosting prices, restraining production, and mitigating competition that oil wealth could be maximized, thus serving as an ample support for the shah's development agenda.

That agenda forms the third theme. Born from the dissatisfaction of Iranian elites after the Constitutional Revolution (1906–1911), the Pahlavi regime was self-consciously concerned with strengthening Iran through economic development. For a regime in search of a legitimizing mission, development offered a path forward that was secular, nationalist, technocratic, and centrally organized – a forceful means of tying the nation together and a way for the Pahlavi monarchy to subordinate the nation's aristocracy, Shi'a clerical class, traditional middle class, intelligentsia, and industrial working class to its authoritarian impulses. While Iran took out loans to pay for postwar programs, revenue from oil constituted the single largest source of state income and served as the major source of funding for a series of development plans run by a semi-autonomous Plan Organization, while also helping to fund the military, historically the state institution closest to the Pahlavi monarchy.[44]

---

[42] For the formation and function of the oil oligopoly in Iran and the Middle East, see Penrose, *The Large International Firm*, 53–86, Shwadran, *The Middle East, Oil and the Great Powers*, 3–12, Theodore H. Moran, "Managing an Oligopoly of Would-Be Sovereigns: The Dynamics of Joint Control and Self-Control in the International Oil Industry Past, Present and Future," *International Organization* 41, no. 4 (Autumn 1987): 575–607; Cowhey, *Problem of Plenty*, 112.

[43] Steven A. Schneider, *The Oil Price Revolution* (Baltimore, MD: Johns Hopkins University Press, 1983), Daniel J. Sargent, *A Superpower Transformed: The Remaking of American Foreign Relations in the 1970s* (Oxford: Oxford University Press, 2015), 131–164.

[44] Homa Katouzian, *The Political Economy of Modern Iran: Despotism and Pseudo-Modernism, 1926–1979* (London: Macmillan Press, 1981), 234–274, Ervand Abrahamian, *Iran between Two Revolutions* (Princeton, NJ: Princeton University Press, 1982), 427–428, Nikki Keddie, *Modern Iran: Roots and Results of Revolution* (New Haven, CT: Yale

0.3 Themes and Structure

Like the American development mission and the companies' coercive dominance of overseas concessions, oil's significance to the Pahlavi government created contradictions. Under Reza Shah (r.1925–1941) and his son Mohammed Reza Pahlavi (r.1941–1979), oil represented foreign influence and the restriction of national sovereignty, due to its nature as a foreign-owned industry. This placed the monarchy and its allies in an awkward position from which they never truly escaped. Eager to avail itself of the wealth created from oil's exploitation but unable to alter the oligopoly's control of the nation's oil industry, the Pahlavi government simultaneously drew in American support for its development program, even as that program ostensibly aimed to legitimize the regime against internal challengers accusing it of acting at the behest of foreign powers. Though not a "Western stooge," the shah had to grapple with the contradictions affecting his oil and development policies, as he leaned on foreign support while consciously characterizing his government in nationalist terms. Studies of Iran's economic growth before the 1973 oil boom tend to emphasize either the "miracle" of rapid industrialization or Iran's status as a "dependent" oil-producer and a nation beholden to Western capital.[45] Both accounts note a key truth: Through oil, Iran was entangled in a global economy managed by Western corporations, while foreign groups played a pivotal role in the management and execution of the shah's development schemes.[46]

Petroleum and Progress in Iran does not cover the entire Pahlavi era (1925–1979). Nor does it attempt to examine the root causes and events leading to the Islamic Revolution of 1978–1979, the fulcrum around which the history of twentieth-century Iran turns. Instead, it focuses on a period where foreign actors, including the US government, engaged with Iran in the process of dual integration, with the Pahlavi petro-state

---

University Press, 2006), 162–163, Ali M. Ansari, *Modern Iran: the Pahlavis and After*, 2nd Edition (New York: Pearson Education, 2007), 231–232, Fred Halliday, *Iran: Dictatorship and Development* (New York: Penguin Books, 1979), 40–41, 139–171, Amin Saikal, *The Rise and Fall of the Shah: Iran From Autocracy to Religious Rule* (Princeton, NJ: Princeton University Press, 1980), 97–134.

[45] Massoud Karshenas, *Oil, State and Industrialization in Iran* (New York: Cambridge University Press, 1990), Jahangir Amuzegar and M. Ali Fekrat, *Iran: Economic Development Under Dualistic Conditions* (Chicago, IL: University of Chicago Press, 1971), and Julian Bharier, *Economic Development in Iran, 1900–1970* (New York: Oxford University Press, 1971). The shah is generally credited for dominated economic policy, particularly after 1973; see Hossein Razavi and Firouz Vakil, *The Political Environment of Economic Planning in Iran, 1971–1983: from Monarchy to Islamic Republic* (London: Westview Press, 1984), 61–62, 90–97.

[46] For insights into the transnational character of Pahlavi Iran, Roham Alvandi, ed., *The Age of Aryamehr: Late Pahlavi Iran and Its Global Entanglements* (London: Gingko Press, 2018).

of the mid-1960s emerging as the outcome of that engagement. A close examination of these years reveals the fragile nature of the Pahlavi government before the years of the shah's *Tamaddon-e Bozorg* ("Great Civilization"). The shah's consolidation of power was by no means assured. It was the result of constant struggle. Though it is facile to draw a direct link between 1941 or 1953 and the events of 1979, it is nevertheless true that the development programs and oil politics embraced by Mohammed Reza Pahlavi and supported by his foreign allies in the United States, the global development movement, and oil oligopoly produced a regime vulnerable to social revolution, as Hossein Mahdavy warned. The dual integration of Iranian oil was a success insofar as it allowed Iran to grow from an agricultural pre-modern state in the 1940s to an industrial and military power in the late 1960s, creating opportunities and raising living standards for some (if not all) Iranians, at the cost of repressing political dissent, concentrating power around the person of the shah, and causing state finances to become dependent on oil exports. This was a form of authoritarianism too brittle to survive serious trauma.[47]

Chapter 1 provides a background to Iran's place in the global oil economy, explaining the origins of US policy in Iran and the birth of dual integration. Chapter 2 explores the initial failure of dual integration through the example of the First Seven-Year Plan, Iran's abortive effort at postwar oil-driven development. Chapter 3 focuses on Mohammed Mosaddeq's nationalization movement and the petro-nationalist challenge to the position of oil capital inside Iran, while also addressing the efforts of the United States to settle the Iranian oil crisis without abandoning Western control of Iran's oil deposits. Chapter 4 provides the hinge: The August 1953 coup d'état and the forced reintegration of Iranian oil into the global oil economy, engineered by the US government, motivated by Cold War concerns, and informed by persistent ideas of Iranian incapacity.

Part II explores the aftermath of the coup, a period when the Pahlavi government embraced dual integration. Chapter 5 examines the Second Seven-Year Plan, a massive project that aimed to legitimize the shah's teetering post-coup regime, through the eyes of the Development and Resources Corporation, managed by American developmentalists Gordon R. Clapp and David E. Lilienthal. Chapter 6 looks at Iran's place amid the changing dynamics of the global oil economy and the rise

---

[47] For oil's role in bringing about the Islamic Revolution, see Katouzian, *Political Economy*, 255–269, Ansari, *Modern Iran*, 229–232, Keddie, *Modern Iran: the Pahlavis and After*, 231–232.

0.3 Themes and Structure

of the Organization of the Petroleum Exporting Countries (OPEC), and the ways the shah's government balanced performative petro-nationalist with its dependence on the oil companies. Chapter 7 examines local integration, the work of American developmentalists to train a cadre of Iranian technocrats, and the clash of ideologies within the US and Iranian governments that played out against the backdrop of the shah's White Revolution, producing a new revolutionary narrative for the shah's rule and satisfying American concerns regarding his regime's stability.

While a broad narrative, *Petroleum and Progress in Iran* is not a comprehensive account of Iranian political history or foreign relations. The focus is on interactions between American and Iranian actors. Though there are British actors who enter the narrative, those hoping for a thorough examination of Anglo-Iranian relations should look elsewhere. "Development" has been deliberately chosen as the term of reference for the material struggle to improve standards of living, rather than "modernization," a concept loaded with epistemological and ontological significance.[48] Access to archives in Iran proved impossible. However, an effort has been made to utilize Persian-language sources. Insights gleaned from what one scholar has called "the crowded panorama of the *zindiqinama* [memoir]" are used with care.[49] Every technocrat and politician who lived during this time was conscious of defending himself (for they were all men) from the attacks of posterity. Yet leaving them out of the story would leave it a tale told exclusively by (and about) foreigners. For this author, that is not a tale worth telling.

---

[48] Ali Mirsepassi, *Intellectual Discourse and the Politics of Modernization: Negotiating Modernity in Iran* (New York: Cambridge University Press, 2000), 54–64.

[49] Siavush Randbjar-Daemi, "Review of Iraj Amini, *Bar Bal-e Bohran* [Flying on the Wings of Crisis] (Tehran: Nashr-I Mahi, 2009)," *Iranian Studies* 44, no. 5 (Sept., 2011): 778.

Part I

1 Iran, Global Oil, and the United States, 1901–1947

In February 1892, a French mining journal published a report on oil seepages at Chia Sorkh, a patch of desert roughly 90 miles west of the Iranian city of Kermanshah. Suspecting that there might be deposits buried nearby, William Knox D'Arcy, an English businessman, sent a delegation to Iran's ruler, the Qajar shah, to secure rights to "obtain, exploit, develop, render suitable for trade, carry and sell" any oil that might be found. The shah accepted D'Arcy's offer of a £20,000 lump sum and 16 percent of "net profits." A team of English drillers discovered oil seven years later in Khuzestan, Iran's southwestern province.[1] By 1920 Iran was a major producer. The oil industry was run by the Anglo-Persian Oil Company (APOC), a British corporation and successor to D'Arcy's original venture. Iran's government had little say in how the company operated – "unaware," wrote Iranian engineer Mustafa Fateh, "except for a few involved in the work"[2] – and received only a slim tithe that rarely amounted to 16 percent of net profits.[3]

Twenty years later, with Iran now under Anglo-Soviet occupation and state finances in disarray, the American financial expert Arthur C. Millspaugh arrived in Tehran. Charged with assisting the bankrupt Pahlavi state after the invasion of 1941, Millspaugh assumed jurisdiction over Iranian finances. Iran was, as he put it, "psychologically and politically unprepared" to operate as a modern nation-state, charging into a modern future "[like] a child forced prematurely to live the life of an adult."[4] Foreign control featured both in how Iran's oil was produced

---

[1] L. P. Elwell-Sutton, *Persian Oil: A Study in Power Politics* (London: Lawrence and Wishart, 1955), 10–25. See Ronald Ferrier, *The History of the British Petroleum Company*, vol. I (Cambridge: Cambridge University Press, 1982), 59–106.

[2] Mostafa Fateh, *Panjah sal naft-e Iran* (Tehran: Entesharat-e Payam, 1979), 235–236.

[3] In 1916, the royalty to Iran was 9 percent of APOC's declared profits; in 1917, it was 1 percent. BP 5193 Memoranda No. 66203, "Total Royalty Paid to the Persian Government under the D'Arcy Concession," June 10, 1933; Shwadran, *The Middle East, Oil, and the Great Powers*, 132–133.

[4] Arthur C. Millspaugh, *Americans in Persia* (Washington, DC: Brookings Institution, 1946), 91.

and in how the riches of oil were spent. Both APOC and Millspaugh reflected the idea that Iran's oil was too valuable to be left in Iranian hands.

This chapter explores the origins of the global oil economy, Iran's relationship with the international oil companies, and the circumstances surrounding the American entry into Iran and policy of dual integration. In the first half of the twentieth century, private corporations constructed systems for extracting oil based on coercive power and the legal regime of the concession. Despite fears that the oil would soon run out, the industry's greatest problems were abundance and the threat that overproduction posed to prices and profits. The challenge of abundance was matched by that of security – specifically the companies' need to secure overseas possessions from resource nationalism. In Iran, the assertive new Pahlavi state sought political legitimacy and financial power by challenging the British oil company. While the company desired cooperation with the Pahlavi shah, it obtained much greater security in 1941 when Anglo-Soviet armies invaded Iran, deposed the shah, and placed the oil fields of Khuzestan under occupation. Control over the oil resources of the Global South was a strategic objective for the Great Powers and a commercial goal of the major oil companies, which combined their dominance of production with collusion at the corporate level to manage output, maintain profits, and mitigate competition. The Pahlavi state attempted to leverage access to oil for its own ends, both to play Great Powers against one another and to secure financial resources and prestige.[5]

For the United States, controlling oil went hand in hand with advancing a developmentalist agenda. Americans treated Iran as a test case for an "enlightened" wartime policy, seeing the country's instability as a sickness caused by elite corruption and foreign imperialism. Wartime advisors arrived in Iran under the belief that administering a cure would require American management, even as American companies made a concerted effort to break the British monopoly over Iranian oil. This confused, and ultimately failed, policy found clarity in the context of the Cold War, where the protection of Iranian territorial integrity and the development goals of the pro-US Pahlavi government were united under

---

[5] This period is very well-documented. See Ferrier, *The History of the British Petroleum Company*, vol. I; J. H. Bamberg, *The History of the British Petroleum Company*, vol. II (Cambridge: Cambridge University Press, 1994); Anand Toprani, *Oil & the Great Powers: Britain and Germany, 1914–1945* (Oxford: Oxford University Press, 2019), 25–136; Shwadran, *The Middle East, Oil, and the Great Powers*, 13–194. For the international oil industry before 1945, see Cowhey, *The Problems of Plenty*, 81–104; Jacoby, *Multinational Oil*, 25–47; Yergin, *The Prize*, 118–286.

the American mission to safeguard Iran and the rest of the oil-producing Middle East from Soviet influence.[6]

Issues of oil and development – of petroleum and progress – were closely intertwined. By 1947 a new American approach had emerged that linked the sale of Iranian oil on the global market to an indigenous development program fostered by Pahlavi technocrats and American developmentalists. The British oil company became the primary instrument of American policy in Iran, as its operations offered the key to ensuring the country's economic development and territorial integrity. Concern for Iran's future stability was paramount. Equally important was maintaining access to oil in order to feed Western consumption and protect the United States and its allies from the danger of shortage.

1.1 Oil Imperialism and Petro-Nationalism

As soon as oil became vital to the functioning of industrial society, fears arose over when it would run out. "The time will come," warned Indiana's state geologist in 1896, "when the stored reserve [of oil] … will have been drained."[7] The first survey of US petroleum reserves conducted in 1908 determined that American oil would be exhausted by 1935.[8] This, of course, did not happen. New deposits were found to replenish national reserves, and the United States remained a net exporter of oil until the 1940s. The "oil scarcity ideology" was based more on fears of future insecurity than on accurate readings of geological data.[9] Chief among those fears was the worry that the United States –

---

[6] For the American experience in Iran during World War II, see Bruce R. Kuniholm, *The Origins of the Cold War in the Near East: Great Power Conflict and Diplomacy in Iran, Turkey, and Greece* (Princeton, NJ: Princeton University Press, 1980); Mark H. Lytle, *The Origins of the Iranian-American Alliance, 1941–1953* (New York: Holmes & Meier, 1987); Ashley Jackson, *Persian Gulf Command: A History of the Second World War in Iran and Iraq* (New Haven, CT: Yale University Press, 2018); Fernand Scheid Raine, "The Iranian Crisis of 1946 and the Origins of the Cold War," in Melvyn P. Leffler and David S. Painter (eds.), *The Origins of the Cold War: An International History*, 2nd ed. (New York: Routledge, 2005), 93–111; Habib Ladjevardi, "The Origins of US Support for an Autocratic Iran," *International Journal of Middle Eastern Studies* 15, no. 2 (May 1983): 225–239; Stephen L. McFarland, "A Peripheral View of the Origins of the Cold War: The Crises in Iran, 1941–1947," *Diplomatic History* 4, no. 4 (October 1980): 333–352; Collier, *Democracy and the Nature of American Influence in Iran*, 10–48.
[7] Quoted in Gerald D. Nash, *United States Oil Policy 1890–1964* (Pittsburgh, PA: University of Pittsburgh Press, 1968), 15.
[8] David T. Day, "The Petroleum Resources of the United States," in Henry Gannett (ed.), *Report of the National Conservation Commission*, vol. 3 (Washington, DC: Government Printing Office, 1909), 446–464.
[9] Roger Stern, "Oil Scarcity Ideology in US Foreign Policy, 1908–1997," *Security Studies* 25, no. 2 (May 2016): 214–257.

which accounted for more than half of world oil consumption in 1919 – would become dependent on imported oil, shackling the nation's future prosperity to foreign interests. In the wake of World War I, the US government encouraged American oil companies to go abroad and secure oil for future domestic consumption.[10]

Though they were wary of direct government oversight, the oil companies formed close ties with Washington and accepted federal help in pushing their interests abroad. "Such cooperation ... may not be in strict accord with the laws of competition," noted Jersey Standard's A. C. Bedford in the *Oil and Gas Journal*, "[but] does not necessarily signify disaster."[11] While public–private cooperation served national needs, the companies cooperated with one another for commercial reasons. Since the nineteenth century, oil markets had been defined by intense fluctuations. Producers tended to increase output as quickly as possible in a rush to out-pump their competitors before prices collapsed. In time, companies adopted vertical integration, growing large enough to control every aspect of oil's production, refining, transportation, and marketing – a model pioneered by John D. Rockefeller's Standard Oil, which by the 1890s controlled roughly 90 percent of the American petroleum market. The companies could also manage the market through horizontal integration, colluding with one another through formal or informal cooperative agreements. Horizontal and vertical integration acted as breaks on oil's volatility, ensuring profitability and mitigating the harmful effects of destructive competition.[12]

By the early twentieth century, the global oil industry was dominated by a small number of vertically integrated companies, known as "majors." The largest were the Standard Oil Company of New Jersey (Jersey Standard) and Royal Dutch / Shell. These firms were later joined by APOC (later AIOC and then BP), the Texas Oil Company (Texaco), Gulf Oil, the Standard Oil Company of California (Socal, later Chevron), and the Standard Oil Company of New York (Socony, later Mobil).[13]

The United States dominated the industry (five of the seven largest firms were American) and possessed domestic reserves to rely upon. For other Great Powers, oil was an imperial venture. In June 1913, as the Royal Navy transitioned from coal to oil, First Lord of the Admiralty

---

[10] Mitchell, *Carbon Democracy*, 94–98; Michael Hogan, "Informal Entente: Public Policy and Private Management in Anglo-American Petroleum Affairs, 1918–1924," *Business History Review* 48, no. 2 (Summer 1974): 187–205.
[11] *Oil and Gas Journal*, April 4, 1918.   [12] Cowhey, *The Problems of Plenty*, 1–23.
[13] Sampson, *The Seven Sisters*, 1–86.

Figure 1.1 Pipelines running through Khuzestan, Iran's oil province, 1950.
BP 78039, Reproduced with permission from the BP Archive

Winston Churchill recommended that His Majesty's Government purchase a controlling stake in APOC to ensure stable access to affordable crude oil in Iran and elsewhere in the Middle East. After discovering oil in 1908, APOC built a refinery on the island of Abadan connected via pipelines to oil fields in Khuzestan (Figure 1.1). By 1927 the company possessed fixed assets of £48 million while Iranian production reached 3,161,000 tons per year (64,519 barrels per day, or bpd). APOC joined Shell, Jersey Standard, and several other American majors as a vertically integrated oil company, albeit one that served political as well as commercial interests.[14] "Persia," as Iran was still known, acted as a strategic petroleum reserve for the British Empire, while APOC also worked to secure a concession in neighboring Iraq – a League of Nations mandate granted to Britain following World War I.[15]

[14] Ferrier, *The History of the British Petroleum Company*, vol. I, 638–639.
[15] Toprani, *Oil & the Great Powers*, 34–36; Marian Kent, *Oil and Empire: British Policy and Mesopotamian Oil, 1900–1920* (London: Macmillan, 1976), 38–49; Gareth G. Jones,

Though Iran was never formally colonized, APOC's presence was unmistakably colonial. In Abadan, European staffers enjoyed social amenities, swimming pools, and social clubs, while the Iranian workforce lived in sprawling slums paying exorbitant rents to predatory landlords. APOC employed Europeans to fill technical jobs and Indians to serve as clerks and administrators, retaining Iranians to run industrial activities without providing them additional education or training. Such dynamics helped to ensure the dominance of the management, which in turn supported stable production and ensured long-term profitability.[16] The global oil industry was dominated by such inequities. The oil fields of Indonesia, which came online in the 1880s, and those of southeastern Texas in the early twentieth century were colonial spaces divided along racial lines.[17] Americans transplanted the forms and functions of Jim Crow to the deserts of Arabia during the 1930s.[18] Abadan, with its comfortable European quarter and sprawling refinery slum, was no different.

APOC carried on its activities without interference from the Qajar government in Tehran. Iran's rulers exerted little influence on the provinces, and the company relied more heavily on local proxies, including pro-British tribes and the Arab sheikh of Mohammerah (the Arabic name for the Iranian port city of Khorramshahr), than on support from the Iranian state.[19] But oil companies could not ignore the central governments entirely, for a simple reason: The oil produced out of the ground was, legally speaking, the property of the state. Companies acquired concessions from the local governments to search for and exploit minerals in a specific area for a specific period of time. The state retained sovereignty over oil and could expropriate or nationalize privately held property through legislative fiat.[20] In practice, however, the legal regimes surrounding concession agreements were bound up in relevant power dynamics. In Mexico, local law was either willfully misinterpreted to suit the oil men's interests or ignored entirely. Reserves worth millions of dollars could be acquired "[for] 300 or 400 pesos," wrote geologist

---

"The British Government and the Oil Companies 1912–1924: The Search for an Oil Policy," *Historical Journal* 20, no. 3 (September 1977): 647–672.

[16] Kaveh Ehsani, "The Social History of Labor in the Iranian Oil Industry: The Built Environment and the Making of the Industrial Working Class (1908–1941)" (PhD thesis, Leiden University, 2014), 141–151, 157–174, 226–256.

[17] Dochuk, *Anointed with Oil*, 81–82, 110–114.   [18] Vitalis, *America's Kingdom*, 18–26.

[19] Stephanie Cronin, "The Politics of Debt: The Anglo-Persian Oil Company and the Bakhtiyari Khans," *Middle Eastern Studies* 40, no. 4 (July 2004): 1–31.

[20] Bernard Mommer, *Global Oil and the Nation State* (Oxford: Oxford University Press, 2002), 9–29.

Everette Lee DeGolyer.[21] Concessionary regimes were lopsided in the favor of companies, which could set the terms of equitability – the substance of a "fair" agreement – with little input from the local governments.

In time, opposition to the imperial influences of the companies increased. In Mexico, hellish working conditions and low pay prompted labor demonstrations in the 1920s. Article 27 of the 1917 constitution asserted national sovereignty over mineral rights: In the realm of oil exploitation, "the dominion of the Nation is inalienable and indispensable."[22] This opposition – combined with the deteriorating geological conditions of most major Mexican oil fields – encouraged the companies to shift their attentions to Venezuela, where output increased from 900 bpd in 1918 to 289,000 bpd in 1928.[23] The experience proved the threat of resource nationalism, but it also illustrated the companies' flexibility. Should a challenge emerge, investment could be shifted elsewhere, so long as oil was abundant. In the words of one official in the US State Department's Office of Petroleum Affairs, the policies of major oil companies "resemble those of the Vatican – both can afford to wait."[24]

While oil's abundance gave the companies flexibility when faced with rising petro-nationalism, it depressed prices and increased destructive competition. As policymakers in London and Washington worried about potential shortage, oil executives contemplated a lack of markets and price wars that would sap profitability. In 1925, the American Petroleum Institute, the major lobbying group for the American oil industry, published a report concluding that there was "no immediate danger" of reserves being depleted, provided prices remained high enough to drive continued investment.[25] The dominance of a few vertically integrated

---

[21] Everette Lee DeGolyer and Nell Goodrich DeGolyer, interview by Cleveland Amory, Lon Tinkle Collection, Box 3, DeGolyer Library, Southern Methodist University. See Myrna I. Santiago, *The Ecology of Oil: Environment, Labor, and the Mexican Revolution, 1900–1938* (Cambridge: Cambridge University Press, 2006), 61–147; Nathan Fagre and Louis T. Wells, Jr., "Bargaining Power of Multinationals and Host Governments," *Journal of International Business Studies* 13, no. 2 (Autumn 1982): 9–23.

[22] 1917 Constitution, Art. 27, accessed via the Library of Congress, www.loc.gov/exhibits/mexican-revolution-and-the-united-states/constitution-of-1917.html; See Mommer, *Global Oil and the Nation State*, 70.

[23] Jonathan C. Brown, "Why Foreign Companies Shifted Their Production from Mexico to Venezuela during the 1920s," *American Historical Review* 90, no. 2 (April 1985): 362–385.

[24] Walton Ferris to Max Thornburg, "The Foreign Oil Policy of the United States," *Office of the Petroleum Advisor*, August 31, 1942, Papers of Max W. Thornburg. My thanks to Norman Seddon for sharing this document.

[25] American Petroleum Institute, *American Petroleum Supply and Demand* (New York: McGraw Hill, 1925), 3.

companies encouraged cooperation to maintain prices and avoid destructive competition. In September 1928, the heads of the three largest majors – John Cadman of APOC, Walter Teagle of Jersey, and Henry Deterding of Shell – met at Achnacarry Castle in Scotland to formalize cooperative management of the global oil industry.[26] "Excessive competition has resulted in the tremendous overproduction of today," they stated.[27] In the Middle East, production would be controlled through a "self-denying" clause known as the Red Line Agreement, while the majors agreed to leave market share "as-is" to mitigate competition.[28] What was imagined was not a cartel, but an oligopoly – a cooperative arrangement of producers who colluded to limit output while continuing to compete with one another under controlled conditions.[29]

There was no "free" oil market. In the oil fields of Iran, Mexico, Venezuela, Indonesia, and elsewhere, colonial regimes ensured foreign control of oil resources which were, legally speaking, the property of the state. Globally, the companies colluded to restrict competition. In 1931, as the Great Depression caused oil demand to plummet, National Guard troops were deployed to shut down oil wells in Texas and Oklahoma. Violence served to produce scarcity, ensuring profitability – the tools of empire were deployed on the American oil patch.[30] The companies were not always comfortable with government intervention but would accept it when necessary. The paramount need, according to W. S. Farish of Humble Oil, was to prevent "unrestrained competition" and permit "orderly production."[31] Yet while the issue of abundance was managed through collusion, the challenge of petro-nationalism remained unresolved, as APOC would discover when a new government rose to power in Iran.

---

[26] Yergin, *The Prize*, 243–248.
[27] Pool Association Agreement, September 17, 1928, from Federal Trade Commission, *The International Petroleum Cartel: Staff Report Submitted to the Subcommittee on Monopoly of the Select Committee on Small Business, United States Senate* (Washington, DC: US Government Printing Office, 1952), 200.
[28] William Stivers, "A Note on the Red Line Agreement," *Diplomatic History* 7, no. 1 (1983): 23–34; Walter Adams, James W. Brock, and John M. Blair, "Retarding the Development of Iraq's Oil Resources: An Episode in Oleaginous Diplomacy, 1927–1939," *Journal of Economic Issues* 27, no. 1 (1993): 69–93.
[29] Theodore H. Moran, "Managing an Oligopoly of Would-Be Sovereigns: The Dynamics of Joint Control and Self-Control in the International Oil Industry Past, Present, and Future," *International Organization* 41, no. 4 (Autumn 1987): 576–607.
[30] Yergin, *The Prize*, 231–242; Matthew Huber, "Enforcing Scarcity: Oil, Violence, and the Making of the Market," *Annals of the Association of American Geographers* 101, no. 4 (2011): 816–826.
[31] "What the Oil Industry Needs," *The Lamp*, vol. 15, no. 1 (June 1932).

1.2 "A Bird That Lost Its Feathers": Oil and Pahlavi Iran, 1921–1941

In February 1921, a column led by the military commander Reza Khan marched into Tehran and overthrew the regime of the Qajar shah.[32] Within several years, the new dictator had rebuilt the army, defeated several insurrections, subdued Iran's semi-autonomous tribes, and brought the state under his control. In 1925, the national parliament, or Majlis, decided to make him the new shah by law. A single deputy, Mohammed Mosaddeq, objected to having executive and royal power placed in the same hands. The deputy's objection was not enough to stop the relentless drive of the new government.[33] Reza Shah Pahlavi I assumed the Peacock Throne in 1926, with his son Mohammed Reza (seven years old, "a wee mite ... without any reserve or nerves" according to APOC chairman Sir John Cadman) at his side.[34]

Iran's *bourgeoisie* hailed the arrival of the military dictator as a turning point in the nation's history. Lying between the rival empires of Russia and Britain, Iran had struggled against pervasive foreign influence throughout the nineteenth century. Popular discontent spiked in 1890 when the Qajar shah ceded control of Iran's tobacco trade to a British interest. A general revolt erupted in 1906, forcing the shah to recognize the country's first constitution and national parliament. The constitutional government survived years of invasion and fiscal crisis, before collapsing in the wake of the 1921 coup d'état. Former revolutionaries like Sayyed Hasan Taqizadeh, who had once argued that Iran "outwardly and inwardly, physically and spiritually, become European," rallied to the dictatorship, hoping to use it as a vehicle for a national revival.[35] Others looked for a more tangible reconstruction. "As long as we refuse to dedicate ourselves to an economic revolution," wrote Ali-Akbar Davar, the shah's minister of justice and author of Iran's first modern legal code, "we will remain a submissive nation of disaster-stricken, starved, and tattered cloaked beggars."[36] Tehran was rebuilt, hospitals and schools erected, and a Trans-Iranian Railroad established

---

[32] Michael Zirinsky, "Imperial Power and Dictatorship: Britain and the Rise of Reza Shah, 1921–1926," *International Journal of Middle East Studies* 24, no. 4 (November 1992): 639–663.
[33] Ansari, *Politics of Nationalism*, 80–81.
[34] BP 70210 Secret Diary of Visit to Persia, February 25–May 26, 1926.
[35] *Kaveh*, January 22, 1920, 2; Afshin Matin-Asgari, *Both Eastern and Western: An Intellectual History of Iranian Modernity* (New York: Cambridge University Press, 2018), 81–87.
[36] Quoted in Majid Sharifi, "Imagining Iran: Contending Political Discourses in Modern Iran," (PhD thesis, University of Florida, 2008), 93.

to connect the capital to the provinces. Reza Shah built a system of state-owned factories and pumped most of the foreign exchange earned through exports into building up the country's industrial base, though he reserved payments from the British oil company for more exotic items, including modern armaments that he purchased from a special account.[37]

While Europe offered a vision of what Iran could become, eliminating foreign influence formed an important part of the new regime's agenda. In 1927, Reza Shah announced the "abrogation of capitulations." Like Article 27 of the Mexican constitution, the law was meant to express Iranian independence from foreign influence.[38] In an important act of fiscal reform, the regime formed a new central bank, the Bank-e Melli, to manage the national money supply, a mandate formerly held by the Imperial Bank of Persia, a British institution. But it was the oil company that received special attention. Touring the oil fields, the shah – an imposing, authoritative figure who made a habit of striking people with his cane when he thought them flippant or disobedient – made it clear that the days of British autonomy were over. "Iran," he declared, "can no longer tolerate the profits of its oil going into foreigners' pockets."[39]

During meetings with APOC chairman Sir John Cadman, Reza Shah's minister of court, the urbane Abdolhossein Teymurtash, described the industry as the "Tree of Life" upon which Iran's financial and economic wellness depended.[40] The oil royalty represented only a portion of Iran's revenue: A study by the shah's American financial advisor Arthur C. Millspaugh estimated APOC's payments constituted between 9 percent and 12 percent of the state budget between 1922 and 1926, while the industry was an enclave detached from the rest of Iran's

---

[37] Ansari, *The Politics of Nationalism in Modern Iran*, 58–67, 83–84; Houchang Chehabi, "Staging the Emperor's New Clothes: Dress Codes and Nation-Building under Reza Shah," *Iranian Studies* 26, no. 3 (1993): 209–233; Stephanie Cronin, "Conscription and Popular Resistance in Iran, 1925–1941," *International Review of Social History* 43, no. 3 (1998): 451–471; and Mehrzad Boroujerdi, "Triumphs and Travails of Authoritarian Modernisation in Iran," in Stephanie Cronin (ed.), *Making of Modern Iran: State and Society under Riza Shah, 1921–1941* (New York: Routledge, 2003), 37–64.

[38] Michael Zirinsky, "Riza Shah's Abrogation of Capitulations, 1927–1928," in Stephanie Cronin (ed.), *The Making of Modern Iran: State and Society under Riza Shah 1921–1941* (New York: Routledge, 2003), 81–98.

[39] Fateh, *Panjah sal naft-e Iran*, 286.

[40] Teymurtash to Cadman, December 12, 1928, in *Asnad va mukatibat-e Taymurtash, vazir-e darbar-e Riza Shah* [The Documents and Correspondence of Teymurtash, Minister of Court to Reza Shah] (Tehran: Sazman-e Chap va Entesharat-e Vezarat-e Farhang va Ershad-e Eslami, 2005), 45–48.

1.2 "A Bird That Lost Its Feathers"

predominantly agricultural economy.[41] Nevertheless, the Pahlavi state was determined to exert pressure on the company in order to secure better terms and more revenue. "We do not say that the Persian government should abolish the concession," explained Teymurtash to Cadman, "but we do say that it should be revised … we have been cheated quite badly in this bargain."[42]

APOC's chairman believed the company needed to change its policies. It was clear, Cadman wrote in 1926, that strong feelings had grown among Iran's elite, "due to the impression that [APOC] was taking huge profits out of the country and doing very little for its inhabitants."[43] A thoughtful and intelligent man, Cadman displayed an astute understanding of Iran's new political status quo. "There is a new Persia to-day and the old method of dealing with her is out of date," Cadman wrote in 1928. The company had to act, Cadman argued, before Iranian demands grew too great: "[W]e are out to save our own skin."[44] In 1932, oil prices crashed amid the global depression. APOC's royalty to Iran fell to just £306,872. Facing a depleted treasury and furious over the slow pace of negotiations, Reza Shah canceled the D'Arcy Concession in November. Shortly thereafter he had Teymurtash arrested. The minister later died in prison.[45]

Cancellation was not nationalization. Despite the rhetoric of the Pahlavi regime, the shah was not prepared to take over the industry. Instead, his government argued that APOC had reduced the royalty through "prodigality and extravagance."[46] It had not, in other words, lived up to its side of the D'Arcy Concession. The British response was one of indignation. Whitehall discussed whether the cancellation warranted a military intervention and additional warships were moved into the Persian Gulf.[47] But Cadman opted for diplomacy. He traveled to Iran in April 1933 and after several days of discussions compelled the shah to intervene personally. According to one account, Cadman promised "essentially what the Shah wanted, if not in the form his ministers

---

[41] Arthur C. Millspaugh, *The Financial and Economic Situation of Persia* (New York: the Persia Society, 1926), 29.
[42] Teymurtash to Greenhouse, June 11, 1931, in *Asnad va mukatibat-e Taymurtash*, 131.
[43] BP 70210 Secret Diary of Visit to Persia, February 25 to May 26, 1926.
[44] BP 87291 Cadman to Barstow, October 14, 1928.
[45] Gregory Brew, "In Search of 'Equitability': Sir John Cadman, Rezā Shah and the Cancellation of the D'Arcy Concession, 1928–1933," *Iranian Studies* 50, no. 1 (2017): 125–148.
[46] BP 96487 Taqizadeh to Jacks, November 27, 1932; BP 88373 Foroughi Letter to APOC, December 12, 1932.
[47] Peter J. Beck, "The Anglo-Persian Oil Dispute 1932–1933," *Journal of Contemporary History* 9, no. 4 (October 1974): 138–140.

and experts recommended."[48] The concession area was reduced by 80 percent, while Iran was promised an annual royalty minimum of £750,000. The agreement came with a hefty lump sum: Payments to the Iranian government for 1933 totaled £4,107,660. In a brief speech, Cadman described the company as "a bird which had lost a great deal of plumage" but that would in time "regain its feathers."[49] "The general feeling," wrote the American minister, "is that the Persian Government has more or less proven its case."[50]

In private, however, Cadman felt he had won a major victory. APOC now had a concession that would not expire until 1993. The company's longtime legal advisor proclaimed it "the best concession he had ever seen."[51] Some of the less favorable articles in the 1901 D'Arcy Concession were eliminated, clarifying the terms of the company's control. Most importantly, the new agreement forbade Iran from changing or withdrawing from the concession agreement without consulting APOC. Cadman successfully concealed the actual extent of the deal's terms. "It was not desirable," he told the Foreign Office, "to stress the many features of the agreement which were favorable to APOC until the appropriate time."[52] By the time observers in Iran realized the scope of the new concession, it was too late.

The cancellation crisis of 1933 established a trend that dominated the relationship of the Pahlavi regime to the international oil industry over the next thirty years. While nationalist rhetoric and invocations of sovereign power allowed Iran's government to pressure the company, the shah was more interested in the appearance of a moral victory – and cash. A new basis in equitability appeared in 1933, thanks to British pressure and Cadman's adroit diplomacy, but it was largely illusory: While APOC paid Iran more money, its control of Iranian oil did not change.

As future Iranian petro-nationalists would point out, Iran's case against APOC was weakened by the terms Reza Shah accepted in April 1933, suggesting the shah colluded with the British.[53] Existing accounts (including the company's own archives) make it very clear that the decision to cancel had been made by the shah himself, partly in a fit of

---

[48] RG 59 Lot File No. 78 D 442, Petroleum Policy Staff Subject File Relating to Iranian Oil and US Middle Eastern Oil Policy, 1921–1951, Box 4, Wadsworth and Jacks Meeting, May 4, 1933, USNA.
[49] BP 96659 Cadman Private Diary, March–April 1933.
[50] RG 59 Lot File No. 78 D 442, Petroleum Policy Staff Subject File Relating to Iranian Oil and US Middle Eastern Oil Policy, 1921–1951, Box 4, Atherton to Hull, May 3, 1933, USNA.
[51] BP 88373 Board Meeting, May 15, 1933; Brew, "In Search of Equitability," 15–16.
[52] BP 69267 Note of Interviews at Foreign Office, May 2, 1933.
[53] Fateh, *Panjah sal naft-e Iran*, 306–307.

pique over the failure of his ministers to reach a new oil deal.[54] As Sayyed Hasan Taqizadeh, the shah's minister of finance, told one APOC official: "[A]ll important matters in this country are decided by the great man of the time."[55] Cadman made sure Iran's great man remained satisfied. Between 1932 and 1941 APOC paid the shah's government £25 million.[56] The company became the "Anglo-Iranian Oil Company," or AIOC, and made an effort to improve living conditions in Abadan. These were token gestures: The company's goal, Deputy Chairman William J. Fraser declared during a meeting of the company's executive leadership, was not to educate or train Iran, "but to exploit its oil resources."[57] The new agreement provided the company a legal basis for doing so for another sixty years.

Cadman died in May 1941. In August, Anglo-Soviet forces invaded Iran, removed Reza Shah from power, and occupied the country. The move, ostensibly meant to purge the country of German influence, ensured Allied control of the Iranian oil fields and the supply line from the Persian Gulf to the Soviet border. As British troops garrisoned Abadan, foreign control over Iranian oil appeared permanent. But the conditions of war upended the fragile truce won by Cadman in 1933. The Anglo-Soviet occupation opened Iran up to a new age of Great Power competition. And the arrival of the United States, with its untested and experimental new policy, produced a set of circumstances which would alter the status quo governing Iranian oil.

1.3 Occupation, "Incapacity," and Expertise: American Advisors in Iran, 1941–1945

Reza Shah's power collapsed amid the Anglo-Soviet invasion of August 1941. In the vacuum left by his departure, Iran split into spheres of influence: Soviet in the north, British in the south.[58] Symbols of the country's modernization were turned toward the war effort. The Trans-Iranian Railway was used to shuttle Allied war material from the Persian

---

[54] For the collusion argument, see Mohammed Gholi Majd, *Great Britain and Rezā Shah: The Plunder of Iran, 1921–1941* (Gainesville, FL: University of Florida Press, 2001), 253–259. For accounts of the shah's decision, see S. H. Taqizadeh, *Zendegi-ye Tufani: khaṭerāt-e Sayyed Ḥasan Taqizādeh* [A Stormy Life: The Memoires of Sayyed Hasan Taqizādeh], 2nd ed., ed. Iraj Afshar (Tehran: 'Elmi, 1993), 231–232; Mihdi Quli Khan Hidayat, *Khatirat va Khatarat* [Memoirs and Dangers] (Tehran, 1950), 500–505.

[55] BP 96487 Note of an Interview, Taqizadeh and M. Fateh, December 2, 1932.

[56] Elm, *Oil, Power, and Principle*, 38.

[57] BP 52889 Notes of a Meeting, November 23, 1933.

[58] Shaul Bakhash, "Britain and the Abdication of Reza Shah," *Middle Eastern Studies* 52, no. 2 (2016): 318–334.

Gulf to the Soviet Union and the British forced the Bank-e Melli to print billions of new rials (the national currency) to fund the occupation. The number of rials in circulation grew from 990 million in 1939 to 6.8 billion by 1944, causing rampant inflation that was further compounded by food shortages and a breakdown in trade.[59] The war was a national calamity, one that would leave a permanent scar on all who lived through it.

Despite the shock of the invasion, the fall of the first Pahlavi liberalized Iranian politics. New political organizations emerged, including the Hizb-e Tudeh, or "Party of the Masses," formed by a group of leftist intellectuals freed from Reza Shah's prisons in 1941. Like the Pahlavi regime, the Tudeh expressed an ideology of national transformation, albeit one influenced by Marxist-Leninist principles. The Engineers' Association, a group of Western-educated doctors, lawyers, and professionals expressed the need for administrative reform and an end to corruption.[60] The *'ulama*, Iran's Shi'a clerical class, also returned to the fore. One tract, *Kashf al-Asrar* (Secrets Revealed), denounced European "decadence" typified by Reza Shah's reforms and called for a return to Islamic governance. The author, a relatively obscure cleric named Ruhollah Khomeini, did not object to the institution of monarchy. But he did suggest the shah be bound by Islamic jurisprudence.[61]

Though frequently at odds with one another, these new dissidents embraced a worldview centered on rejecting foreign influence over domestic political affairs (though this would change in the case of the Tudeh Party). The position was expressed eloquently by the nationalist Majlis deputy Mohammed Mosaddeq, the same man who had opposed Reza Khan's ascension in 1925. In 1944 Mosaddeq suggested Iran adopt a position of "passive balance" (*muvazanah-e manfi*) also referred to as "negative equilibrium." Trying to balance foreign interests – like offering additional oil concessions to balance the AIOC position in Khuzestan, for example – was like "asking a man, who has lost one of his arms, to cut his other arm for the sake of balancing his body."[62] Iran should adopt a neutral position and forge an independent course, he argued.

---

[59] Stephens to Garner, September 30, 1949, Attachment No. 1, Van Zeeland Report, Iran – General – Correspondence 04, 1805822, WBGA; Stephen L. McFarland, "Anatomy of an Iranian Political Crowd: the Tehran Bread Riot of December 1942," *International Journal of Middle East Studies* 17, no. 1 (February 1985): 51–65.

[60] Abrahamian, *Iran between Two Revolutions*, 188–189; HIOHP, Sanjabi Interview, Tape 5, 12–13.

[61] Ruhollah Khomeini, *Kashf al-Asrar* [Secrets Revealed] (Lost Angeles, CA: Ketab Corporation, 2009); Matin-Asgari, *Both Eastern and Western*, 128–135.

[62] George C. McGhee, "Recollections of Dr. Muhammed Mussadiq," in W. Roger Louis and James Bill (eds.), *Musaddiq, Iranian Nationalism and Oil* (London: Tauris, 1988),

1.3 Occupation, "Incapacity," and Expertise

Amid such foment, the Iranian elite – aristocrats, merchants, and landowners who dominated the Majlis – shared power between themselves and the new shah, twenty-one-year-old Mohammed Reza Pahlavi, the first Pahlavi's eldest son. Despite the dissent from the right and left, the elite directed most of their attention toward securing foreign patronage in the belief that balancing British and Soviet interests would allow Iran to remain nominally independent, a political philosophy known as "positive equilibrium." Some saw the need to attract a "third force," to counter the Anglo-Soviet presence. For a small clique led by the young shah, the United States of America seemed a natural choice. An American presence would balance that of the Soviets and British and permit Iran to retain its independence once the war was over.[63]

President Franklin D. Roosevelt received the first Iranian request for assistance in January 1942. There were compelling strategic reasons to respond favorably. Protecting the "Persian Corridor" was a major wartime objective.[64] A larger American presence in Iran would facilitate "the steady transportation of American supplies to Russia."[65] The British, who thought a US presence would strengthen their position in the oil fields, endorsed a more active American role in managing the supply line. Iran was filled with "reactionary politicians with unsavory reputations," said the British ambassador. It could do with some political guidance.[66]

While US troops helped manage the supply line, American advisors assisted the Iranian government manage the fallout from the occupation. Missions were sent for the army, which after the invasion had been left "demoralized, inefficient ... and almost disintegrated," and to the *gendarmerie*, the latter led by Colonel H. Norman Schwarzkopf, the former chief of the New Jersey State Police.[67] By 1943, there were missions assisting Iran's government with everything from police training to grain distribution. Americans were in positions of authority throughout Iran's

---

301; Kay-Ustuvan, *Siyasat-e muvazanah-e manfi dar Majlis-i Chahardahum* [Negative Equilibrium in the Fourteenth Majlis], vol. I (Tehran, 1949), 182–185.

[63] Abrahamian, *Iran between Two Revolutions*, 169; Fakhreddin Azimi, *Iran: The Crisis of Democracy: from the Exile of Reza Shah to the Fall of Musaddiq* (London: IB Tauris, 2009), 1–80.

[64] T. H. Vail Motter, *The Persian Corridor and Aid to Russia* (Washington, Office of the Chief of Military History, Dept. of the Army, 1952).

[65] *FRUS 1942, IV*: 222–223.   [66] *FRUS 1942, IV*: 225–226.

[67] RG 59 891.20/165, Dreyfus to Hull, August 14, 1942, USNA; Thomas M. Ricks, "US Military Missions to Iran, 1943–1978: The Political Economy of Military Assistance," *Iranian Studies* 12, no. 3/4 (Summer-Autumn 1979): 163–193; see also Bill, *The Eagle and the Lion*, 15–27; Lytle, *The Origins of the Iranian-American Alliance*, 41–46; Louise L'Estrange Fawcett, *Iran and the Cold War: The Azerbaijan Crisis of 1946* (Cambridge: Cambridge University Press, 1992), 110–122.

administration. "We shall soon be in a position," noted the State Department's Wallace Murray, "of actually 'running' Iran."[68]

Americans found the country baffling. "There are so many different Irans," wrote *New Yorker* correspondent Joel Sayre. Apart from missionaries who had traveled to Iran to establish schools or the occasional oil executive looking to crack the British monopoly, very few Americans visited Iran (or "Persia" as it was still widely known) before the war. Sayre described a country that fit the American image of a romantic Orient, but only from certain angles. The men in Western business suits walking the streets of Tehran, speaking Persian-accented French while smoking cigarettes and sipping coffee, bore little in common with the "ancient people" loading ass-carts near the port of Khorramshahr.[69] A guide for US Army personnel helpfully pointed out that Iranians "belong to the so-called Caucasian race, like ourselves," and were to be treated with the courtesy and respect owed to white Europeans.[70] At the same time, Americans saw Iran as a place of backwardness, suffering from "the evils of greedy minorities, monopolies, aggression and imperialism," according to Patrick J. Hurley, Roosevelt's Middle East envoy.[71] There was an unmistakable sense of otherness attached to the country and its inhabitants that suffused official US discourse, particularly among those like Hurley who lacked any background in Iranian history, language, or culture.

For a time, American policy toward Iran was surprisingly ambitious, considering the country's relative lack of importance to traditional US interests. Troubled by Iran's economic distress and political instability, officials focused on two culprits: foreign imperialism and elite corruption. A report from the military attaché in November 1942 described Iranians as "appallingly illiterate," led by a political class who welcomed US help "[to] save them from the British and Russians."[72] Iran was riddled with mismanagement and graft, on the verge of "economic chaos and possible revolution."[73] In an important State Department memorandum, Middle East specialist John Jernegan argued in early 1943 that Iran had fallen victim to imperialism and

---

[68] *FRUS 1942, IV*: 242.
[69] Joel Sayre, *Persian Gulf Command: Some Marvels on the Road to Kazvin* (New York: Random House, 1945), xv, 32–33.
[70] *A Pocket Guide to Iran* (Washington, DC: War and Navy Departments, 1943), 10.
[71] *FRUS 1943, IV*: 420–426.
[72] RG 84 USLETCGR, 1941–1945, Box 2, Report No. 31, John G. Ondrick, November 27, 1942, USNA.
[73] RG 59 891.51A/1-645, Lewis to Stettinius, Enclosure No. 1 Letter from Hudson to Allen, December 22, 1944, USNA.

1.3 Occupation, "Incapacity," and Expertise

needed to be rebuilt with help from American experts, acting as a "test case" for a new foreign policy based on the principles of the Atlantic Charter. An aid campaign and expanded advisory missions could preserve Iran "as an independent nation ... self-reliant and prosperous, open to the trade of all nations and a threat to none."[74]

For a time, such ideas found purchase at the highest levels of government. Hurley wrote in late 1943 that Iran required a course of "nation building," with teams of US advisors reconstructing the Iranian administrative state from scratch.[75] Roosevelt, who paid more attention to Hurley than to his own State Department, visited Tehran for the Big Three conference in December and was struck by the rampant inequality, "[where] less than one percent of the population owns practically all the land."[76] Egged on by Hurley, Roosevelt secured Churchill and Stalin's signatures to a "Declaration for Iran," which recognized "the assistance which Iran has given in the prosecution of the war," and promised that once the war was over, Iran's economic problems would be given "full consideration."[77] It is unclear whether the British or Soviet leaders thought much of the declaration, but Roosevelt seemed to take it seriously. He confessed himself "rather thrilled with the idea of using Iran as an example" of what the United States could accomplish "by an unselfish foreign policy." The president admitted the challenge was immense: "We could not take on a more difficult nation than Iran."[78]

Alarmed by the disorganization in Iranian state finances, the United States dispatched a large mission to assist the shah's Ministry of Finance. The mission was led by Arthur C. Millspaugh. Among the many Americans sent to Iran during the war, Millspaugh was unique in the sense that he had real experience with Iranian internal affairs. Twenty years earlier, Millspaugh had served as financial advisor to the government of Reza Khan. From 1921 to 1927, Millspaugh reordered Iran's budget, producing one of the first studies of the Iranian economy ever published in English.[79] Millspaugh arrived in Tehran in the wake of the 1921 coup, praised by Iranian newspapers as "the last doctor called to the death-bed of a sick person." Millspaugh had mixed feelings about his new home. "A weak ... immature country," with a "primitive and

---

[74] *FRUS 1943, IV*: 330–336.
[75] *FRUS 1943, IV*: 420–426. See also Collier, *Democracy and the Nature of American Influence in Iran*, 33–37.
[76] Memo for the President, January 12, 1944, Box 1, President's Official File, FDRPL.
[77] *FRUS 1943, IV*: 413–414.
[78] Memo for the President, January 12, 1944, Box 1, President's Official File, FDRPL.
[79] Arthur C. Millspaugh, *The Financial and Economic Situation of Persia* (New York: The Persia Society, 1926).

medieval" economy dominated by "reactionary" elements, Iran seemed to struggle against the tide of history.[80] Millspaugh did not think Iranians racially inferior – "apart from the superficialities of dress and manner, they look, think, talk, and act like the rest of us," he wrote. But he doubted the Pahlavi government's ability to manage state finances efficiently, despite the "strong will" of its ruler. Finance was a "difficult piece of machinery for a representative government to operate," and Iran appeared to lack "enlightened and effective public opinion in support of honest, efficient and law-observing administration."[81]

In 1942, Roosevelt's State Department asked Millspaugh to return to Iran and resume his role as financial advisor. He took the assignment with considerable reluctance. Time and lingering bitterness over his ejection from Iran in 1927 had made Millspaugh cantankerous. He was more dismissive of Iran's capacity for self-government than he had been twenty years earlier. "Morale is low among Iran's young men," he warned one Iranian diplomat. "They need someone who can protect them when they do good work and discipline them when they go wrong."[82]

Millspaugh arrived in Iran and set about reordering state finances as he saw fit. His team imposed rigid guidelines on the budget, mandating new rules in the bazaar and managing the nation's financial affairs with little input from the Majlis or the shah's ministers.[83] Millspaugh's attempts to cut military spending irritated the shah, who regarded the army as his personal sphere of influence, while the mission's proposed progressive income tax threatened the interests of the aristocracy and merchant class.[84] Bank-e Melli Governor, Abolhassan Ebtehaj, lambasted Millspaugh for taking over the country's financial system and freeing up billions of rials for the importation of luxury items "like silk fabrics and toothbrushes."[85] Millspaugh, in response, demanded the authority to fire Ebtehaj, who left for the Bretton Woods Conference in July 1944 promising to have Millspaugh removed as soon as he returned.

---

[80] Arthur C. Millspaugh, *The American Task in Persia* (New York: The Century Co., 1925), 3, 15.
[81] Millspaugh, *The American Task in Persia*, 43, 91, 16, 140–141.
[82] RG 84 USLETCGR, 1941–1945, Box 2, Alling to Dreyfus, Enclosed Letter from Millspaugh to Schayesteh, October 12, 1942, USNA.
[83] Collier, *Democracy and the Nature of American Influence in Iran*, 23–26; Simon Davis, "'A Projected New Trusteeship?' American Internationalism, British Imperialism, and the Reconstruction of Iran, 1938–1947," *Diplomacy & Statecraft* 17, no. 1 (2006): 31–72.
[84] Fawcett, *Iran and the Cold War*, 117; RG 59 891.51A/1-645, Lewis to Stettinius, Enclosure No. 1 Letter from Hudson to Allen, December 22, 1944, USNA.
[85] Abolhassan Ebtehaj, *Khatirat-e Abu'l-Hasan Ebtehaj* [The Memoirs of Abolhassan Ebtehaj] Vol. I (London: Alireza Arouzi, 1991), 114.

1.3 Occupation, "Incapacity," and Expertise

The drama surrounding the American advisor dominated Tehran's press and limited the amount of work Millspaugh was able to accomplish. The growing anti-foreign chorus within Iran's fractured political scene saw Millspaugh as emblematic of Iran's continued weakness. In a fiery address to the Majlis on July 6, 1944, Mosaddeq declared the Millspaugh mission to be "incompatible with the constitution." The Americans had taken control of the Iranian state, reducing the shah's finance minister "to the status of an advisor," and using their power to print "an unlimited quantity of notes," causing inflation and hardship, Mosaddeq argued. If Millspaugh was not willing to subordinate himself to the government, he must step down.[86] In early 1945, the State Department bowed to Iranian pressure and withdrew its support for the financial mission, forcing Millspaugh to leave Iran.[87]

The Millspaugh mission embodied an important element within the American advisor campaign. For all its idealism, the missions considered the Iranians as patients to be treated, rather than as equal partners. In Millspaugh's view, Iran needed to be saved, both from the imperialists and from itself. Such direct intervention provoked a strong reaction among Iranians who were determined to limit foreign interference in internal affairs. All Iranians from the shah to administrators like Ebtehaj and nationalists like Mosaddeq opposed the Millspaugh mission. Though they recognized Millspaugh's shortcomings and did not regret his departure, other American officials tended to find fault in his Iranian hosts. "The primary reason" for Millspaugh's failure, concluded an embassy official in March 1945, "[was] a total lack of cooperation on the part of all classes of Iranians."[88] The aristocracy had conspired against Millspaugh: "[C]orrupt and selfish political elements," wrote one report, "stand to lose personally" had the advisor succeeded in passing his intended reforms.[89] This confirmed the belief, widespread among the Americans, that the Iranian elite stood in the way of the country's reform and stability. "I am convinced," wrote Ambassador Leland Morris, "that no influential group ... desires foreign financial or economic advisors."[90] The onus was placed on the Iranians themselves, who had shown "a regrettable lack of clarity," by first requesting advisors

---

[86] RG 84 USLETCGR, 1941–1945, Box 5, Speech Against Dr. Millspaugh by Deputy Mohammed Mossadegh, July 8, 1944, USNA.
[87] Kuniholm, *The Origins of the Cold War in the Near East*, 172–173.
[88] RG 84 USLETCGR, 1941–1945, Box 8, C. V. Ferguson, Memo for Ambassador Morris, March 1945, USNA.
[89] Quoted in Fawcett, *Iran and the Cold War*, 118.
[90] RG 59 891.51A/2-345, Morris to State, No. 70 February 3, 1945, USNA.

and then rejecting them when they overstepped their authority.[91] The patient, in the American view, had turned away the medicine.

Though they drew on previous experiences by missionaries and financial advisors, the wartime missions constituted the first substantive form of development assistance offered by the United States to Iran. They began an era of engagement that would last more than twenty years. The experience, however, revealed several major sources of friction. For Americans, Iran appeared immature, unstable, and in need of foreign assistance. The key causes of its instability were imperialism, elite corruption, and administrative incompetence. These were not controversial points. Many Iranians, particularly among the educated middle-class, agreed that the country's government was poorly run and there was widespread opposition to the influence of the British in the south and Russians in the north. But the American conception of Iranian incapacity would pose significant challenges to cooperation, both in the 1940s and in the future. While Iran appeared incapable of administering its own reform, indigenous reactions to direct assistance rendered the effectiveness of that assistance limited, as the Millspaugh mission illustrated. These elements imbued future American development endeavors with a distinctly ambivalent attitude – how to save a country if the inhabitants turned away your aid?

For these reasons, the missionary spirit proved fleeting. By 1945, the drive to assist Iran through advisors had dissipated. Figures like Hurley and Jernegan lost out to a group of policymakers – Dean Acheson, Loy W. Henderson, and a series of new US ambassadors to Iran – who were skeptical of advisors. Eugene Rostow scoffed at the missions as "an innocent indulgence in messianic globaloney," while Acheson regarded Hurley's program of assistance with deep suspicion: Sending out "indoctrinated amateurs, ignorant of the politics and problems of the Mohammedan world," to transform countries like Iran seemed the height of folly.[92] There was nevertheless a recognition of Iran's importance to American interests. As Roosevelt's advisor, Harold Hoskins, noted in early 1945, the United States ought to increase its commitment to Iran's progress, "not for any sentimental reasons," but for the sake of national security.[93] Iran's significance to the United States lay in its position athwart the world's largest and most valuable oil fields.

---

[91] RG 59 891.51A/2-345, Grew to Morris, No. 65, February 10, 1945, USNA.
[92] RG 59 891.00/2844, Acheson to Stettinius, January 28, 1944, USNA; Lytle, *Origins of the US-Iranian Alliance*, 93–94; Dean Acheson, *Present at the Creation: My Years at the State Department* (New York: Norton, 1969), 133.
[93] RG 84 USLETCGR, 1941–1945, Box 7, Harold B. Hoskins, "Economic Aid to Iran," January 13, 1945, USNA.

This view grew clearer once the context of an ideological struggle against communism solidified in 1946 – a conflict where Iran was to be an important battleground.

1.4 Oil, Iran, and the Cold War

As it entered World War II, US oil reserves equaled 46 percent of the world total. The United States accounted for two-thirds of global oil production.[94] Large domestic discoveries and access to oil in Latin America left the United States and the major US oil companies with enough crude to supply the domestic economy and fuel the global war effort. However, fears of a postwar shortage preoccupied policymakers. Consumption outpaced the rate at which new fields were discovered, and it was estimated the United States would become a net importer by the late 1940s. While there were initiatives that aimed at bringing the US government directly into the oil industry, wartime oil policy supported efforts by private companies to seek new concessions and secure reserves held overseas, in the hope that it would improve American energy security in the postwar period.[95]

Conscious of the American interest in overseas oil, the Pahlavi government extended an invitation to the Standard Vacuum Oil Company (StanVac), a venture co-owned by Jersey Standard and the Standard Oil Company of New York (Socony), to offer a bid on areas outside the AIOC area in early 1943. Like the advisory missions, this was intended to draw in American support for Iran as a counter to the influence of the British and Soviets. "It has long been the wish of the Government," explained Iran's ambassador in Washington, "to have American companies represented in the development of Iran's petroleum resources."[96] The young shah, eager to obtain a more meaningful US commitment, insisted to the US *charge d'affaires* that they could count on his "sympathetic consideration," noting how Iran "needs money badly."[97] The thinking was straightforward: An oil concession would solidify the US presence and balance the AIOC concession in the south. It would also buttress state finances. While payments from AIOC still constituted less than 15 percent of the state budget, the oil industry had become an important source of foreign exchange. A concession,

---

[94] Painter, *Oil and the American Century*, 9.
[95] Michael B. Stoff, *Oil, War, and American Security: The Search for a National Policy on Foreign Oil, 1941–1947* (New Haven, CT: Yale University Press, 1980), 22–33; Painter, *Oil and the American Century*, 32–47.
[96] RG 59 891.6363/808, P. W. Parker (StanVac) to Alling, October 20, 1943, USNA.
[97] RG 59 891.6363/830, Ford to Hull, March 13, 1944, USNA.

moreover, would be permanent, securing a lasting US commitment to Iranian independence – the policy of positive equilibrium in action.

The companies were interested. Both Jersey and Socony were "crude short": They had plenty of markets (and would have more once the war was over), but not enough oil to feed them all. StanVac served as the companies' distribution subsidiary in the eastern hemisphere and needed access to Middle East oil to meet postwar demand. Apart from a thin share of the concession in Iraq, neither Jersey nor Socony had access to Middle East reserves. The AIOC monopoly had vexed American companies for years – Jersey attempted twice in the 1920s and 1930s to break into Iran, without success.[98] But the companies demurred, waiting for State Department permission before sending executives to Tehran. Given the importance of preserving the Anglo-American alliance, there were risks involved in permitting US companies to enter Iran. Officials at the embassy warned that an oil concession would irritate the British and potentially trigger a Russian reaction.[99]

Such concerns were ignored. The State Department "looks with favor upon the development of all possible sources of petroleum," Secretary of State Cordell Hull told StanVac executives.[100] Hull, a fierce advocate for American commercial interests, believed further penetration of the Middle East by American companies would ensure postwar energy security. He was also interested in seeing oil form a part of the general US program to rebuild Iran. As he explained to Roosevelt, it was in the US interest that Iran be able "to stand on her feet without foreign control." While the advisory missions would shore up Iran in the short-term, the nation's independence would be ensured if the United States made its interest explicit through an oil concession. "From a more directly selfish point of view," Hull wrote, it was in the interest of the United States "that no great power be established on the Persian Gulf opposite the important American petroleum development in Saudi Arabia," where Socal and Texaco, two other US majors, were developing a concession.[101] Iran's oil was important, but the country's strategic location was arguably of greater importance. The desire to dominate Middle East oil compelled the United States to seek a concession in Iran.

---

[98] Michael A. Rubin, "Stumbling through the 'Open Door': The US in Persia and the Standard-Sinclair Oil Dispute, 1920–1925," *Iranian Studies* 28, no. ¾ (Summer-Autumn 1995): 203–229.

[99] RG 59 891.6363/807, Dreyfus to Hull, November 15, 1943, USNA.

[100] RG 59 891.6363/807, Hull to Dreyfus, November 23, 1943, 891.6363/808, Berle to Parker, November 17, 1943, USNA.

[101] RG 891.00/2042A, Hull to Roosevelt, "American Policy in Iran," August 10, 1943, USNA. See also Painter, *Oil and the American Century*, 76–77.

1.4 Oil, Iran, and the Cold War

The concession scramble played out in chaotic fashion. Royal Dutch/Shell, an Anglo-Dutch company, was another "crude short" firm with an interest in expanding its Middle East access. Shell executives arrived in Tehran in early 1944 and began approaching Majlis deputies, promising a concession with a $1 million lump-sum payment to sweeten the deal.[102] StanVac arrived in Iran to find Shell with a considerable head start. The situation grew more complicated when another US company, Sinclair Oil, joined the fray. As Shell had the most favorable negotiating position, the concession scramble sent off alarm bells among the more Anglo-phobic US officials fearful that American capital was about to get shut out. Persian Gulf oil constituted "the greatest single prize in human history," wrote John Leavall, the petroleum attaché in Cairo, but British tampering had produced a situation "combining the worst features of feudal economy and capitalism." Unless living conditions improved, oil nations of the Middle East would succumb to revolution, while American oil concessions "would cease entirely to be under our nation's control."[103] To Leavall's chagrin, Hull would not back either StanVac or Sinclair, as an intervention might undermine the principal of free enterprise.

Before the Majlis could consider any of the new concession offers, a Soviet delegation arrived in Iran to discuss a concession covering the northern provinces. Where the Anglo-American proposals were commercial, the US ambassador believed a Soviet concession would function as an "agreement between states," and cement Moscow's control over Iran's north.[104] The Soviet intervention worried the Iranians. Rather than open up the situation to a three-sided Great Power competition, Prime Minister Mohammed Sa'ed suspended concession discussions until after the war. Nationalist deputies led by Mosaddeq then pushed a bill through the Majlis that made it illegal for Iran's prime minister to offer concessions until after the occupation – all foreign troops had to vacate Iranian territory before any new bids could be considered.[105] The move tied the government's hands and halted the concession scramble.

With negotiations on hold, the Americans puzzled over the Soviet move. On the face of it, a Soviet oil concession in northern Iran made sense. The Soviet Union shared a border with Iran that was over 1,000 miles long. Soviet oil production was depressed due to the war and Moscow would need new sources to facilitate the postwar economic

---

[102] RG 59 891.6363/816, Stewart to Sheeds, January 1, 1944, USNA.
[103] RG 59 891.6363/8-2644, Memorandum by Leavall, August 26, 1944, USNA.
[104] RG 59 891.6363/10-244, Morris to Washington, October 2, 1944, USNA.
[105] RG 59 891.6363/11-544, Morris to State, November 5, 1944, USNA.

recovery.[106] Herbert Hoover Jr., the son of the former president and an oil advisor to the Iranian government, thought that the only natural market for Iran's northern oil was the Soviet Union. If Iran wished to utilize this oil, it would have to do business with Moscow.[107] "The Russians are still suspicious of the US advisory program," a report from the Office of Strategic Services concluded, while the Office of Petroleum Advisor determined that "pragmatic economic interest" motivated the Russian move.[108] Given their position in Khuzestan, the British were circumspect over the threat of a Russian concession. According to the ambassador in Tehran, there should be no objection, "provided that [the] concession is granted ... freely and not under pressure."[109] Britain was prepared to accept a permanent partition of Iran so long as it protected AIOC's position.[110]

The Soviet move in Iran prompted concern among a group of US officials who viewed communism as an existential threat to the United States and the postwar international order.[111] According to the *charge d'affaires* George F. Kennan in Moscow, "apprehension of potential foreign penetration" motivated Soviet policy. Iranian oil was important not as an economic asset, "but as something it might be dangerous to permit anyone else to exploit."[112] Loy W. Henderson, head of the State Department's Near East division and an ardent anti-communist, rejected the idea of entertaining Russian demands for a concession, "regardless of how reasonable," and declared that the United States would not deal with the Soviets "behind the back of a small country." In a long memo written in August 1945, Henderson insisted that the United States protect Iran from threats to its sovereignty, which he felt were "implicit in the Russian desire for access to the Persian Gulf."[113] Wallace Murray,

---

[106] Vladislov M. Zubok, "Stalin, Soviet Intelligence, and the Struggle for Iran, 1945–1953," *Diplomatic History* 44, no. 1 (January 2020): 22–46; Natalia Egorova, "Stalin's Oil Policy and the Iranian Crisis of 1945–1946," in Jeronim Perovic (ed.), *Cold War Energy: A Transnational History of Soviet Oil and Gas* (Cham, Switzerland: Palgrave Macmillan, 2017), 79–104.

[107] RG 59 891.6363/10-1144, Statement of Herbert Hoover Jr. on Oil Negotiations in Iran, October 11, 1944, USNA.

[108] RG 84 USLETCGR, 1941–1945, Box 8, "Report on Iranian Oil as Potential Source of Political Conflict," May 9, 1944; RG 59 891.6363/12-1145, "Oil Concessions and the Problems in Iran," December 11, 1945, USNA.

[109] FO 371/52728 Bullard to Eden, No. 179, February 4, 1946, UKNA.

[110] Fawcett, *Iran and the Cold War*, 173–175.

[111] Kuniholm, *The Origins of the Cold War in the Near East*, 188; Melvyn P. Leffler, *Safeguarding Democratic Capitalism: US Foreign Policy and National Security, 1920–2015* (Princeton, NJ: Princeton University Press, 2017), 133–143.

[112] RG 59 891.6363/11-744, Kennan to Stettinius, November 7, 1944;

[113] RG 59 891.00/8-2345, Loy Henderson, "United States Policy towards Iran," August 23, 1945, 891.6363/12-1145, Memorandum, December 11, 1945, USNA.

the ambassador in Tehran, felt a Soviet concession in Iran's northern provinces would threaten "our immensely rich oil holdings in Saudi Arabia."[114]

Kennan emphasized Russian territorial ambitions in his famous "Long Telegram" from February 1946, suggesting that firm resistance to such advances would cause Stalin to reconsider. As the breadth of Soviet ambitions became clear after the Potsdam Conference of July 1945, Iran emerged as a point where the United States could resist the threatening spread of Soviet hegemony. In the words of historian Louise Fawcett, "In Eastern Europe it was already too late, in Iran it was not."[115]

Events in March 1946 appeared to justify American concerns. While British and American troops withdrew, Soviet forces remained and backed separatists in the northern province of Azerbaijan. Stalin told Tehran that the troops would leave once he was promised an oil concession. Officials at the US embassy warned of an imminent Soviet offensive while the American consul in Tabriz delivered panicked reports of a three-pronged attack on Iraq, Turkey, and Iran.[116] President Harry S. Truman perceived in the Soviet actions a "giant pincers movement against the oil-rich areas of the Near East."[117] Ambassador to Iran George V. Allen warned that Iran could become a "Russian puppet state," that "slavish Soviet tools and unscrupulous adventurers" might facilitate a coup d'état. The Persian Gulf would become a realm of "intense international rivalry ... with control of all Middle East oil as one of the vital matters at stake."[118] While the United States coordinated a response in the United Nations, the British considered ways to protect their position in the Iranian oil fields.[119] Defending AIOC's profits was "imperative ... for our commercial and economic well-being," according to Defense Minister Emanuel Shinwell.[120] With the Soviets entrenched in Azerbaijan and the British determined to retain control over the oil fields of Khuzestan, Iran's permanent partition loomed.

---

[114] *FRUS 1945, VIII*: 417–420. [115] Fawcett, *Iran and the Cold War*, 121.
[116] *FRUS 1946, VII*: 340; McFarland, "Peripheral View of the Cold War," 347.
[117] Harry S. Truman, *Memoirs, Vol 1: Year of Decisions* (New York: New American Library, 1965), 523.
[118] RG 59 891.00/6-446, Allen to Byrnes, June 4, 1946, USNA.
[119] Stephen G. Galpern, *Money, Oil and Empire in the Middle East: Sterling and Postwar Imperialism, 1944–1971* (Cambridge: Cambridge University Press, 2009), 1–22. See also Alexander Nicholas Shaw, "'Strong, United and Independent': The British Foreign Office Anglo-Iranian Oil Company and the Internationalization of Iranian Politics at the Dawn of the Cold War, 1945–1946," *Middle Eastern Studies* 52, no. 3 (2016): 505–524.
[120] FO 371/52723 Shinwell to Bevin, July 31, 1946, UKNA.

The Pahlavi government was not a passive participant in the crisis. Anxious to stave off further Soviet aggression, the shah's Prime Minister, Ahmed Qavam, traveled to Moscow in April and met with Stalin personally. An experienced politician known for his intelligence and strength under pressure, Qavam flattered the Soviet leader, promised him an oil concession, and suggested turning Iran into a republic.[121] Having secured the Soviet promise to withdraw, Qavam returned to Tehran and publicly embraced the Tudeh Party, bringing several communists into this government. The prime minister, drawing on support from his followers in the Majlis, also drew up plans for an ambitious economic program. Before departing Moscow, Qavam convened a gathering of Iran's most eminent economic minds in March 1946.[122] "The standard of living of the great masses of the Iranian people," he declared, "though extremely low before the war, has become still worse." He proposed that Iran launch a national program of economic revitalization. Offering another fig leaf to Iran's communists, Qavam took a page out of the Soviet book and called his new program the Seven-Year Plan.[123]

While he appeased Moscow, Qavam's real plan was to maintain American support for Iran's territorial integrity. He continued to meet with both British and American ambassadors throughout the crisis. His Seven-Year Plan, meanwhile, was part of a general push by the Pahlavi government to secure US financial assistance. "Patriots," explained Ebtehaj to Ambassador Allen, were trying to save the country from Soviet conquest, and a US declaration of physical assistance would have "considerable moral effect."[124] Ebtehaj signed a deal with an American firm, Morrison & Knudsen Inc., to prepare an economic survey on which the plan could be based. In October 1946 Husayn 'Ala, Iran's representative to the United Nations, sent a note to the International Bank of Reconstruction and Development – the US-backed financial institution better known as the World Bank – requesting a loan of $250 million for the new national development plan.[125] The shah repeatedly invoked Iran's need for social and economic reform to Allen, while still pushing for an oil concession to balance the one Qavam would offer to the Soviets. Allen reported the odd spectacle of a foreign leader "begging

---

[121] Zubok, "Stalin, Soviet Intelligence, and the Struggle for Iran," 29.
[122] HIOHP, Sanjabi, Tape No. 8, 7–8.
[123] "Supreme Economic Council," *Ettela'at*, March 30, 1946.
[124] RG 59 891.502-51A /9-2146, Allen to State, September 21, 1946, USNA.
[125] RG 59 891.51/10-2646, Aide-Memoire from Iranian Embassy, October 26, 1946, USNA.

Americans to take an oil concession."[126] The Seven-Year Plan was a tool to lure American support back into Iran, after the failures of the advisory missions and the oil concession scramble.

The United States shifted to a stance of active containment toward the Soviet Union in 1946.[127] Yet there were doubts on whether direct assistance to Iran was prudent. Henderson thought that concrete aid for Iran was vital for preserving its territorial integrity. "Unless we show ... that we are seriously interested" in assisting Iran, he concluded, the Iranian people would become "so discouraged that they will no longer be able to resist Soviet pressures."[128] At the same time, means for assisting Iran seemed limited. The idea of an American oil concession had lost its appeal, with the State Department warning American oil executives to steer clear of Iran until the crisis over the Soviet concession had been resolved. Though the Soviet actions in Azerbaijan gave credence to the growing concern in Washington that confrontation with the Soviets was inevitable, the response of the Truman administration was cautious and focused largely on marshaling support for Iran in the United Nations.[129] In November, Assistant Secretary of State Dean Acheson assured Allen that the United States was prepared to furnish Iran with more military aid and would support its independence with "appropriate acts."[130]

The onset of the global Cold War clarified the US position on Iran, as it did with the Middle East in general. The region, though a British sphere of influence, was crucial for meeting the energy needs of the United States and the Western world as a whole. Iran, like the region's other states emerging from various stages of colonialism, required support to ward off the threat of communism. Yet if US policymakers determined the need to assist Iran, they had not yet settled on a means. Both the advisory missions and oil concession search had proven to be dead ends. While Soviet forces left Iran and the shah's troops successfully reoccupied the separatist province of Azerbaijan in December 1946, for the United States a definitive solution to the crisis – an answer to Iran's state of instability – had not presented itself. Fortunately, at that moment the oil oligopoly came to the rescue, providing a solution tailored to the needs of the US government.

---

[126] RG 59 891.6363/7-3146, Allen to State, July 31,1946, USNA; *FRUS 1946, VII*: 509–510.
[127] Richard Pfau, "Containment in Iran, 1946: The Shift to an Active Policy," *Diplomatic History* 1, no. 4 (Fall 1977): 359–372.
[128] *FRUS 1946, VII*: 533–536.
[129] Leffler, *Safeguarding Democratic Capitalism*, 144–146.
[130] *FRUS 1946, VII*: 546–547.

1.5 The Dual Integration of Iranian Oil

In late 1946, the global oil market stood on the verge of another crisis. Despite the rapid decline in military consumption, civilian consumption was set to rise dramatically, driven by demand for motor fuel and oil products for heating.[131] Prices rose and fears mounted that supply would be unable to meet demand. To secure the orderly exploitation of the major Middle East oil fields and prevent destructive competition, the largest oil companies came together for a series of accords historians would dub the "great oil deals."[132]

The deals were motivated by commercial concerns. The colossal abundance represented by the Middle East oil fields threatened markets with instability and overproduction, as most of it was in the hands of a few companies with inadequate market outlets. AIOC, for example, produced 408,000 bpd yet anticipated markets for only 224,000 bpd after the war.[133] Socal and Texaco, which together held the concession over Saudi Arabia, were in a similar position. Socony, Jersey Standard, and Shell all lacked oil for their markets, a commercial quandary that had driven them toward obtaining a concession in Iran in 1944. As competition loomed, the companies decided to share the spoils of the Middle East between them. The resulting agreements remade the global oil economy and imposed a form of international cartelization that would endure for nearly three decades.

Jersey Standard and Socony made a deal with Socal and Texaco for participation in Saudi Arabia, forming a new company, the Arabian American Oil Company (Aramco). Jersey and Socony also agreed to fund a pipeline with AIOC, in return for 134 million tons of AIOC crude purchased over twenty years. Shell secured a long-term contract for oil from Gulf, AIOC's partner in Kuwait.[134] The companies were now bound up in mutual agreements to share Middle East oil among themselves: four US majors shared Saudi Arabia; Iraq was split among the US companies, AIOC, Shell, and a French firm; Kuwait was split between Gulf Oil and AIOC, while Iranian oil would now flow to Shell, Jersey,

---

[131] Painter, *Oil and the American Century*, 97–98.
[132] Painter, *Oil and the American Century*, 102–110; Yergin, *The Prize*, 392–394.
[133] T 273/359 Note of Conversation, Oil and Foreign Exchange, January 23, 1945, UKNA; BP 72339 "AIOC Policy" July 22, 1946.
[134] RG 891.6363/12-3146, Robertson to US Embassy Tehran No. 13, January 8, 1947, USNA. The deals were modified in subsequent years. AIOC's pipeline with Jersey was canceled after the Iraqi government refused to allow construction on the companies' terms. AIOC did become a major seller to the other majors, however: By 1951, StanVac was the company's single largest outside customer, purchasing nearly 20 percent of AIOC's output from Iran.

1.5 The Dual Integration of Iranian Oil

and Socony, thus ending their interest in an Iranian oil concession. As the largest and most mature Middle East oil producer, AIOC was guaranteed a market. Overall, the deals achieved what State Department officials called "orderly development," along lines that were unmistakably cartelistic.[135] This process provided the oligopoly a firm basis for controlling the flow of oil in a way that would ensure profitability and mitigate competition. The deals also served American strategic interests and gave the United States an escape from its awkward position in Iran in the wake of the Azerbaijan crisis.

When news of the deals broke in late December 1946, Ambassador Allen was ecstatic. The deals would increase Iran's revenue "and consequently contribute to the economic stability of Iran for which we are working."[136] The deals meant that the United States could gracefully decline further entreaties from the shah regarding a US oil concession. On March 12, 1947, President Harry S. Truman promised US assistance to any friendly government threatened by communism.[137] Yet Iran would get no aid, for practical reasons. Despite Truman's rhetoric and the preponderance of American power internationally, the United States had no interest in antagonizing the Soviet Union in Iran and did not wish to waste limited resources. Greece and Turkey were offered financial assistance. Iran, meanwhile, would have to subsist on oil revenues and loans from the World Bank.

Iran's omission from the new US policy prompted a startled response from Qavam. Iran, he argued, "must have the strength and means of resisting ... Communist infiltration by raising the standard of life of the people."[138] But Qavam's entreaty fell on deaf ears. The prime minister was falling out of favor with US officials like Allen, who found the young shah a much more promising potential ally. Mohammed Reza Pahlavi scored a considerable moral victory in late 1946 when he led troops into separatist Azerbaijan, reclaiming control of the province. According to Allen, who played tennis with the shah once a week, the larger US goal of maintaining Iran's "territorial integrity" could best be achieved through a policy that supported "[the] improvement of conditions of Iran's workers and peasants" through the Seven-Year Plan. This would counter Soviet accusations that the United States supported "only [the] reactionary

---

[135] Miller, *Search for Security*, 158–172; Anderson, *Aramco, the United States, and Saudi Arabia*, 144–159.
[136] RG 59 891.6363/12-2946, Allen to Marshall, No. 1636, December 29, 1946, USNA.
[137] Melvyn P. Leffler, *A Preponderance of Power: National Security, the Truman Administration, and the Cold War* (Stanford, CA: Stanford University Press, 1992), 141–146.
[138] RG 59 891.50/6-2447, "Assistance to Iran," June 24, 1947, USNA.

ruling class," who Qavam seemed to represent.[139] The shah's government, meanwhile, "has little to gain by granting us an oil concession," wrote Under Secretary of State Robert A. Lovett, since Iran could now fund its postwar economic recovery through the funds provided by AIOC, "in harmony with the spirit of the Seven Year Plan of economic development," formerly announced in March 1947.[140]

AIOC had unexpectedly become the single most important factor in the Anglo-American campaign to build up Iran to the point that it could "stand on its own feet." Given the company's attachment to British imperialism and the rising petro-nationalist opposition within Iran, the US dependence on AIOC was very risky. The company pinned its future profitability on a steady expansion in Iranian production: From 1947 output was expected to increase 8 percent per year, reaching 40 million tons (816,400 bpd) by 1953. "Politically and strategically, Iran is at present the key to the whole Middle East," wrote one company report.[141]

As the British-owned oil industry increased in commercial and strategic importance, it grew into an important target for Iranian nationalists. According to one Iran Party member, after the Azerbaijan Crisis attention turned to the British oil concession, "the most important source of our national wealth and a source of pain for the country."[142] In October 1947, the Majlis rejected the Soviet oil concession offer. At the same time, the assembly passed a bill prohibiting any new oil concessions and called on the government to examine Iran's sovereign rights "in regard to the southern oil concession."[143] The bill was a clear legal challenge to AIOC. Harold Pyman of the Foreign Office felt that the law would be used as the basis for some "tiresome" action against AIOC, which had also contended with a spike in labor militancy, including a major strike in July 1946, and growing public criticisms of its housing and welfare policies in the oil city of Abadan.[144]

This rise in Iranian petro-nationalism elicited shrugs from American officials like Allen. There was likely to be "some difficulties" over the British concession, "but we shall ride them out as best we can," he wrote,

---

[139] RG 59 891.50/9-2547, Allen to State, September 25, 1947, USNA.
[140] RG 59 891.6363/8-1847, Lovett to Allen, August 18, 1947, USNA.
[141] BP 72339 AIOC Policy in Iran, July 22, 1946, G. H. Coxon, Future Production Target for Iran, June 23, 1948.
[142] HIOHP, *Sanjabi*, Tape 8, 7.
[143] RG 59 891.6363/10-2947, US Embassy Tehran No. 539, October 29, 1947, USNA.
[144] RG 59 891.6363/10-2747, Douglas to State, October 27, 1947, USNA; BP 80924 Seddon to Rice, October 29, 1947.

"without much damage."[145] The fact that Iran had now outlawed the very idea of an oil concession did not trouble Allen. Once the Soviet threat to Iranian oil was resolved in late 1947, attention from Washington began to drift. Iran, in the British area of responsibility, would be left to "put its own house in order," according to the State Department, with help from AIOC and other proxies.[146]

1.6 Conclusion

Foreign control had been the hallmark of the Iranian oil industry since the days of the D'Arcy Concession. The oligopoly, acting through the Anglo-Iranian Oil Company, solidified its hold over Iranian oil first by negotiating equitability and eventually through coercion, leaning on British military power to secure the oil fields of Khuzestan in 1941. The war opened up the Iranian state to the influence of American advisors, who had found Iran a baffling venue in which local nationalism and evident incapacity blunted the effect of direct assistance. The Pahlavi state, to ensure its survival, attempted to secure a lasting American commitment through an oil concession. But the United States avoided making its own commitment. By 1947, American policy in Iran was based on the expansion of Iranian oil production and the assumption that oil would help pay for Iran's development. Assistance would come from proxies, the most important being the British oil company.

Local development and global oil were closely linked. Through AIOC and the oil deals of 1946, Iran was smoothly integrated into a postwar petroleum order that fed Middle East oil into the economic reconstruction of Western Europe and Japan – delivering oil to the Marshall Plan and generating stupendous profits for the oligopoly. The companies ordered the oil market as they wished, preserving the cartelization of the 1920s and ensuring profits while limiting competition. In the view of the Pahlavi government and its Great Power benefactors, oil wealth would help pay for the Seven-Year Plan, an indigenous development program which the Anglo-American powers would assist indirectly through private actors and proxies like AIOC.

Officials like US Ambassador George V. Allen doubted the weight of Iranian petro-nationalist attacks: "[T]he Iranian economy," noted Allen,

---

[145] RG 84 USLETCGR, 1945-1951, Box 14, Folder 8, Allen to Jones, October 29, 1947, USNA.
[146] RG 59 891.50/1-848, Marshall to Wiley, January 8, 1948, USNA; Goode, *The United States and Iran, 1946–1951*, 23–24; Ricks, "US Military Missions," 176.

"made the uninterrupted exportation of oil a necessity."[147] Consciously or not, Allen's position mirrored that of John Cadman years before. The Iranians, the thinking went, needed the revenue from AIOC's operations to carry out their economic development plan. They would never endanger such a lucrative source of income. Foreign control over Iranian oil resources formed a crucial part of the American strategy. It was only through the mechanisms of the companies and the management of the oligopoly that Iranian oil wealth could be ensured.

Similarly, US officials felt that foreign experts would be needed to guide Iran's economic development plan. Allen spoke for many US officials when he observed Iran's need for a "complete revolution ... of management."[148] John Jernegan, whose 1943 memo had suggested Iran as a test case for the Atlantic Charter, embraced a more authoritarian vision four years later, suggesting at one point that the United States back a "strong-man" to shepherd Iran's development program, the Seven-Year Plan. "Iran is a backward country," he argued, "and not fully prepared for democratic processes."[149] The legacy of Millspaugh lingered within the new US policy, feeding a growing belief that Iran required foreign assistance or, at the very least, a strong central government in order to carry out successful oil-based development. By 1947 the basis of a new strategy in Iran had been established. American expertise would guide the plan, funded through the operations of the British oil company. Oil's global expansion would power the local transformation of Iran and prevent its fall to communism. It was the dawn of dual integration.

---

[147] *FRUS 1947, V*: 936–937.
[148] RG 59 891.60/6-2847, Allen to State, June 28, 1947, USNA.
[149] *FRUS 1947, V*: 991–993.

2 "We Have Done Nothing"
The Seven-Year Plan and the Failure of Dual Integration in Iran, 1947–1951

On March 20, 1947, Prime Minister Ahmed Qavam delivered a New Year's address to the nation of Iran. The country had passed through the "dark days" of war and occupation, but peace had finally returned. It was time for "essential economic and social reforms ... for the progress and welfare of the people." The Seven-Year Plan would correct Iran's "imbalance" and implement "a fair distribution [among] all people."[1] The plan included ten hydroelectric dams, hundreds of miles of paved roads, railway links, modernized agriculture, new mines and factories, a national Iranian oil company, and a public health program. At $650 million, it was at the time the most expensive and ambitious project in Iran's modern history.

The Seven-Year Plan represented more than just well digging and roadbuilding. The plan signified an important shift in how Iran chose to utilize oil revenues. Iran's chief developmentalist Abolhassan Ebtehaj imagined the transformation of oil wealth into lasting economic growth. The plan would act as a conduit for funneling the riches of oil into projects benefiting the rural peasantry, Iran's poorest demographic. Economically, it would revolutionize the country's agriculture and lay a basis for an expansion in private capital investment. Politically, the plan would bolster the legitimacy of Mohammed Reza Pahlavi, the shah of Iran, who muscled Qavam out in late 1947, by reducing inequality in the countryside and eliminating a potential source of social unrest and communist agitation. In more immediate terms, the plan promised to deepen the connection between the Pahlavi regime and the United States, to which the shah and his allies looked to for material and moral support.

In 1947, US policy focused on maintaining Iranian territorial integrity and encouraging "social and economic development as a means of

---

[1] Printed in *Democrat-i Iran*, March 22, 1947; FO 371/62001 Le Rougetel to Foreign Office, March 28, 1947, UKNA. New Year in Iran falls on the spring equinox of each year.

ensuring greater stability."[2] Unlike its neighbors Greece and Turkey or the industrialized states of Western Europe, Iran would not receive substantive economic aid. There would be no "Marshall Plan for the East," both because the Truman administration did not wish to expend the financial and political capital and because Iran was deemed too wealthy to warrant aid. Instead, while the US government remained aloof, foreign developmentalists would help Iran apply its oil revenues to economic development. Cold War concerns were fundamental to the American embrace of Iran's oil-backed program, which appeared to be Iran's best hope of resisting Soviet pressure in the wake of the Azerbaijan crisis. The goal was dual integration, tying Iran's growing oil wealth to projects that would strengthen the central government and deliver economic and social reform, thus mitigating the threat of communism.[3]

Generally disregarded in economic histories of Iran or diplomatic histories of the US-Iranian relationship, the First Seven-Year Plan failed to achieve its lofty ends.[4] Scholars point to the 1951 nationalization as the reason for the plan's demise, when the shutdown of Iran's oil industry removed the program's chief financial support.[5] Yet the plan's shortcomings were evident in the years preceding 1951 and go beyond a shortage of funds. Despite the enthusiasm of Ebtehaj and other technocrats, the Pahlavi government did not unite behind the plan. The development cause faced obstruction in the Majlis where it threatened the interests of the landed class. Development vied with competing priorities, particularly the shah's desire to build up Iran's military.

Domestic obstacles could have been overcome had the shah's government received more help from the United States. Rather than engage directly, the Truman administration opted to act through proxies. The strategy did not go as planned. The World Bank, which Ebtehaj looked to for financial aid, was a cautious and conservative institution that operated on strict commercial principles. Guided by a view of Iranian incapacity, the bank would only offer assistance if the plan came under foreign management. The American developmentalists sent to assist Ebtehaj, led by former oil executive Max W. Thornburg, hoped to take over the plan and facilitate Iran's penetration by American capital. Finally, AIOC doomed the plan to bankruptcy when it stubbornly refused to alter the terms of the 1933 Concession during the crucial

---

[2] *FRUS 1947, V*: 592.
[3] James F. Goode, *The United States and Iran, 1946–1951: The Diplomacy of Neglect* (New York: St. Martin's Press, 1989); Lytle, *The Origins of the Iranian-American Alliance*, 80–192; Collier, *Democracy and the Nature of American Influence in Iran*, 49–81.
[4] Goode, *The United States and Iran*, 41–45.
[5] Amuzegar and Fekrat, *Iran: Economic Development Under Dualistic Conditions*, 41–42.

negotiations of 1949.⁶ While divisions within the shah's government and opposition from the Majlis slowed the plan's progress, ultimately it was the lack of foreign assistance that proved decisive. The first effort at dual integration in Iran failed due to the hubris of AIOC, the inaction of the US government, and the misplaced priorities of foreign developmentalists who tried to commandeer the Seven-Year Plan while doubting whether Iran could successfully manage its own economic development without their guidance.

2.1 Development in Iran

Immediately after World War II, "development" was an idea in search of a definition. Before the war, European empires and the Soviet Union experimented with forms of social, political, and economic transformation on their peripheries. For the United States, prewar "modernization" crystallized around the twin projects of exporting American technical achievements, primarily to "stagnant" countries such as China, Haiti, and the Philippines, and furthering progress at home through projects like the Tennessee Valley Authority (TVA).⁷ Countries that fell within the US sphere of influence combined elements of the New Deal with other, more esoteric concepts that would become more familiar during the neoliberal era of the 1970s.⁸ But there was no hard doctrine for how development should look, even if the end result – American-style liberal capitalism – was often taken for granted.⁹

The playbook was diverse but the strategic end defined by Cold War ideology. While they avoided direct armed confrontation, the Soviet Union and United States waged a war for hearts and minds throughout

---

⁶ While there is no study of the World Bank's relationship with Iran in the 1946–1951 period, the bank's important role in postwar development is widely recognized. See Edward S. Mason and Robert E. Asher, *The World Bank since Bretton Woods* (Washington, DC: The Brookings Institution, 1973); Amy L. S. Staples, *The Birth of Development: How the World Bank, Food and Agriculture Association, and the World Health Organization Changed the World, 1945–1965* (Kent, OH: Kent State University Press, 2006), 22–45; Michele Alacevich, "The World Bank and the Politics of Productivity: The Debate on Economic Growth, Poverty, and Living Standards in the 1950s," *Journal of Global History* 6 (2011): 53–74. For Max Thornburg and the First Plan, see Linda W. Qaimmaqami, "The Catalyst of Nationalization: Max Thornburg and the Failure of Private Sector Developmentalism in Iran, 1946–1951," *Diplomatic History* 19, no. 1 (January 1995): 1–31. AIOC's relationship with Iran and the negotiations of the Supplemental Agreement are covered in Bamberg, *Vol. II*, 383–409.
⁷ Ekbladh, *The Great American Mission*, 50–76.
⁸ Amy Offner, *Sorting Out the Mixed Economy: The Rise and Fall of Welfare and Developmental States in the Americas* (Princeton, NJ: Princeton University Press, 2019).
⁹ Lorenzini, *Global Development*, 1–8; Latham, *Right Kind of Revolution*, 1–22.

the Global South, deploying financial aid and technical expertise through state institutions and affiliated proxies. Processes of improvement were facilitated through expertise. The United States exported money and technology, but its chief tool was knowledge. Technicians, economists, social scientists, and engineers claimed the "know-how" necessary to transform backwardness into a form of modernity based on the American model.[10]

In Iran, development had prewar antecedents. Reza Shah attempted a transformation of the country through top-down projects, pairing institution building with expanding access to education while growing the nation's incipient industrial base through state-owned manufacturing plants. Oil was detached from this endeavor – royalty payments were sequestered in special accounts while major development projects, such as the Trans-Iranian Railroad, were funded through taxes and customs duties. The goal was a form of modernization based on the example of the industrial West and Iran's neighbor Turkey, from which Reza Shah drew inspiration.[11]

The political freedom afforded by the fall of Reza Shah in 1941 facilitated new discussions regarding the economic future of the country. Groups such as the Iran Party and the Tudeh Party advocated for programs linked to land reform, the dissolution and redistribution of landed estates, and the elimination of the aristocracy. An emphasis on rural issues reflected dominant socio-economic realities. Iran in 1946 was a country of villages: A total of 50,000, scattered across a landmass half the size of Europe, contained some 70 percent of the population. Most arable land was controlled by a handful of major families, who retained 80 percent of the crop. The aristocracy, together with the bazaar merchant class and Shi'a clergy, had a vested interest in maintaining the existing economic order. They valued keeping land prices high, inflation low, and the prevailing social hierarchy firmly in place. As a result, most were skeptical of development and opposed to land reform.[12]

---

[10] Gilman, *Mandarins of the Future*, 3–17; Michael Adas, *Dominance by Design: Technological Imperatives and America's Civilizing Mission* (Cambridge, MA: Harvard University Press, 2006), 219–281.

[11] Touraj Atabaki and Erik Zürcher, eds., *Men of Order: Authoritarian Modernization Under Ataturk and Rezā Shah* (London: IB Tauris, 2004), 3–7; Abrahamian, *Iran between Two Revolutions*, 122–123; Ansari, *The Politics of Nationalism in Modern Iran*, 58–67, 83–84.

[12] For a breakdown of estimates, see Afsaneh Najmabadi, *Land Reform and Social Change in Iran* (Salt Lake City: University of Utah Press, 1987), 46–47; Ann K. Lambton, *Landlord and Peasant in Persia* (Oxford: Oxford University Press, 1953), and her later work, *The Persian Land Reform 1962–1966* (Oxford: Clarendon Press, 1969), 1–30; Eric J. Hooglund, *Land and Revolution in Iran, 1960–1980* (Austin, TX: University of Texas Press, 1982), 3–35; Abrahamian, *Iran between Two Revolutions*, 58–61.

2.1 Development in Iran

Mohammed Reza Pahlavi was as an outspoken advocate for economic development. Educated in Switzerland, fluent in English and French, Reza Shah's eldest son was twenty-one when he ascended the throne in 1941. To foreign observers as well as to the old guard of Iranian politics, the young shah seemed inexperienced and overly ambitious. "Young, timid ... exacerbated by his own superficiality," the shah was "affable ... full of good intentions ... [with] little conception of how to put them into action."[13] Despite a reputation for indecision, the Pahlavi monarch displayed a shrewd grasp of his own political vulnerabilities. Upon taking the throne, the shah agreed to return the lands his father had seized during the 1930s. In 1946, his prestige soared when Iranian troops recaptured the separatist province of Azerbaijan. 'Alinaqi 'Alikhani, a student in 1946, recalled how the shah's jeep was blocked in the streets of Tehran by jubilant crowds: "The Shah was at the height of his political popularity."[14]

In 1947 the shah emerged as the country's dominant political personality, pushing out the powerful Qavam and appointing a royalist as prime minister. He drew strength from his position as commander in chief of the armed forces; the prestige of the Crown and the ability to dispense royal patronage; and the disunity of his opponents, which allowed him to exert influence over a fractious Majlis.

While the shah concentrated on military matters and expanding his constitutional prerogatives, he saw utility in Qavam's Seven-Year Plan. He installed his half brother Adboreza as the head of the Sazman-e Barnameh, or "Plan Organization," a new government body created to oversee the development program. Eager to draw in greater support from the United States, the shah felt a policy of development could serve his own interests. "Iran had lost a great deal of time," he told US officials in March 1948, "[and] was ripe for communist penetration. Something had to be done and he, the shah, could not do it alone."[15] This interest stemmed partly from genuine enthusiasm – throughout his life, Mohammed Reza Pahlavi showed an interest in development projects and was ardently anti-communist. But by framing Iran's development in Cold War terms, the shah astutely connected the US strategic objectives with his own personal ambition to expand the power of the central state.

---

[13] Homa Katouzian, *Musaddiq and the Struggle for Power in Iran* (London: Tauris, 1990), 48; State Department, "Background Memoranda on Visit," November 1, 1949; Harry S. Truman Papers, White House Confidential File, Box 40, HSTPL; Azimi, *Crisis*, 192; Bill, *Eagle and the Lion*, 192–197.

[14] FISDS, *Siyasat va siyasatguzari-ye eqtesadi dar Iran, 1340–1350* [Ideology, Politics, and Process in Iran's Economic Development, 1960–1970].

[15] *FRUS 1948*, V, 117–121.

Crucial to the shah's development push were technocrats within the Pahlavi state. These individuals inherited the philosophy of the first Pahlavi's courtiers – indeed, many were pupils of 'Ali-Akbar Davar, author of Iran's modern legal code, while others came from the Iran Party, a prominent organization of professionals, lawyers, bureaucrats, and intellectuals.[16] Prince Adboreza drew in a circle of Western-trained Iranians, including Dr. Taqi Nasr, an economist with a US degree who was regarded as Iran's brightest economic mind. But the real ideological leader of the development effort was Iran's "first technocrat," the Bank-e Melli's Governor, Abolhassan Ebtehaj. "One of the most intelligent and influential men in Iran," who was also on very good terms with the shah, Ebtehaj was widely regarded as Iran's most distinguished economist.[17] Ambassador George V. Allen, writing to World Bank President John J. McCloy, regarded Ebtehaj as "the most able and energetic Iranian official both in the field of public finance and public administration."[18] He attended the Bretton Woods Conference in 1944 and was welcomed into the boardrooms of major corporations, development organizations, and international institutions like the International Monetary Fund and World Bank. Famously cantankerous, with a tendency to brush aside contrary opinions, Ebtehaj was something of a contradiction – a nationalist who imagined himself to be progressive, he was a staunch royalist and never wavered in his loyalty to the Pahlavi dynasty, which he had served since joining the Bank-e Melli in the early 1930s.

"I have come to the conclusion," Ebtehaj remarked in 1938, "that it is impossible for a country to develop without a program."[19] The development of Reza Shah's day consisted of state-funded industrialization and construction projects. What had been missing was a plan (*barnameh*) that would direct public investment and an authority independent from the government with the power to expend funds on long-term projects. Ebtehaj's thinking was bound up in the "politics of productivity," a view emanating from the work of early development economists like Paul N. Rosenstein-Rodan. Societal gains could be achieved by increasing

---

[16] Abbas Milani, *Eminent Persians: The Men and Women Who Made Modern Iran, 1941–1979*, Vol. I (Syracuse, NY: Syracuse University Press, 2008), 63–65; Abrahamian, *Iran between Two Revolutions*, 188–189.

[17] RG 84 USLETCGR, 1945–1951, Box 23, Thorp to McGhee, September 14, 1949, USNA; Ebtehaj, *Khatirat*, 399, 403; Frances Bostock and Geoffrey Jones, *Planning and Power in Iran: Ebtehaj and Economic Development under the Shah* (London: F. Cass, 1989), 38–41.

[18] George V. Allen to McCoy, IBRD, August 16, 1947, Records of the Middle East and North Africa Regional Vice Presidency, Iran – General – Correspondence 01, 1805819, WBGA.

[19] Ebtehaj, *Khatirat*, 301.

2.1 Development in Iran

output and raising the gross national product (GNP), with state-spending driving a "big push" toward self-sustaining growth.[20] According to his associate Khodadad Farmanfarmaian, Iran's first technocrat believed that raising productivity would erase Iran's political problems: "[P]eople would become more straightforward, more cooperative ... you would get true social, political change."[21] Ebtehaj's views were tailored to his specific context and reflected the political needs of the Pahlavi state. Ebtehaj hoped that the plan would increase national income, "raising the standard of living of individuals and increasing the country's agricultural exports," thus delivering benefits to the rural peasantry, Iran's poorest inhabitants.[22]

Oil was central to Iran's development program. Under Reza Shah, oil royalties – £60 million between 1913 and 1945 – were spent on non-productive enterprises, expensive imports, and military equipment.[23] Ebtehaj and his supporters hoped to change that. "Oil is like the blood which runs in the veins of our country," wrote Musharaf Naficy, a colleague and protégé of Ebtehaj, and a nation "which has sold its blood for a fixed payment has no right to spend its blood on non-productive expenditure."[24] For Iran's big push to be successful, earnings from petroleum, a wasting asset, would have to be applied to productive enterprises. Naficy's plan draft from early 1948 called for oil revenues to contribute 7.8 billion rials to the total plan budget of 21 billion rials, the equivalent of $650 million (Figure 2.1). But oil would not be enough. Ebtehaj planned to fund one-third of the plan through internal financing, facilitated by devaluing the rial and issuing new banknotes through the Bank-e Melli. The last third of plan spending would come from a loan of $250 million that Ebtehaj planned to secure from the World Bank.[25]

Ebtehaj and Naficy recommended an independent agency, the Plan Organization, administer the program. Legislation would direct oil revenues toward development rather than the general state budget, freeing it from interference from the Majlis. This was both a practical decision,

---

[20] Bostock and Jones, *Planning and Power*, 90–93; Paul Rosenstein-Rodan, "Problems of Industrialisation of Eastern and South-Eastern Europe," *The Economic Journal* 53, no. 210/211 (June–September 1943): 202–211; Alacevich, "The World Bank and the Politics of Productivity," 53–74.

[21] HIOHP, Farmanfarmaian, Tape 3, 25.

[22] Ebtehaj, *Khatirat*, 318; Letter to 'Ala, 21 Aban 1325.

[23] Bamberg, *Vol. II*, 325; Shwadran, *Middle East, Oil, and the Great Powers*, 132–133; Amuzegar and Fekrat, *Iran: Economic Development under Dualistic Conditions*, 16–23.

[24] BP 80924 F. Rouhani to London, Translation of Naficy Report, January 25, 1948.

[25] Svoboda to Bayne, Question of Iran's Capacity to Finance Seven-Year Plan in Initial Phase, July 18, 1949, Table III, Iran – General – Correspondence 04, 1805822, WBGA; RG 59 891.50 SEVEN YEAR PLAN/2-648, US Embassy Tehran No. 33, Naficy's Preliminary Report, February 6, 1948.

Plan Divisions	Expenditures
Agriculture	5.3
Transportation	5
Industries & Mines	3
Oil	1
Social Welfare	6
Misc.	0.7
Total	21

Funding Source		Amount	Percent
Oil		7.8	37.1
Sale of Govt. Property		1.0	4.8
Private Participation		1.0	4.8
Loans	Bank-e Melli	4.5	21.4
	World Bank	6.7	31.9
Total		21.0	100

Figure 2.1 The First Plan: Expenditures and funding (billion rials)[26]

meant to improve efficient operation of plan activities, and a political imperative. Beyond the shah and this relatively narrow circle, there was little enthusiasm for the Seven-Year Plan. Members of Iran's bureaucracy looked upon Ebtehaj's independent Plan Organization and its assembly of foreign contractors with "pessimism and severe concern," Ebtehaj recalled in his memoirs.[27] There was a distaste in the Majlis for foreign loans, which conjured up memories of the Qajar-era capitulations. Conservatives led by elder statesman Sayyed Hasan Taqizadeh opposed the plan on the grounds that it would produce budget deficits and depress land values, weakening the basis of the elite's economic and political power. They opposed Ebtehaj's efforts to devalue the rial on the same grounds. The shah, unlike his father, could not count on the total support of the Majlis, where debates in 1948 and 1949 often centered on deputies' fears of encroaching "dictatorship." The plan appeared to act as a vessel for spreading royal power and despite the shah's attempts to wrangle support many deputies viewed it with suspicion.[28]

Even Iran's ally, the United States of America, approached the Seven-Year Plan with a degree of ambivalence. "It is generally recognized," concluded James Somerville at the embassy, "that conditions among the Iranian peasants ... are deplorable and, as a result, they are particularly

---

[26] Plan Organization, Iran, *Review of the Second Seven Year Plan Program in Iran* (Tehran, March 10, 1960), 4.
[27] Ebtehaj, *Khatirat*, 322.
[28] Bamberg, *Vol. II*, 384–385; Abrahamian, *Iran between Two Revolutions*, 316–317, 328–371.

susceptible to communistic propaganda."[29] The results of failure appeared grim. "Iran is in desperate need of economic development," concluded Somerville's colleague Randall S. Williams, "and ... in the absence of constructive progress, eventual absorption ... into the Soviet sphere is a probability."[30] But the US government was wary to intervene directly. Iran appeared to possess resources – $160 million in gold and sterling as of February 1948 and a strong balance of payments position supported by its oil revenues, which gave it a large trade surplus, at least on paper – and did not need sizable US economic assistance.[31] Rather than offer financial aid or intervene in a way that might bring a Soviet response, the United States remained aloof, dispensing a limited amount of military aid while encouraging Iran to make use of its own resources.

After the US assistance of the war years, the postwar decision to withhold aid was bitterly disappointing to Iranians. "We expected the US would contribute," recalled Karim Sanjabi of the Iran Party, "as part of the promise made to Iran during World War II."[32] Instead, Iran would be left, as Qavam declared, "to set its house in order."[33] But it would not be left alone. According to Under Secretary of State Robert A. Lovett, the shah's government would welcome experts or technicians, "especially when provided by private companies."[34] Support for the local integration of Iranian oil would have to come from proxies, particularly the International Bank of Reconstruction and Development (IBRD), better known as the World Bank.

2.2 "Know-How": The World Bank, Max Thornburg, and the Plan, 1947–1949

In its approach to development, the World Bank represented an uncomfortable union of disparate ideologies. Economists and administrators witnessed state-supported economic policies during the Great Depression, where notable experiments like the TVA illustrated the use of state power to promote successful development.[35] But in the context of the Cold War, where "planning" came under criticism for its

---

[29] RG 59 891.50 SEVEN YEAR PLAN/2-2048, US Embassy Tehran No. 51, February 20, 1948, Enclosure No. 2, "Betterment of Conditions in Persia," February 16, 1948, USNA.
[30] Preliminary Analysis of Proposed Iranian Application for a World Bank Loan, Randall S. Williams, Attache, Undated, Iran – General – Correspondence 01, 1805819, WBGA.
[31] RG 59 891.515/2-2748, Doherty to Dunn, February 27, 1948, USNA.
[32] HIOHP, Sanjabi, Tape No. 8, 11.   [33] *FRUS 1946, VII*: 558.
[34] RG 59 891.00/9-1948 Lovett to Wiley, No. 948, October 1, 1948, USNA.
[35] Ekbladh, *Great American Mission*, 76–77.

association with communism, New Deal development was blunted by the politics of productivity, which emphasized investment by private capital and the inculcation of a free market ethos.[36] Created at the Bretton Woods Conference of 1944, the bank was not initially meant as a tool for development but rather as an instrument of reconstruction – its interests lay in rebuilding the shattered industrial cores of Western Europe and Japan, and it was only gradually that bank projects came to encompass the Global South. Bank officers hailed from Wall Street, while upper-level officials like Vice President Robert L. Garner, formerly of General Foods, held a dim view of TVA-style projects.[37] The bank's first two presidents Eugene Meyer (1946) and John J. McCloy (1947–1949) built an institution that conceived of itself as a supranational, commercially oriented tool for promoting free enterprise.[38] It operated, in other words, like a bank, and one with a fundamentally conservative character.

Husayn 'Ala, Iran's representative to the United Nations, the shah's minister of court and a personal friend of Ebtehaj, requested a loan from the World Bank in October 1946. The request came in the context of the Azerbaijan crisis and the Truman administration encouraged the bank to consider Iran's application. On paper, Iran appeared a strong candidate for a development loan. The country reported a trade surplus, with exports exceeding imports by 1.8 billion rials ($56 million) in 1945. Much of this, of course, was due to oil. Iran was the second-largest exporter of oil products in the world, behind the United States. In 1948, the Abadan refinery produced $312 million derived from 17.9 million tons of refined goods. The value of these products, of course, passed through AIOC. While Iran received an annual royalty from the British oil company, it earned additional foreign exchange from AIOC's operations through employee incomes, purchases of raw materials, customs duties, and other miscellaneous payments, sufficient to cover a non-oil trade deficit that grew from 1.3 billion rials in 1945 to 2.5 billion rials in 1948.[39] World Bank Executive Director, Emilio G. Collado,

---

[36] Amy L. S. Staples, "Seeing Diplomacy through Bankers' Eyes: The World Bank, the Anglo-Iranian Oil Crisis, and the Aswan High Dam," *Diplomatic History* 26, no. 3 (Summer 2002): 397–418, and *The Birth of Development*, 8–21.

[37] Michele Alacevich, "The World Bank and the Politics of Productivity: The Debate on Economic Growth, Poverty, and Living Standards in the 1950s," *Journal of Global History* 6 (2011): 53–74; Charles S. Maier, "The Politics of Productivity: Foundations of American International Economic Policy After World War II," *International Organization* 31, no. 4 (Autumn 1977): 607–633.

[38] Lorenzini, *Global Development*, 94–95.

[39] Synopsis of the Report on Program for the Development of Iran, November 2, 1947, Iran – General – Correspondence 02, 1805820, US Embassy Tehran, Annual Economic

suggested in April 1947 that Iran presented "a real opportunity for modest, carefully-planned development," though he noted how the oil industry had been "superimposed upon a primitive, even biblical economy."[40]

The bank tended to view Iran through the lens of incapacity, which encouraged a conservative attitude. While officers at the bank liked and admired Ebtehaj, they noted "the lack of administrative and technical skills, and the general inefficiency and corruption" in Iran's government.[41] Iran could not "digest" a large loan: "[it] possesses neither the technical expertise … nor the experience in economic coordination" to apply sizable sums to a program on the scale of the Seven-Year Plan.[42] Such attitudes existed beyond the bank. The engineers at Morrison–Knudsen, who conducted the first economic survey of Iran in 1946, did not believe the Seven-Year Plan would succeed. "The country is at present in such a backward state," the company's managers felt that mismanagement would lead quickly "to dissipation of available assets."[43] Arthur C. Millspaugh, former financial advisor to Iran and a consultant for the bank, came to the same conclusion. Without reforms to the central government, better tax collection practices, less corruption, and more accountability, any investment in Iran "will simply go down the drain, as much of Iran's public expenditure have gone in the past."[44] There was a general sense that money spent on Iran would be money wasted.

Reluctance to extend loans to Iran stemmed from a belief that the country's development program could not be carried out successfully without foreign expert assistance. Ebtehaj resubmitted Iran's loan request in 1947, arguing that Iran's strategic significance together with the lack of formal aid from the US government justified a large loan.[45] During a tense meeting in September, the bank refused to consider the application until Iran possessed a more detailed outline of the plan's

Report on Iran, 1948, February 15, 1949, Iran – General – Correspondence 03, 1805821, WBGA.

[40] Collado to McCloy, April 21, 1947, Iran – General – Correspondence 01, 1805819, WBGA. In 1947, Collado left the bank to take a position with Jersey Standard: He retired in 1975, having served nearly thirty years as a director.
[41] Memorandum, October 6, 1947, Iran – General – Correspondence 01, 1805819, WBGA.
[42] Consolo to Hill, January 22, 1948, Iran – General – Correspondence 02, 1805820, WBGA.
[43] J. Madigan and F. A. Console to Walter Hill, November 10, 1947, Iran – General – Correspondence 02, 1805820, WBGA.
[44] The Morrison-Knudsen Report, AC Millspaugh, February 1948, Iran – General – Correspondence 02, 1805820, WBGA.
[45] Ebtehaj, *Khatirat*, 320–321.

projects.[46] Bank officers agreed with the conclusions of Morrison–Knudsen: Once Iran possesses "rationalized agriculture" and an adequate communication system, "private enterprise will find the requisites for a development of industrial processes." Loan repayment would be tied to Iran's oil revenues, "the only kind of international guarantee Iran can present."[47] A loan was contingent on Iran retaining Western specialists who could guide the plan to success. Ebtehaj reached out in 1948 to request the assistance of an economic advisor. The bank suggested Max Thornburg.[48]

No one exemplified the dissonance of American postwar developmentalism better than Max Weston Thornburg. An eloquent advocate for expanding aid and technical assistance abroad, Thornburg was also a corporate animal with a keen sense of self-interest honed over decades in the international oil industry. As an executive for Socal during the 1930s, Thornburg secured for the company a concession in Bahrain. Ingratiating himself with the ruler, Thornburg was awarded a private island that he used as a personal base from which to pursue new commercial opportunities. A gregarious smooth talker, Thornburg's connections were wide-ranging and included corporate lawyers like Allen Dulles and prominent businessmen Nelson Rockefeller and John J. McCloy, president of the World Bank from 1947 to 1949. During World War II Thornburg acted as petroleum advisor to the State Department, a position he held while still drawing a Socal salary.[49]

After leaving the State Department in 1943, Thornburg rebranded himself as an international consultant versed in oil economics and development. He first appeared in Tehran in May 1946, scouting the country on behalf of American aviation and oil interests.[50] He met with Ebtehaj and discussed plans to harness Iran's oil wealth to a program of economic reconstruction, where he bragged that American companies could "match dollars to the devil" and would be eager to help Iran's

---

[46] Notes on Meetings with Ebtehaj, September 10 and 13, 1947, Iran – General – Correspondence 01, 1805819, WBGA.

[47] Consolo to Hill, September 25, 1947, Iran – General – Correspondence 01, 1805819, WBGA.

[48] Collier, *Democracy and the Nature of American Influence in Iran*, 54–55; Qaimmaqami, "The Catalyst of Nationalization," 1–31.

[49] Painter, *Oil and the American Century*, 14–31; Stoff, *Oil, War, and American Security*, 62–70; Mark Seddon, "Incorporating Corporations: Anglo-US Oil Diplomacy and Conflict Over Venezuela, 1941–1943," *Journal of Transatlantic Studies* 10, no. 2 (June 2012): 134–149.

[50] RG 59 891.6363/5-2046, Allen to Byrnes, May 20, 1946, USNA.

2.2 "Know-How"

economic agenda, particularly where oil was concerned.[51] In 1948 Thornburg returned to Iran to help draft the first outline of the Seven-Year Plan.

Like Ebtehaj, Thornburg supported state-driven development as a way to encourage private investment. The greatest contribution the United States and its proxies could make to the plan "is in the field of managerial skill," making up for Iran's insufficiencies.[52] He also believed the plan needed to be insulated from Iranian politics to ensure efficient administration. Allowing Majlis politicians to tamper with the plan would undermine the productivity focus: True progress would be "neglected in favor of spectacular undertakings aimed chiefly at enhancing political prestige."[53] Thornburg's reasoning was self-serving. Pulling the plan away from Majlis influence would allow foreign consultants to exert greater influence over its execution.

While he commanded a large salary and wielded influence within the Plan Organization offices, Thornburg's official position was as liaison for Overseas Consultants Inc. (OCI), a group of engineering and construction firms that acted as technical advisors to the Seven-Year Plan. Thornburg had first approached Nelson Rockefeller's International Basic Economy Corporation (IBEC), but the scion of oil's wealthiest family demurred, worrying that Iran was too risky an environment so soon after the Azerbaijan crisis. Thornburg turned next to OCI, which had a sterling reputation, having spearheaded the postwar reconstruction of Japan. Plying the executives with cocktails in August 1948, Thornburg convinced them to reform OCI, promising fat contracts from the Seven-Year Plan's $650 million budget.[54]

Thornburg's philosophies were reflected in OCI's initial report published in January 1949. Conditions in the Iranian countryside were deteriorating, "[and] the mass of people is generally under-nourished, disease-ridden, indigent and illiterate." The Seven-Year Plan could improve these conditions. But Iran faced a dearth of "honest and efficient administration." Without expert guidance, "the Plan will do no more than limp and stumble along ... fortunately, [this is] a field in which we

---

[51] RG 59 891.50/5-3046, Allen to Byrne, May 30, 1946, Attached Letter from Thornburg, May 20, 1946, USNA.

[52] RG 59 891.50 SEVEN YEAR PLAN/6-2248, US Embassy Tehran No. 179, June 22, 1948, Enclosure No. 3, Thornburg, "Memorandum on the Naficy Plan," March 12, 1948, USNA. See also Nathan J. Citino, *Envisioning the Arab Future: Modernization in US-Arab Relations, 1945–1967* (New York: Cambridge University Press, 2017), 68–71.

[53] RG 59 891.50 SEVEN YEAR PLAN/6-2248, US Embassy Tehran No. 179, June 22, 1948, Enclosure No. 1, Thornburg to Somerville, May 22, 1948.

[54] Thornburg to Burland (IBRD), August 4, 1948, Iran – General – Correspondence 03, 1805821, WBGA.

have had wide experience."[55] OCI's mission followed a three-phase program. Phase one involved a survey; phase two, a complete outline of all plan projects; and phase three, implementation of the plan under OCI supervision.

For the World Bank, OCI's involvement would guard against Iranian incapacity. With OCI and Thornburg guiding the process, Iran would eventually be ready for a supporting loan. President McCloy made this clear to Ebtehaj during a meeting in October 1948. The impatient technocrat would have to wait for OCI to do its work, and if the bank was satisfied Ebtehaj could expect financial assistance "compatible with Iran's needs."[56] Ebtehaj accepted McCloy's verdict and retreated from developmental politics, focusing instead on his currency devaluation bill in the Majlis. Thornburg, meanwhile, worked to entice "top-flight men" to reform the plan's finances, which he felt were "extremely vague."[57] Among the specialists drawn to Iran was Allen Dulles, a lawyer, intelligence operative, and Thornburg's particular friend. Dulles spent weeks reviewing the country's economic laws with the Plan Organization's Karim Sanjabi, with an eye toward opening the country up to American investment.[58]

After several months of work, OCI drafted a blueprint for the Seven-Year Plan in June 1949. The report laid out hundreds of projects, which contractors would manage "with almost complete responsibility" independent of Iranian authorities.[59] As compensation, OCI would be paid $600,000 per year for the duration of the Seven-Year Plan, including a $50,000 salary and $10,000 tax-free stipend for Thornburg. Under OCI's supervision, the plan would be reconfigured into a vehicle through which American capital could penetrate Iran's economy – with ample room left for Thornburg to profit himself.

Thornburg and OCI were backed by the shah, Ebtehaj, and the United States. Otherwise, the group lacked support inside Iran. "Small-minded, jealous and suspicious as mice," according to one British critic, the US executives were not "shirt-sleeves ambassadors" typically found doing development work on the global frontier. They represented Wall Street and other "American business interests," and rarely strayed from their

---

[55] OCI to Saed, January 12, 1949, Iran – General – Correspondence 03, 1805821, WBGA.
[56] Memo of Meeting, John J. McCloy and Ebtehaj, October 2, 1948, Iran – General – Correspondence 03, 1805821, WBGA.
[57] US Embassy Cairo to State, March 17, 1949, For Iliff from Garner, Iran – General – Correspondence 03, 1805821, WBGA.
[58] HIOHP, Sanjabi, Tape No. 8, 9–10.
[59] OCI, *Report on the Seven Year Development Plan for the Plan Organization of the Imperial Government of Iran* (New York, 1949), Vol I, 3–7; Vol. V, 239.

2.2 "Know-How"

comfortable offices in Tehran.[60] Majlis deputies decried the OCI salaries as a waste and Ebtehaj as an American tool. That the bank director's financial policies put him at odds with bazaar merchants did not help matters.[61]

The Majlis refused to commit funds for the plan until February 1949, when an assassination attempt on the shah temporarily boosted his prestige and allowed him to push through a plan bill. Nevertheless, competing interests limited plan funds. Convinced by his Finance Minister Abbasqoli Golshayan and Army Chief of Staff 'Ali Razmara to prioritize military funding, the shah agreed to release only 60 percent of the 1949 AIOC royalty for plan projects. "His Majesty," confessed Dr. Taqi Nasr, Plan Organization manager, "wants a strong army, which results in diverging funds from economic development."[62] Total spending on development for that year would be £9.8 million, rather than the £15 million originally earmarked.[63]

Visiting Iran in March 1949, Garner framed the situation in Cold War terms. "In view of the Russian menace," he wrote to McCloy, "prompt and positive steps must be taken to improve the conditions of the masses." Without such action, "Iran may blow up." Hope lay in the OCI contract, which would give foreign developmentalists the authority "to organize, supervise, and in some cases, direct all the development work" once the plan commenced in earnest. "This seems absolutely essential," he concluded. The reason, Garner noted, was the "habitual lethargy and weakness for action of the Iranians," which Garner also blamed for the relative lack of progress on the plan.[64]

Garner's report clarified the bank's stance. Loan assistance would be contingent on the shah's government handing control of Iran's development over to foreign interests like OCI. In effect, the bank and OCI were slowly engineering an American takeover of the Seven-Year Plan. An assumption of Iranian incapacity and a confidence in American expertise informed the bank's policy and the OCI mission. This left the question of financing unresolved. American officials told the bank that financial

---

[60] FO 371/75484 Report from Murray, April 25, 1949, FO 371/75485 Ross to Bevin, May 31, 1949, "Interim Report to the Plan Organization," OCI May 16, 1949, Report by Maitland, May 1949, UKNA.
[61] Engert to Iliff, August 26, 1949, Iran – General – Correspondence 04, 1805822, WBGA.
[62] RG 59 891.50 SEVEN YEAR PLAN/8-149, US Embassy Tehran No. 174, July 1, 1949, Enclosure No. 1, Memo of Conversation, "Status of Economic Development Plan," June 29, 1949.
[63] RG 59 891.50/6-249, Memo of Conversation, June 2, 1949.
[64] Garner to McCloy, March 15, 1949, Iran – General – Correspondence 03, 1805821, WBGA.

assistance for Iran was "out of the question."[65] The bank would not proceed with a loan. Ebtehaj's efforts to secure internal financing through a rial devaluation stalled in the face of Majlis opposition. That left only one avenue of financial support – the royalty payments of the Anglo-Iranian Oil Company. The success of development in Iran thus hinged on the Pahlavi government's negotiations for an increase in the AIOC royalty.

2.3 Paying for the Plan: AIOC and Iran, 1946–1949

In October 1948, the Pahlavi government presented AIOC with twenty-five grievances. The chief complaint regarded the distribution of oil profits, which the Pahlavi regime felt had grown deeply inequitable. To add weight to their argument, Pahlavi negotiators drew on the discourse of development and the significance of the Seven-Year Plan. "We are meeting a great danger," argued Iranian negotiator Husayn Pirnia. "The best name we can give it is poverty and misery ... the best way of meeting this danger is to have an economic plan ... to a very large extent the plan could be carried out by means of receipts from the Company."[66] The time had come to revise the terms of Sir John Cadman's 1933 agreement with Reza Shah, with the specific goal of freeing up more revenue for the funding of Iran's economic development.

AIOC was under pressure to deliver better terms to the Iranian government. After five years under the watchful eye of British soldiers garrisoning Abadan, the company's wartime comfort came to an abrupt end in July 1946, when thousands of its workers went on strike for higher wages and better living conditions.[67] The incident alarmed AIOC executives and the British government. Hobbled by the war and on the verge of losing its empire in India, Britain had become increasingly dependent on earnings from overseas investments. AIOC's operation in Iran was a large contributor to the national balance of payments and the value of sterling.[68] Losing access to Iranian oil "would ... have disastrous economic consequences," warned Foreign Secretary Ernest Bevin.[69] AIOC would have to forge closer ties to the Pahlavi government, adopt

---

[65] Stephens to Files, June 15, 1949, Iran – General – Correspondence 03, 1805821, WBGA.
[66] BP 126420 Notes of Meeting, October 3, 1948.
[67] Habib Ladjevardi, *Labor Unions and Autocracy in Iran* (Syracuse, NY: Syracuse University Press, 1985), 121–136.
[68] Galpern, *Money, Oil, and Empire*, 88–90.
[69] FO 371/52714 Bevin to Le Rougetel, June 14, 1946, UKNA.

2.3 Paying for the Plan: AIOC and Iran, 1946–1949

Figure 2.2 Aerial view of Abadan, the world's largest refinery, 1950.
BP 78039, Reproduced with permission from the BP Archive

"an enlightened policy," and work to represent its operations as vital to the future economic prosperity of Iran.[70]

Bevin's concern was justified. The company lacked houses for most of its workers, who lived in shanties crammed into slums to the east of the massive Abadan refinery (Figure 2.2). AIOC's European management continued to enjoy amenities and a quality of life reminiscent of the Indian Raj, complete with servants, bungalows, and strict racial and social divisions. British officials monitoring the company found the

---

[70] FO 371/52723 Cabinet Conclusions, August 7, 1946.

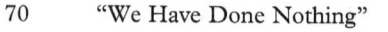

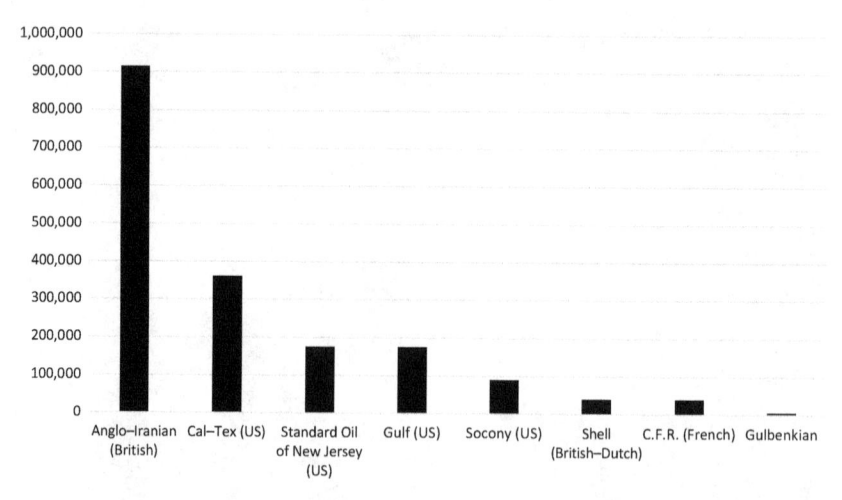

Figure 2.3 Share of Middle East production, 1950 (barrels per day)[71]

situation unnerving. According to one report from a Foreign Office visitor, the company was "guilty of complacency, not to say neglect," in ensuring proper housing and sanitary conditions for its workers.[72] The imperial atmosphere was clearly no longer sustainable. "The contrast between the British and Persian staffs," wrote Ambassador John le Rougetel, "provide[s] fertile ground" for communist agitation.[73] Furthermore, AIOC began to realize windfall profits following the great oil deals in late 1946. As the company with the largest share of Middle East oil, it stood to gain financially from the cooperative effort by the oligopoly to increase regional production after 1946 (Figure 2.3). Profits in 1947 and 1948 reached historic levels.

The company's wealth in the midst of Iran's economic deprivation made AIOC a lightning rod for opposition groups. According to Tudeh Party leaders, AIOC had erected a colonial edifice through bribery and intimidation "assimilating two-thirds of the homeland with the help of their domestic servants, the Iranian government."[74] Nationalists like Majlis deputy Mohammed Mosaddeq railed against the company while the press published editorials excoriating the company's exploitation of

---

[71] *FRUS 1950, V*: 174–175.
[72] FO 371/52726 Col. Wheeler Report, December 1, 1946.
[73] FO 371/52714 Dispatch from Abadan Tour, Undated, UKNA.
[74] "The Text of the Collective Defense of the Leaders of the Tudeh Party of Iran in a Military Court Regarding the Events of 23 Tir 1325 in Abadan," from Farajollah Mizani Javanshir, *Hamase-ye 23-e tir. Gushe'i az mobarezat-e kargaran-e naft-e khuzestan* (N.p. 1980): 21–26. Thanks to Mattin Biglari for bringing this text to my attention.

2.3 Paying for the Plan: AIOC and Iran, 1946–1949

Iranian workers. In the Majlis, attacks on AIOC grew frequent in 1947 and 1948; even deputies inclined to be pro-British felt compelled to denounce the company to avoid attacks from petro-nationalists.[75]

On January 19, 1949, one deputy launched a withering attack on Sayyed Hasan Taqizadeh, who as Reza Shah's finance minister had signed the agreement with Cadman in 1933. Buckling under the pressure, Taqizadeh publicly disavowed the concession: "No one ... could stand against the will of the Almighty Ruler – there was no alternative."[76] Discontent toward the company was boiling over into outright hatred, to the point that Pahlavi officials and politicians loyal to the shah were wary of speaking out in its defense.

AIOC was confident it could manage this pressure. Construction on new living quarters for Iranian workers accelerated in the wake of the July 1946 strike. The company spent £22 million on housing and services between 1946 and 1949 (compared to £37 million paid to Iran in royalties[77]) and it expected to spend another £3.5 million in 1950.[78] By the end of 1950, AIOC had constructed 43 staff clubs, 19 cinemas, 20 swimming pools, 11 restaurants and canteens, 389 shops, and 70 miscellaneous amenity buildings.[79] The company launched a program to hire more Iranians to technical and management positions, a so-called Iranianization drive, and published glossy pamphlets in the Iranian press to trumpet their achievements in housing, welfare, training, and education.[80] Much of this campaign was coordinated by Neville Gass, AIOC's director for Iranian affairs. Born in India, Gass served long stints in Abadan as the company's troubleshooter. Yet Gass also classified Iranian demands for better housing and more jobs as "[a] method of blackmail," from a government looking for "some special gesture ... to placate public opinion."[81]

Gass' confidence betrayed the complacency pervading the company's entire management structure. Backed by the prestige of the British government, AIOC possessed considerable power inside Iran, influencing the press, bribing Majlis deputies and local notables, and generally acting as a "state within the state" in the words of US Ambassador John

---

[75] BP 80924 Seddon to Rice, April 28, 1948, Northcroft to Rice, August 30, 1948, Seddon to Rice, May 5, 1948; *Ettela'at*, April 29, 1948 and August 30, 1948.
[76] Katouzian, *Musaddiq*, 67–68; Taqizadeh, *Zendegi-ye tufani*, 551–553.
[77] Bamberg, *Vol. II*, 325.
[78] BP 68186 Chairman's Statement to Stockholders, March 21, 1951.
[79] BP 68186 Report on Amenity Buildings, April 3, 1951.
[80] BP 44242 "The AIOC in Iran," May 1948, "A Tour Through the Abadan Refinery of the Anglo-Iranian Oil Company Ltd," April 1948.
[81] BP 71726 Gass to Fraser, December 3, 1947.

C. Wiley.[82] Welfare measures were regarded as a necessary expense to maintain the security of the concession, but the company did not feel obliged to do more than was necessary to meet the demands from Bevin in London or Pahlavi officials in Tehran. While it worked to contain the fallout of the July 1946 strike, the company's attention focused predominantly on negotiations to revise the 1933 Concession.[83] If the demands of the Pahlavi government were met, other threats to the security of the company's investment – and the financial security and economic well-being of Great Britain – could be managed.

The main Pahlavi complaint regarded the annual royalty. According to Iranian officials, the amount paid to Iran was inequitable compared to AIOC profits and taxes paid to the British government. The numbers bore out this accusation. Owing to Britain's wartime tax regimen, AIOC paid £75 million in taxes and only £37 million in royalties to Iran.[84] In February 1949, Minister of Finance Abbasqoli Golshayan suggested a formula to AIOC negotiator Neville Gass whereby Iran would receive half of the "gross profits," covering AIOC's global operations.[85] The model for Golshayan's suggestion was an agreement signed between major oil companies and Venezuela in 1948. Rather than calculate a royalty based on production, paying Iran a sum on each ton of oil exported, AIOC would divide its profits "fifty-fifty" paying half to Iran while retaining the other half for itself (Figure 2.4).

There was much to recommend a fifty-fifty agreement. It promised Iran much higher revenue. After signing an agreement on profit sharing in 1943, Venezuela's earnings rose from $80 million to $242 million in 1944. By 1948, Caracas earned $0.77 per barrel compared to Iran's 7s/9d per ton (roughly $0.20 per barrel).[86] Under Iranian calculations, should a fifty-fifty formula be applied to AIOC's profits the result for Iran would be payments roughly equal to what was earned in Venezuela.[87] Fifty-fifty carried an unmistakable air of equitability, which the shah's government could sell as an upgrade from the unpopular 1933 Concession. By March 1949 both Golshayan and Prime Minister Mohammed Sa'id had expressed their support for a fifty-fifty deal.

---

[82] RG 59 891.6363/5-648, Wiley to Henderson, May 6, 1948, USNA.
[83] Bamberg, *Vol. II*, 347–382.   [84] Bamberg, *Vol. II*, 325.
[85] Fateh, *Panjah sal naft-e Iran*, 390–392.
[86] Stephen G. Rabe, *The Road to OPEC: United States Relations with Venezuela, 1919–1976* (Austin, TX: University of Texas Press, 1982), 88–91, 104; Painter, *Oil and the American Century*, 128–135; George Philip, *The International Political Economy of Oil* (Edinburgh: Edinburgh University Press, 1994), 100.
[87] FO 371/75496 Minute by Clinton-Thomas, March 30, 1949, UKNA.

2.3 Paying for the Plan: AIOC and Iran, 1946–1949

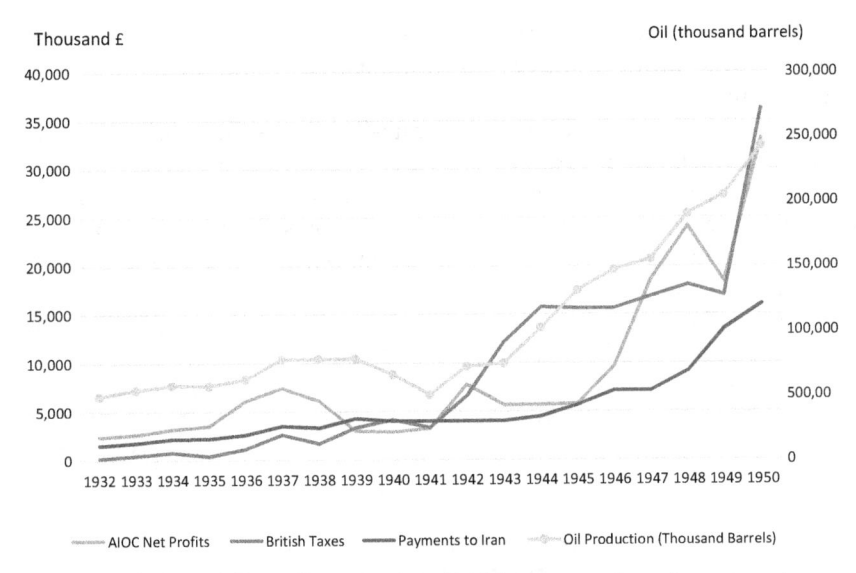

Figure 2.4 Iran oil production, British taxes, and royalty payments, 1932–1950[88]

In meetings with Ambassador Wiley, Max Thornburg agreed that a new concession awarding Iran at least 20s per ton (or roughly $0.55 per barrel) would satisfy Iran's financial needs. Fifty-fifty was fast becoming the new "standard of equitability" and AIOC would be foolish to reject it. Wiley suspected Thornburg himself was pushing Golshayan to demand a fifty-fifty deal, as doing so would free up more money for the Seven-Year Plan.[89] AIOC came under additional pressure from Bevin in London, who felt that Iran had "some legitimate grievances" regarding royalty payments, and that it was important "from the political point of view" that Iran receive "an equitable return from the exploitation of their resources."[90] Other officials in the Foreign Office felt that the impasse could be solved through "fifty-fifty ... which will ensure a sharing of profits," though officials in the Treasury argued that Iran's demands

---

[88] Zuhayr M. Mikdashi, *A Financial Analysis of Middle Eastern Oil Concessions, 1901–1965* (New York: Praeger, 1966), 109–110; Mostafa Elm, *Oil, Power, and Principle: Iran's Nationalization and its Aftermath* (Syracuse, NY: Syracuse University Press, 1992), 38; Galpern, *Money, Oil, and Empire*, 88; Bamberg, *Vol. II*, 515.

[89] RG 59 891.6363 AIOC/5-2749, Wiley to State, May 27, 1949, USNA. Thornburg claimed in February 1949 that he would not become involved in Iran's negotiations, but it seems very likely that he encouraged Golshayan to push for a fifty-fifty agreement, which he had been instrumental in negotiating while a US official in Venezuela in 1943. See RG 59 891.6363/2-2549, Wiley to State, February 25, 1949.

[90] FO 371/75495 Bevin to Cripps, February 18, 1949.

per barrel exceeded what was reasonable.[91] The US government did not get involved but supported any deal that increased Iran's access to oil revenues.

In sum, most parties agreed that a fifty-fifty deal would help end the rift between AIOC and Iran while ensuring an increased source of funds for the Seven-Year Plan. At the very least, the company should offer Iran something approaching an equitable division of profits. By the spring of 1949 fifty-fifty had become an "obsession" within Iran according to Golshayan, and he warned AIOC's negotiators that anything less would have trouble obtaining the approval of the Majlis, which would have to ratify any new arrangement before it could be signed into law by the shah.[92]

The company resisted. Throughout the lengthy negotiations from February to May 1949, AIOC executives rejected the idea of a fifty-fifty formula as "unfair and unsound and unworkable."[93] Instead, AIOC suggested an increase in the per-ton royalty and an added annual payment from the company's general reserve, which would translate into 12s/9d per ton or $0.35/barrel. While not a fifty-fifty deal, the offer would double Iran's royalty for 1948 and 1949, delivering an immediate payment £40 million.[94] In London, the Foreign Office yielded to pressure from the Treasury and agreed it would be "unwise" to push AIOC further.[95] The United States took no action, choosing to let AIOC manage the negotiations.

Pressure to accept the company's offer was strong. Persuaded by Golshayan to divert most of that year's oil royalty to the military, the shah had left the Plan Organization with only a few million in sterling while Ebtehaj's attempts to devalue the rial had run up against Majlis opposition. Thornburg and the rest of OCI were on the verge of a mutiny, as the entire operation was in danger of being shut down for want of funds.[96] While members of the cabinet including Golshayan encouraged him to stand strong and demand better terms from AIOC, financial concerns convinced the shah to accept Gass' offer so that both the military build-up and plan could be funded together. Despite his reservations, Golshayan signed the deal on July 17 and sent it to the

---

[91] FO 371/68732 Note from Berthoud, November 8, 1948.
[92] BP 126409 Gass to Fraser, March 2, 1949.
[93] BP 126409 Fraser to Gass, February 21, 1949; for the negotiations, see Bamberg, *Vol. II*, 383–399.
[94] BP 126409 Gass to Fraser, Memo of AIOC Offer, March 11, 1949; FO 371/75497 Le Rougetel to FO, May 12, 1949, Le Rougetel to Wright, May 16, 1949, Record of a Meeting, May 19, 1949, UKNA.
[95] FO 371/75496 Note from Chadwick, April 6, 1949 Note for Bevin, February 9, 1949; FO 371/75496 Note on Financial Payments from AIOC to Iran, April 1, 1949, UKNA.
[96] RG 59 891.50/5-3049, Wiley to State, May 30, 1949, USNA.

2.3 Paying for the Plan: AIOC and Iran, 1946–1949

Majlis for ratification. The company's campaign to resist a fifty-fifty agreement succeeded. As Cadman had done in 1933, AIOC used the Pahlavi government's need for money to its advantage, simultaneously playing off the regime's diverging priorities and Iran's internal political divisions.

Was the Supplemental Agreement equitable?[97] In the short term, it would deliver a cash infusion of £40 million to Iran while promising higher royalties linked to annual production. According to the World Bank, the agreement would allow Iran to commit 1.17 billion rials to the Seven-Year Plan by March 1950 and 1.95 billion rials in the following year. Should AIOC's production increase as anticipated, total plan spending by 1954 would be almost 14 billion rials. Even without foreign loans, Iran's ability to fund its development plan seemed "reasonably assured," so long as the agreement won Majlis ratification.[98] AIOC argued that the Supplemental Agreement was as equitable as a fifty-fifty arrangement. William J. Fraser, AIOC's chairman, insisted that Cadman's per-ton formula would protect Iran from fluctuations in the price of oil, sheltering the annual royalty from potential falls in the company's profits. During a meeting with Iran's prime minister in May, Fraser invoked the world market, as Cadman had done. Profitability was not "what the Majlis, or the public or the government expected," but what the market decreed.[99] Neither Fraser nor Gass acknowledged the degree of control AIOC exerted over the global oil market as a member of the oligopoly, of course.

Opponents of the deal argued a fifty-fifty deal would net Iran more revenue per year. Scholars sympathetic to Iran and critical of AIOC have made the same point.[100] In March 1951, AIOC accountants estimated the total value of crude and refined products exported from Abadan at £164 million. Less operating expenses of £54 million, profits equaled £110 million, from which Iran would net £55 million from a fifty-fifty deal but only £40 million from the Supplemental Agreement.[101] Yet comparing figures yields little insight into why AIOC refused to consider a fifty-fifty offer in 1949. The company's reasons were tied to convenience and reflected arrogance and complacency rather than pure avarice. Applying fifty-fifty to Iran would have required a reorganization of the company's structure, including the formation of a new affiliate to manage

---

[97] For text of the Supplemental Agreement, see Hossein Makki, *Kitab-e Siyah* [The Black Book] Vol. I (Tehran: Sazman-e Intisharat-e Naw, 1970), 38–43.
[98] Svoboda to Bayne, Question of Iran's Capacity to Finance Seven-Year Plan in Initial Phase, July 18, 1949, Iran – General – Correspondence 04, 1805822, WBGA.
[99] Quoted in Bamberg, *Vol. II*, 394–395.   [100] Elm, *Oil, Power, and Principle*, 55.
[101] BP 66900 "Royalty, 50/50 Participation, Estimate for 1951," March 29, 1951.

operations in Iran. This affiliate would then split its profits fifty-fifty with Iran, preserving the rest of AIOC's global operations. Fraser acknowledged the possibility of AIOC "segregating" its operations in Iran, but he did not support the idea in principle.[102]

In Venezuela, fifty-fifty applied only to crude oil, for which a benchmark existed – the so-called posted price – which companies could use to calculate payments. Two-thirds of AIOC's Iranian output was in refined products, for which no effective profit-sharing benchmark existed. Finally, fifty-fifty was not attractive to AIOC from the point of view of savings on tax. The US tax code allowed taxes paid to foreign governments to be deducted from domestic taxes. AIOC was a British company, however, and the British tax code reflected postwar austerity. Fraser believed that the Treasury would not offer tax credits to a company as profitable as AIOC.[103] "We cannot seek special exemption" for any taxes paid to Iran, he warned Gass.[104] From his point of view, fifty-fifty was not a good fit.

Sorting through the figures and dollars-per-barrel obscures the basic premise behind AIOC's strategy in 1949. The company was unwilling to alter the major components of the 1933 Concession, an agreement which promised AIOC control of Iran's oil until 1993 and contained a clause prohibiting either party from withdrawing unilaterally. AIOC negotiators found Iranian demands for 30s or 20s per ton to be ridiculous. Despite the strike of 1946 and mounting Iranian pressure, AIOC was confident in its position. Fraser planned to increase Iranian output from 19 million tons to 37 million tons by 1954 and 58.5 million, or 1.1 million bpd, by 1960. "A continuous expansion of Iranian production," he declared, "is of primary importance."[105] Iran was clearly in need of money and the company retained London's backing. Against such odds, the challenge from the Pahlavi state or Iran's nascent petro-nationalist movement felt insignificant. Chairman Fraser, famed for his stubbornness, did nothing to conceal his contempt for the "Persians." To him, the Iranians were only interested in "more money," while Golshayan was "just a trader," and would yield when AIOC offered Iran more than £15 million per year.[106] Backed by the British government and facing a divided and cash-

---

[102] BP 126409 Fraser to Gass, March 11, 1949.
[103] BP 142640 "Fifty-Fifty and Tax Relief for UK Oil Companies 1953," Robert Brown and JA Bowden, 1983.
[104] BP 126409 Fraser to Gass, March 2, 1949.
[105] BP 72339 Notes from Chairman Meeting of January 20, 1949, Production Capacity in Iran, June 29, 1949.
[106] FO 371/75497 Le Rougetel to FO, May 12, 1949, Le Rougetel to Wright, May 16, 1949, Record of a Meeting, May 19, 1949, UKNA.

strapped Pahlavi government, AIOC oozed confidence. Once it made its offer in the spring of 1949, it refused to back down. It would prove to be a grievous error in judgment.

2.4 The Collapse of Dual Integration, July 1949–March 1951

The Seven-Year Plan collapsed between July 1949 and March 1951. The failure of Iran's first oil-based development program was linked to the drama surrounding the Supplemental Agreement, a slow-motion economic crisis, and a political challenge stemming from the rise of a new petro-nationalist movement. The United States and its proxies were slow to respond to these mounting dangers. When they did take action, it was uncoordinated and ill-timed.

First, the Supplemental Agreement failed to secure Majlis ratification. The deal had little support in the assembly and Finance Minister Golshayan declined to defend it in public. The deal's opponents, meanwhile, arrived on July 24 determined to block a vote. The journalist and orator Hossein Makki led a small group of deputies in a filibuster.[107] AIOC had conducted the discussions "behind a curtain of secrecy," suppressing all criticism "at the point of the bayonet ... I pray to God to set all those who have betrayed this country on the flames of oil," Makki roared.[108] The Majlis adjourned without submitting the Supplemental Agreement to a vote.

AIOC declined to restart discussions and held the £40 million owed to Iran in reserve, vowing to release the funds only when the new Majlis ratified the agreement. The company's opponents mobilized in the aftermath of July's filibuster, as famed nationalist leader Mohammed Mosaddeq returned from a brief retirement to form a new political coalition, *jebhe-ye melli*, "Popular Movement" or National Front, that opposed further compromise with AIOC and instead pushed for the nationalization of the oil industry.[109]

---

[107] Hossein Makki, *Naft va nutq-e Makki: jarayan-e muzakirat-e naft dar Majlis-e Panzdahum dar barah-e qarardad-e naft-e Iran va Ingilis* [Oil and the Speeches of Makki: The Course of Discussions in the Fifteenth Majlis Regarding the Anglo-Iranian Oil Concession] (Tehran: Intisharat-e Amir Kabir, 1978), 213–215.
[108] *Muzakirat-e Majlis* [Meetings of the Majlis] Vol. XV, July 23–27, 1949; Makki, *Naft va nutq-e Makki*, 202–214, 220–406, 411–514.
[109] Fu'ad Ruhani, *Zindagi-ye siyasi-ye Musaddiq: dar matn-e nahzat-e milli-ye Iran* [The Political Life of Musaddiq: in the National Front Movement of Iran] (London: Intisharat-e Nahzat-e Muqavamat-e Milli-ye Iran, 1987), 123–127; Katouzian, *Musaddiq*, 71–77; Fateh, *Panjah sal naft-e Iran*, 403–404; HIOHP, Sanjabi, Tape No. 8, 14–15, Tape No. 9, 1–7.

This troubling development came at a time when the Seven-Year Plan encountered new bureaucratic and financial obstacles. After a long delay, the plan received Majlis approval in July, with a budget of 1 billion rials for the period lasting until March 1950. Plan Director Dr. Taqi Nasr, a confidante of the shah's brother and Plan Organization head Prince Abdoreza, received £3 million in foreign exchange from the annual oil revenues, with the rest of the £9 million going to military expenses.[110] Faced with Majlis gridlock over both the Supplemental Agreement and the plan budget, Taqi Nasr made the ill-timed decision to take over Iran's state-owned factories as a way to kick-start an industrialization drive. The move was meant to be a splashy and decisive gesture by the Plan Organization, which had thus far accomplished very little concrete development work. But the acquisition sapped the plan of its cash reserves and triggered a palace coup organized by Ebtehaj to remove Taqi Nasr and replace him with Naficy, Ebtehaj's acolyte.[111] Administrative confusion made plan progress almost impossible, as cabinet positions rapidly changed hands and funds were allocated "according to the taste of the prime minister," a position which switched hands five times between December 1947 and June 1950.[112] Plan disbursements in the second half of 1949 totaled a mere 365 million rials.[113]

The confusion within the plan hinted at the more general economic crisis sweeping the country. Two bad harvests in 1948 and 1949 depressed rural areas and contributed to rising unemployment. Ebtehaj used his position at the Bank-e Melli to run a deflationary policy, hoarding rials for use on plan projects. This served to boost the bank's reserves but produced a slump in exports. State spending, meanwhile, spun out of control, doubling from 4.4 billion rials in 1946 to 8.9 billion rials in 1949. The main reason was an explosion in the size of the state bureaucracy, which grew from 60,000 in 1939 to 130,000 in 1949, and

---

[110] Taqi Nasr to Black, July 11, 1949, Iran – General – Correspondence 04, 1805822, WBGA.
[111] RG 59 891.50 SEVEN YEAR PLAN/7-149, US Embassy Tehran No. 174, July 1, 1949, Enclosure No. 1, Memo of Conversation, June 29, 891.50 SEVEN YEAR PLAN/7-849, US Embassy Tehran No. 179, July 8, 1949, Enclosure No. 1, Discussion with Ebtehaj, July 5, 1949; FO 371/75485 Le Rougetel to Bevin, July 4, 1949; FO 371/75486 Lawford to FO, August 23, 1949; Ebtehaj, *Khatirat*, 327–331.
[112] Ja'far Sharif Imami, *Khatirat-e Ja'far Sharif Imami: nukhust-e vazir 1339–1340 va 1357* [Memoirs of Ja'far Sharif Imami, Prime Minister of Iran 1960–1961] Habib Ladjevardi, ed. (Cambridge MA: Center for Middle Eastern Studies of Harvard University and Distributed by Ibex Books, 1999), 141.
[113] Svoboda to Bayne, Question of Iran's Capacity to Finance Seven-Year Plan in Initial Phase, July 18, 1949, Iran – General – Correspondence 04, 1805822, WBGA.

2.4 Collapse of Dual Integration, July 1949–March 1951

the shah's preoccupation with expanding Iran's military.[114] Between July 1949 and March 1950, Iran's financial position deteriorated while its economy slipped into recession.

The World Bank watched the situation in Iran with growing alarm. Cornelius van Engert noted that between the "absurdly overvalued" national currency and the slim chance of a bank loan, Iran was fast becoming dependent on AIOC as a source of foreign exchange. "I don't think this is at all a healthy thing for a country's economy," he wrote in October 1949, "but I don't know what can be done about it."[115] In November, the bank dispatched Edward A. Bayne to Tehran.[116] His reports were grim. The Plan Organization had devolved into a tool for political patronage "[and] the financial relief of powerful interests." The bulk of funds went to industrial projects, contradicting the original emphasis on agriculture, where budgeted spending for the year fell from 619.8 million rials to 187.4 million rials. "Disparity between actual income and authorized programs," Bayne concluded, "defeat[s] the whole purpose of a plan of expenditure .... The Plan has become a misnomer."[117] Thornburg blamed the worsening economic picture on Iranian mismanagement. "There has been enough money wasted during the past year ... to have paid for everything," he grumbled in March 1950. The problem, in his view, rested with the failure of Iranian administrators: "the practical difficulty of turning money, ideas and good intentions into real works ... by people who don't know how to do it."[118]

The Iranian New Year began on March 21, 1950. By that time, the US government had become concerned with the state of the shah's government. The US ambassador in Tehran warned that Iran was "crumbling away ... the Seven Year Plan will not save the situation .... Time is of the essence."[119] An increase in Cold War tensions, born from the communist revolution in China and the explosion of a Soviet nuclear device in late 1949, caused the Truman administration to take a harder

---

[114] Stephens to Garner, September 30, 1949, Attachment No. 1, Van Zeeland Report, Iran – General – Correspondence 04, 1805822, WBGA.

[115] Engert to Iliff, October 16, 1949, Iran – General – Correspondence 04, 1805822, WBGA.

[116] Bayne penned a glowing paean to the shah's modernizing sensibilities twenty years later. See E. A. Bayne, *Persian Kingship in Transition* (New York: American Universities Field Staff, 1968).

[117] Bayne to Campbell, December 22, 1949, Iran – General – Correspondence 04, 1805822, WBGA.

[118] Thornburg to US Ambassador, March 5, 1950, Iran – General – Correspondence 05, 1805823, WBGA.

[119] *FRUS 1950*, V: 470–471.

look at Iran. Belatedly abandoning its aloof posture, the US government took action in 1950 to rescue the plan and resume dual integration.

The first step would be to replace the shah. According to Assistant Secretary of State George C. McGhee, the young monarch, "has exhibited he has neither the character nor the ability to offer his people guidance ... his indecision is monumental and his moral courage debatable."[120] The embassy in Tehran reported that the "immediate improvement in the lot of the people cannot be accomplished" without the rise of a "strong man" who could push through reforms "without regard for democratic processes."[121] The new American Ambassador Henry F. Grady made it clear to the shah that the United States would support a government led by Army Chief of Staff Hajj 'Ali Razmara.

A seasoned intriguer, Razmara was known to be decisive, ambitious, and on poor terms with the shah. He was on very good terms with Thornburg, however, whom he had been secretly meeting throughout the spring to discuss development issues. Thornburg noted that during a meeting held on May 30, both he and Razmara assumed that the general would soon be named prime minister.[122] How much pressure the United States placed on the shah and what tools were used to orchestrate his compliance are not clear. In any event, the shah named Razmara as prime minister on June 26, despite his distaste for the former general and his concern that the appointment would threaten the Crown. Grady promised the new government a $25 million loan and support in new negotiations with AIOC. Razmara's first priority, however, would be to revive the Seven-Year Plan. In that regard, he relied on advice from Thornburg, who reached the apex of his influence in Tehran as Razmara's special advisor on economic and financial policy.[123]

Thornburg proposed a new-and-improved Seven-Year Plan that would emphasize small scale "impact" programs aimed at Iran's countryside – well digging, road construction, sanitation, and health projects meant to deliver quick results. "I know that Persia is financially solvent," wrote Thornburg. "All we have to do is keep the bird-brains and the crooks away from the cash register." Thornburg had confidence in Razmara, "[who] thus far has accepted every recommendation that we

---

[120] *FRUS 1950, V*: 509–518.
[121] RG 59 888.00/3-650, US Embassy Tehran No. 87, March 6, 1950, USNA.
[122] RG 59 888.00/4-1050, US Embassy Tehran No. 153, April 10, 1950, 888.00/6-2350, Embassy Dispatch No. 391, June 23, 1950, Enclosure No. 3, Memo of Conversation, May 30, 1950.
[123] Qaimmaqami, "The Catalyst of Nationalization," 22–31.

2.4 Collapse of Dual Integration, July 1949–March 1951

have made."[124] The new development strategy did not please everyone, however. Ebtehaj resigned in July, muscled out by Razmara. Dr. Taqi Nasr, whose poor judgment had bankrupted the plan a year before, resigned in September, shifting even more power to Thornburg, now the effective manager of the country's economic development program.[125]

Thornburg's new scheme ground to a halt in the face of AIOC stubbornness. Razmara needed concessions from the British to bring the Supplemental Agreement back to the Majlis, and he also needed funds to pump into the plan while balancing the general budget. Fraser refused to reopen discussions on either issue, insisting instead that Iran ratify the Supplemental Agreement as written. The company "[has] already conceded too much and should concede nothing more."[126] Pressure came down on Fraser from every direction, as London, Washington, and Tehran all worked to convince the chairman to change his tune. Assistant Secretary of State and former oil executive, George C. McGhee, warned the British company that US firms were close to concluding a "sweeping" deal with Saudi Arabia reflecting the new basis of equitability. Once that happened, the Supplemental Agreement would become obsolete: "Time is running out."[127]

Thornburg, acting as Razmara's envoy, came to London in December for a secret meeting with AIOC, in order to convince them to work toward funding the plan and bolstering Iran's new premier. He found them immovable.[128] The prime minister, growing frustrated, told the British and Americans his new plan would be to dissolve the Majlis, impose martial law "until tranquility was assured," and rule by decree.[129] Democracy, in its barest form, would be suspended until dual integration was restored.

On December 30, 1950, Aramco announced a fifty-fifty deal in Saudi Arabia. On January 11, 1951, the Majlis oil committee chaired by Mosaddeq rejected the Supplemental Agreement and the National Front stepped up its calls for nationalization. The World Bank, which had been stalling for months, now decided to act. "Iran is an oil economy," concluded the bank's preparatory memo. "If a new oil agreement is consummated, development in Iran in the short-term future could be

---

[124] Thornburg to Garner, July 30, 1950, Iran – General – Correspondence 06, 1805824, WBGA.
[125] FO 371/82342 Shepherd to FO, No. 425, September 8, 1950.
[126] RG 59 888.2553/1-2150, Wiley to State, January 21, 1950, 888.2553/2-350, Holmes to State, February 3, 1950, USNA.
[127] *FRUS 1950, V*: 593–600.
[128] RG 59 888.2553/12-2750, Parker to McGhee, December 27, 1950, USNA; FO 371/82377 Note from Furlonge, December 9, 1950, UKNA.
[129] FO 371/82377 Shepherd to Foreign Office, December 27, 1950, UKNA.

financed."[130] The British finally surrendered the Supplemental Agreement and offered a fifty-fifty contract, contingent on Razmara's public denunciation of nationalization. The bank would offer $19 million, so long as he permitted fiscal reforms overseen by Thornburg. Such a situation would give the United States and its allies considerable leverage over Razmara's government. It would also serve as a culmination to Thornburg's machinations from the year before: The plan would be placed under American control. "We are witnessing in dramatic fashion the death of the Seven Year Plan," Bayne wrote to Razmara. "The dream of development is lost in conflict of political pressures," which Razmara could settle so long as he reached an agreement with AIOC and submitted to foreign supervision.[131]

The powerless prime minister relented, delivering a speech on March 4, 1951, that denounced Mosaddeq and nationalization. Razmara used words drafted by the AIOC representative in Tehran, in the hopes that it would lead to a fifty-fifty deal and financial relief for his cash-strapped government.[132] Before he could move any further, Razmara was assassinated on March 7 while exiting a mosque in Tehran. The bank, unsure of whether a new government would honor their commitment to Razmara, withdrew its loan offer. Any hopes that Iran could continue to draw support from oil resources vanished on April 27, when the Majlis passed comprehensive nationalization legislation, supported by Iran's new Prime Minister, Mohammed Mosaddeq.

Once Iran set out on the course to nationalize its oil industry, the Seven-Year Plan receded from view, as did the Supplemental Agreement and fifty-fifty. Bereft of political or financial support, the Plan Organization limped along for the next three years, though most activities were suspended in 1951 once Mosaddeq made Iran's nationalization official and AIOC began its embargo on Iranian oil. The plan ended before it began. Dual integration had failed.

2.5 Conclusion

The First Seven-Year Plan did not meet the lofty expectations of its planners. In most accounts it is dismissed as a stillborn effort at

---

[130] Memo on the Financing of Development, January 16, 1951, Memo, Iran, January 18, 1951, Iran – General – Correspondence 07, 1805825, WBGA.
[131] FO 371/91485 EP 1112/14 Bayne to Razmara, January 18, 1951, UKNA.
[132] For text of Razmara's speech, see *Ettela'at*, March 4, 1951; BP 126353 Rice to Northcroft, March 2, 1951, Northcroft to Rice, No. 652, March 3, 1951, Northcroft to Directors, Rice, No. 8396, March 4, 1951, Northcroft to Rice, No. 8398, March 6, 1951.

2.5 Conclusion

economic development.[133] According to estimates, the Plan Organization spent 4 billion rials, or roughly $125 million, out of its intended budget of 21 billion rials.[134] The plan established ties between the Pahlavi government and the World Bank, a relationship that would prove crucial in future years: Despite the bank's dismissive attitude and its preoccupation with Iranian incapacity in the 1940s, over the next twenty years the institution would lend over $600 million to Iran, serving as the nation's single largest creditor.[135] The plan completed agricultural programs, an expansion of the national railroad and road network, and the beginnings of an irrigation dam at Karkheh in Khuzestan. But to label the First Plan even a partial success ignores the calamitous events of early 1951. Despite the efforts of the Pahlavi government and its foreign allies, Iran's first oil-driven development project ended in failure.

The plan failed for a variety of reasons. Despite support from the shah and his technocrats, most factions on the left and right opposed the plan. Ebtehaj blamed his countrymen's suspicion of foreigners and their discomfort with economics: "[B]ureaucrats ... did not believe in the principles of planning and did not trust it," he wrote years later.[136] While many distrusted the plan or opposed it on the grounds of self-interest, others objected to the sweeping powers the plan conferred onto foreign experts like Thornburg and OCI. Western observers fell back on the idea of Iranian incapacity to explain the plan's slow progress and eventual failure. Opposition to the OCI mission was blamed on an "unscrupulous minority" that used political obstruction "to sabotage the Plan and preserve their parasitical way of life," according to one OCI executive.[137] These accusations served to reiterate the key lessons of the Millspaugh mission, which had collapsed under similar circumstances. Other factors including bureaucratic intrigues and an aloof shah slowed the plan's progress.

Had the Pahlavi government united behind the plan, it likely would have accomplished more even with its limited funds. But to imagine greater success ignores the very real political fissures which existed in Iran before the 1951 nationalization. The shah supported development, but he had to contend with a suspicious Majlis. He was inclined to direct

---

[133] Bharier, *Economic Development in Iran*, 89–90.
[134] Plan Organization, Iran, *Review of the Second Seven Year Plan Program in Iran* (Tehran, March 10, 1960), 4–5.
[135] World Bank, "Current Economic Position and Prospects of Iran, Vol. I: The Main Report," May 18, 1971, Report No. SA-23a.
[136] Ebtehaj, *Khatirat*, 328–329.
[137] Clifford S. Strike, "A Plan That Failed," *Vital Speeches of the Day* 18, no. 4 (December 1, 1951): 125–127.

more money toward the military, leaving the development plan underfunded. Bureaucratic battles left the effort rudderless, a situation made worse by the efforts of Thornburg and OCI to profit from the plan's execution and bring it under American control.

The plan failed due to American neglect. The US government remained detached, trusting its designated proxies to carry out dual integration. According to Grady, Thornburg "could not subordinate his personal interest to the interests of his government." The former oil man's scheming proved counterproductive; both he and the OCI were jettisoned from Iran in March 1951 following Razmara's death.[138] The World Bank chose a cautious course of action, refusing Iran a loan until it had proven the plan's viability. This conservatism, as well as its support for Thornburg and OCI, was grounded in a preoccupation with Iranian incapacity. Bank officials did not consider Iran a viable investment until it had placed the development program under foreign management, a requirement which made the plan more unpopular with Iranians. Edward Bayne, writing in *Foreign Affairs* in July 1951, suggested that greater official US involvement could have made the difference. But no action was taken: "[T]he Bank, being a bank, did not find Iran a suitable risk."[139]

The chief blame for the failure of the First Plan rests with the Anglo-Iranian Oil Company. The company refused to acknowledge the new standard of equitability and stuck to terms that served its narrow interests. The frantic effort to restart the plan under Razmara failed because the company refused to alter its terms, though the prime minister was also undermined by the country's deteriorating economic situation and his fractious relationship with the shah. The United States, despite its preponderant international power, proved incapable of pushing any of the proxies toward a constructive policy. The result, Grady lamented, was paralysis: "We have done nothing .... I just cannot understand the general attitude of our Government toward this vital spot."[140]

The Seven-Year Plan had been designed to serve a political, as well as economic purpose. By bringing the Iranian people together around the cause of economic development, the plan would turn oil into a source of national prosperity, ensuring the stability of the Pahlavi regime. Though it ostensibly served a popular aim, the thrust of the plan was essentially undemocratic. Ebtehaj and the shah worked around the Majlis, which

---

[138] Grady to Bechtel, April 19, 1951, Papers of Henry F. Grady, Box 2, HSTPL.
[139] Edward A. Bayne, "Crisis of Confidence in Iran," *Foreign Affairs* 29, no. 4 (July 1951): 578–590.
[140] Grady to Bechtel, March 16, 1951, Papers of Henry F. Grady, Box 2, HSTPL.

2.5 Conclusion

they regarded as corrupt and obstructionist. American development groups sought to place the plan under foreign management. When the United States intervened in 1950, it was to support a strongman government. The plan's political achievements were an even greater disappointment than its contributions to Iran's economy. The first attempt at postwar development failed for want of funds, but its political appeal was insignificant compared to the program of nationalization.

3 The Mosaddeq Challenge
Nationalization and the Isolation of Iranian Oil, 1951–1952

Torkild "Captain" Rieber was a controversial figure best known for selling crude oil to Spanish fascists before World War II. Gruff and argumentative, the former chairman of Texaco came to Tehran in February 1952 with a specific goal in mind: convince Iran's government, led by populist hero Mohammed Mosaddeq, that it was incapable of running its own oil industry. Rieber did his utmost, debating with Mosaddeq's oil advisor Kazem Hasibi for hours, days, and eventually weeks. "I like Mr. Hasibi," Rieber declared, "I consider him a good friend ... and I have been trying to beat some sense into his head for the past six weeks."[1] Rieber's boss, World Bank Vice President Robert L. Garner, was in despair. Iran "has shown little understanding of the realities of the international oil business," he moaned.[2] Garner could not understand why Iran's petro-nationalists insisted on retaining control over their oil, when surrendering that control would yield millions in oil revenue.

In his history of Iran's oil crisis, Fu'ad Ruhani described the showdown between Mosaddeq and the British as a dispute "over what it means to nationalize."[3] Among the most studied episodes in Iran's modern history, the nationalization crisis is a transitional point in Iranian politics – the moment a secular, nationalist, and middle-class movement took control of the government, briefly interrupting the decades-long dominance of autocracy – and the cataclysm that set the stage for the coup of August 1953.[4] Yet in a fundamental sense, the crisis was over terminology and the precise meaning of "nationalization."

---

[1] *Foreign Relations of the United States, 1952–1954, Iran, 1951–1954, Volume X* [hereafter *FRUS X*], 355–356.
[2] Informal Memo for Mr. Nasser, November 24, 1952, Iran – General – Secret and Confidential Files – Negotiations – Volume 4, 1806454, WBGA.
[3] Fu'ad Ruhani, *Tarikh-e milli shudan-e san'at-e naft-e Iran* [The History of the Nationalization of the Oil Industry of Iran] (Tehran: Kitabhaye Jibi, 1973), 5.
[4] James F. Goode, *The United States and Iran: In the Shadow of Musaddiq* (New York: St. Martin's Press, 1997); Mary Ann Heiss, *Empire and Nationhood: The United States, Great Britain, and Iranian Oil, 1950–1954* (New York: Columbia University Press, 1997); Mostafa Elm, *Oil, Power, and Principle: Iran's Nationalization and Its Aftermath*

Expelling the British from Iran was Mosaddeq's political goal. But nationalization was also an expression of economic self-determination, the idea that the rewards of oil exploitation could, and should, be predominantly enjoyed by the oil-producing nation. Mosaddeq hoped that Iran could act as a member of the oligopoly, producing oil in a quantity and selling it at a price of its own choosing. In that sense nationalization served as a rejection of dual integration, which contended that a foreign-run oil industry was more economically beneficial to the producer state than a nationalized industry. Iran's prime minister and his advisors were confident their plan would succeed, for two reasons: They did not believe the global oil market could survive without Iranian oil, and they trusted the United States would rescue Iran in the event of a major crisis.

For the British government and the oil companies, nationalization posed a serious threat. The loss of control over Iranian oil threatened British finances as well as its fragile postwar prestige.[5] Nationalization would disrupt the oligopoly's carefully calculated system established to mitigate competition, manage price, and ensure profitability. The United States hoped to resolve the crisis through negotiation, fearing that aggressive action would drive Mosaddeq's nationalists toward communism. Policymakers worried that a prolonged oil shutdown would weaken Iran and potentially bring about its collapse. It would be a mistake, however, to characterize the Truman administration as an "honest broker" searching for a "middle ground," as historians have done in the past.[6] Throughout discussions from May 1951 to February 1952, the United States consistently took the side of Britain and the companies against Iran's fledgling nationalist government. The Truman administration used the appeal of dual integration – suggesting Iran had more to gain economically from a deal with the oil companies than from nationalization – to push Mosaddeq toward terms that the British could accept. When that proved impossible, the United States assisted the British and the companies with suspending dual integration, embargoing Iran and replacing its oil on the global market, in the hope that it would either

---

(Syracuse, NY: Syracuse University Press, 1992); Steve Marsh, *Anglo-American Relations and Cold War Oil: Crisis in Iran* (New York: Palgrave Macmillan, 2003); W. Roger Louis and James Bill, eds., *Mosaddeq, Iranian Nationalism, and Oil* (London: Tauris, 1988); Malcolm Byrne and Mark J. Gasiorowski, eds., *Mohammed Mosaddeq and the 1953 Coup in Iran* (Syracuse, NY: Syracuse University Press, 2004); Homa Katouzian, *Musaddiq and the Struggle for Power in Iran* (London: Tauris, 1990).

[5] For oil's importance to Britain's postwar economy, see Galpern, *Money, Oil, and Empire*, 23–141.

[6] Heiss, *Empire and Nationhood*, 76–106; Elm, *Oil, Power, and Principle*, 106.

convince Mosaddeq to abandon the fight or force him from power altogether.

Throughout the crisis, both Americans and British contended that Iran was incapable of running its own oil industry. Evidence suggests that this was a convenient myth spread to discredit Iran's nationalization. The crisis revealed the coercive power at the heart of the postwar petroleum order, the stability of which rested on the cooperative efforts of the oligopoly and Anglo-American governments to suppress petro-nationalism and preserve their favorable access to the oil of the Global South. For the companies and Anglo-American governments, nationalization was a disease. Iran, the patient, had to be quarantined to prevent the infection from spreading elsewhere.

3.1 Mosaddeq and "Nationalization"

By 1951, nationalizing foreign-owned oil industries was an established legal concept. Mexico nationalized its industry in 1938, following a precedent set by other Latin American countries years earlier. Great Britain nationalized many of its major industries under the Labour Party's postwar government. In Iran, calls for canceling the 1933 Concession became common in the 1940s, as the agreement was broadly unpopular and seen as a betrayal of the national interest. Such calls were distinct from "making the industry national" (*melli shudan*), which did not enter into public discourse until the late 1940s.[7] Far from a "vacuous slogan," the Iranian conception of nationalization was a coherent theory of anti-imperialist action combining a political program of rejecting foreign influence with an economic agenda aimed at strengthening the nation through the exploitation of its most valuable resource.[8] It drew its power from Iranian nationalism, the growing hatred of the British oil company, and the personal prestige of Mohammed Mosaddeq (Figure 3.1), perhaps the most mythologized figure in modern Iranian history.[9]

Though a landowner and member of the Qajar dynasty, Mosaddeq was not a typical aristocrat. A staunch advocate of constitutional government, Mosaddeq served in the Majlis during the 1920s. Alone among his peers, he rejected the ascension of Reza Khan to the throne in 1925. He continued to oppose the autocracy of the first Pahlavi, which he regarded

---

[7] Katouzian, *Musaddiq*, 67–68; Makki, *Naft va nutq-i Makki*, 174–194.
[8] For the companies' critique of nationalization as a "vacuous slogan," see RG 59 888.2553 AIOC/5-1751, Brewster Jennings (SONJ) to McGhee, May 17, 1951, 888.2553 AIOC/5-1851, BB Howard (SONJ) to McGhee, May 18, 1951, USNA.
[9] Ansari, *Modern Iran*, 130–131; Fateh, *Panjah sal naft-e Iran*, 515–517.

3.1 Mosaddeq and "Nationalization"

Figure 3.1 Mohammed Mosaddeq (middle) with Ambassador Henry F. Grady (left), 1951.
Photo ID 66-8020, HSTPL

as contrary to the spirit of the 1906 Constitution that the shah should reign, not rule. As the Majlis deputy for Tehran – a seat that he won through a free and fair election, a rarity at the time – Mosaddeq authored the 1944 bill on foreign oil concessions, rejected the Millspaugh financial mission on the grounds that it constituted a breach of Iran's national sovereignty, and delivered passionate speeches against the British oil company.[10] His doctrine of negative equilibrium called for Iran to remain neutral in foreign affairs. While the British dismissed him as a demagogue, Mosaddeq's political bona fides were firmly established by 1944, with the American embassy noting he enjoyed "an enormous

[10] Parsa Yamagani, *Karnamah-e Musaddiq* [The Addresses of Mosaddeq] (Tehran: Ravaq, 1978), 15–34, 35–78, 117–128; Katouzian, *Musaddiq*, 1–77, and Mohammed Musaddiq, *Musaddiq's Memoirs*, trans. Homa Katouzian (London: JEBHE, 1988), 1–25; Hossein Makki, *Duktur Musaddiq va nutq'ha-ye tarikhi-ye* [Dr. Musaddiq and His Historical Speeches] (Tehran: Sazman-e Intisharat-e Javidan, 1985), 116–119, 168–172, 172–199; Kay-Ustavan, *Siyasat-e muvazanah-e manfi*, vol. I, 20–35.

amount of prestige" among both the elite and the general population.[11] He was known as a patriotic, passionate politician. He was also believed to be incorruptible.

After a brief retirement, Mosaddeq returned to politics in the aftermath of the July 1949 Majlis filibuster to reject the Supplemental Agreement. He formed a new political coalition, the National Front, in November 1949.[12] The coalition was loosely organized and included such groups as the socialist-technocratic Iran Party and the followers of populist cleric Ayatollah Abolqassem Kashani. But its members were united around a shared commitment to nationalizing the oil industry and the rejection of British influence in Iran. In 1950 Mosaddeq's prestige as an elder statesman won him a seat on the Majlis oil committee that he led as chairman. From this lofty perch, Mosaddeq orchestrated the National Front campaign against the Supplemental Agreement and the Razmara government, while consistently advocating for nationalization rather than further negotiation with AIOC.[13]

Mosaddeq won the premiership through a series of unexpected events. Following Razmara's death from an assassin's bullet on March 7, 1951, Mosaddeq used the subsequent confusion in the capital to propose a resolution declaring the nationalization of the oil industry. His oil committee had already ruled against the Supplemental Agreement and had recommended nationalization before Razmara's demise. Pressure from the National Front deputies compelled the Majlis to pass the resolution on March 20.[14] The shah, still grappling with a financial crisis, wanted to avoid nationalization at all costs. He worked with the British ambassador to prepare the Majlis to vote for Seyyed Zia, the British favorite, as prime minister. During a Majlis election on April 27, the assembly overwhelmingly chose Mosaddeq, who accepted the position on the condition that the assembly vote on a new "Nine-Point" nationalization bill that spelled out how the industry would be transferred to Iranian ownership. The Majlis passed the Nine-Point Bill on April 27, 1951, and the shah signed it on May 1.[15]

Mosaddeq was no radical. He was not overtly anti-Western. He did not oppose Western-style modernization or relations with the West. His

---

[11] RG 59 891.00/3022, Ford to State, March 10, 1944, USNA.
[12] Abrahamian, *The Coup*, 48–54; Ebtehaj, *Khatirat*, vol. I, 286–287; 'Ali Shayegan, *Sayyed 'Ali Shayegan: Zendagi-nama-ye siasi* [Sayyed 'Ali Shayegan: A Political Biography] Vol. I (Tehran 2006), 329–339, 349–350; HIOHP, Azar, No. 1, 1–16.
[13] Katouzian, *Musaddiq*, 90; Makki, *Naft va nutq-e Makki*, 402–411.
[14] Katouzian, *Musaddiq's Memoirs*, 32; Ruhani, *Tarikh-e milli shudan-e san'at-e naft-e Iran*, 116–122.
[15] Azimi, *Crisis*, 253–258; Katouzian, *Musaddiq's Memoirs*, 33–34.

philosophy of negative equilibrium argued for a non-aligned Iran that pursued self-sufficiency. Like other prominent nationalists of the Global South, Mosaddeq did not fit neatly on either side of the Cold War, though he considered American friendship preferable to the influence of the Soviet Union. Iranian communists, as well as their sponsors in Moscow, regarded him as a "bourgeois nationalist" and a tool of the United States.[16] Older constitutionalists like Taqizadeh respected Mosaddeq as an "honest, trustworthy, and patriotic" figure while castigating him as a "rabble-rouser" who used anti-British sentiment to whip up popular support.[17] He was "indigestible," from a political point of view, "both a patrician and a populist."[18] Once in office, Mosaddeq retained notable conservatives in key cabinet positions and showed deference to the shah, despite his conviction that the monarch should remain bound by the constitution.[19] Mosaddeq and nationalization were wildly popular, enjoying support from "95–98 percent" of all Iranians according to one American estimate.[20] The shah and the rest of Iran's elite were too cowed by Mosaddeq's prestige to resist what was clearly the most appealing political program in Iran's modern history.

For the National Front, nationalization was an "absolute sovereign right, universally recognized."[21] The core of nationalization's political power lay in an emotional appeal to Iran's history of subjugation at the hands of foreign powers. "Nobody denies that all the sorrows of Iran," declared Kashani, "are all the results of British politics. The Nationalization of the oil industry … is the sole remedy of our ills."[22] In 1949, Karim Sanjabi argued that Britain had nationalized its coal industry after World War II and would thus be bound to recognize nationalizations in other nations: "there was no question that it was legal."[23] It was for this

---

[16] Memorandum, "The National Front in Iran," October 28, 1949, trans. Jamil Hasanli, Wilson Center Digital Archive, www.digitalarchive.wilsoncenter.org/document/119116; Maziar Behrooz, "Tudeh Factionalism and the 1953 Coup in Iran," *International Journal of Middle East Studies* 33, no. 3 (August, 2001): 364.

[17] Taqizadeh, *Zendegi-ye tufani*, 366.

[18] Katouzian, *Musaddiq's Memoirs*, 9; Ansari, *Politics of Nationalism*, 130, 11 and *Modern Iran*, 131–134.

[19] Karim Sanjabi, *Omidha va Namidha: Khatirat-e Siyasi* [Hopes and Despairs: A Political Life] (London: Nashr-e Kitab, 1989), 174; Afkhami, *The Life and Times of the Shah*, 117–125; Milani, *The Shah*, 150–151.

[20] *FRUS X*: 79–81.

[21] Jahangir Bushehri, "Nationalization of the Iranian Oil Industry – An Outline of Its Origin and Issues," February 15, 1952, 30, in Iran – General – Correspondence, 1806440, WBGA; BP 126464A Mosaddeq Speech, September 27, 1951.

[22] Kashani, "Declaration on the Question of Nationalization," *Ettela'at*, December 21, 1950.

[23] HIOHP, Sanjabi, Tape No. 8, 14–15.

reason that "nationalization" was adopted as the group's slogan instead of "cancellation" or "repossession," on the assumption that the international community (particularly the United States) would have to accept it as a fait accompli. Nationalization was first and foremost a political program designed to expel foreign influence from Iran.

Yet the economic importance of nationalization weighed nearly as much as its political significance. Iranian grievance over its measly share of AIOC's oil profits had appeared as early as the 1920s and Cadman's showdown with Teymurtash. According to one estimate, AIOC deprived Iran of $1.2 billion over the lifetime of the concession.[24] In 1950, Iran produced 30 million tons of oil. If sold at $1.75 per barrel (the so-called posted price used by the companies to value oil produced in the Persian Gulf), this equaled roughly $391 million. "The revenue derived from oil," explained Kashani, "can remedy the prevailing disastrous condition of our country ... the only way to put an end to poverty and misery of the Iranian nation."[25] Nationalization was the National Front's response to the country's socio-economic crisis, a new program after the public failure of the Seven-Year Plan. Its wild popularity was built upon the idea that it would bring national prosperity.

While foreign observers argued it was a vague, imprecise, and emotional program, Mosaddeq and the National Front were aware of the more practical implications of their scheme. Iranian petroleum engineer Parviz Mina noted that nationalization had three interrelated goals: assert Iranian ownership of oil reserves and facilities, take control of the industry, and "enter international oil markets ... engaging in commercial and distribution activities."[26] The nationalization bill signed by the shah on May 1, 1951 did not articulate a seizure but rather a transfer of assets. All of AIOC's staff would be invited to work for National Iranian Oil Company (NIOC) so that Iran could benefit from "the experience and knowledge of the former oil company."[27] AIOC would be paid compensation. Mosaddeq, the first Iranian to obtain a PhD in law from a European university, prepared counterclaims based on decades of underpaid royalties to insure against an onerous obligation to AIOC.[28]

---

[24] Bushehri, "Nationalization of the Iranian Oil Industry – An Outline of its Origin and Issues," 20–23, in Iran – General – Correspondence, 1806440, WBGA.
[25] Kashani, "Declaration on the Question of Nationalization."
[26] FISDS, *Tahavvul-e san`at-e naft-e Iran: negahi az darun* [The Evolution of Iran's Oil Industry: An Insider's Account], Interview with Parviz Mina.
[27] BP 126464 Aide Memoire from Minister of Finance, May 30, 1951.
[28] Mosaddeq asked for 'Ali Shayegan's assistance in crafting the laws creating the new oil company. See Shayegan, *Sayyed 'Ali Shayegan: Zendagi-nama-ye siasi*, vol. I, 468–469. FISDS, *Tahavvul-e san`at-e naft-e Iran*, Interview with Mina.

3.1 Mosaddeq and "Nationalization"

Nationalization was a gamble, as it was sure to infuriate the British and anger the major oil companies. But Mosaddeq felt he had the upper hand. The National Front believed that the global oil market would collapse without Iranian oil. This was not a controversial position. Iran was the fourth-largest oil producer in the world and Abadan the world's largest refinery. High-ranking US officials like George C. McGhee and Dean Acheson regarded Iran's oil as irreplaceable.[29] Kashani boasted that Iran could survive without oil, and Mosaddeq himself utilized this argument at times during his meetings with US officials.[30]

But while Kashani may have believed his own rhetoric, Mosaddeq was eager to sell oil abroad. His thinking was influenced by Kazim Hasibi, his chief oil advisor, a graduate of the Ecole Polytechnique well-versed in oil's production and refining.[31] A founding member of the Iran Party, Hasibi had spent the years from 1948 to 1951 researching nationalization and AIOC's record in Iran and regarded himself as an expert on the subject.[32] Both Hasibi and Mosaddeq felt that Anglo-American corporate competition, which had been on vivid display during the 1944 concession scramble, would allow Iran to find customers, particularly among smaller American companies excluded from the oligopoly. Compensation for AIOC would be paid "with American money," boasted one Iranian official.[33] Mosaddeq did not really intend for Iran's oil-industry to shut down: He hoped that production and exports would continue, with the benefits flowing down to the Iranian people. Finally, Mosaddeq believed that the US commitment to stopping communism would oblige the Truman administration to intervene. As he explained to Ambassador Henry F. Grady several weeks after taking office, "if the industry collapses and no money comes and disorder and communism follow, it will be your fault."[34]

Mosaddeq was an experienced politician with a distinct and carefully organized agenda. Nationalization, by the same token, was a coherent political and economic strategy that had accumulated popular support and the cooperation (or at least non-opposition) of Iran's political establishment. Its fatal flaw lay in the belief that competition within the

---

[29] *FRUS 1951, V*: 313–314.   [30] *FRUS X*: 178–179.
[31] Ebtehaj, *Khatirat*, 286–287. For Kazem Hasibi's biography, see Amir Tayarani, *Namah'ha va yaddasht'ha-ye Muhandis Kazim Hasibi, mushavir-e arshad-e duktur Musaddiq dar umur-e naft* [The Letters and Diaries of Engineer Kazem Hasibi, Senior Advisor to Dr. Musaddiq for Petroleum Affairs] (Tehran: Gam-e Naw, 2011), 7–19.
[32] Tayarani, *Namah'ha va yaddasht'ha-ye Muhandis Kazim Hasibi*, 33–42.
[33] FO 371/91497 Minute by Logan, May 2, 1951, UKNA.
[34] RG 59 888.2553/5-3151, Memo of Conversation, May 31, 1951, USNA.

international oil industry was stronger than was in fact the case, or that solidarity within the oligopoly would not be sufficient to keep American oil companies from doing business with Iran. Mosaddeq also mistakenly believed that the United States would prioritize Iran's security from communism over its commitments to Britain and the oil companies. Though both Mosaddeq and nationalization failed to achieve their intended goals, it is important not to fall into the trap left by contemporary commentators and dismiss both the man and the movement as driven by visions of an unrealistic utopian ideal. Though he appeared an odd character to the Western media – an aristocrat who wore pajamas and held sensitive negotiations in his bed chambers – Mosaddeq was sincere in his convictions and resolute in his determination to carry out his program despite the considerable risks to himself and his country.[35]

In the British view, Mosaddeq was a "mad man." Nationalization was driven by xenophobia and irrational demagoguery.[36] "We do not ... dispute the right of a Government to acquire property in their own country," declared Foreign Secretary Herbert Morrison in the House of Commons on May 2, 1951, "but we cannot accept that [AIOC's] whole position in Persia should be radically altered by unilateral action."[37] The 1933 Concession forbade unilateral cancelation – nationalization, according to the British government, was illegal. This contrivance masked anxiety. British finances rested on a precarious foundation of invisible earnings and overseas assets. Should Mosaddeq succeed, his example might inspire nationalizations of other British possessions, such as the Suez Canal or the oil concessions in Iraq or Kuwait.[38] Determined in 1949 to hold on to Abadan without changing the terms of the concession, AIOC and the British government were prepared to abandon Iran rather than yield to terms that might be demanded elsewhere. The British

---

[35] Mary Ann Heiss, "Real Men Don't Wear Pajamas: Anglo-American Cultural Perceptions of Mohammed Mossadegh and the Iranian Oil Nationalization Dispute," in Peter Hahn and Mary Ann Heiss eds., *Empire and Revolution: The United States and the Third World Since 1945* (Columbus, OH: Ohio State University Press, 2001), 178–191; Dietrich, *Oil Revolution*, 33–39.

[36] Examples of this attitude are easy to find in British documents: see FO 371/91530 Franks to FO, May 3, 1951, FO to Shepherd, May 6, 1951; FO 371/91531 Note on Persia, May 4, 1951, Note to Shepherd May 9, 1951, UKNA; see also Marsh, *Anglo-American Relations*, 47–50.

[37] Quoted in Alan W. Ford, *The Anglo-Iranian Oil Dispute of 1951–1952: A Study of the Role of Law in the Relations of States* (Berkeley, CA: 1954), 56.

[38] W. Roger Louis, *The British Empire in the Middle East, 1945–1951: Arab Nationalism, the United States, and Postwar Imperialism* (Oxford: Clarendon Press, 1984), 667; Galpern, *Money, Oil and Empire*, 80–141.

3.1 Mosaddeq and "Nationalization"

government rejected Mosaddeq, argued his political power was ephemeral, and worked continuously to remove him from power.[39]

The oligopoly's members were similarly resolute in their opposition. "By arbitrarily breaking its own contract," declared Jersey Standard's Brewster Jennings, Iran had undermined "faith in binding international agreements."[40] In violating the so-called sanctity of contracts, Iran had imperiled the basis of economic exchange throughout the Free World. Such high-minded language concealed straightforward self-interest. The companies increased Middle East production by more than 1 million barrels a day between 1946 and 1950.[41] The members of the oligopoly produced at a paltry $0.10 or $0.20 per barrel but valued the crude at $1.75–$2.00, realizing windfall profits. From AIOC's point of view, "any resolution which pays lip service ... to nationalization will make endless difficulties" in other concessionary areas.[42] Royal Dutch/Shell, in a note to the British government, acknowledged that some form of nationalization would have to be recognized, but on restricted terms, "so that control of future operations ... remains in the hands of [AIOC]."[43] The whole premise of the postwar petroleum order was the companies' control of Middle East oil. To admit the legality or validity of nationalization would be to put that control in jeopardy.

The US approach to nationalization was cautious, reflecting Cold War strategic priorities and a desire to preserve the dual integration of Iranian oil. Since 1950, the United States had worried over Iran's internal stability. Razmara's death left the Truman administration with few options, as the shah was regarded as a weak figure and Iran's conservative elite broadly rejected as out-of-touch and corrupt.[44] In a political vacuum, the organized and Soviet-backed Tudeh Party might attempt a takeover of the government. A few CIA officials, including Middle East chief Kermit Roosevelt and deputy director Allen Dulles, felt Iran might fall to communist control within a year.[45]

These concerns conditioned US assessments of the National Front and nationalization. Mosaddeq, according to one CIA report, was "a dramatic demagogue ... without particular wisdom or background for

---

[39] FO 248/1514 Shepherd to Morrison, July 4, 1951; FO 371/191548 Berthoud, "Persia," June 15, 1951, UKNA; Louis, *The British Empire in the Middle East*, 660–661.
[40] "Comments on the Iranian Case," Brewster Jennings, October 22, 1951, Box 2.207/E184, Exxon-Mobil Collection, Briscoe Center for American History.
[41] Leeman, *Price of Middle East Oil*, 269.
[42] BP 126353 Rice to Northcroft, March 2, 1951.
[43] BP 28341 Hopwood to Butler, June 1, 1951.
[44] Heiss, *Empire and Nationhood*, 15, 36.
[45] Mark J. Gasiorowski, "US Perceptions of the Communist Threat in Iran during the Mossadegh Era," *Journal of Cold War Studies* 21, no. 3 (Summer 2019): 12–13.

government." But he was not a communist.[46] A variety of factors, including the fall of Czechoslovakia in 1948 and the communist revolution in China in 1949, encouraged a cautious approach from Truman administration officials like Secretary of State Dean Acheson and Assistant Secretary of State George C. McGhee. Rejecting nationalization might push Iran's nationalists toward a Soviet alignment or throw the country into greater instability. American officials insisted to their British counterparts that a solution to the crisis had to protect "the stability of Iran and ... the uninterrupted flow of oil to its normal markets."[47] In a sense, Mosaddeq was correct – the United States would do all it could to prevent Iran's fall to communism, including supporting a settlement that prevented a shutdown of the oil industry.

Nevertheless, no one in the Truman administration would acknowledge nationalization on Mosaddeq's terms. A statement issued by the US government on May 11, ten days after the nationalization bill became law, condemned the "unilateral cancellation of clear contractual relationships."[48] Ambassador Henry F. Grady, widely regarded as sympathetic to Iranian nationalism, thought of Mosaddeq's working definition of nationalization as "confiscation," one that "flew in the face of established ... ideas of free trade and enterprise."[49] The seizure of private property by sovereign governments, while legally possible, was a clear threat to American commercial interests, including other oil concessions. The loss of AIOC constituted a major political and economic blow to Great Britain, the most important US ally in the Cold War.

American officials imagined a settlement that defined the terms of nationalization in a way that would leave the *status quo ante* essentially unaltered. McGhee, a former oil executive, believed this could be done through some altered terminology. "As in Mexico, the word 'concession' must be abandoned," he concluded. A new arrangement would place Iran's oil resources "ostensibly under the control of some Iranian authority," while preserving "operational control" for AIOC, what McGhee regarded as the "ultimate objective" of negotiations.[50] Arguments would be premised on notions of Iranian incapacity – the idea that the Iranians could not run the oil industry without help from AIOC – and the assumption that maintaining dual integration was in Iran's economic

---

[46] *Foreign Relations of the United States, 1952–1954, Iran, 1951–1954, Second Edition* [hereafter *FRUS Retrospective*], 73–75.
[47] RG 59 888.2553/4-2051, Memo from McGhee to Acheson, April 20, 1951, USNA.
[48] *Department of State Bulletin*, May 28, 1951.
[49] RG 59 888.2553/5-1351, Grady to Acheson, May 13, 1951; BP 126353 Interview with Grady, March 17, 1951.
[50] *FRUS 1951, V*: 288–291.

interests. Between May 1951 and February 1952, the United States sponsored three major attempts to define nationalization. The hope was that Mosaddeq would agree to a deal that acknowledged Iranian incapacity to manage the oil industry, the need for foreign management, and continued corporate control of Iranian oil.

3.2 Defining Nationalization: Negotiations, June 1951–March 1952

After some prodding from the Truman administration, the British government instructed AIOC to send a delegation to Iran to commence negotiations in June 1951. AIOC chairman William J. Fraser chose Basil Jackson, a widely respected figure within the company, to lead the negotiating team. Upon his arrival in Tehran, Jackson stated to the press that his mission was to determine "what … exactly is meant by 'nationalization'."[51] The British government would hold off on punitive measures – including a military strike then being formulated in the Ministry of Defence – until AIOC and Iran had discussed a diplomatic resolution to the crisis. The United States watched from the sidelines.

Ostensibly, Jackson would find common ground with Iran. But his instructions contained elaborate descriptions of what might happen to Abadan should AIOC withdraw, including technical breakdowns and unstoppable fires "[with] many hundreds of people burned to death." Having scared the Iranians with such apocalyptic imagery, Jackson would offer Iran a cash incentive to accept a fifty-fifty agreement – the same terms which AIOC had refused to offer since 1949, but which were now necessary owing to the recent fifty-fifty deal in Saudi Arabia – and AIOC's continued control of the industry.[52] A draft agreement suggested a preamble "[with] suitable recitals setting out the Company's acceptance … of the principle of nationalization."[53] AIOC's proposed definition of nationalization, in other words, barely escaped the bounds of Cadman's contract with Reza Shah from 1933. The company's strategy was the same as it had been twenty years before: A combination of pressure and cash incentives would bring about Iranian cooperation. The US Ambassador Henry F. Grady thought it a "most liberal offer."[54]

---

[51] RG 59 888.2553 AIOC/6-1251, Grady to Acheson, June 12, 1951, USNA.
[52] BP 72363 "Abadan Refinery: Withdrawal of British Staff," June 11, 1951, "Effect of the Withdrawal of British Staff," Pattinson to Gass, Undated, "Abadan Refinery: Note on Complexity of Operations".
[53] BP 28341 Copy of Heads of Agreement, June 25, 1951.
[54] RG 59 888.2553/6-1551, Grady to Acheson, June 15, 888.2553/6-1951, Grady to Acheson, June 19, 1951, USNA.

Unsurprisingly, talks between Jackson and Mosaddeq's government broke down almost immediately. Kazem Hasibi, Mosaddeq's oil advisor, insisted AIOC obey the articles of Iran's nationalization laws and turn over all revenue earned since March 20, setting aside 25 percent in a separate account to cover compensation. Iran's minister of finance argued that they had no wish to "paralyze the Company's operations," and once control over operations was transferred business would resume "under the same mechanism as had hitherto been in operation." AIOC staff would remain in Iran and continue their duties under the management of NIOC. Jackson scoffed at the Iranian position. He asked whether they were prepared to export crude and refined products without access to the "vast and highly complex" marketing organization of AIOC. Jackson asserted that Iran could not profit from its oil industry without AIOC's help, and that the industry would shut down without British expertise. But Hasibi dismissed Jackson's threats of a shutdown. "The Iranian oil industry," he argued, "was a child which the Western world would fondly nurture in any circumstances." Even if Iran exported less oil than it had under AIOC, eliminating the British middleman would allow the government to realize "eight or nine times" more revenue than it had received as royalty.[55] His arguments illustrated the confidence Mosaddeq's supporters felt regarding the execution of nationalization, the financial windfall it would produce, and the fact that the United States (to which Hasibi was referring) would not allow Iran to slip into financial ruin. Talks ended on June 20 and Jackson left Tehran the following day.

With Jackson's departure, AIOC's position inside Iran deteriorated. Suspecting company agents were bribing Majlis deputies and distributing propaganda to undermine the nationalization effort, National Front investigators raided the AIOC information office and discovered a trove of compromising material.[56] The company's representative was forced to flee to Iraq, his suitcases crammed with documents.[57] In Abadan, a committee headed by National Front leader Hossein Makki demanded the company turn over its account books and acknowledge Iranian ownership of exports.[58] Citing the interference of Makki's oil

---

[55] BP 72363 Meeting at Ministry of Finance, June 14, 1951, Notes on a Second Meeting Held at the Summer Office of the Prime Minister, June 17, 1951.
[56] For the documents taken from the AIOC information office, see *Asrar-e khanah-e Siddan* [Records from the House of Seddon] (Tehran: Mu'assasah-'e Intisharat-e Amir Kabir, 1979).
[57] BP 72363 Seddon to Rice, No. 78, July 9, 1951, Seddon to Northcroft, No. 83, July 16, 1951.
[58] RG 59 888.2553 AIOC/6-1951, Grady to Acheson, June 19, 1951, USNA; Bamberg *Vol. II*, 427; BP 101108 Drake to Fraser, June 11, 1951; Fateh, *Panjah sal naft-e Iran*, 549–551.

3.2 Defining Nationalization

commission, Fraser gave the order to begin winding down operations. "The only alternative," according to Abadan manager Eric Drake, "was acceptance ... of oil nationalization."[59] Payments of royalties to Iran ceased. The British believed that economic warfare and internal political pressure from the shah and other conservatives would bring about the fall of the Mosaddeq government in relatively short order.[60] After Jackson's departure, British officials and agents in Iran actively began working toward that end.[61]

Jackson's failure troubled the United States. Secretary Acheson worried a shutdown in oil exports would bring chaos to Iran, while the National Security Council concluded that eventual communist rule was "a distinct possibility" if the nationalization crisis was not resolved.[62] "The Iranian government and AIOC desperately need each other," wrote Ambassador Grady, yet the British seemed content to let the situation spiral out of control, confident that an end to oil revenues would force Mosaddeq to resign.[63] McGhee felt a British withdrawal would be a mistake. "Any test of will ... in the light of the highly irrational and emotional view of the Iranians, [would] not be successful," he warned.[64] Both sides, recalled Acheson, were pushing their luck "to the point of suicide."[65] A few isolated voices, including CIA deputy director Allen Dulles and his friend Max Thornburg, backed the British plan to force Mosaddeq out of office.[66] But the chief of the CIA station in Tehran Roger Goiran vetoed the idea, arguing Mosaddeq was in a strong position while the conservative opposition remained divided and disorganized.[67] With no alternatives, the United States forged ahead with a new round of talks.

Mosaddeq hoped to avoid a full oil shutdown. Driving out AIOC satisfied members of the National Front like Makki, but Mosaddeq grasped the economic significance of keeping the oil flowing. He wrote to President Truman on June 28 and invited US participation in further negotiations that could establish a basis for keeping the industry in

---

[59] BP 72363 Drake to Fraser, June 24, 1951.
[60] This argument was laid out in an important cable from Ambassador Sir Francis Shepherd on July 4. The Foreign Office printed the cable for distribution. See FO 248/1514 Shepherd to Morrison, July 4, 1951, UKNA.
[61] Louis, "Britain and the Overthrow of the Mosaddeq Government," in Byrne and Gasiorowski eds., *Mohammed Mosaddeq*, 138. British covert operations to remove Mosaddeq began in earnest after June 20.
[62] *FRUS X*: 67–68, 72–73.
[63] RG 59 888.2553/6-3051, Grady to Acheson, June 30, 1951, 888.2553/7-151, Grady to Acheson, July 1, 1951, USNA.
[64] *FRUS X*: 89–91.   [65] Acheson, *Present at the Creation*, 507.
[66] *FRUS Retrospective*: 87; Memo of Conversation, July 6, 1951, Dean Acheson Papers, HSTPL.
[67] *FRUS Retrospective*: 86–87.

operation.[68] Truman sent Averell Harriman, a prominent American diplomat and former ambassador, to act as mediator. Truman urged Harriman to find some "common denominator" that could act as a foundation for a new agreement. Yet Harriman's goal, as he assured the British before his arrival in Tehran, was to convince Mosaddeq that oil "could not be sold without British help."[69]

Harriman arrived in Tehran on July 14. After several meetings with Mosaddeq, Harriman recognized that the prime minister's rigid position stemmed from political considerations: Anything less than full nationalization might enrage his supporters. Ayatollah Kashani promised Harriman that "blood would flow" if anything was done to reverse nationalization.[70] Harriman dismissed British arguments that Mosaddeq's government would fall to internal political intrigue or economic pressure.[71] Instead, he repeated language used by the Jackson mission in June. He stressed to Mosaddeq the "disastrous results" that were sure to befall Iran should the Abadan refinery shut down, in the hope that he could persuade the prime minister to avoid a course of action that would cause oil exports to cease.[72]

While Harriman conducted high-level diplomacy, the task of "educating" the Iranians on why nationalization was sure to fail fell to his advisor, Walter J. Levy. A renowned oil expert, Levy had worked for the Marshall Plan, directing its efforts to stabilize world oil prices.[73] Totting a "huge loose-leaf binder" crammed with statistics and charts, Levy struck a pose as the consummate oil-man – a disinterested professional advisor who nevertheless tried his utmost to push the Iranians toward an interpretation of nationalization that suited AIOC and US interests.

Presuming that Hasibi would be unmoved by technical arguments given his knowledge of petroleum production and refining, Levy focused on oil's international dimension. Iran's crude, he explained, was "valueless." Only with the "technical knowledge" of the major companies was it transformed into a profitable commodity. Selling 8 or 10 million tons (163,000–204,000 bpd) to independent buyers as Hasibi proposed was unrealistic, Levy argued, as those customers could buy from the major companies at lower prices through long-term contracts. Iran would have

---

[68] *FRUS X*: 77–79.
[69] CAB 128-21-12 Minute of Meeting July 16, 1951, UKNA; Heiss, *Empire and Nationhood*, 82.
[70] Memo of Conversation, July 25, 1951, Papers of Averell Harriman, Box 292, Library of Congress.
[71] *FRUS X*: 97–98, 101–102, 104–105; Heiss, *Empire and Nationhood*, 85.
[72] *FRUS X*: 93–95.
[73] Walter Levy, "Iranian Royalty Question Serious Problem," *Oil Forum*, February 1951.

3.2 Defining Nationalization

to offer steep discounts to entice customers away from the oligopoly, negating any economic benefits of nationalization. Mosaddeq did not have the credibility to sell oil in commercial quantities, argued Levy. Iran would have to convince the global industry of its good intentions and establish "confidence and cooperation" with the oligopoly. To accomplish this, Iran had to make peace with AIOC.[74]

Levy's arguments had their intended effect. On July 23, Mosaddeq admitted that Iran could not market oil internationally without help from AIOC. Conservatives in the Majlis, together with the shah, were applying gradual pressure to the prime minister, who feared what a shutdown would do to the nation's economy and his own political position. He agreed to Harriman's formula to restart negotiations: If AIOC accepted the principle of nationalization as legally valid, Iran would accept a settlement that ensured the effective management of the oil industry. "The principle of nationalization" referred to the March 20 nationalization resolution, which had simply stated Iran's ownership of the industry, rather than the May 1 law that was more detailed. "Effective management" euphemistically referred to British control of the oil fields and Abadan refinery.[75] Harriman's formula appeared expansive enough to accommodate Iran's interests, but upon closer inspection was skewed to facilitate a deal that would satisfy the British and maintain foreign control of global oil reserves.

While Mosaddeq appeared willing to negotiate, the British remained confident he would eventually fall from power. A new government would then accept the Jackson proposal, "dressed up" with some additional "sweetenings."[76] When Harriman commenced talks between Mosaddeq and the British envoy, Sir Richard Stokes, in August, the British position had changed little. Stokes delivered an eight-point proposal to the Iranians on August 13. His proposal acknowledged Iranian ownership of the "installations, machinery, plant and stores." The plan established an operating company to manage those assets, with a board of two British, two Iranian, and two neutral members. AIOC would purchase all Iranian crude oil from the operating company at a discounted price and on a long-term contract of twenty-five years. A profit-sharing mechanism would deliver half of the profits to Iran. Stokes explicitly noted that

---

[74] RG 59 888.2553/8-3151, "Technical Oil Discussions," Conversation with Hasibi and Saleh, July 16, 1951, 888.2553/7-1951, Eakens for Levy, July 19, 1951, USNA.

[75] *FRUS X*: 99–100, 105–107, 109–113, 115–116; RG 59 888.2553/7-2151, Harriman to State, July 21, 1951, 888.2553/7-2251, Note from Harriman, July 22, 1951, USNA.

[76] FO 371/91575 Minute by Logan, July 31, 1951, Ramsbotham, Record of Meeting, July 31, 1951, Gass to Bowker, July 31, 1951; T 236/2828, "Lord Privy Seal's Mission to Persia," Undated, UKNA.

such an arrangement "is the only basis upon which [Iran's] oil industry ... could hope to maintain itself." In exchange, Mosaddeq would recognize AIOC's right to compensation and Iran's need "for the services of the British staff" for the marketing and distribution, "in order to deal with the maximum of oil and so benefit the Iranian exchequer."[77] The offer was predicated on a minimal recognition of Iran's ownership of the industry, continued AIOC control, and an admission of Iran's inability to manage the industry without British assistance. From the outset, Stokes took a hard line, telling the shah on August 16 that if Mosaddeq did not accept the proposal, "there would be nothing for me to do but to go home."[78] Harriman thought the offer could provide sufficient "camouflage" for AIOC to remain, though he worried that some elements would prove inimical to Iranian nationalism.[79]

As Harriman feared, neither the form nor the substance of the British proposal proved acceptable. Mosaddeq objected to the price structure, where Iran sold oil at a discount to manufacture a fifty-fifty split. He insisted that sales be at the posted price of $1.75 per barrel – what the oil was ostensibly worth, according to the oligopoly.[80] Mosaddeq and his advisors disagreed with the concept of a purchasing agreement, which would constitute a return of AIOC to its old position as the sole purchaser of Iranian oil: "a concession in disguise," according to the prime minister.[81] Finally, Mosaddeq was wary of the issue of compensation, which had to be addressed to assure the legality of nationalization. Both AIOC and Stokes had avoided discussing the issue, even as internal memos suggested Iranian compensation to AIOC could be as high as $2 or $5 billion, accounting for the value of physical assets and future profits over the lifetime of the concession.[82] Such terms would effectively negate the economic value of nationalization and load Iran with an immense financial obligation. Mosaddeq would not agree to terms that left compensation undefined.

---

[77] BP 126364 Outline of Suggestions Submitted by the British Delegation (8-Point Offer), August 13, 1951, "Eight Point Proposal – Child's Guide Edition," Memo, "Next Step in Tehran."
[78] FO 371/91580 Notes with Meeting with the Shah, August 16, 1951, UKNA.
[79] *FRUS X*: 140–142.
[80] RG 59 888.2553/8-1351, Grady to Acheson, Note from Harriman August 13, 1951, USNA; BP 126364 Reply of the Persian Delegation to the Proposals of the British Delegation, August 18, 1951; Ruhani, *Tarikh-e milli shudan-e san'at-e naft-e Iran*, 188–209.
[81] *FRUS X*: 139–142.
[82] BP 91031 "Compensation for AIOC Assets," and "Persia–Compensation," August 28, 1951.

3.2 Defining Nationalization

With talks on the verge of breaking down, Harriman intervened on behalf of the British. He insisted that a "large income" would accrue to Iran if Mosaddeq accepted Stokes' proposal. His government could achieve solvency and revitalize the moribund Seven-Year Plan, "and thus improve [the] health and welfare" of the Iranian people.[83] The American diplomat urged Mosaddeq to preserve dual integration. Under pressure from the shah and members of his own cabinet, Mosaddeq relented once again. He agreed to let a purchasing company manage the industry, so long as British staff agreed to become employees of NIOC. He maneuvered to put the matter to one side, asking that Stokes and Harriman consider questions of price and production before returning to the politically fraught question of allowing British technicians to operate the oil industry. Once Stokes determined that Mosaddeq would not accept the "elementary and fundamental principle" of British management, however, he ended discussions and left Tehran on August 23.[84]

The Jackson and Stokes-Harriman missions represented a concerted effort by AIOC and the Anglo-American governments to push Mosaddeq away from his original definition of nationalization and toward one that maintained AIOC's position. All operations had to be conducted in a way that guaranteed the British "absolute control."[85] The definition of nationalization was restricted to Iranian ownership of the oil in the ground and the assets already present in the country. Stokes took a firm position, trusting that it would result in a breakdown in talks and the fall of Mosaddeq government. "I felt obliged to go as far as possible to meet Musaddiq," he wrote to Prime Minister Clement Attlee, "if only to convince Harriman and public opinion ... . I had made every effort."[86] While Mosaddeq had shown a certain flexibility, in the end it was British intransigence that doomed the talks.

The US government, however, felt Mosaddeq was responsible for the breakdown.[87] The outcome of talks confirmed for the Americans the importance of Iranian incapacity as a barrier to a successful settlement. An assessment on August 29 concluded that Mosaddeq did not understand "the complexities of the technical problems" involved in nationalization.[88] "In his dream world, the simple passage of legislation

---

[83] *FRUS X*: 142–144.
[84] FO 371/91580 Shepherd to Foreign Office, August 22, 1951, UKNA.
[85] BP 126364 Note from Elkington to Stokes, August 22, 1951.
[86] FO 371/91580 Stokes to Attlee, August 22, 1951, UKNA.
[87] Quote from Elm, *Oil, Power, and Principle*, 142.
[88] "Developments in Iranian Oil Negotiations," August 29, 1951, RG 59 Lot File No. 78 D 442: Petroleum Policy Staff Subject File Relating to Iranian Oil and US Middle Eastern Oil Policy, 1921–1951, USNA.

nationalizing [the] oil industry creates [a] profitable business," Harriman fumed.[89] Ambassador Grady felt it was "hopeless" trying to reason with Mosaddeq, though he dissuaded the British ambassador from supporting covert measures to oust the prime minister, warning that they would likely backfire.[90] British military action to retain control of Abadan was out of the question. On October 3, the last British staff were evacuated from Abadan.[91]

A final attempt to define nationalization came from an unexpected quarter. In October, Mosaddeq visited New York City, where he addressed the United Nations Security Council. While in Washington, DC some weeks later, Mosaddeq met with Robert L. Garner of the World Bank. Garner suggested the bank take over management of the industry on an interim basis. "The Bank has no intention of engaging in oil operations ... as a business venture," Garner wrote to Mosaddeq, "[and its] sole concern with the Iranian oil question is to avoid the economic loss caused by interruption of oil operations."[92] Mosaddeq expressed an interest and suggested the bank send a delegation to Iran to begin discussions in January.[93]

By the time the bank chose to intervene, the nationalization crisis was more than six months old. Two previous efforts at negotiation had failed – AIOC had left Iran, and the companies had imposed an embargo on Iranian oil. Confidence in a negotiated solution to the crisis was waning, with the British maintaining their determination to remove Mosaddeq and negotiate with a more conservative replacement. Garner's offer was vague in its particulars. Along with arranging the management of the refinery to a "qualified neutral individual or organization," the bank would purchase crude and refined products for an (unspecified) price and distribute them to (unspecified) customers, splitting the profits with Iran while placing an (unspecified) amount in escrow to cover compensation claims by AIOC. For reasons that are difficult to fathom, Garner felt the return of hundreds of foreign technicians would be palatable to Mosaddeq. "As a matter of practical necessity," most would have to be British, provided by AIOC, which still had 600–700 former Abadan

---

[89] *FRUS X*: 144–145. [90] FO 248/1514 "Interview with Dr. Grady," August 30, 1951.
[91] Norman Kemp, *Abadan: A First-Hand Account of the Persian Oil Crisis* (London: Wingate, 1953), 239–250.
[92] RG 59 Box 5506 Nitze-Linder Papers, Garner Memo to IBRD Board, November 16, 1951, 888.2553/12-2851, Garner to Mossadeq, December 28, 1951, USNA.
[93] For the bank's role in the crisis, see Amy L. S. Staples, "Seeing Diplomacy through Banker's Eyes: The World Bank, the Anglo-Iranian Oil Crisis, and the Aswan High Dam," *Diplomatic History* 26, no. 3 (Summer 2002): 397–418.

3.2 Defining Nationalization

engineers on its payroll.[94] His information came directly from AIOC, which briefed him on Iran's need for 1,100 British technicians during meetings held in early December.[95] In effect, the bank would act as an intermediary overseeing the return of AIOC to its previous position. American officials did not have tremendous confidence in Garner's judgment. The bank seemed "very sensitive" to commercial issues but showed little appreciation of the "political risks" in Iran.[96] Events proved this assessment correct.

Garner dispatched the bank's loan officer Hector Prud'homme and oil advisor Torkild "Captain" Rieber on a fact-finding mission to Iran in late December 1951. Rieber, in his early seventies but "young in spirit," cut an interesting figure in Tehran, liberally passing around $50 bills to wait staff at his hotel while commenting on how Iranians "don't know how to do a damn thing."[97] He visited Abadan in January 1952 and was astonished by what he found: A refinery in perfect working condition, marred only by a lack of spare parts.[98] Sending hundreds of British technicians back to Iran was both politically unsound and technically unnecessary, as the Iranians needed only a small team of foreign engineers to handle the refinery's more complex components. Politically, it would be impossible for Mosaddeq to accept AIOC technicians. It was clear to Rieber that the prevailing logic in London was "unrealistic."[99]

Now that the bank approach looked like a dead end, Acheson tried to convince the British that a new agreement combining compensation for AIOC and management of production by Iran stood a better chance than Garner's proposal. Still fearful of what pressure on Mosaddeq would do to Iran's internal political scene and anxious to get Iranian oil flowing again, the Truman administration even suggested AIOC buy back the stocks of oil and products held in storage at Abadan, an idea Prud'homme had already pitched to Garner.[100] The British resisted all

---

[94] Minutes of Meeting, November 21, 1951, Record of a Meeting, November 30, 1951 Iran – General – Memoranda of Meetings – Correspondence, 1806448, WBGA.
[95] Notes of a Meeting, December 1, 1951, Notes of Meeting, December 5, 1951, Notes for Negotiations, February 6, 1952, Iran – General – Calculations – Correspondence, 1806456; Refined Products, December 24, 1951, Iran – Anglo Iranian Oil Company – Correspondence, 1806432, WBGA.
[96] RG 59 Box 5506 Nitze-Linder Notes, Linder to Acheson, November 28, 1951, USNA; FRUS X, 287–288.
[97] Interview of Hector Prud'homme, May 2, 1985, by John Muir, WBGA.
[98] RG 59 888.2553/2-1152, US Embassy Tehran No. 909, February 11, 1952, USNA.
[99] RG 84 USLETCGR, Box 40, Prud'homme to Garner, January 1, 1952, Prudhomme for Garner, No. 2462, January 4, 1952, USNA; FRUS X: 321–322.
[100] Prud'homme to Garner, January 31, 1952, Iran – General – Secret and Confidential Files – Negotiations – Volume 3, 1806452, WBGA.

these proposals.[101] Instead, they pushed the bank's existing proposal, despite Rieber's misgivings. Eden himself admitted that Garner's stance on management "is likely to render the plan unacceptable."[102] But no deal was preferable to a bad deal that was too lenient and did not conform to the preferred, restricted definition of nationalization.

Thus, when Garner arrived in Iran in February 1952, his chances of success were slim. "I am pessimistic," wrote Prud'homme.[103] Garner pushed the incapacity argument, arguing that without British help there would be no way "[to] get a substantial amount of oil flowing within a reasonable time."[104] His stiff stance baffled Prud'homme and the US Ambassador Loy W. Henderson, who felt a more lenient position was appropriate since Iran had made the "surprising concession" of giving the bank the right to manage its oil properties.[105] In his final note to Mosaddeq, Garner urged the prime minister to see the matter from a commercial point of view: "If Iran is to really benefit from its oil resources, the industry must be operated on a business-like basis." Unless Iran's industry was operated by foreign technicians, "it will inevitably fall behind in the competition and fail to give Iran the benefits which she ought to enjoy."[106] But Mosaddeq was adamant: The British could not be permitted to return. Garner and his team left Iran in March 1952.

The bank failed for several reasons. It received limited support from the United States, which believed Garner's approach to Mosaddeq was flawed. Support provided by the British was counterproductive, as AIOC offered advice that ensured Garner's proposals would be rejected. Garner, a former executive for General Foods and Wall Street banker, had little knowledge of oil or the Middle East. He approached the problem as one of commerce, not politics. Garner admitted in March 1952 that the bank "was not interested in rewarding Iran for tearing up its contract ... since this would be a bad example for all countries with foreign investments."[107] The bank posed as a mediator but very clearly favored the British side. Like the British, the bank presumed Mosaddeq

---

[101] Heiss, *Empire and Nationhood*, 121. [102] *FRUS X*: 344–346.
[103] PH to "Dave," February 19, 1952, Iran – General – Secret and Confidential Files – Negotiations – Volume 3, 1806453, WBGA.
[104] Garner to Black, March 6, 1952, Iran – General – Secret and Confidential Files – Negotiations – Volume 3, 1806453, WBGA.
[105] RG 59 888.2553/2-2152, Henderson to Acheson, February 21, 1952, USNA.
[106] Garner to Mossadegh, April 4, 1952, Iran – General – Secret and Confidential Files – Negotiations – Volume 3, 1806453, WBGA.
[107] Digest of a Meeting, Robert L. Garner, "The Role of the International Bank as a Mediator in the Iranian Crisis," March 18, 1952, Records of Meetings, Vol. 17, Archives of the Council on Foreign Relations (CFR). My thanks to David S. Painter for bringing this document to my attention.

could be lured with the promise of oil revenues, not realizing that Iranian control of the industry, together with the expulsion of the British technicians, had taken on immense political significance and were issues on which Mosaddeq could not retreat.

The collapse of the bank intervention concluded the last attempt to define nationalization. In July 1952, the International Court of Justice in The Hague ruled that the British case against Iran was baseless. It no longer mattered how "nationalization" was to be defined. Legally speaking, Iran's actions would have to be accepted as a fait accompli, so long as Iran provided AIOC compensation for its lost assets.[108] The ruling was a victory for Mosaddeq. In practical terms, however, it changed very little, as Mosaddeq was unable to sell oil due to the embargo.

The United States gave up on discussions with Mosaddeq after the bank intervention. The reasons for the US retreat stemmed from the apparent deterioration of Mosaddeq's financial position (a subject covered in more detail in Chapter 4). Negotiations were abandoned both because the gap between the British and Iranian positions seemed too wide to bridge, but also because the United States did not believe the Mosaddeq government would last much longer in office. Torn between maintaining Iran's internal stability through dual integration and backing the British and the companies, the United States chose the latter. All assumed that financial and political pressure would eventually force Mosaddeq from power. The most important source of pressure was through the oil embargo. To ensure Mosaddeq's failure, the companies and Anglo-American governments cooperated to isolate Iran from the global oil economy.

3.3 Embargo: Iran's De-integration and the Myth of Iranian Incapacity

Opponents of nationalization based their arguments on an assumption of Iranian incapacity. Iran could not manage its own oil industry, they contended, due to the nation's lack of technical expertise. "Nationalization," declared Razmara's minister of finance in January 1951, "would bring to our country the same consequences as Mexico," spreading mass unemployment and "misery."[109] Once it became clear AIOC would withdraw, these same arguments were used to prophesy the failure of Mosaddeq's experiment. "The British theme in almost all

---

[108] International Court of Justice, Anglo-Iranian Oil Co. Case, Judgement of July 22, 1952: 112, 115.
[109] RG 59 888.2553/1-1251, US Embassy Tehran No. 544, January 12, 1951, USNA.

conversations," reported one American visitor to Abadan, "is that the Iranians will not be able to operate the industry."[110] The complexities of the Abadan refinery were assumed to be beyond the bounds of the Iranian mind. "Oil refining, if not oil producing, is an extremely technical matter," wrote Victor Butler in the Ministry of Fuel and Power, "and the poor Persians will be left way behind us."[111] "Everybody assumed that Abadan ... had been completely cannibalized," recalled Hector Prud'homme of the World Bank, who instead found the refinery in pristine condition when he visited Abadan with Torkild Rieber in January 1952.[112]

Local incapacity was a common refrain in the international oil industry. The oligopoly premised their dominance of oil production in the Global South on a carefully cultivated reputation of technical expertise.[113] They used this assumption as a tool to combat petro-nationalism. Iran's ownership of the oil reserves was undeniable, according to existing precedents of international law. But as Eugene Holman, president of Jersey Standard, explained to shareholders, without "capital, technical skill, accumulated experience and marketing outlets ... the oil would be of use to no one – neither the people of Iran, nor the rest of the world."[114] Oil could be nationalized. But it was worthless until it had passed into the hands of companies. Such an argument was imbued with cultural prejudice and ethnocentric bias, reflecting a concept which historian Megan Black has termed "resource primitivism."[115] It was also speculative – there was no evidence to suggest that Iranian engineers could not operate the Abadan refinery or produce enough oil to market internationally.

Parviz Mina, an engineer with NIOC, recalled the excitement that accompanied the expulsion of the British, when Iranian managers earned the freedom to operate the industry without foreign supervision.[116] Forty years of industrial activity, together with AIOC's training program and Pahlavi-era educational advancements, produced a class of technically

---

[110] RG 84 USETCGR, 1950–1952, Box 39, Cuomo to Richards, September 20, 1951, USNA.
[111] POWE 33/1929 Minute by Butler, January 29, 1952, UKNA.
[112] Interview of Hector Prud'homme, May 2, 1985, by John Muir, WBGA.
[113] For discussions of petro-knowledge, see Rudiger Graf, *Oil and Sovereignty: Petro-Knowledge and Energy Policy in the United States and Western Europe in the 1970s*, trans. Alex Skinner (New York: Berghahn Books, 2018), 31–34; Katayoun Shafiee, *Machineries of Oil: An Infrastructural History of BP in Iran* (Boston, MA: MIT Press, 2018), 61–67.
[114] *The Oil Forum*, Vol. V, No. 7, July 1951.
[115] Megan Black, "Interior's Exterior: The State, Mining Companies, and Resource Ideologies in the Point Four Program," *Diplomatic History* 40, no. 1 (January 2016): 81–110.
[116] FISDS, *Tahavvul-e san'at-e naft-e iran*, Interview with Mina.

3.3 Embargo: Iran's De-integration

proficient Iranians that included Kazem Hasibi, engineers like Mina and Baqer Mostowfi, and dozens more. When Abadan came under Iranian control, little about the day-to-day life of the refinery changed. The menu at AIOC's guest house still featured "under-done beef and over-done cabbage," according to one American visitor.[117] More importantly, the refinery continued to operate, albeit at a reduced level given the lack of market outlets. Unlike the drama in Abadan, the hand off of AIOC's small refinery at Kermanshah occurred without any violence whatsoever.[118] Iran's engineers were capable of producing crude oil and refining enough products, from kerosene for lighting to gasoline for transportation, to meet domestic need. Iran possessed the technical capacity to produce oil and products for export. An internal AIOC intelligence report from December 1951 indicated Iran could manage 8–10 million tons (163,000–204,000 bpd).[119] In private, American oil-man James Terry Duce of Aramco admitted Iran could produce 100,000–150,000 bpd of crude.[120] Should Iran attract 190 experts to run Abadan's more advanced components, Rieber was confident NIOC could manage AIOC's former level of 30 million tons a year without difficulty.[121]

Iranian incapacity was a myth spread by the British and oligopoly to undermine the cause of nationalization. This fact is essential to understanding Mosaddeq's failure. Shortly after nationalization, Iran established a marketing office that began soliciting customers around the world. Around 5 percent of Iran's output had formerly gone to customers outside AIOC and the rest of the oligopoly, including national buyers like Argentina.[122] Italy and Japan, two large industrial markets with refinery capacity but no crude oil of their own, showed interest in purchasing Iranian oil at a low price, as did small companies and cooperatives in Europe and the United States. But apart from a few minor successes, Iran's efforts to market its oil abroad failed. It was not that Iran could not produce oil for export. Rather, Iran was *prevented* from doing so. After nationalization the oligopoly and Anglo-American governments worked to de-integrate Iran from the global oil economy. Market power and coercion were used to stymie nationalization's success. These efforts began in May 1951 and were largely completed by February 1952, just as the World Bank's intervention reached its denouement.

---

[117] RG 59 888.2553/2-1152, US Embassy Tehran No. 909, February 11, 1952, USNA.
[118] BP 72363 Seddon to Rice, July 2, 1951.
[119] BP 67280 Report on the Situation: Abadan and Fields, December 1951.
[120] *FRUS 1952–1954, IX, Part 1*: 610–613.
[121] RG 59 888.2553/2-1152, US Embassy Tehran No. 909, February 11, 1952, USNA.
[122] BP 28341 Annex II, "His Majesty's Government Sanctions."

The embargo was a British creation. As soon as the Nine-Point Law passed on May 1, the British government began contemplating economic sanctions against Iran. These would include freezing Iran's ability to convert sterling into dollars and halting shipments of materials such as sugar, Iran's single largest import item. The most significant move would be embargoing Iranian oil. This would have several economic and political effects. Iran would suffer financially, 50,000 oil workers would be idle, and Mosaddeq's experiment would look like a failure, undermining his position and potentially forcing him from power. The British knew that such measures would "horrify" the United States by creating "economic chaos" inside Iran, but felt the move was necessary to compel Mosaddeq to offer suitable terms or resign from office.[123] After the failure of the Jackson mission, AIOC instructed tankers to avoid Abadan. Production continued until July 31, when the US embassy reported refinery operations had halted due to a lack of storage space.[124] All industry functions ceased in September before AIOC's final withdrawal in early October. The company issued a notice on September 4 threatening legal action against any company or government which purchased Iran's "stolen" oil.

AIOC weathered the storm of its Iranian ejection fairly well. The company was the chief purchaser of Iranian oil, taking 74 percent of Iran's output for its marketing subsidiaries. The Iranian crude offtake of 7.5 million tons (153,000 bpd) accounted for about one-third of AIOC's total crude production. The company owned shares in Iraq (23.75 percent) and Kuwait (50 percent), while total non-Iranian crude capacity totaled 18 million tons.[125] By December 1951 production had increased in the company's other concessions.[126] The loss of Abadan was a blow to the company's prestige. But changes in the industry, including demands in oil consuming countries that the companies import crude rather than refined products, thus saving valuable foreign exchange, reduced the commercial significance of the world's largest refinery. "[While] some months ago it had seemed of primary importance to get Abadan going," wrote Prud'homme of the World Bank in April 1952, retaining the refinery now seemed "of decreasing importance" as the company shifted

---

[123] FO 371/91497 Minute by Logan, May 2, 1951, Furlonge to Burrows, May 24, 1951, Economic Sanctions, May 24, 1951, Note from Furlonge, May 30, 1951.
[124] RG 59 888.2553/8-1351, US Embassy Tehran No. 197 August 13, 1951, USNA.
[125] BP 72363 Effect of the Withdrawal of British Staff on Producing and Refining Operations in Persia, June 1951.
[126] "Anglo-Iranian Oil Co, Ltd. Expands Activities to Compensate for Iran Losses," *World Petroleum*, December 1951.

3.3 Embargo: Iran's De-integration

to other assets, including a new refinery in Aden and its concessions outside of Iran.[127]

To make the embargo work, AIOC would need the cooperation of the rest of the oligopoly. For decades, AIOC had zealously guarded its position in the Middle East. Behind closed doors, the rest of the oligopoly criticized AIOC for its failure to retain control of its concession.[128] But nationalization threatened them all. After the Jackson mission failed in late June, the other majors – which purchased 20 percent of Abadan's output – ceased taking on Iranian oil.[129] When the embargo became official in October, Brewster Jennings of Jersey Standard and Sidney A. Swensrud of Gulf suggested to McGhee that it might be better to let Iran fall to communism than to let nationalization spread to other countries.[130] The oligopoly formed a united front in opposition to Mosaddeq, despite the very clear friction between AIOC and the other companies.

Cooperation was crucial to the success of the embargo. More than 70 percent of the world's tanker fleet was under oligopoly control. Out of 1,600 tankers on the seas, only about 100 operated on "spot" contracts, with the rest shipping oil for the majors.[131] Without tankers, there was no way for Iran to move its oil. And since the oligopoly dominated the global oil market, set the price, and controlled the cheapest sources of available crude, even if Mosaddeq found buyers he would have great difficulty selling at a profit.

While the oligopoly applied their market power, the British deployed other means of staunching the flow of Iranian oil. For one of the last times in its history, Great Britain flexed its economic, diplomatic, and military muscles on a global scale. In June 1952, when the Italian tanker *Rose Mary* defied the embargo and took on a load from Abadan, the Royal Air Force scrambled fighter jets and escorted the tanker into Aden, a British protectorate, where a local judge had the cargo

---

[127] Prud'homme for Files, April 30, 1952, Iran – General – Secret and Confidential Files – Negotiations – Volume 3, 1806453, WBGA; RG 59 888.2553/10-1851, Aden to State Dept. No. 45, October 18, 1951, USNA.
[128] FO 371/98709 EP 15319/1, "Some Observations on the Anglo-Iranian Experience," George H. Freyermuth, Standard Oil Company of New Jersey, UKNA.
[129] BP 91031 Northcroft to London, June 18, 1951.
[130] RG 59 888.2553 AIOC/5-1751, Brewster Jennings (SONJ) to McGhee, May 17, 1951, 888.2553 AIOC/5-1851, BB Howard (SONJ) to McGhee, May 18, 1951, USNA; Memo of Conversation, October 10, 1951, Acheson MemCons, Dean Acheson Papers, HSTPL.
[131] RG 59 Lot File No. 78 D 442 Petroleum Policy Staff, Iranian Oil and U.S. Middle Eastern Oil Policy, 1921–1951, Box 2, *The World Today: Chatham House Review*, August 1951, "World Tanker Fleet;" Box 5506 Nitze-Linder Working Group, Memorandum, January 24, 1952, USNA.

impounded.[132] British diplomats applied pressure to the Italian government to "hold the line on the oil question," much to the chagrin of Italian oil-men like Enrico Mattei who yearned to break the oligopoly's stranglehold on the global oil trade.[133] Argentina, which had depended on Iran for 50 percent of its crude imports in 1950, came close to buying oil from Mosaddeq in late 1951, until the British convinced Buenos Aires to take Kuwaiti crude instead.[134] In Europe, South America, South Asia, and throughout the sterling zone, the British government used every weapon at its disposal to prevent the flow of Iranian oil.

These victories would be meaningless without US cooperation. The American position on the embargo was complex. The US government believed the only way to end the crisis was through a settlement between Iran and the companies, which would allow Iran to sell oil in large quantities that would provide sufficient revenue to help stabilize the nation politically. An agreement was needed, in other words, to restore dual integration. Iran might succeed in selling a small amount of oil, but this appeared an issue of "minor importance," compared to the risk of Iran offering oil to the Soviet Union.[135] This concern recurred throughout the crisis and reflected Washington's preoccupation with Cold War strategic issues. Secretary of Defense Robert A. Lovett noted in September 1951 that the Soviet Union possessed enough tankers to move "substantial quantities" of Iranian oil to Eastern Bloc consumers.[136] The United States hoped to keep Iranian oil moving "in the interest of the West" and prevent Mosaddeq from selling to the Soviets.[137]

Despite this view, the United States did not openly break with the British over the embargo. The State Department received dozens of inquiries from small firms interested in purchasing Iranian oil.[138] In each instance, it dissuaded Americans from approaching Mosaddeq, citing the unstable political situation in Iran and the British threat of legal action. American support of the embargo may have been reluctant, but it proved

---

[132] Mary Ann Heiss, "The International Boycott of Iranian Oil and the Anti-Mosaddeq Coup of 1953," in Mark J. Gasiorowski and Malcolm Byrne, eds., *Mohammed Mosaddeq and the 1953 Coup in Iran* (Syracuse, NY: Syracuse University Press, 2004), 196–198.
[133] FO 371/98653 Franks to Foreign Office, January 6, 1952, UKNA.
[134] RG 59 888.2553/9-651, US Embassy London, September 3, 1951, USNA.
[135] RG 59 888.2553/11-1752, Byroade to Bruce, Matthews, November 17, 1952, USNA.
[136] *FRUS X*: 163–164.
[137] RG 59 888.2553/10-951, Villard to Nitze, Policy Planning Staff, October 9, 1951, "Soviet Influence in Iran and Possible Measures to Offset It," USNA.
[138] For one such example, see RG 888.2553/10-2551, Memo of Conversation, October 25, 1951. The International Cooperative Petroleum Association (ICPA) and its chief Howard Cowden made repeated attempts to obtain Iranian oil for cooperatives in the United States and Europe.

3.3 Embargo: Iran's De-integration

decisive, particularly when combined with actions taken to insulate the global oil market from the sudden impact of the Iranian embargo.

Before nationalization, Iran produced 150,000 bpd of crude and 460,000 bpd of refined products, 7 percent and 5.3 percent of world supply, respectively. Iran's customers included the British Admiralty (1.56 million tons), Jersey Standard (1.7 million tons), Shell (3.8 million tons), and AIOC's marketing subsidiaries (11.5 million tons).[139] Western Europe received 31 percent of its refined products and 16 percent of its crude oil from Iran; South Asia counted on Iran for 70 percent of its needs. Refinery capacity in 1951 was near its limit and the market for refined products lay in "very delicate balance," according to energy specialists in Washington.[140] The Iran crisis illustrated the danger of a sudden, unexpected interruption to the flow of global oil.

As it had done in the past, the US government turned to the oil companies for help. The US Department of the Interior established the Petroleum Administration for Defense (PAD) in January 1951. On June 25, as Iran slid toward a shutdown, PAD formed the Foreign Petroleum Supply Committee (FPSC), made up of representatives from nineteen different oil and gas companies. In late July PAD adopted Plan of Action No. 1, which mandated close cooperation with all US companies, "to organize their schedules of production, refining, transportation and distribution," so that energy requirements could be met without serious disruption.[141] PAD and the FPSC represented a conscious effort by the United States to mitigate the impact of the Iran shutdown.

First, crude oil production would have to be increased. This was a relatively simple proposition due to the spare capacity that existed in the Middle East. Conscious of the supply gap created by the Iranian crisis, other states seized the opportunity to improve the terms of their concessions. Iraq secured new terms in February 1952 that gave it slightly more per-barrel than Saudi Arabia, where a fifty-fifty deal had been signed in December 1950. After considerable haggling, Kuwait reached its own

---

[139] BP 66900 Report on Offtake, May 16, 1951; "Importance of Iran in World Oil Industry," January 28, 1952, Iran – General – Calculations – Correspondence 1806456, WBGA.

[140] RG 312 PAD Foreign Supply and Transportation Division (FSTD), Box 2, "History of Foreign Branch, PAD;" RG 59 888.2553/4-1751, Memo of Conversation, April 17, 1951; RG 59 Box 5506 Nitze-Linder Working Group, Background Paper, Funkhouser, December 18, 1951, USNA; *FRUS Retrospective*: 115–118.

[141] Memo, "Supplying Petroleum to Free World Without Iran," July 12, 1951, Papers of Oscar L. Chapman, Box 99, HSTPL; RG 312 PAD FSTD, Box 1, Snodgrass to R. R. Ellen, Aus. Embassy, August 10, 1951, Box 2, "History of Foreign Branch, PAD," USNA.

114   The Mosaddeq Challenge

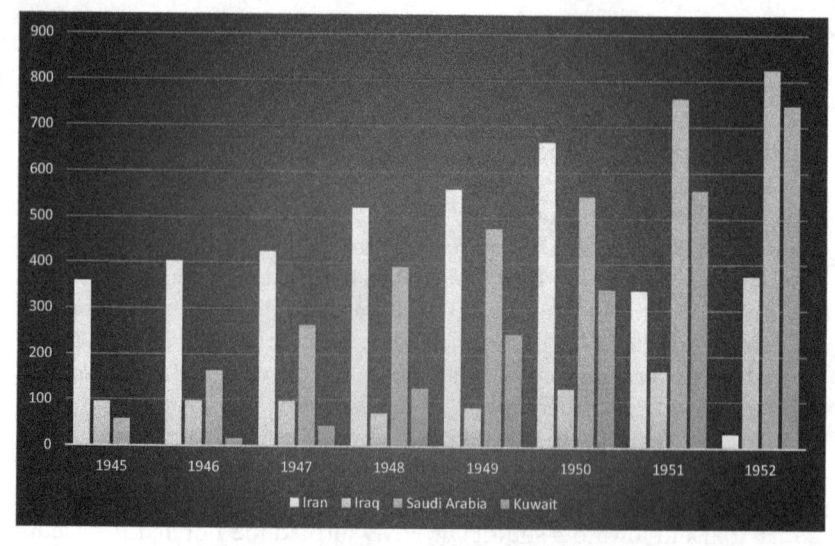

Figure 3.2 Middle East production, 1945–1952[142]

fifty-fifty deal with Gulf and AIOC in mid-1952.[143] By early 1952 crude output in Kuwait, Iraq, and Saudi Arabia was up 395,000 bpd.[144] Ironically, Mosaddeq's act of defiance allowed oil producers to secure a better standard of equitability and boost their production and revenues – all at Iran's expense (Figure 3.2).

A harder problem was managing the loss of Abadan. The world's largest refinery was a major component of the energy economy east of Suez. Australia, Rhodesia, and India faced shortages of refined products. British companies, which had formerly purchased products from Abadan, were now buying from US refiners, leaving a gap in American supply. Abadan had formerly supplied the United States with 18,000 bpd of aviation gasoline that American refineries (which were already operating at nearly full capacity) would have a difficult time replacing. In August 1951, PAD officials worried about a products deficit of 301,000 bpd by the end of the year.[145]

---

[142] Leeman, *Price of Middle East Oil*, 269. [143] *FRUS 1952–1954, IX, Part 1*: 596–599.
[144] "Importance of Iran in World Oil Industry," January 28, 1952, Iran – General – Calculations – Correspondence 1806456, WBGA.
[145] RG 59 888.2553/5-2951, US Embassy London No. 5763, May 29, 1951, RG 312 PAD ADA FPO, Box 4, Foreign Petroleum Operating Committee, Meeting No. 8, July 31, 1951, Operating Program: Foreign Petroleum Industry, Fourth Quarter 1951, August 9, 1951; RG 312 PAD FSTD, Box 3, Memorandum, Snodgrass to Brown, August 17, 1951, USNA.

3.3 Embargo: Iran's De-integration

While crude came from global sources, the United States made up the deficit in refined products, increasing exports by 135,000 bpd.[146] European refiners and stocks made up the rest. Spot shortages in certain products appeared in the second half of 1951 and 1952, but the supply crisis PAD thought would create deficits did not materialize.[147] A study by the World Bank found the crisis resolved in early 1952. "The impact on the world petroleum position," the bank concluded, "[was] less than might have been expected."[148]

Industry expertise was credited with the victory. According to PAD, private oil companies had managed the loss of 150,000 bpd in crude and 460,000 bpd in products, as well as a demand increase of 320,000 bpd, without any major disruptions.[149] The utility of having oil industry executives assist a federal agency staffed by ex-oil-men was not lost on the oil-men themselves. James Terry Duce of Aramco noted to PAD official C. Stribling Snodgrass that countries around the world would likely follow the US example, forming commissions like the FPSC, "for the handling of supply problems," and to avoid the "numerous political questions" that arose when governmental organs became involved: "I feel certain that the industry itself will see that such crises are remedied with the least damage."[150]

Collaboration between the Anglo-American governments and the major oil companies prevented the sale of nationalized Iranian oil. The embargo was a smashing success. Between May 1951 and May 1953, Iran exported eight cargoes of oil – a single Italian and seven Japanese tankers – totaling 495,000 barrels of crude and refined products, less than the output of Abadan on a normal working day under AIOC.[151] While other oil-producing nations profited from Iran's isolation, the crisis revealed the coercive power that formed the foundation of the oligopoly's domination of the global oil economy. Local incapacity was a convenient myth. Control of markets and tankers, not mastery of

---

[146] RG 59 Box 5506, Nitze-Linder Working Group Papers, Funkhouser, Background Paper, December 18, 1951; RG 312 PAD FSTD, Box 1 "Responsibilities and Functions of the Foreign Branch, PAD," Undated, USNA.

[147] RG 312 PAD Assistant Deputy Administrator Foreign Petroleum Operations (ADAFPO), Box 4, Foreign Petroleum Operating Committee Meeting, July 31, 1951, USNA.

[148] "Importance of Iran in World Oil Industry," January 28, 1952, Iran – General – Calculations – Correspondence 1806456, WBGA.

[149] RG 312 PAD FSTD, Box 1 "Responsibilities and Functions of the Foreign Branch, PAD," Undated, USNA.

[150] RG 312 PAD ADAFPO, Box 1, James T. Duce to CS Snodgrass, February 27, 1952, USNA.

[151] *International Petroleum Trade*, vol. 22, no. 5, May 1953.

technology, formed the basis of the oligopoly's power and the chief deterrent against petro-nationalism. So long as the West retained private control of global oil through the oligopoly, nationalizations could be dealt with. "Possession of markets," wrote one official in the Ministry of Fuel and Power, "is the best safeguard against the repetition of Persia's action."[152] And while PAD experts acknowledged the power of the oligopoly in keeping Iran isolated, "should Iranian oil begin to move ... there is no doubt that it would find an instant market."[153] Market power and the conditions produced by the oligopoly, not Iranian incapacity, stymied the commercial success of nationalization.

3.4 Conclusion

Mosaddeq's confidence in the ultimate success of nationalization stemmed from his belief that US companies wanted Iranian oil, while his supporters felt that the United States would not abandon Iran for fear of losing it to communism. Both assumptions proved mistaken. The United States did encourage a negotiated settlement but would only accept a resolution that maintained the *status quo ante* and left AIOC in control of the oil industry. Even when Mosaddeq was willing to compromise – as he was during the Harriman–Stokes talks of August 1951 – British intransigence and American skepticism of Iran's ability to run its oil industry prevented a settlement. The US government worried over Iran's stability, but it ultimately sided with the British and the companies, opting to isolate Iran rather than risk letting nationalization spread elsewhere. The Jackson mission, Harriman–Stokes discussions, and World Bank intervention revealed that a definition of nationalization that would satisfy both sides in the dispute was unobtainable.

The oligopoly's victory over Mosaddeq appeared total. But it was not permanent. In July 1952, oil expert Walter J. Levy wrote a report for PAD. His tone was grave. "There are significant signs that foreign oil may, in the future, be no longer so readily available." The reason was rising petro-nationalism tied to decolonization, declining British prestige, and the ideological atmosphere of the Cold War. Over time the pressure from local governments to take full control would become unstoppable: "[A]s the producing countries are actually unable to direct the complex technical and commercial operations of the oil industry, such interference would greatly hamper the development of the free

---

[152] FO 371/98695 Note for Strang, August 27, 1952, UKNA.
[153] RG 59 Box 5506, Nitze-Linder Working Group Papers, Background Paper, December 18, 1951, USNA.

3.4 Conclusion

world's oil resources." The answer, according to Levy, was doubling down on dual integration and tying the companies more directly into producer states' economic development strategies. In most cases, the oil industry stood out as the only industrial enterprise, "[amidst] otherwise [an] ancient ... and underdeveloped economy."[154] If the companies made themselves indispensable to the economic future of the Global South, producer states would have no reason to nationalize and would remain bound to the West economically as well as strategically.

In the short term, the oligopoly was content. The British expected Mosaddeq's eventual fall from power in mid-1952. For the United States, this raised new concerns. In May, US ambassador Loy W. Henderson concluded that an oil agreement with Mosaddeq was no longer possible.[155] But that still left Iran without an operating oil industry. Dual integration remained suspended. The embargo proved conclusively that the world of oil could survive without Iran. For the United States, a more important question now loomed: How long would Iran survive without oil?

---

[154] "The Progressive Threat to the US Position in Foreign Oil," July 25, 1952, Papers of Oscar L. Chapman, Box 102, HSTPL.
[155] *FRUS X*: 381–383.

4 The Collapse Narrative
The Coup and the Reintegration of Iranian Oil, 1952–1954

On August 19, 1953, the streets of Tehran exploded into violence. Crowds of ruffians armed with clubs descended on the offices of the National Front and its allies. The mobs looted newspaper headquarters while pro-shah military units mobilized in the city center and seized control of the national radio station. An armored column surrounded the home of Prime Minister Mosaddeq, peppering it with machine gun fire. Shouts of "Zendebad shah!" or "Long live the shah" filled the air as Mosaddeq's government fell from power. From the ashes rose a new government, led by former general Fazlollah Zahedi and Mohammed Reza Pahlavi, who returned from a brief exile on August 22. While various Iranian factions took part, the 1953 coup would not have been possible without the active participation of the US Central Intelligence Agency (CIA) and the British secret services.[1]

Thanks to the work of a generation of scholars, accounts of the coup's planning, preparation, execution, and aftermath exist and are readily available.[2] What is less understood, however, is *why* the coup was launched in the first place. According to the official narrative included in internal histories of the operation drafted with the approval of the CIA, the coup prevented a communist takeover of Iran. Scholars examining the decision to remove Mosaddeq in the context of the Cold War

---

[1] A small number of scholars have attempted to revise this narrative. For a detailed response to this revisionism, see Fakhreddin Azimi, "The Overthrow of the Government of Mosaddeq Reconsidered," *Iranian Studies* 45, no. 5 (2012): 693–712.

[2] David S. Painter and Gregory Brew, *The Struggle for Iran: Oil, Autocracy, and the Cold War, 1951–1954* (Chapel Hill: University of North Carolina Press, 2023); Mark J. Gasiorowski, "The 1953 Coup D'etat in Iran," *International Journal of Middle East Studies* 19, no. 3 (August 1987): 261–286, and Gasiorowski, "The 1953 Coup d'Etat Against Mossadeq," in Gasiorowski and Byrne, eds., *Mohammed Mossadeq*, 227–260; Ali Rahnema, *Behind the 1953 Coup in Iran: Thugs, Turncoats, Soldiers, and Spooks* (New York: Cambridge University Press, 2015); Ervand Abrahamian, *The Coup: 1953, The CIA, and the Roots of Modern US-Iranian Relations* (New York: New Press, 2013), and Abrahamian, *Oil Crisis in Iran: From Nationalism to Coup d'Etat* (New York: Cambridge University Press, 2021). As of 2022, the British government has not admitted its involvement in the coup or declassified relevant records.

emphasize the importance of the communist threat in motivating Operation TPAJAX, the coup's CIA code-name.[3] Yet there are problems with this explanation. Analyses from 1952 to 1953 indicated that the Tudeh Party – Iran's domestic communist organization, closely affiliated with Moscow – was not in a position to take over Iran's government at any time before August 1953.[4] After the successful coup of August 19, the shah's forces crushed the Tudeh in a matter of weeks, with help from the CIA, suggesting the party's strength at that time was illusory.[5] Evidence suggests the narrative emphasizing the communist threat is simplistic. If the coup was not meant to forestall an imminent communist uprising, why then was it necessary?

This chapter does not examine Operation TPAJAX itself. It focuses instead on the question of why the United States decided to remove Mohammed Mosaddeq, install the shah, and force Iran and the oligopoly to commit to a new oil agreement. The key to understanding these decisions is not American preoccupation with communism – though that was a factor – but the concern over allowing Iran to continue as an "oil-less" state led by Mosaddeq's National Front government.

Following the brief interregnum of Ahmed Qavam's July 1952 premiership, Mosaddeq returned to power and launched a series of initiatives designed to fortify Iran against the impact of the ongoing embargo. Incorporated into this campaign were the efforts of American developmentalists working through the Point Four technical assistance program. While Mosaddeq's policies may have worked in time to detach Iran from oil's influence, the notion of an oil-less Iran filled the United States with dread. Policymakers believed the National Front was not capable of running Iran without foreign help or oil-based financial

---

[3] Roosevelt, *Countercoup*, 3; Donald Wilber, *CIA Clandestine Service History: "Overthrow of Premier Mossadeq of Iran, November 1952–August 1953,"* published on-line by National Security Archive, November 29, 2000, accessed March 23, 2017, 1–3, www.nsarchive2.gwu.edu/NSAEBB/NSAEBB28/; Scott A. Koch, *"Zendebad Shah!": The Central Intelligence Agency and the Fall of Iranian Prime Minister Mohammed Mossadeq, August 1953* (Washington, DC: CIA, June 1998) and *The Battle for Iran*, published on-line by National Security Archive, June 27, 2014 www.nsarchive2.gwu.edu/NSAEBB/NSAEBB476/ [Accessed March 28, 2018]. Gasiorowski's 1987 article and 2003 chapter largely hold up this interpretation. See also Marsh, *Anglo-American Relations*, 152–153; Frank J. Gavin, "Politics, Power, and US Policy in Iran, 1950–1953," *Journal of Cold War Studies* 1, no. 1 (Winter 1999): 56–89.

[4] This point is made very persuasively by Mark J. Gasiorowski in his appraisal of the declassified documents. See Gasiorowski, "US Perceptions of the Communist Threat in Iran During the Mossadegh Era," *Journal of Cold War Studies* 21, no. 3 (Summer 2019): 1–37.

[5] *FRUS Retrospective*: 746–747, 766–768.

resources. This narrative predicated Iran's "collapse," a vague but ominous concept, on continued oil-lessness.

The collapse narrative lay upon two assumptions: That oil-less economics were not sustainable for Iran in the long term, and that without an oil agreement, the National Front government was not capable of managing Iran. Though hard evidence of an imminent catastrophe was limited, officials became convinced that an oil-less Iran under Mosaddeq's management was unsustainable – that in the absence of action, a cataclysm would occur threatening not just the security of Iran but the security and stability of the entire oil-producing Middle East. To reverse Iran's oil-lessness, the United States organized a coup with the assistance of Great Britain and anti-Mosaddeq forces within Iran. The ultimate success of the coup rested upon Iran's reintegration into the global oil economy. For that, an agreement between the shah's post-coup government and the oligopoly was essential. Funds from the oligopoly's reintegration of Iranian oil could then go toward economic development and the stabilization of the shah's pro-Western regime. The goal, as Eisenhower later argued, was to "save Iran from communism."[6] But the actions undertaken by the United States – replacing a popular constitutionalist leader with an authoritarian monarch – were also meant to save Iran from an oil-less fate. The coup was necessary to re-establish the dual integration of Iranian oil. There could be no progress without petroleum.

4.1 "Oil-Less" Economics

On May 26, 1952, Mohammed Mosaddeq addressed the nation. Three months after the end of the World Bank's intervention and a year after nationalization, the prime minister called for "patience and steadfastness." Mosaddeq acknowledged the sense of crisis pervading the land: a shuttered oil industry, creeping economic malaise, and recent Majlis elections fraught with accusations of vote tampering. He blamed their predicament on an "economic blockade and … subversive activities" carried out by foreign agents, but hoped that in time the nations of the world would recognize Iran's plight. The embargo would end. Oil would flow once again.[7]

Behind the scenes, Iranian officials painted a grimmer picture. All attempts to sell oil had failed. On June 6, engineer Mehdi Bazargan resigned from his position at the National Iranian Oil Company

---

[6] *FRUS 1955–1957, XII*: 895.
[7] RG 59 888.2553/5-2652, Henderson to Acheson, May 26, 1952, USNA.

4.1 "Oil-Less" Economics

(NIOC), complaining of interference from National Front figures like Kazem Hasibi, who boasted to the press of deals to sell oil to Poland, Argentina, Brazil, and small American companies – all of them fabrications designed to boost public morale.[8] The finance minister admitted to the US embassy that Iran's state budget deficit had ballooned to 3 billion rials.[9]

To forestall a budget crisis, Mosaddeq undertook emergency financial action. Between March 1951 and March 1952, 4.5 billion rials out of total budget expenditures of 10.87 billion rials came from stopgap measures.[10] But by the summer of 1952, these sources had been exhausted. According to the US embassy, Iran would have to tackle a combined budget deficit of 6 billion rials for the fiscal year starting in March 1952.[11] A worsening financial situation accompanied growing political instability as Mosaddeq tried to hold together his fractioning coalition while resisting efforts by the British and their allies to remove him from power.

The premier was at an impasse. Mosaddeq lacked a strong majority in the Majlis and could not get approval to issue more rials or reduce the budget. Without emergency financial assistance, the Mosaddeq government faced insolvency. The Truman administration continued to worry that economic pressure from the embargo might push Mosaddeq toward the Soviets, but – as noted in Chapter 3 – did not break with the British. Instead, observers waited to see whether Mosaddeq would successfully hold onto power. Expectations were not high. In June 1952, US officials predicted that Mosaddeq would be out of office "in a few weeks," and put plans together to extend emergency aid to a successor government "determined to settle the oil controversy."[12] "We didn't see how the Mosaddeq government," recalled Ambassador Loy W. Henderson, "could last out the summer."[13]

A veteran with thirty years of experience in Iranian politics, Mosaddeq chose to gamble. Facing an imminent showdown over the budget, he

---

[8] *Kayhan*, June 8, 1952; RG 59 888.2553/6-1652, US Embassy Tehran No. 1322, June 16, 1952, USNA. Bazargan later led the Liberation Movement, an organization similar to Mosaddeq's National Front, and protested the shah's rule throughout the 1960s and 1970s. He was head of the provisional government following the shah's departure in January 1979 and resigned in November 1979.

[9] *Ettela'at*, June 18, 1952; FO 371/98625 Middleton to FO, June 23, 1952, UKNA.

[10] FO 371/98625 UK Embassy to FO, May 19, 1952, UKNA.

[11] RG 84 USLETCGR, 1950–1952, Box 36, Henderson to State No. 3781, Drafted by Carr, April 4, 1952, USNA.

[12] RG 59 Subject Files Relating to Iran, 1951–1958, Box 9, Memo of Conversation, June 1, 1952, USNA.

[13] *FRUS Retrospective*: 605–607.

started a political crisis by demanding the right to appoint the Minister of War, a position traditionally (though not constitutionally) left to the shah. The shah, who had been patiently biding his time while outwardly supporting the popular prime minister, seized an opportunity to be rid of the National Front. He refused Mosaddeq's demand and the prime minister resigned on July 17. The shah then replaced him with Ahmed Qavam, an aged but ambitious political mainstay who had guided Iran through the Azerbaijan crisis. Qavam had been courting Anglo-American support for several months. While the shah distrusted Qavam, his candidacy was backed by Henderson and British chargés d'affaires George Middleton. In general, the reaction in Washington was enthusiastic. Acheson felt Qavam would need help, "if he is to remain in power and work out [an] agreement with Britain," and authorized $26 million in emergency aid.[14]

But before any progress could be made, demonstrations broke out in Tehran. Crowds called for Mosaddeq's return, as Tudeh Party organizers cooperated with the National Front in defiance of the new government. The shah's support for Qavam wavered and he secretly began talks with National Front leaders even as Henderson and the British embassy urged him to approve a declaration of martial law permitting Qavam to clear the streets. On July 21, after a morning of clashes between police, National Front demonstrators, and Tudeh street fighters, Qavam resigned in frustration. The shah reappointed Mosaddeq to the premiership the following morning after a Majlis vote of confidence.[15]

The July Uprising, as it was known, marked a turning point in Iran's politics. Conservative opposition had been squashed and the shah relegated to the periphery. Mosaddeq had proven his vitality and mustered the force of the street, albeit with tactical support from Iran's communists. The Tudeh Party henceforth adopted a less hostile stance toward the prime minister. Having failed to oust their nemesis through parliamentary means, the British were convinced after July that only a military coup d'état could remove Mosaddeq and began working toward that end.[16] The United States was forced to re-evaluate its stance and consider new oil negotiations. In more immediate terms, Mosaddeq's triumph granted him the political capital to shore up his government's financial position.

---

[14] RG 59 888.2553/7-1952, Memo from Byroade to Acheson, July 19, 1952, USNA; *FRUS Retrospective*: 246–251, 266–267, 268–269, 269–270, 273–274.

[15] Bamberg, *vol. II*, 472–473; Azimi, *Crisis*, 288–293; Husayn Makki, *Vaqayi'-e 30 Tir 1331* [Events of 30 Tir, 1331] (Tehran: Bungah-e Tarjumah va Nashr-e Kitab, 1982), 24–26, 39–57, 62–91.

[16] Rahnema, *Behind the Coup*, 22–23.

4.1 "Oil-Less" Economics

Once back in power, he forced a Majlis vote on a ruling granting him emergency powers to rule by decree for six months. He used his powers to pass a raft of reform legislation. The centerpiece of the reforms was "oil-less economics" (*iqtisad-e bidun-e naft*), a new and sweeping plan to insulate Iran from the British embargo and move the country toward lasting economic stability without the need for oil revenues.[17]

Development formed a part of the new economic initiative. On August 24, Mosaddeq issued a letter to the director of the Plan Organization, authorizing the expenditure of 2 billion rials on projects meant to stimulate agricultural production.[18] Three billion rials would be diverted to a new "Five-Year Plan," meant to make Iran self-sufficient in sugar and tea, two large import items, while the government set aside 450 million rials to encourage Iranian non-oil exports.[19] The First Seven-Year Plan was still technically in progress, though at a much reduced pace. According to figures supplied to the US embassy, the Plan Organization disbursed about 800 million rials in 1951 from total receipts of 1.1 billion rials.[20] Along with these economic measures, Mosaddeq embarked upon a wide-ranging program of fiscal and labor reforms, promoted a free press and a more competent judiciary, Iran's first substantive land reform law, and legislation designed to appeal to the middle class, urban workers, and rural peasantry.[21]

While it was not openly stated, the government met its budget needs through deficit spending. In August 1952, Mosaddeq ordered the Bank-e Melli to secretly begin releasing new bank notes. The US embassy estimated 2 billion rials entered circulation between August 1952 and January 1953.[22] This de facto devaluation caused the market exchange

---

[17] Katouzian, "Oil Boycott and the Political Economy," in Bill and Louis, eds., *Musaddiq*, 203–227; Hasan Tavanayan-Fard, *Duktur Mosaddeq va iqtisad* [Dr. Mosaddeq and the Economy] (Tehran: Sazman-e Intishrat-e 'Alavi, 1983), 5–12.

[18] The letter was reprinted in *Ettela'at*; see RG 84 USLETCGR, 1953–1955, Box 60, US Embassy Tehran No. 824, April 8, 1953, USNA.

[19] RG 84 USLETCGR, 1950–1952, Box 36, US Embassy Tehran No. 470, October 4, 1951, and No. 80, July 30, 1952; RG 84 USLETCGR, 1953–1955, Box 60, Iran Economic Paper No. 16, January 15, 1953, "The Seven Year Plan, the Plan Organization and OCI," No. 2, "Government Budget," January 1953, USNA; Tavanayan-Fard, *Duktur Mosaddeq va iqtisad*, 129–173.

[20] RG 84 USLETCGR, 1950–1952, Box 39, US Embassy No. 574, "Effects of the Cessation of AIOC Operations on the Iranian Budget," October 31, 1951; RG 84 USLETCGR, 1953–1955, Box 60, Iran Economic Papers No. 16, The Seven Year Plan, The Plan Organization and OCI, January 15, 1953.

[21] Ladjevardi, "Constitutional Government and Reform Under Musaddiq," in Bill and Louis, eds., *Musaddiq*, 76–90.

[22] RG 84 USLETCGR, 1953–1955, Box 60, US Embassy Iran No. 46, July 18, 1953; RG 84 USLETCGR, 1950–1952, Box 36 501 Henderson to State, No. 1245 September 23, 1952; FO 371/98625 EP 1112/29, Middleton to FO, No. 292 (E), September 22, 1952,

rate to change from 50 rials to 100 rials per $1 by August 1953 (the formal rate continued to be 32 rials to $1).[23] The move contravened Iranian economic orthodoxy, which had tended toward a hard-money view – every rial in circulation was backed by either foreign exchange or gold – and was a reversal for the prime minister, who had once called devaluation "a cure worse than the disease."[24] Yet the move was not as extreme as it might have appeared. Economic analyses from the World Bank and US embassy before 1952 had advocated for rial devaluation. Bank-e Melli Governor Abolhassan Ebtehaj had tried for years to pass a devaluation bill through the Majlis. A weaker rial stimulated the economy in the short term, freeing up credit and ending the business depression which had begun in 1949.

In the struggle to accomplish oil-less development, Mossadeq received help from an unexpected quarter: the US government, acting through the Technical Cooperation Administration (TCA), better known as Point Four. The Truman administration established Point Four in 1949 to assist nations in the Global South with development efforts through technical assistance. Rather than fund large projects, Point Four would act as a guide for private capital – like Max Thornburg's work for the First Plan, Point Four worked to advertise US liberal capitalism as the superior alternative to socialism.[25] Focusing on small-scale rural improvements – well-digging, health and sanitation, and education – would insulate Point Four from accusations that it acted as a vessel for American imperialism.[26] Iran signed a Point Four agreement in December 1950 in the chaotic final months of the Razmara government. While the United States denied Mosaddeq large-scale economic assistance, believing aid would discourage him from reaching an oil settlement, the Point Four program remained untouched, allocating $23 million for rural improvement and relief work in 1952 and again in 1953.[27]

UKNA. According to figures later released by the Plan Organization, the total rial issue increased from 7.27 billion in 1950 to 10.49 billion in 1953. See Dadkhah, "Oil Nationalization Movement," 96.

[23] Patrick Clawson and Cyrus Sassanpour, "Adjustment to a Foreign Exchange Shock: Iran, 1951–1953." *International Journal of Middle Eastern Studies* 19, no. 1 (February 1987): 5.

[24] Kay-Ustavan, *Siyasat-e muvazanah-e manfi*, vol. I, 114.

[25] Lorenzini, *Cold War Development*, 26–29.

[26] Latham, *The Right Kind of Revolution*, 30–32.

[27] For Point Four in Iran, see Richard Garlitz, *A Mission for Development: Utah Universities and the Point Four Program in Iran* (Salt Lake City, UT: Utah State University Press, 2018); Najmabadi, *Land Reform and Social Change in Iran*, 59–75; H. Motamen, "Development Planning in Iran," *Middle East Economic Papers* 3 (1956): 98–111.

4.1 "Oil-Less" Economics

For some developmentalists, oil was a distraction from the main issue: Rescuing Iran's peasantry from a state of backwardness. "Inequality of wealth is becoming more pronounced," wrote the embassy's agricultural advisor Gideon Hadary, while reports warned the shutdown of the Seven-Year Plan had made Iran's rural population "restless [and] dissatisfied."[28] The strategic concerns of the Cold War continued to guide the agenda. "Mass undernourishment, disease, ignorance, and poverty provide fertile breeding ground for Communist propaganda," according to one Point Four assessment.[29] The emphasis of Point Four was overwhelmingly on agricultural issues. The mission's chief William E. Warne was a veteran agrarian specialist from Southern California, where he had worked on the Imperial Valley irrigation scheme.[30] The ranks of Warne's mission (which at its height employed more than 200 Americans) were drawn from the farms and agricultural colleges of Utah, where soil and climate conditions were similar to those of the Iranian countryside.[31]

Perhaps because of its niche focus and insulation from the drama of the oil crisis, Point Four fit awkwardly into the political dynamics of Mosaddeq-era Iran. The prime minister saw the program as a useful symbol of American support for his government but was wary of allowing it too much latitude. Among other things, he forbade Point Four from operating too close to the Soviet border, as he hoped to avoid giving his government an overtly pro-US affiliation, in keeping with his philosophy of negative equilibrium. Many Iranians suspected Point Four acted as a vehicle for US commercial and strategic interests. It was natural, noted Point Four translator Abdolreza Ansari, "that a country such as Iran, with a history of foreign interference in its internal affairs, would view foreign aid in general with distrust."[32] The Tudeh Party targeted the mission as a symbol of American imperialism. While there were sporadic demonstrations and "Yankee Go Home" graffiti spread across walls in

---

[28] Gideon Hadary, "The Agrarian Reform Problem in Iran," *Middle East Journal* 5, no. 2 (Spring 1951): 181–196; RG 469 Records of US Foreign Assistance Agencies (RUSFAA) Technical Cooperation Administration (TCA): Iran Division, Subject Files (IDSF) 1951–1954, Box 15, Point Four Country Program Authorization, Iran FY 1953, USNA.

[29] RG 469 RUSFAA TCA IDSF 1951–1954, Box 16, "The Point 4 Program in Iran," May 6, 1953, USNA.

[30] William Warne, *A Mission for Peace: Point 4 in Iran* (New York: Bobbs-Merrill, 1956).

[31] Jessie Embry, "Point Four, Utah State University Technicians, and Rural Development in Iran, 1950–1964," *Rural History* 14, no. 1 (2003): 99–113; Garlitz, *A Mission for Development*, 34–55.

[32] FISDS, *Umran-e khuzistan* [Khuzistan's Development] Interview with Abdolreza Ansari.

most major cities, local support was strong in rural areas where the bulk of the mission's practical work was carried out.[33]

Though Warne's memoirs portray a problematic relationship with Mosaddeq, dispatches and reports from the period suggest a degree of cooperation between Point Four and the National Front government. In December 1951, Point Four received $4.5 million to implement the village council program outlined in Mosaddeq's agrarian wealth distribution bill.[34] Warne himself grew close to members of Mosaddeq's government – he made plans, in fact, to dine with Mosaddeq's son on the night of August 19, 1953.[35] From a relatively small budget, Point Four drew up plans for irrigation projects, sprayed thousands of villages with DDT, launched anti-malaria campaigns, and established seed exchanges to increase crop yields. There is evidence to suggest that Point Four's projects contributed to Mosaddeq's oil-less economic policy. Between August 1952 and February 1953, Point Four assisted with sugar imports totaling 60,000 tons, at a cost of $4 million. Warne himself guessed that Point Four expenses were keeping rial rates down in mid-1953 while its import credits forestalled a major sugar shortage: Point Four assistance "clearly provided important foreign exchange relief."[36]

Mosaddeq's economic measures, combined with the efforts of Point Four, met some of Iran's needs in the second half of 1952. Imports plummeted while non-oil exports increased from 1.4 billion rials to 2.8 billion rials.[37] The balance of payments deficit declined from 2.7 billion rials to only 399 million rials in 1952. Good harvests in 1951–1952 and 1952–1953 improved rural employment.[38] There was no appreciable

---

[33] RG 59 888.00TA/4-453, US Embassy Tehran No. 62, April 4, 1953; RG 84 USLETCGR, 1953–1955, Box 60, US Embassy Tehran No. 847, April 17, 1953, USNA.

[34] Tavanayan-Fard, *Duktur Mosaddeq va iqtisad*, 263–266; RG 84 USLETCGR, Box 60, US Embassy Tehran No. 555, "Quarterly Economic and Financial Review, Iran, Fourth Quarter, 1952," January 17, 1953.

[35] RG 469 RUSFAA, Iran Branch, Subject Files 1952–1959, Box 5, Warne to TCA, Weekly Report, August 23, 1953. The plans were canceled that morning, hours before pro-shah military forces began shelling Mosaddeq's house.

[36] RG 84 USLETCGR, 1953–1955, Box 60, Warne to Silver, "Information Requested on November 24, control 2139," July 9, 1953, Iran Economic Paper No. 9, Balance of Payments, January 1953; RG 59 888.00TA/10-3052, Point Four Tehran, No. 24, October 30, 1952; RG 469 RUSFAA, Near East Central Files, Iran Project Files, 1951–1957, Box 1, Project Agreement No. 14, June 10, 1952, Henderson to State, No. 3815, April 8, 1952, Project Plan and Justification of Karkheh Dam, May 12, 1953.

[37] Elm, *Oil, Power, and Principle*, 273; Clawson and Sassanpour, "Foreign Exchange Shock," 10–11.

[38] RG 84 USLETCGR, 1953–1955, Box 60, Iran Economic Papers, No. 8, "Imports and Exports," USNA.

increase in the Bank-e Melli's cost of living index, though one banker told the US embassy the figures were falsified at the behest of the prime minister.[39] The army and civil servants were paid promptly with newly issued rials and development work continued at the slow but steady pace of the pre-nationalization era. With higher exports and agricultural yields, it is possible Mosaddeq may have been able to reduce deficit spending, particularly if he coupled such moves with reductions to the bloated administrative and military budgets. Had the oil-less economy continued it is likely Iran would have recovered from the initial shock of the oil shutdown and stabilized its finances in 1954.[40]

This is clear with the benefit of hindsight. Mosaddeq turned to oil-less economics because he had no other option. Reducing Iran's foreign exchange gap and paying the government's bills through deficit-spending helped shore up his position in the short term. But Mosaddeq strove to secure an oil agreement with the United States and saw Washington's support as crucial for the survival of his government. He did not support an oil-less Iran in perpetuity. In August 1952, even as he passed his oil-less economic package, Mosaddeq maneuvered for new talks with the Americans. This attitude also explains why he worked hard to maintain good relations with Point Four. After a violent attack by a mob on the Point Four office in Shiraz in April 1953, Mosaddeq wrote a letter to Warne exhibiting his "sincere appreciation for your continuous and consistent efforts" while noting that Point Four had "opened new doors of hope" for the Iranian people.[41] The rural assistance mission represented a tangible US commitment to Iran's stability. Even as official American support for his position disappeared, the prime minister held out hope for aid, oil purchases, or some other concrete sign that the United States supported his regime.

Unfortunately for Mosaddeq, the US government viewed Point Four as peripheral. While officials were ready to maintain the mission, no one thought it a solution to the problems created by nationalization. Ambassador Loy W. Henderson argued that technical assistance could not cure Iran's "economic ills," though he praised Warne's efforts at

---

[39] RG 84 USLETCGR, 1953–1955, Box 60, US Embassy Tehran No. 824, April 8, 1953, USNA.
[40] Clawson and Sassanpour, "Foreign Exchange Shock," 10–11; Katouzian, "Oil Boycott and the Political Economy," 212–214.
[41] RG 59 888.00 TA/7-353, US Embassy Tehran No. 2, July 3, 1953; RG 469 RUSFAA TCA IDSF, 1951–1954, Box 17, Press and Public Affairs File, June Critique by Warne, Mosaddeq to Warne, July 28, 1953.

relieving rural poverty.[42] The program provided a convenient façade of American consideration for the life of the Iranian peasant, preserving the notion that development remained at the core of the US mission. But façade it was, despite Warne's enthusiasm and willingness to work closely with members of the Mosaddeq government.

By early 1953, the United States had abandoned all plans to support Mosaddeq and instead turned to a policy of regime change via covert action. As TPAJAX proceeded, Warne's presence grew embarrassing: He was "swimming against the general current," in the words of CIA operative Kermit Roosevelt.[43] Point Four suggested what might have been possible, had the United States undertaken a different set of policies and assisted Mosaddeq with transitioning Iran away from dependence on oil. But that would have flown in the face of the consensus in the embassy in Tehran as well as in Washington: The feeling that, sooner or later, an oil-less Iran would succumb to collapse.

4.2 Judging Collapse: Analyzing the Oil-Less Economy

The collapse narrative formed in response to a simple question: Did Iran need oil? Any assessment of oil's importance to Iran ultimately rested on economic data. Acquiring accurate statistics on Iran's economy and state finances was difficult and figures for the 1951–1954 period were (and remain) fragmentary and unreliable. American policymakers depended on information from the US embassy, particularly the political analysis of Ambassador Loy W. Henderson, to judge the situation. When it came to judging "collapse," Henderson himself depended on embassy economic counselor Robert M. Carr.

A dour, unglamorous man who manned the economic desk from 1951 to 1954, Carr worked with his staff and British counterparts to collect, dissect, analyze, and translate economic data gathered from Iran's government, the Bank-e Melli, and other sources. The finished reports were, according to Carr, "the most recent and comprehensive compilation of economic information which exists in respect to Iran."[44] Judging the oil-less economy and estimating Iran's ability to survive under National Front administration were among Carr's most important duties. The figures he compiled in his reports painted a picture not of a

---

[42] RG 84 USLETCGR, 1953–1955, Box 60, Henderson to State, February 15, 1953, USNA.

[43] *FRUS Retrospective*: 635, footnote 2.

[44] RG 84 USLETCGR, 1953–1955, Box 60, Carr to Henderson, April 17, 1953. These papers were completed in January 1952 and updated in January 1953. The originals can be found in RG 469 RUSFAA, Iran Branch, Subject Files 1952–1959, Box 1, USNA.

petro-state per se, but of a country that by 1951 came to rely on oil in myriad ways. His conclusions were crucial in forming a view of Iran that emphasized the threat of collapse through oil-lessness, Iranian economic mismanagement, and the rising threat of communist subversion. This narrative was repeated, reimagined, and reprocessed by others throughout the US policymaking apparatus, creating a consensus resting on two fundamental precepts: That oil-less economics was not a viable long-term course of action; and that without an oil agreement the National Front government was not capable of managing Iran's affairs, creating a situation where increasing Tudeh influence became more and more likely.[45]

Before nationalization, oil revenues flowed into Iran's national development program, the Seven-Year Plan. From January 1949 to March 1951, AIOC paid £39 million to Iran in royalties. The plan absorbed £30 million, equal to 2.95 billion rials, while the rest were used for general budget expenses.[46] Iran earned income taxes on AIOC salaries (though British employees were exempt), collected customs duties on British imports, and earned rials by charging AIOC a higher exchange rate for expenses the company paid in sterling.[47] Foreign exchange contributions from oil allowed Iran to manage a large non-oil trade deficit, which grew to 1.2 billion rials by 1948. Oil payments and AIOC purchases accounted for between 60 and 80 percent of total foreign exchange earnings. The idea that Iran enjoyed a positive balance of payments – frequently repeated before 1951 and used as a justification by the Truman administration for withholding aid – was a fallacy. Without AIOC, the country's trade pattern was unsustainable.[48]

Based on existing statistics, Carr presented an estimate of Iran's oil-related finances in April 1951, just before nationalization and the embargo. For the Iranian fiscal year of March 1951–March 1952, had nationalization not occurred, the government would have earned £10 million worth of rials from AIOC operating expenses, another

---

[45] A version of this argument appears in Gregory Brew, "The Collapse Narrative: The United States, Mohammed Mossadegh, and the Coup Decision of 1953," *Texas National Security Review* 2, no. 4 (November 2019): 38–59.

[46] RG 84 USLETCGR, 1953–1955, Box 60, Iran Economic Paper No. 16, January 15, 1953, "The Seven Year Plan, the Plan Organization and OCI,"; RG 59 888.00 SEVEN-YEAR/1-2451, US Embassy Tehran No. 575, Drafted by Carr, January 24, 1951, 888.00 SEVEN YEAR/5-251, US Embassy Tehran No. 882, Drafted by Carr, May 2, 1951, USNA.

[47] Bostock and Jones, *Power and Planning*, 64–69.

[48] US Embassy Tehran, Annual Economic Report on Iran, 1948, February 15, 1949, Iran – General – Correspondence – vol. 3, 1805821 WBGA; RG 59 888.00/3-650 US Embassy Tehran No. 87, March 6, 1950, USNA.

Excise Tax	Income Tax	Electricity	Customs	Royalty	Foreign Exchange Sales
£6,598,972	£1,047,234	£207,874	£2,151,176	£28,000,000	£12,200,000
Total	£50,005,256 4.5 billion rials				
State Budget	9.55 billion rials				

Figure 4.1 AIOC contribution, 1951–1952 (estimated)[49]

£12.2 million from sales of sterling earned through charging AIOC a higher exchange rate, and £15.9 million in royalties, or £28 million under the Supplemental Agreement, for a total of £50 million or $140 million. Under these conditions, AIOC would contribute 4.5 billion rials, more than one-third of the entire estimated budget, including projected development expenses (Figure 4.1).[50]

Carr and Ambassador Loy W. Henderson, who transmitted his counselor's figures to Washington, chose to express the final figure as "40 percent of the total government budgetary revenues."[51] AIOC's withdrawal and the oil embargo shut off these sources of revenue and foreign exchange. The shutdown also burdened the state with AIOC's former expenses, including wages for 50,000 oil workers. According to the embassy figures, Iran faced a trade crisis, a state budget crisis, a balance of payments crisis, and a defunct development plan, all of which would occur more-or-less simultaneously.

As Chapter 3 illustrates, there were significant concerns in 1951 within the US government that the oil nationalization crisis, if left unresolved, would lead to Iran's fall to communism. Carr's reports worked to allay the hysteria. He emphasized Iran's "considerable resistance" to the shock

---

[49] RG 59 888.2553/4-2751, US Embassy Tehran No. 866, Contributions of the AIOC to the Iranian Embassy, April 27, 1951, USNA.
[50] RG 59 888.2553/4-2751, US Embassy Tehran No. 866, Contributions of the AIOC to the Iranian Embassy, April 27, 1951, USNA. For additional figures, see RG 84 USLETCGR, 1950–1952, Box 39, US Embassy Tehran No. 574, October 31, 1951, 1953–1955, Box 60, Iran Economic Paper No. 2, Government Budget, January 1953; RG 59 888.2553/3-551, US Embassy Tehran No. 712, March 5, 1951, USNA. The budget cited here was Razmara's anticipated budget for the fiscal year 1951–1952; in reality Iran spent far less than 9.55 billion rials during this fiscal year.
[51] *FRUS X*: 260–262.

4.2 Judging Collapse: Analyzing the Oil-Less Economy

of oil de-integration. AIOC may have covered nearly half of all state expenditures and three-quarters of Iran's foreign exchange, but the overvalued rial, Iran's gold reserves, and the primitive state of Iran's agricultural economy convinced Carr that collapse would take some time to materialize.[52] Both the British and the World Bank agreed with this assessment.[53] Mosaddeq himself remained anti-communist, and while the Tudeh was an evident threat, its capacity to infiltrate the government appeared limited.[54] Collapse, if it came at all, was still many months away.

This attitude changed following the events of July 1952. Carr was unimpressed by the oil-less economic plan Mosaddeq rolled out that August. The legislation seemed a "half-baked project," one that displayed "the ultimate limit of improvisation."[55] Plans to offset imports and save foreign exchange would require increasing production to 110,000 tons of sugar and 6,500 tons of tea per year – astronomic figures, given Iran's dependence on imported commodities. Iran was able to endure a period of low imports because merchants had built up large inventories during the 1949–1950 depression.[56] When these inventories ran out Iran would have no choice but to look to the Soviet Union for assistance: Trade with the USSR had already increased from $1 million in 1950 to $28.2 million in 1951.[57] The increased note issue and a strong harvest provided a short-term benefit, as did the global export boom – the Korean War caused a spike in demand for most traded goods – but the change was of a "superficial nature," masking symptoms of an "economic and financial deterioration."[58] The idea that the Iranian state could manage an oil-less economic transition did not appear credible to Carr and his staff.

---

[52] RG 59 888.2553/7-2351, "Prospects for Economic Stabilization in Iran After Oil Nationalization," July 23, 1951; RG 84 USLETCGR, 1950–1952, Box 35, US Embassy Tehran No. 185, October 4, 1951, Box 36, Henderson to State, No. 3781, Drafted by Carr, April 4, 1951, USNA.

[53] FO 371/98625 Middleton to FO, June 19, 1952, Bailey to Carrell, July 26, 1952, UKNA; Bank-i Melli Role in Iranian Government Financing, May 6, 1952, Iran – General – Correspondence 1805826, WBGA.

[54] Gasiorowski, "US Perceptions of the Communist Threat," 14–19; Siavush Randjbar-Daemi, "'Down with the Monarchy': Iran's Republican Moment of August 1953," *Iranian Studies* 50, no. 2 (2017): 293–313.

[55] RG 84 USLETCGR, 1950–1952, Box 35, US Embassy Tehran, October 25, 1952, USNA.

[56] RG 84 USLETCGR, 1953–1955, Box 60, US Embassy Tehran No. 847, April 17, 1953, USNA.

[57] RG 84 USLETCGR, 1953–1955, Box 60, Iran Economic Paper No. 15, USSR Economic Interests in Iran, January 1953, USNA.

[58] RG 84 USLETCGR, 1953–1955, Box 60, US Embassy Tehran No. 555, January 17, 1953, USNA.

The position on devaluing the rial underwent a subtle shift after July 1952. Whereas analyses in 1949 and 1950 had emphasized Iran's need for a more competitive currency, Carr's reports from 1952 to 1953 highlighted the danger of inflation and Mosaddeq's use of deficit spending. The figures released in the oil-less budget, including 9.25 billion rials in spending against 9.77 billion rials of revenue and 2.5 billion rials in economic development, appeared "dubious" and "unduly optimistic."[59] Carr estimated Iran would face a budget deficit of 5.6 billion rials if Mosaddeq went ahead with plans to invest 2.5 billion rials into new economic development projects.[60] The only way to cover this gap would be to print new rials, eroding the currency's purchasing power and eventually creating spiraling inflation that would raise prices, destroy business activity, and plunge the country into chaos, according to the embassy.

Carr and his staff pushed the concept of Iranian incapacity. They doubted the competence of Mosaddeq and the National Front to manage the oil-less economy. There was a "woeful lack of competent or experienced personnel" in the central ministries, the Plan Organization, and the Bank-e Melli.[61] Mosaddeq's advisors hailed from the Iran Party, which embassy officials like Carr and Ambassador Loy W. Henderson held in deep suspicion due to the group's Left-leaning ideology.[62] Mosaddeq's proposals suggested growing state involvement in the management of the economy, characterized by interventions from the "already overgrown and none-too-competent bureaucracy."[63] Before July 1952, the embassy relied on career government officials, "pro-Western in sympathies and conservative in outlook," for information on Iran's state finances and overall economic health. After July, most of those friendly to the embassy were marginalized, replaced by National Front appointees such as Baqer Kazimi and Kazem Hasibi who in Carr's

---

[59] RG 84 USLETCGR, 1953–1955, Box 60, Iran Economic Paper No. 2, Government Budget, January 1953, US Embassy Tehran No. 555, January 17, 1953, USNA.

[60] RG 59 888.00TA/3-1753, US Embassy Tehran No. 766, Robert M. Carr, March 17, 1953, USNA.

[61] RG 84 USLETCGR, 1953–1955, Box 60, US Embassy Tehran No. 847, April 17, 1953, USNA.

[62] Henderson was particularly skeptical of Allahyar Saleh, a prominent moderate within the National Front who the shah had suggested in May 1952 as a potential replacement for Moṣaddeq. For Henderson's views of Saleh, see *FRUS Retrospective*: 239–241, 243–246, 252–258.

[63] RG 84 USLETCGR, 1953–1955, Box 60, US Embassy Tehran No. 555, January 17, 1953, USNA.

4.2 Judging Collapse: Analyzing the Oil-Less Economy

view had "little sympathy with the West," and were politicians rather than effective bureaucrats.[64]

Carr was repulsed by the "new men" in charge at the capital, "apostles of the typical 'bureaucratic revolution,' complete with the statism, controls and neo-Keynesian economics which have become increasingly questioned elsewhere."[65] While the embassy believed the National Front was peopled by demagogues and socialist technocrats, Carr admitted that a government possessed of greater will, "sufficiently able, demagogic and dictatorial," could balance the budget and survive without oil revenues, perhaps indefinitely.[66] Such a government would either come in the form of military rule or a dictatorship by the Tudeh Party. Not only were the new managers of Iran's economy incompetent – they were also crypto-communists, at least in Carr's eyes.

Carr's reports were amplified by Ambassador Loy W. Henderson, who took over from Henry F. Grady in September 1951 and served until 1955. Henderson was a career foreign service officer who had led the State Department's Near East division during the Azerbaijan crisis and was among the department's most aggressively anti-communist voices.[67] Before July 1952, Henderson wrote in countless reports how the threat of collapse in Iran demanded urgent action. "Iran is [a] sick country," he wrote in January 1952, "and [Mosaddeq] is one of its most sick leaders."[68] For Iran to resist communism, there needed to be "honest and efficient" government, "with a positive program of reform" that would weaken Tudeh appeal. Such a government would need funds, "and the best source of income is from the country's vast oil resources."[69] Until an agreement was reached, no government could improve "the miserable social and economic conditions" pervasive

---

[64] RG 84 USLETCGR, 1953–1955, Box 60, US Embassy Tehran No. 808, "Impact of Political Change on Iran's Economic Affairs during 1331," April 3, 1953, USNA; 'Ali Amini, *Khatirat-e 'Ali Amini: nukhust vazir-e Iran, 1340–1342* [Memoir of 'Ali Amini, Prime Minister of Iran 1961–1962], Habib Ladjevardi, ed. (Cambridge, MA: Center for Middle Eastern Studies of Harvard University and Distributed by Ibex Books, 1995), 62–71; Muhammed Ibrahim Amir Taymur Kalili, *Khatirat-e Muhammed Ibrahim Amir Taymur Kalali* [Memoirs of Mohammed Amir Teymour Kalali], Habib Ladjevardi, ed. (Cambridge, MA: Center for Middle Eastern Studies of Harvard University and Distributed by Ibex Books, 1997), 93–94.

[65] RG 84 USLETCGR, 1950–1952, Box 36, US Embassy Tehran No. 555, January 17, 1953, USNA.

[66] RG 84 USLETCGR, 1950–1952, Box 36, US Embassy Tehran No. 1362, June 26, 1952, USNA.

[67] H. W. Brands, *Inside the Cold War: Loy Henderson and the Rise of the American Empire* (New York: Oxford University Press, 1991), viii–xi.

[68] *FRUS X*: 301–303. [69] *FRUS X*: 260–262.

through the country; "[the] discontent of [the] people is bound to attract them towards extreme of Communism."[70]

After July 1952, the ambassador grew concerned that Mosaddeq was turning to the Tudeh Party for support, moral or otherwise. The idea of Mosaddeq's incompetence formed part of his reasoning. An oil-less economy would need "skillful, strong and ruthless dictatorship," the kind only the Tudeh "was capable of furnishing."[71] The National Front, meanwhile, would find it exceedingly difficult to carry out any kind of internal reform campaign "because of the varying objectives of its leaders."[72] While policymakers in Washington argued that Mosaddeq represented a meaningful opposition to the Tudeh Party, Henderson dissented, basing his case in part on observations of Iranian incapacity. Since the National Front took power, "there has been a marked deterioration of forces making for steady administration and for [the] stability [of the] country," he wrote. Henderson believed that Mosaddeq received "Tudeh-slanted advice," and that several of his cabinet members were "Tudeh tools." Communist influence within the government, while apparently quite small, could grow quickly under the right circumstances: "infiltration of this kind might result in communists creeping almost imperceptibly into power."[73]

By late 1952 and into early 1953, these views were becoming well-represented elsewhere in the US government. As Secretary of State Dean Acheson recalled in 1954, Iran's economic situation was "deteriorating ... various people put it at four, six, seven or eight months," but sooner or later, "we would reach ... the point of no return."[74] The National Security Council policy document completed in November 1952 concluded that "nationalist failure to restore the oil industry has led to ... deficit financing to meet current expense, and is likely to produce a progressive deterioration of the economy at large."[75] Secretary of Defense Robert A. Lovett felt urgent action was needed, "to save Iran."[76] Following the November 1952 election, Truman, Acheson, and Averell Harriman briefed President-elect Dwight D. Eisenhower. The situation in Iran, they said, had developed to a "critical point." The National Front could survive for a year if they acted "reasonably," but Acheson, Truman, and Harriman no longer thought

---

[70] RG 59 888.2553/11-2051, Henderson to Acheson, November 20, 1951, USNA.
[71] RG 84 USLETCGR, 1950–1952, Box 36, Henderson to Acheson, November 5, 1952, USNA.
[72] *FRUS Retrospective*: 310–314.   [73] *FRUS X*: 513–517.
[74] Princeton Seminar, May 15, 1954, Papers of Dean Acheson, Box 81, HSTPL.
[75] *FRUS Retrospective*: 422–425.
[76] RG 59 888.2553/11-1252, Lovett for Acheson, November 12, 1952, USNA.

that likely: "They would act emotionally ... [and] in a very short time might have the country in a state of chaos."[77] Immediate US action – an intervention – was needed to stop Iran from suffering a collapse, one that would presage a communist takeover.

Economic data formed little part of the US assessment. Even the figures available to Carr indicated an economy which had come to rely upon oil but which would survive, and possibly even prosper, if proper reforms were made. At no point between July 1952 and April 1953 (the approximate time when the coup was authorized) did the Iranian economy appear on the verge of cataclysm. Even without an oil agreement or foreign aid, Iran could pay for all its essential imports through 1953, "unless there is a serious crop failure or an unfavorable export market," according to the November 1952 national intelligence estimate.[78] Looking back, Acheson admitted that panic had set in: "[W]e thought disaster was closer to us than it probably turned out to be."[79] Fear of the future, skepticism of Iranian capacity for self-government, and an overriding sense that the Tudeh would profit from maintaining the status quo formed an omnipresent anxiety that gripped the US government. But if collapse was certain, what could be done to avert it? Three courses lay open: aid Mosaddeq, bring Iran and Britain back to the negotiating table, or use covert action to remove the National Front from power.

4.3 Making the Coup Decision, August 1952–March 1953

On August 20, 1952, the director of the CIA's Psychological Strategy Board held an unusual meeting. In attendance was Edward Bayne, formerly of the World Bank, and Max W. Thornburg, the international consultant and oil executive now moonlighting as an Iran "expert." Since losing his position as advisor to the prime minister of Iran, Thornburg had appeared on television, playing the commentator on Eleanor Roosevelt's talk show and Longines' *Chronoscope*, where he criticized the US government's policy in Iran.[80] Thornburg's situation improved somewhat when his friend and former OCI tax lawyer Allen Dulles became deputy director of the CIA in August 1951. A year later, Dulles brought Thornburg in as an advisor on Iranian issues.

---

[77] *FRUS Retrospective*: 420–421.   [78] *FRUS Retrospective*: 407–416.
[79] Princeton Seminar, May 15, 1954, Papers of Dean Acheson, Box 81, HSTPL.
[80] *The Eleanor Roosevelt Program*, June 8, 1951, Interview segment with Max Thornburg. For transcript, see Eleanor Roosevelt Papers Project, George Washington University Libraries, www.scholarspace.library.gwu.edu/concern/gw_works/kw52j838h.

"The oil question," said Thornburg at the August meeting, "could not be settled until there was a government in Persia that wanted to settle it." Thornburg also believed such a government would have to demonstrate both the desire and the ability "to make effective use of the revenues" for projects of economic development. Fortunately, "there is a responsible segment of the governing class ... that wants the same thing that we do." A new government could be supported, he argued, "dedicated to the welfare of its people ... the most promising figure around whom a responsible government can be built in Persia today is the shah."[81]

Thornburg – who had no experience in covert operations – kept his details vague. "The essence of the plan" he explained in a memo prepared for the CIA, "is that the shah take control," rule by decree, suppress all dissent, and carry out economic reforms, before settling the oil dispute "on a rational basis."[82] After the failure of July 1952, there was no point in trying to get anything done through the Majlis, while the National Front clearly could not be trusted. Like Carr and Henderson, Thornburg believed that a dictatorial government could enforce stability in Iran, crush the communists, re-establish ties with the oil companies, and restart the national development plan – in other words, revive dual integration. The necessary corollary to this result was the removal of Mosaddeq from office.

Thornburg's suggestion did not come as a shock. There had been talk within the Truman administration of removing Mosaddeq since the beginning of the crisis. In 1951 just days after Mosaddeq took office, Dulles suggested steps ought to be taken to "throw out Mossadeq, close the Majlis ... at a later date a premier could be installed with our help."[83] In October 1952, British agents tried to support a military coup led by Fazlollah Zahedi and a group of ex-military officers. Before the coup could proceed, Mosaddeq closed the British embassy.[84] Having lost their foothold inside Iran, the British turned to the United States. Using the threat of communism as their chief rationale on the theory that it would prove more effective at eliciting US interest, the British suggested replacing Mosaddeq with a more "reliable" prime minister, one who could be trusted to subdue the Tudeh.[85] According to one British agent, the suggestion was favorably received by Dulles and Frank Wisner of the CIA.[86]

---

[81] *FRUS Retrospective*: 321–325.   [82] *FRUS Retrospective*: 330–334.
[83] *FRUS Retrospective*: 87.   [84] Rahnema, *Behind the Coup*, 24–26.
[85] RG 59 888.2553/10-2352, Memo Jernegan to Matthews, October 23, 1952, 788.00/11-2652, Byroade to Matthews, November 26,1952, 788.00/12-352, Memo of Conversation, December 3, 1952, USNA. Thanks to the National Security Archive for bringing these documents to public attention.
[86] C. M. Woodhouse, *Something Ventured* (London: Granada, 1982), 117–118.

4.3 Making the Coup Decision, August 1952–March 1953

Worried that the Tudeh Party's influence had increased in the wake of the July Uprising, the Truman administration expanded the agency's remit to operate inside Iran. The national security policy adopted in November 1952 included provisions for "special political operations" to support non-communist forces, and the CIA began assembling weapons to combat communists inside Iran in the event that conditions deteriorated further.[87] The agency concluded in 1953 that enough arms and cash had been assembled to outfit a force of 10,000 soldiers.[88]

Recommendations for regime change did not translate into policy for a simple reason: Most US officials could see no viable alternative to Mosaddeq. After Qavam's failure, analysts in the CIA's intelligence-gathering division concluded that there were no strong figures "around whom a coup might be engineered."[89] The anti-communist forces marshaled by the agency's operatives were not anti-Mosaddeq and could not be counted on to support a coup. There were fears that with Mosaddeq gone, a more extreme figure like Ayatollah Abolqassem Kashani would seize power. The shah had lost all credibility due to his failure to back Qavam. Former Ambassador George V. Allen, who remained on good terms with his former tennis partner, felt the shah was "virtually a prisoner" in Tehran. The capabilities of the army, his sole reliable bastion of support, "are wholly unclear," as many of the low-ranking officers were believed to be pro-Mosaddeq while upper-level command positions were gradually being filled with National Front supporters.[90] The CIA special estimate from October 1952 agreed with Allen's assessment.[91] Thornburg's notions of propping up the shah seemed "ill-informed and unrealistic."[92] When the British suggested a covert operation to remove Mosaddeq, State Department officials thought it too risky.[93] Officials dismissed a coup not because they supported the Mosaddeq government, but because the chances of an operation producing a favorable outcome seemed remote.

Instead of a coup, the Truman administration opted for one last round of negotiations. According to Paul Nitze of the Policy Planning Staff, Iran needed to be pushed into a deal that would provide "sufficient revenues to meet its economic problems."[94] It was a bold plan. Using the authority of the Defense Production Act, the United States would

---

[87] *FRUS Retrospective*: 424–425.
[88] Mark J. Gasiorowski, "The US Stay-behind Operation in Iran, 1948–1953," *Intelligence and National Security* 34, no. 2 (2019): 170–188.
[89] *FRUS Retrospective*: 301.
[90] *FRUS Retrospective*: 359–362.
[91] *FRUS Retrospective*: 367–370.
[92] *FRUS Retrospective*, 331, ft. 2.
[93] RG 59 788.00/12-352, Memo of Conversation, December 3, 1952, USNA.
[94] RG 59 888.2553/11-652, Nitze for Acheson, November 6, 1952, USNA.

buy $100 million in Iranian oil, and in exchange Mosaddeq would agree to allow the World Court to determine a compensation award for AIOC's nationalized assets. The embargo would end, nationalization would be recognized, and Mosaddeq's government would receive a large infusion of American aid. While Iran would agree to sell oil to the oligopoly, it would enjoy total freedom over the management of its oil industry.[95] Discussions between Henderson and Mosaddeq kicked off in late December 1952.

Success hinged on securing British cooperation. When it came time to negotiate, Foreign Secretary Anthony Eden – who remained convinced Mosaddeq would have to be removed from office – stalled for time. He took an unyielding stance on compensation for AIOC, the last issue over which his government had any control. According to Eden, the company would have to be promised money covering its "loss of enterprise," beyond the physical assets in Iran. Like nationalization, this was a nebulous term with multiple potential definitions. For Mosaddeq, it meant AIOC would receive compensation for all the profits it might have made over the lifetime of the original concession, covering 1951–1993. This figure was anything from $1 billion to $5 billion, according to US and AIOC projections.[96] Eden's move effectively sabotaged discussions. Acheson later wrote that the British were "determined on a rule-or-ruin policy," and their refusal to negotiate on compensation terms was probably linked to their desire to see Mosaddeq removed.[97] On January 15, 1953, Mosaddeq rejected the proposal.[98]

After January 20, a new administration assumed control. Neither President Dwight D. Eisenhower nor Secretary of State John Foster Dulles were ready to give up on negotiations. Allen Dulles, now CIA director, still supported a coup. Dulles took steps to bring the collapse narrative to the top of the policymaking process, in the hopes of convincing the president and his brother the secretary of state to support covert action against Mosaddeq. Before Eisenhower took office, Dulles had the intelligence estimate for Iran altered to emphasize how "unexpected events" like a sudden crop failure "would increase Tudeh capabilities

---

[95] RG 59 888.2553/12-2652, Acheson to Henderson, December 29, 1952, 888.2553/12-2952, Acheson to US Embassy London, Note for Eden, December 29, 1952, USNA.
[96] BP 91031 "Compensation for AIOC Assets," and "Persia – Compensation," August 28, 1951; RG 59 Box 5506 Nitze-Linder Working Group, Basic Premises of US Good Offices Proposals, November 1951, USNA.
[97] Dean Acheson, *Present at the Creation: My Years at the State Department* (New York: Norton, 1969), 682.
[98] RG 59 888.2553/1-1653, Henderson to Acheson, January 16, 1953, USNA.

4.3 Making the Coup Decision, August 1952–March 1953

greatly."[99] On February 19, Dulles forwarded a letter by Max Thornburg to Walter Bedell Smith, the outgoing CIA director and Eisenhower's new under secretary of state. The key issue, wrote Thornburg, "is not how to make an oil agreement that will bolster up the government in Persia, but how to bolster up the government in Persia so it can make an oil agreement." Thornburg admitted that taking the actions necessary to bring about this outcome "might involve 48 hours of tough going for some people," but it was preferable to watching Iran "drift behind the Curtain."[100]

Thornburg's letter synthesized the central components of the collapse narrative. Mosaddeq and his supporters were incompetent. Moreover, they were communist sympathizers. An authoritarian government with US support could stabilize the situation, and more importantly, facilitate an oil agreement that could keep Iran from falling to communism. Political events in Iran seemed to confirm Dulles and Thornburg's position. In late February, Mosaddeq demanded the shah end his political interference and subordinate himself to the government. The shah responded by threatening to leave the country. The prime minister's sudden move against the shah pushed Henderson into a direct intervention. "I dislike remaining inactive," he wrote defiantly, "when [the] monarchical institution ... is in grave danger."[101] In a breach of diplomatic protocol, Henderson met with Mosaddeq and made it clear that the shah's departure would "weaken [the] security [of the] country." As Henderson left, crowds organized by Ayatollah Kashani, Mosaddeq's ally-turned-rival, attacked the prime minister's house, forcing him leap over a ten-foot fence to take refuge in the Point Four office next door.[102] Pro-Tudeh crowds emerged and clashed with Kashani's supporters. Mosaddeq blamed Henderson for interfering in Iranian politics, while Secretary John Foster Dulles approved Henderson's "energetic measures" to bolster the shah, who agreed to remain in the country.[103]

The events of February had an impact on US thinking. Henderson's warnings of an alliance between the Tudeh and Mosaddeq now appeared prescient. When the National Security Council met on March 4, President Eisenhower was preoccupied with Iran's collapse, evidence that the narrative had percolated to the top of the administration. "If ... I had $500,000,000 of money to spend in secret, I would give

---

[99] *FRUS Retrospective*: for the original NIE, see 407–416; for the January draft, see 438–447.
[100] *FRUS Retrospective*: 450–452.   [101] *FRUS Retrospective*: 464–465.
[102] Rahnema, *Behind the Coup*, 49–60.
[103] *FRUS Retrospective*: 458–459, 462–463, 466, 468–472. For the events of the February crisis, see Rahnema, *Behind the Coup*, 49–60; Azimi, *The Crisis of Democracy*, 311–319.

$100,000,000 of it to Iran right now," he mused. Allen Dulles emphasized the consequences of an Iranian collapse: The loss of the Middle East, "with some 60 percent of the world's oil reserves," to Soviet domination.[104] At the same time, Dulles pushed Thornburg's proposal. The events of February proved that the monarchy "may have more popular backing than was expected," indicated by the strong show of support for the shah by the crowds in February – crowds organized by Kashani and encouraged to use pro-shah chants, though Dulles did not mention this. Dulles then reported the CIA had resources inside Iran, "a considerable supply of small arms … [and] a considerable amount of cash," which could be quickly supplemented.[105]

On March 11, Eisenhower convened his National Security Council a second time. The meeting's tone was markedly different from that of March 4. Eisenhower now felt an oil agreement with Mosaddeq "might not be worth the paper it was written on." The United States had no military options. Should Iran be lost, the entirety of the Middle East's oil resources would be lost with it.[106] After the meeting, Secretary Dulles instructed Henderson to end all negotiations with Mosaddeq.[107] Discussion in Washington reflected the feeling that "[the] situation [had] materially altered," and assets "which could be rallied to support a replacement" should be cultivated.[108] In May, Henderson met with Secretary Dulles in Karachi. The embassy sent along notes on the situation inside Iran, drawn from the analysis of Carr's economic staff. "The need for foreign exchange has become acute … local currency needs have been met in the printing press route … the inflationary effect of this is only just beginning to be felt." On the political side, the confrontation in February had increased Mosaddeq's reliance on the Tudeh Party, "the only organization which can give him the kind of support in the streets." There were several potential courses of action, which included breaking off negotiations, proceeding with emergency aid, or removing Mosaddeq through covert action. Doing nothing, however, would cause Iran to "drift into chaos."[109]

The decision to remove Mosaddeq was made sometime in March or April, with Henderson's May meeting with Dulles a final consultation. By June, Operation TPAJAX was in motion and Eisenhower and Dulles gave their approval on the operational details on July 11.[110] All talk of

---

[104] *FRUS Retrospective*: 480–489.   [105] *FRUS Retrospective*: 475–478.
[106] *FRUS Retrospective*: 495–499.
[107] RG 59 888.2553/3-1353, Dulles to Henderson, March 13, 1953.
[108] *FRUS Retrospective*: 504, 504–511.   [109] *FRUS Retrospective*: 570–574.
[110] A meeting between Henderson and several CIA officials, including Kermit Roosevelt, on June 6 makes it clear that the ambassador was aware of the operation. See *FRUS*

aiding Mosaddeq or working out a new oil agreement disappeared. Once the order was given, an atmosphere of inevitability consumed American policymaking. According to an internal CIA history, "[material] incompatible with the planned covert political action ... did not dissuade the President, Secretary of State ... from executing TPAJAX."[111] At least one report on the limitations of US resources in Iran was produced but never utilized: Dulles either ignored the report or had it suppressed.[112] Interestingly, Ambassador Henderson, who had little faith in an oil agreement and even less in Mosaddeq, did his best to deter the coup plan, suggesting it would be better to explore other options: "I do not believe the problem can be solved merely by attempts to unseat Mosaddeq."[113] This warning was ignored.

Instead, Eisenhower and Secretary Dulles gave public statements distancing the US government from Mosaddeq, as a CIA team led by Kermit Roosevelt distributed bribes to Majlis deputies and army generals while publishing propaganda designed to discredit the prime minister and his government. A recalcitrant shah finally agreed to cooperate in July when a final coup plan was approved. Thornburg, Dulles, and the British had gotten their wish – Mosaddeq would go.

4.4 Settling Accounts

Why did the United States decide to overthrow the government of Mohammed Mosaddeq? The coup's semi-official justification was that it stopped the fall of Iran to communism. After an abortive first attempt on August 16, TPAJAX ended in success on August 19. The National Front collapsed, as Mosaddeq's enemies had him arrested and the shah named coup leader Fazlollah Zahedi prime minister through a *firman*, or royal decree, printed and distributed with help from Roosevelt and his contacts.[114] The Tudeh Party took very little action in the day's events, for reasons that remain unclear. In the sense that TPAJAX was an anticommunist operation – and it is impossible to argue otherwise, given the overwhelming evidence indicating concerns regarding communism in

---

Retrospective: 589–593. Roosevelt's memoir includes a meeting held on June 25 when high-level approval was given, but no record has been found elsewhere. See Roosevelt, *Countercoup*, 1–10. Two CIA histories mention authorization for TPAJAX was given by Secretary Dulles and President Eisenhower on July 11. See *FRUS Retrospective*: 916–918.

[111] Koch, *Zendebad Shah!* Appendix E, 118–120. [112] *FRUS Retrospective*: 478, ft. 1.
[113] RG 59 888.2553/5-853, Memo by Stuteseman, May 8, 1953, Attachment, Henderson to State, May 7, 1953, USNA.
[114] *FRUS X*: 748-752; Wilber, "Overthrow of Prime Minister Mossadeq," ix–xiii, 39–77; Gasiorowski, "The 1953 Coup D'etat in Iran," 261–286.

American archives – the outcome was precisely what the United States, Great Britain, and their Iranian allies had planned. The Tudeh Party was crushed and the National Front reduced to a rump as a new political constellation arose centered on the military and the shah, backed materially and financially by the United States.

Justifying TPAJAX as an anti-communist operation carried over into subsequent accounts of the coup. According to one internal history, "[Iran] seemed headed for an economic collapse and political anarchy," a state of affairs that would inevitably lead to its transformation into a "Soviet satellite."[115] In his self-serving memoir, Kermit Roosevelt stated bluntly that Mosaddeq had "formed an alliance of his own with the Soviet Union," and recounted the moment he warned John Foster Dulles "Iran would fall to the Russians … if we do nothing."[116] Eisenhower voiced this position in a meeting some years after the coup: "Whatever we have done, good or bad … we can at least have the satisfaction that we saved Iran from communism."[117] Retold in accounts and emphasized in memoirs, the collapse narrative became the official narrative, justifying the actions of all those involved in TPAJAX.

What makes this simple narrative hard to swallow is the evidence disproving the basic premise of the American policy. Intelligence reports from the March–August 1953 period consistently concluded that the Tudeh Party was not ready to seize control of the government. The CIA had been steadily combatting the Tudeh since 1948. By 1953 the party's upper echelons had been compromised and its communiques were frequently intercepted and delivered to agency personnel. While the Tudeh had broad support in the cities, it had not penetrated the government or the combat units of the military.[118] Mosaddeq never made good on his threat of offering oil to the Soviet Union. While he did meet with the Soviet ambassador in March 1953, Russian archives reveal that his goal was to end the embargo; better relations with Moscow were meant to apply pressure on the United States. The Soviet leadership, in a state of confusion following Stalin's death in early March 1953, continued to view Mosaddeq as pro-American.[119] The communist threat in Iran remained inchoate, at best.

---

[115] *The Battle for Iran,* 1. See also Wilber, *Clandestine Service History*: 1–2; Koch, *Zendebad Shah*, 16.
[116] Roosevelt, *Countercoup*, 2, 14. [117] *FRUS 1955–1957, XII*: 892–899.
[118] Gasiorowski, "Perceptions of the Communist Threat," 36–37; Mark J. Gasiorowski, "The CIA's TPBEDAMN Operation and the 1953 Coup in Iran," *Journal of Cold War Studies* 15, no. 4 (Fall 2013): 4–24.
[119] Zubok, "Stalin, Soviet Intelligence, and the Struggle for Iran," 38–43.

4.4 Settling Accounts

American officials in late 1952 and 1953 warned of an economic collapse so long as Iran remained oil-less. But with help from Point Four, Mosaddeq was managing the worst of Iran's economic problems in 1953. An economic analysis conducted just weeks before the coup noted an exchange rate of 89 rials per $1, a rising foreign exchange balance in the Bank-e Melli, and an excess of exports over imports "for the first time in recent history." The embassy warned of continued government deficit financing, but determined a major breakdown was months away. The embassy report from July 1953 repeated Carr's warnings from months before: The trend in Iran pointed to "a dictatorship with a rigidly planned economy ... it would be most difficult in that eventuality to find in Iran men who are qualified by training, experience, or competence to do any economic planning that would be either effective or consistent."[120] Whether the National Front had the competence to run the government is obviously a subjective determination, though it aligns with expressions of Iranian incapacity that had influenced American thinking in the past. Mosaddeq's government proved adept enough to manage the nationalization of the oil industry, a lengthy campaign by Great Britain to destabilize Iran's internal politics, and a prolonged business recession. Had Iran continued along the trajectory plotted by Mosaddeq it likely would have followed a neutralist course modeled on Nehru's India or Sukarno's Indonesia rather than accept Soviet sponsorship. From the point of view of the United States, of course, this would have been a highly unsatisfactory state of affairs in a country of such strategic importance.

There is evidence to suggest John Foster Dulles and Eisenhower were concerned about the impact of Mosaddeq "dumping" oil on the global market. Mosaddeq threatened to do so in February 1953, though he never followed up on this threat. There were fears that Iranian oil sold at rock-bottom prices would undercut the oligopoly's existing price system.[121] While British documents point to the American fear of oil dumping, the British themselves were unconcerned, as were the major companies.[122] British pressure does not appear to have played a part in the American coup decision, which was made through internal consultations. However, an important antecedent – the failed oil negotiations of

---

[120] RG 84 USLETCGR, 1953–1955, Box 60, US Embassy Iran No. 46, July 18, 1953.
[121] For the former position, see RG 59 888.2553/1-253, Jernegan to Acheson, January 2, 1953. For the latter, see RG 59 888.2553/2-1053, Dulles to Holmes, February 10, 1953, 888.2553/2-2053, Holmes to Dulles, February 20, 1953, 888.2553/2-1853, CIA Allen Dulles, Memo for Secretary of State, February 18, 1953, USNA.
[122] FO 371/104612 Makins to FO, February 10, 1953, FO to Makins, February 18, 1953, UKNA; Brew, "Collapse Narrative," 54.

January–February 1953 – stemmed from British unwillingness to alter their position on compensation. British intractability on the oil issue and the need to maintain Anglo-American relations was a factor in compelling Eisenhower to pursue a regime change policy. As the president noted during the March 4 meeting of his National Security Council, the losses from a "bad deal" to buy Iranian oil "were likely to overweigh any gain ... we certainly don't want to break with the British."[123] The British did not convince the United States to remove Mosaddeq, but they did contribute to circumstances that produced the ultimate decision.

The Eisenhower administration remained committed to preserving the postwar petroleum order and the oligopoly's control over global oil and prioritized the alliance with Britain over maintaining the Mosaddeq government. It was for these reasons that further oil negotiations or unilateral aid to Mosaddeq was not contemplated after March 1953. Once these options had been taken off the table, Allen Dulles' proposal of covert action was the only viable alternative. The urgency of the collapse narrative made it imperative to act quickly – a determination bolstered by fears of what Iran's nationalized oil might do to the global oil market – but the strategic goal remained as it had been before: Maintain access to the oil of the Middle East by propping up a pro-Western government in Iran, one that would be committed to maintaining dual integration.

If protecting the global oil economy was important, what proved more important in the motivation of the coup was concern regarding oil's impact *inside* Iran. Though he was not a key decision-maker within the government, Max Thornburg accurately summed up the core impulse of TPAJAX. The dispute between Mosaddeq and the British was keeping Iran oil-less. It fueled political unrest, weighed down the economy, and produced conditions that encouraged Iranian nationalists to turn to Moscow for help. As the minutes of the March 4 and 11 National Security Council meetings illustrate, senior US officials believed the loss of Iran would make the entire Anglo-American position in the Middle East untenable.[124] Allowing Iran to remain oil-less would lead to collapse, communism, and the nightmare of a Soviet-controlled Middle East. Rather than negotiate, the Eisenhower administration chose to remove Mosaddeq and replace him with a government that could maintain Iran's pro-Western strategic alignment, secure an oil agreement, and stave off collapse. Thornburg receded from view after the coup, dying in relative obscurity in 1962 at the age of sixty-nine. But his suggestion that

---

[123] *FRUS Retrospective*: 480–489. [124] *FRUS Retrospective*: 480–489, 495–499.

4.4 Settling Accounts

the United States place its faith in oil, the shah, and development would provide the crux of US policy in Iran for the next ten years.

It is for this reason that the first priority of the United States after the coup of August 19 was a deal reintegrating Iran into the global oil economy. While Iran's new Prime Minister Zahedi needed time to crush the Tudeh and consolidate his position, Secretary Dulles told Henderson that the United States would move "at the earliest possible date" to secure an oil agreement "[that] would lessen the danger" of losing Iran.[125] A deal would come on the oligopoly's terms. A corporate lawyer whose firm had represented major US oil companies, Dulles had no sympathy for nationalization's political or economic aspirations. As far as he was concerned, a "partial negation of Iranian nationalization," and the reintegration of Iran on the companies' terms was the only suitable course of action.[126]

In October, Under Secretary of State and former oil-man Herbert Hoover Jr. came to Iran to explain the situation to Zahedi and the shah. An arrangement would ensure Iran "income in [the] immediate future from its oil," but effective control would be exercised by a consortium of oil companies.[127] According to Manuchehr Farmanfarmain of NIOC, Hoover's proposal was essentially an ultimatum: If the "principle" of foreign control was not admitted, there would be no deal and no additional aid.[128] Morally, politically, and financially Zahedi and the shah needed US support. They had no choice but to accept.

By nearly every estimation, the Consortium Agreement of October 1954 was inferior to the deal offered to Mosaddeq in January 1953. The shah's finance minister 'Ali Amini, who had negotiated the final settlement, argued that the terms were the best they could obtain. "We must adopt a realistic attitude," he told the Majlis, "and cease laboring under delusions."[129] Yet the new arrangement was itself a delusion. Iran retained ownership of all oil in the ground, but exploration, production, and refining would be handled by a consortium of companies that included all of the seven major firms. The entire oligopoly would now have a stake in Iranian oil. Through imagined transactions, Iran would sell oil to the consortium while receiving 50 percent of profits, thus ensuring Iran the fifty-fifty profit-sharing terms that now dominated the

---

[125] RG 59 888.2553/8-2553, Dulles to Henderson, August 25, 1953, USNA.
[126] *FRUS X*: 802–803.
[127] RG 59 888.2553/10-2253, Henderson to Dulles, October 22, 1953, 888.2553/10-2353, Henderson to Dulles, October 23, 1953, USNA.
[128] Farmanfarmain, *Blood and Oil*, 302–303.
[129] *Muzakirat-e Majlis*, vol. XVIII, October 19–21, 1954.

oil-producing Middle East. But the oil would never pass out of consortium control. Nationalization was effectively reversed.[130]

Though he publicly hailed the deal as "the best agreement yet made," the reinstated shah chafed at the constraints of the Consortium Agreement.[131] Nor were the companies entirely satisfied with the arrangement. While AIOC had been eager to return to Iran, the US companies had little interest in increasing Iranian production when markets were in a state of oversupply. "From the strictly commercial viewpoint," wrote Jersey's Orville Harden to Secretary Dulles in December 1953, "our company has no particular interest in entering such a group."[132] Pressure from the Eisenhower administration forced the companies into the consortium, "to permit the reactivation of the petroleum industry in Iran and to provide to the friendly government of Iran substantial revenues."[133] The companies were given protection from anti-trust laws but were obliged to increase Iran's exports from zero to 30 million tons by 1957 – a significant undertaking, considering how the market remained saturated with oil from other sources. The companies knew that their terms were being forced onto the shah: "deep down," noted Harden, "the Iranians don't want us."[134]

For the United States, that was beside the point. As soon as the shah's handpicked Majlis confirmed the Consortium Agreement, the Eisenhower administration announced a new program of economic and budgetary aid to tide Iran over until the Pahlavi government had "concrete plans regarding its economic development."[135] Hoover wrote to Iran's foreign minister, offering his congratulations: The news marked a "significant victory" for those "dedicated to the principle that Iran is to move toward social and economic development."[136] Dulles was satisfied, while Henderson retired from his post after months of grueling work. The Tudeh Party had been effectively wiped out, the military and conservative elite were back in control, and Iran was guaranteed a steady

---

[130] Gregory Brew, "De-nationalized: Mohammed Reza Pahlavi, the Consortium, and Global Oil, 1954–1964," in Matthew Shannon, ed., *American-Iranian Dialogues: From Constitution to White Revolution, c. 1890s–1960s* (New York: Bloomsbury Academic, 2022), 97–102.
[131] Milani, *The Shah*, 196–197.
[132] US Senate Committee on Foreign Relations, *The International Petroleum Cartel, the Iranian Consortium, and US National Security* (Washington: US Government Printing Office, 1974), 58.
[133] Printed in *Multinational Oil Corporations and US Foreign Policy*, Committee on Foreign Relations, US Senate (Washington, 1975), 68.
[134] BP 126490 Minutes of Principals Meeting June 2, 11 and 15, 1954.
[135] RG 59 888.2553/10-2954, Dulles to Henderson, October 29, 1954, USNA.
[136] *FRUS X*: 1063.

supply of oil revenue on which a new development plan could be based. The coup had worked. Collapse had been averted. Dual integration was restored.

4.5 Conclusion

There were many reasons why the Eisenhower administration opted for covert action in Iran in 1953. The president had campaigned on a platform of fervent anti-communism and had publicly committed to toughening the US stance against Moscow. Eisenhower and Secretary Dulles would show little support for nationalist governments in the Global South over the course of the next eight years, and their willingness to undertake covert action in Iran reflected the new administration's thinking toward the Third World as a whole.[137] By early 1953 the military balance of power in the global Cold War had swung in favor of the West thanks to the rearmament programs launched in 1950. Eisenhower felt much more confident in attempting a potentially dangerous unilateral move, one without precedent in the history of US policy in the Middle East, due to the expansion in American military power.[138]

Arguably the most significant factor was the fear of what might happen if the United States did nothing. The predictions of Robert Carr, Loy W. Henderson, and Max Thornburg all pointed to disaster as long as Mosaddeq was left to govern and the oil industry remained idle. The chances of resolving the crisis through diplomacy faded after British obstruction prevented a settlement in January 1953, while the February confrontation between Mosaddeq and the shah hinted that the National Front government was poised to move Leftwards. The United States desired a government in Iran that could be trusted to suppress the Tudeh Party. But the coup was primarily meant to create the conditions necessary for the reintegration of Iranian oil so that the long-term stability of the new pro-US government could be assured. Operation TPAJAX resolved the nationalization crisis. It represented a sudden and decisive shift in US policy. After the confusion of the war years, the proxy strategy under the Seven-Year Plan, and mediating the definition of nationalization, the United States chose to intervene deliberately, decisively, and violently in Iran's internal politics.

---

[137] Salim Yaqub, *Containing Arab Nationalism: The Eisenhower Doctrine and the Middle East* (Chapel Hill, NC: University of North Carolina Press, 2005); William I. Hitchcock, *The Age of Eisenhower: America and the World in the 1950s* (New York: Simon & Shuster, 2018), 148–175.
[138] Gavin, "Politics, Power, and US Policy in Iran," 88–89.

In the long term, the coup was a disastrous mistake for the United States. The middle-class movement symbolized by Mohammed Mosaddeq had been dealt a devastating defeat. The National Front may have been fractious, but it represented a commitment to constitutional government and possessed a broad base of support. Henceforth, US policy would be bound to the parties elevated in August 1953, specifically the shah, the military, and a thin slice of the national elite. Iranians remembered the coup as the moment the United States, hitherto a respected and benign international influence, supplanted the British as the power dedicated to upsetting their country's internal affairs. The coup may have been a tactical success, but it left the United States with virtually no allies within Iran other than the shah and his immediate followers.

In the near-term, the deficiencies of this position were clear to US officials, who after 1954 began pushing the shah's government toward a new, grand program of economic development that could legitimize his shaky rule. Military aid could not create "real stability."[139] Lasting growth would depend "on the effective application," of oil riches, according to the US embassy in 1955.[140] The coup was a short-term solution to a long-term problem. Iran could not remain a garrison state indefinitely. American policymakers and the shah were both conscious of this fact.

In the meantime, however, there was cause for celebration. The regime's reintegration into the global oil economy through the 1954 Consortium Agreement preceded a tidal wave of US economic and military aid. According to Carr's successor, most aid was wasted and its positive economic effect "sterilized." Yet the psychological impact of regime change would offset the waste: "the economy of Iran has considerable resistance and flexibility ... political factors are often more important than economic." Deficit spending could probably continue for months, "perhaps even a year or so," before becoming "disastrous."[141] The collapse narrative did not disappear – many US officials and developmentalists continued to worry about Iran's stability – but the urgency was gone. The prognostication of Allen Dulles and Thornburg had come true. Iran, apparently unprepared for democracy and vulnerable to "unreasonable" demagogues like Mosaddeq, would be safer in the hands of a pro-Western authoritarian monarch. More importantly, it would never again be "oil-less." Henceforth the fate of the Pahlavi state would be closely tied to that of the global oil economy.

---

[139] *FRUS Retrospective*: 874–899, 921–924.   [140] *FRUS 1955–1957, XII*: 715–722.
[141] RG 469 RUSFAA Iran Branch, Subject Files 1952–1959, Box 2, Barnes to Henderson, Conversion of US Aid Dollars to Rials, September 21, 1953, Barnes to Warne and Henderson, Utilization of Grant Aid Funds, October 14, 1953, USNA.

Part II

5 The Petrochemical Paradise
Oil-Driven Development and the Second Plan, 1954–1963

On January 30, 1961, Professor Robert M. Adams addressed the Oriental Institute at the University of Chicago. His audience, a crowd of archaeologists, academics, and members of Hyde Park's intellectual elite, listened as Adams described the work of Development and Resources Corporation (D&R), a company managed by David E. Lilienthal, former director of the Tennessee Valley Authority (TVA). In the arid deserts of southwestern Iran, teams of American engineers, agronomists, technicians, and scientists were merging Iran's past with its future. A hydroelectric dam and irrigation area covered a swath of land "where dozens of ancient village mounds stand as mute witnesses"; a new sugar refinery sat in the very spot where techniques for turning cane into sugar emerged "more than twelve hundred years ago." "Evidence of the great periods of Iran's past are omnipresent" within the Khuzestan Development Service (KDS), a $140 million plan to transform Iran's poorest province into a thriving industrial and agricultural hub. "In the dramatic setting that Khuzestan offers," said Adams, "both past and future seem tantalizing near at hand."[1]

In the aftermath of TPAJAX, Iran was a land of opportunity for Iranian and American developmentalists. Flush with oil wealth and US aid, the government of Mohammed Reza Pahlavi funneled oil revenues, foreign loans, and private capital into the Second Seven-Year Plan in the belief that economic growth would support the regime's shaky post-coup claim to legitimacy. Iran's chief technocrat Abolhassan Ebtehaj returned to the fore to manage the Second Plan and overcome his country's apparent problems through oil-based development. "Is there time?" Ebtehaj asked one audience in San Francisco. "We believe there is time – provided, however, that our program … responds to the spur of urgency."[2]

---

[1] Robert M. Adams, Address to the Oriental Institute, January 30, 1961, DELP Box 426, SGMML.
[2] "Public and Private Enterprise in the Development of Iran" International Industrial Development Conference, San Francisco, October 17, 1957, DELP Box 406, SGMML.

For foreign observers, what Iran lacked was not the will to achieve progress, but the capacity. This shortcoming could only be remedied through outside assistance. After the US government intervened to alter Iran's political system in 1953, the myth of Iranian incapacity continued to hold strong. Developmentalists angled not just for contracts and opportunities, but for power – the power to shape a country of Cold War importance, one that had officially invited American influence, expertise, and direction.

Among the organizations that flocked to Iran after 1954 was Development and Resources Corporation. Founded by American liberal David E. Lilienthal and managed by his right-hand man Gordon R. Clapp, from 1956 to 1963 D&R ran the Khuzestan Development Service, a multipurpose dam, irrigation, and petrochemical project that consumed 10 percent of total Second Plan spending, or more than $100 million. Envisioned by Lilienthal, Clapp, and Ebtehaj as a road map for the transformation of Iran's impoverished rural provinces, the KDS was among the most ambitious operations in the history of the Cold War-era modernization movement.[3]

This chapter situates the work of D&R inside the context of the Second Plan and US support for the post-coup Iranian development program. Lilienthal and Clapp's project embodied dual integration: It was a campaign to link Iran's globally derived oil wealth to its internal development, guided by American experts and informed by a view of Iranian incapacity, all in service of US Cold War strategic objectives. The KDS was unique in the way that it linked fossil fuels to agrarian development, irrigation, and the plight of Iran's peasantry. Yet its story is a cautionary tale – an example of how developmentalist plans to guide the progress of another nation could fall short. KDS symbolized a political aspiration and was meant to burnish the legitimacy of the Pahlavi state. The fate of Lilienthal and Clapp's ambitious designs depended on the political priorities of the shah's government. When those priorities changed amid financial and political challenges, both D&R and the Second Plan became scapegoats for the broader struggles of the Pahlavi

---

[3] Steven M. Neuse, *David E. Lilienthal: The Journey of an American Liberal* (Knoxville TN: University of Tennessee Press, 1996), 266–274; Christopher T. Fisher, "'Moral Purpose Is the Important Thing': David Lilienthal, Iran and the Meaning of Development in the US, 1956–1963," *The International History Review* 33, no. 3 (2011): 431–451; Katayoun Shafiee, "Cost-Benefit Analysis at the Floodgates: Governing Democratic Futures Through the Reassembly of Iran's Waterways," *Social Studies of Science* 50, no. 1 (2020): 94–120; Razavi and Vakil, *Political Environment of Economic Planning*, 22–25; Bill, *Eagle and the Lion*, 120–127. The broader work of D&R, particularly its work in Colombia, is explored in Offner, *Sorting Out the Mixed Economy*.

	Military Aid	Economic Aid	Government Spending	Military Spending
1953	20.6	31.9	N/A	41.5
1954	25.6	84.5	183.3	50.3
1955	15.5	75.2	293.1	64.7
1956	23	74.7	308.9	81.9
1957	82.5	56	406.6	138.1
1958	104.9	52.1	524.1	168.6
1959	84.6	48	632.3	207.2

Figure 5.1 US aid to Iran and total Iran government spending (million $)[4]

regime. The shah's commitment to maintaining his authority superseded the interests of Ebtehaj, Lilienthal, and Clapp in furthering Iran's economic development. Ultimately dual integration worked only when it upheld the dominance of Iran's monarch.

5.1 After AJAX: Pahlavi Power Post-coup

After August 1953, the Eisenhower administration turned the shah's Iran into a US client state. Economic aid, loans, and grants totaled $422 million between 1953 and 1959. In addition to economic assistance, the United States furnished the shah with $353 million in military support between 1954 and 1959 (Figure 5.1).[5] The *Sazman-e Etaalaat va Amniyat-e Keshvar* (Organization of National Intelligence and Security) or SAVAK, established with help from the CIA in 1957 monitored civil society and rooted out dissent. Everything from Tudeh Party cells to mundane gatherings of young Western-educated intellectuals were subject to surveillance and repression.[6] In 1957, the CIA secured the shah's permission to establish listening posts near Iran's border with the Soviet Union to monitor Soviet nuclear tests.[7] The purpose of American support was threefold: stabilize Iran's economy, shore up the shah's

---

[4] Gasiorowski, *Iran as a Client State*, 102–103, 112.
[5] Figures above can be found in Gasiorowski, *US Foreign Policy and the Shah*, 93–95, 101–103, 109–126; see also Stephen McGlinchey, *US Arms Policies Towards the Shah's Iran* (New York: Routledge, 2014), 9–18; Bill, *Eagle and the Lion*, 114.
[6] Abdolreza Ansari notes in his memoirs how the "New Iran" tea parties organized by himself, Houshang Ram, and future-Prime Minister Jamshid Amuzegar were shut down by SAVAK, for fear that it would draw attention away from the state-sponsored Melliyun and Mardom political parties. "If we wanted to drink tea and discuss issues," Ansari recalled the head of SAVAK explaining, "we better join one of the parties and drink our tea with them." Abdolreza Ansari, *The Shah's Iran, Rise and Fall: Conversations with an Insider*, trans. Katayoon Ansari-Biglari (London: IB Tauris, 2017), 76–80.
[7] Roham Alvandi, "The Shah's Détente with Khruschev: Iran's 1962 Missile Base Pledge to the Soviet Union," *Cold War History* 14, no. 3 (2014): 431.

confidence and the capacity of his government to maintain internal security, and retain Iran's strategic alignment with the West. In all respects, the policy was successful.

The chief beneficiary of this policy was Mohammed Reza Pahlavi. Crouched in the American ambassador's office in Baghdad on August 17, 1953, having fled Iran in the wake of the failed first coup attempt on August 16, the shah seemed a defeated man. US officials did not regard the second Pahlavi as a particularly forceful personality and were leery of his qualifications to serve as head of a new government. Ambassador Loy W. Henderson suggested at one point that he could be replaced with one of his brothers.[8] Weighing his options in exile, the shah talked of relocating to America and taking on personal employment, "as he has a large family and very small means."[9] It was the lowest point in his reign. On August 19 a second coup attempt succeeded, and on August 22 the shah returned to the capital "a new man," his confidence restored by what he chose to see as a popular uprising to restore him to power.[10] Defying the low expectations set for him during the build-up to TPAJAX, the shah moved aggressively to take control of the Pahlavi state, rising to a position of authority that rivaled that of his father Reza Shah during the autocratic days of the 1930s.[11]

In 1955 the shah replaced coup leader Fazlollah Zahedi with longtime supporter and advisor Husayn 'Ala. Henceforth, the office of the prime minister was occupied by a loyalist with close ties to the Crown. The Majlis was filled with pro-shah deputies chosen through rigged elections. The shah created two political parties, Mardum and Melliyun, and parliamentary debates were carefully handled to mask the authoritarian approach to governance. The shah approved all laws beforehand. The regime's power rested first and foremost upon the army. Iran's military budget doubled to 4 billion rials in 1956 and doubled again to 8.2 billion rials by 1959.[12] Anxious to retain the goodwill of the officer corps, the shah showered his soldiers with funds, honors, and high-tech equipment.

---

[8] *FRUS Retrospective*: 589–593. While the shah's name is redacted from the exchange, the context very clearly implies he is the topic of discussion.

[9] *FRUS Retrospective*: 678–680. In his memoirs, the shah portrayed his flight to Rome as part of the coup operation: "I believed it would force [Mosaddeq] and his henchmen to show their real allegiance, and ... crystallize Persian public opinion." If so, he did not make this clear to anyone in Rome or Baghdad during his brief exile. See Mohammed Reza Pahlavi, *Mission for My Country* (London: Hutchinson, 1961), 104.

[10] *FRUS Retrospective*: 763–764.

[11] Afkhami, *The Life and Times of the Shah*, 187–189, 200–204.

[12] World Bank, *Recent Economic Developments in Iran and the Progress of the Third Plan*, Department of Operations, South Asia & Middle East (February 6, 1964), 6.

5.1 After AJAX: Pahlavi Power Post-coup

Additional political support came from those who had opposed Mosaddeq and backed the August coup: the landowning aristocracy, bazaar merchants, and Shi'a clergy.[13] Royal forces crushed the Tudeh and Iran's Leftists were kept under close surveillance by SAVAK. The National Front, decimated after August 1953, lingered on in diminished form.[14]

Yet even with SAVAK, a stronger military, and US assistance, the shah did not rule as a true autocrat. He shared some of his power with a handpicked group of elder statesmen while his autonomy was constrained by the needs to grow the economy and maintain cordial relations with the United States.[15] The effective end of democracy did not conceal the simmering discontent in most sections of Iranian society, particularly among Iran's urban middle-class, Mosaddeq's old constituency. While the shah outwardly believed the "uprising" against Mosaddeq in August 1953 proved his popular support, he was keenly aware of how his government would need to satisfy the unrest left over from the nationalization crisis and the coup. State propaganda promoted the shah's concept of "positive nationalism," containing what historian Cyrus Schayegh has called the "politics of promise." Attention focused on the improvement of material conditions at the expense of press freedom, political expression, or free elections.[16] The Pahlavi state could crush and repress its Leftist opposition. The middle class, however, it would buy off.

For a time, this strategy appeared to work. Oil and US aid provided a sturdy foundation for an economic expansion. After the Consortium Agreement of October 1954, the oil companies made good on their promise and increased Iran's oil output. From the oil-less days of the

---

[13] In return for their cooperation, the Pahlavi regime permitted the Shi'a leadership to crack down on religious minorities inside Iran, particularly members of the Baha'i sect. In 1955–1956, the shah's security forces took no action as mobs organized by the clergy converged on Baha'i centers throughout the country. Hundreds of Baha'i were killed and thousands more forced to recant. See Bill, *The Eagle and the Lion*, 101–102.

[14] Shapur Bakhtiyar, *Khatirat-e Shapur Bakhtiyar: nukhust-e vazir-e Iran, 1357* [Memoirs of Shapour Bakhtiyar: Prime Minister of Iran, 1979] ed. Habib Ladjevardi (Cambridge MA: Center for Middle Eastern Studies of Harvard University and Distributed by Ibex Books, 1996), 40–44.

[15] Cyrus Schayegh, "Mohammed Rezā Shah Pahlavi's Autocracy: Governmental Constraints, 1960s–1970s," *Iranian Studies* 51, no. 6 (2018): 895–896; Ansari, *Modern Iran Since 1921*, 125; Milani, *The Shah*, 225.

[16] While he began popularizing "positive nationalism" in press interviews in the mid-1950s, the shah explained the concept at length in his first book, published in 1961. See Mohammed Reza Pahlavi, *Mission for My Country* (New York: McGraw Hill, 1961), 111–131; Cyrus Schayegh, "Iran's Karaj Dam Affair: Emerging Mass Consumerism, the Politics of Promise and the Cold War in the Third World," *Comparative Studies in Society and History*, liv (July 2012), 612–643.

Mosaddeq era, revenues from petroleum accounted for 37–51 percent of all government receipts between 1954 and 1963.[17] Ample cash created an atmosphere conducive to a rapid expansion in credit: Iran's domestic debt grew by 35.7 billion rials between 1954 and 1962.[18] Lax import requirements and access to credit powered a private sector boom while public spending increased dramatically. Cars and buses filled thoroughfares once trafficked by ass-carts. Millions of Iranian families bought televisions, radios, refrigerators, and gas-fired stoves. Abadan, the old British company town, represented the broader changes in Iranian urban life: blue jeans, machine-rolled cigarettes, and Coke-a-Cola became staples of Iranian society.[19]

While cities prospered, Iranians in rural areas saw sluggish growth. As development and modernization programs targeted urban areas, the issues that had historically preoccupied both Iranian and foreign developmentalists – the plight of the rural poor and the need for land reform – remained prevalent. This was a product of political constraints: While he focused on mollifying the middle class, the shah avoided antagonizing the country's major landowning elite. The regime did not pursue substantive efforts to alter prevailing landowning patterns. As a result, few in Iran's rural peasantry enjoyed the fruits of the post-coup economic boom.

Despite this hesitation, Mohammed Reza Pahlavi made a new national development initiative a major priority in the years following the coup. According to Khodadad Farmanfarmaian, a US-trained economist who returned to work for the Plan Organization in 1958, "political pressure ... was directed in full force" toward development.[20] As with the First Plan, the program welcomed foreign assistance. Development groups that had shunned the Mosaddeq government now flocked to Iran, confident of a welcoming atmosphere and unperturbed by the overt authoritarianism of the Pahlavi government. This rush of activity was spurred on by an ideological consolidation within the foreign assistance community around a new development philosophy: modernization theory.

---

[17] World Bank, *Recent Economic Developments in Iran and the Progress of the Third Plan*, Department of Operations, South Asia & Middle East (February 6, 1964), 6.
[18] Farhad Daftary, "The Balance of Payments Deficit and the Problem of Inflation in Iran, 1955–1962," *Iranian Studies* 5, no. 1 (Winter, 1972): 8.
[19] Christian Rasmus Elling has explored the transformation of Abadan during the mid-twentieth century: See "Abadan: Oil City Dreams and Nostalgia for Past Futures in Iran," Ajam Media Collective [Accessed June 12, 2019] www.ajammc.com/2015/02/16/abadan-oil-city-dreams/
[20] Khodadad Farmanfarmaian, "Report on the Formation and Development of Economic Bureau, 1336–1342," 12, FFR, Unpublished Reports, Box 559, RAC.

5.2 Modernization Theory, Ebtehaj, and the Second Plan

In the 1950s, fostering economic growth in the Global South came to be viewed from the perspective of a unifying concept of historical change. "Development" was imagined to be systematic progress toward a societal model exemplified by the United States, a *weltanschauung* spread throughout the social sciences, government bureaucracy, and international development community that has come to be known as modernization theory.[21] The struggle of the global Cold War defined modernization's message. As social scientist Walt V. Rostow explained in *The Stages of Economic Growth: A Non-Communist Manifesto*, "traditional societies" progressed economically and culturally until they reached a "take-off" point, when their growth became self-sustaining.[22] The final stage mirrored the affluence, technological sophistication, and perceived political and social stability of post-war America. "Materialism without class conflict ... democracy without disobedience," according to historian Nils Gilman, was the desired end goal.[23]

Modernization theory's emphasis on "self-help" shaped the outlook on foreign assistance. Experts contended that aid was only useful if it helped to inculcate a culture conducive to free enterprise. Economic changes would in time bring democracy. "The keystone of political and social stability," argued William N. Rogers of the Middle East Institute in March 1954, "is primarily economic stability – not the reverse."[24] This ethos informed US aid policy, much of which benefited authoritarian anti-communist regimes. While the US government provided funds and defined the bounds of strategy, it was up to non-state actors – organizations like the Ford Foundation and World Bank – to engineer change on the ground.[25]

Eugene Black, president of the World Bank (1949–1963), argued that for modernization to become effective one needed "a deal more than money." True change only came with "promoting the right economic

---

[21] Gilman, *Mandarins of the Future*, 1–17; Gendzier, *Managing Political Change*, 1–13; Ekbladh, *The Great American Mission*, 1–12, 101–113; Latham, *The Right Kind of Revolution*, 34–61.
[22] Walt W. Rostow, *The Stages of Economic Growth: A Non-Communist Manifesto* (Cambridge: Cambridge University Press, 1960), 4–16.
[23] Gilman, *Mandarins of the Future*, 13.
[24] William N. Rogers, "A Program for International Economic Cooperation through the US of Private Institutional Agencies," March 20, 1954, MEI 8th Annual Conference, Papers of George C. McGhee Papers, Box 21, Georgetown University.
[25] For the work of private development firms, see Staples, *The Birth of Development*, 1–7; Matthew Connelly, *Fatal Misconception: The Struggle to Control World Population* (Cambridge MA: Harvard University Press, 2010), 18–45.

and financial policies," and offering aid and support to governments who first showed an interest "in thrashing out the difficult and inescapable conditions for making that aid effective."[26] Expertise opened the door to the potential locked away in countries like Iran, creating opportunities for local peoples and American capital while demonstrating the superiority of the liberal capitalist system. "The fundamental approach to the problems of the Middle East," declared former oil executive and State Department troubleshooter George C. McGhee, "lies in a thorough knowledge of the resources ... its manpower, land, water, minerals." The goal of the West should be to direct "our geologists, geographers, climatologists, hydrologists, agricultural experts, and anthropologists ... [toward] an understanding of the use to which these assets can be put."[27] While developmentalists imagined improving conditions in the impoverished Global South, engineering change presumed the superiority of American technology and methods.

A firm believer in the need to wed financial assistance to free enterprise was Iran's new development czar Abolhassan Ebtehaj. Following his dismissal by 'Ali Razmara in May 1950, Ebtehaj had gone into unofficial exile. The shah's return to power augured well for the technocrat, who enjoyed a good relationship with the Pahlavi monarch. The shah, conscious of Ebtehaj's international renown and anxious to make use of his reputation as an honest bureaucrat, offered him a choice between chairmanship of the National Iranian Oil Company or a position as managing director of the reconstituted Plan Organization. Ebtehaj chose the latter: He was to be "the de facto ruler of the planning process."[28]

Ebtehaj's boundless energy matched the atmosphere of urgency surrounding the shah's development program. According to Ebtehaj, it was useless to wait for the economy to develop itself: "Iran is the patient who will die if not operated upon."[29] Undeterred by the failure of the First Plan, Ebtehaj quickly drew up designs for the Second Seven-Year Plan. Budgeted at $930 million or 70 billion rials (later raised to $1.1 billion or 84 billion rials, roughly twice the size of the First Plan), the plan included large allocations for transportation and infrastructure, including dams for

---

[26] "What Answer to the Challenge of International Poverty?" Eugene Black, April 20, 1959, DELP Box 413, SGMML.
[27] George C. McGhee, March 19, 1954, "Challenges to Middle East Development," Papers of George C. McGhee Papers, Box 21, Georgetown University.
[28] Ebtehaj, *Khatirat*, 329–330; FISDS, *Umran-e khuzistan*, Introduction by Gholam Reza Afkhami.
[29] Ebtehaj, *Khatirat*, 396, Ebtehaj, San Francisco October 1957/Mehr 1336, quoted in *The Unified Development of the Khuzestan Region*, August 28, 1958, 108, DELP Box 409, SGMML.

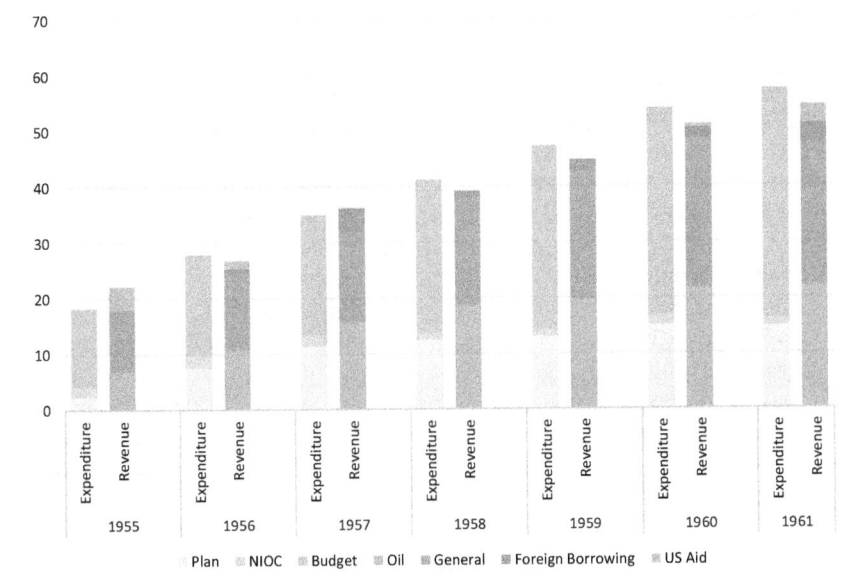

5.2 *Modernization Theory, Ebtehaj, and the Second Plan* 159

Figure 5.2 Iran's expenditures and revenues (billions rials), 1955–1961[30]

irrigation and electricity. Like the First Plan, Ebtehaj's new program would encourage public investment in agriculture, to increase productivity in Iran's largest economic sector and reduce social unrest in rural areas. Oil would provide support on a scale that exceeded the First Plan, where oil would have covered roughly one-third of total expenditures. The Plan Organization would receive 60 percent of oil revenues before March 1958 and 80 percent thereafter (Figure 5.2). Loans to cover spending gaps would be sought from the World Bank, which had shed some of its past conservatism. Revenues from oil "appear to be adequate" to cover the weight of the program, according to a bank estimate in 1957.[31] The bank would eventually provide $167.8 million in loans to Iran between 1956 and 1960.[32]

---

[30] Data from World Bank, *The Economic Development Program of Iran: An Appraisal, Part I, Main Report* (April 17, 1963), 15.
[31] World Bank, *Iran – Economic development (English)*, Asia Series, No. AS 55. (Washington DC: World Bank, 1957), 2.
[32] World Bank, *The Economic Development Program of Iran: An Appraisal, Part I, Main Report* (April 17, 1963), Report No. AS-93a, Table 22; Kamran Mofid, *Development Planning in Iran: From Monarchy to Islamic Republic* (Outwell UK: Middle East & North African Studies Press, 1987), 40, 90–95; Katouzian, *Political Economy of Modern Iran*, 203–204.

The plan's design reflected Ebtehaj's core beliefs: Large-scale projects built up over a period of several years could produce a "take-off." Public funds would spur private investment. To overcome the political barriers that had beset the First Plan, Ebtehaj obtained autonomy from the shah. "The wedge approach," as Farmanfarmaian termed it, involved directing oil wealth in a way that would avoid the corruption and venality Ebtehaj felt dominated the central government ministries. As with the First Plan, Iran's new development program would be a centrally run affair free from interference. The plan director's "greatest fight," according to Farmanfarmaian, was to keep money "out of the hands of the ministries," where he feared it would be wasted on vanity projects or distributed as largesse for political purposes.[33]

Despite the Second Plan's purpose, only around 50 percent of oil revenues between 1954 and 1962 actually went to plan projects. The rest was syphoned off to the general budget or utilized for special development initiatives, or *bongahs*, operated out of the central ministries. Try as he might, Ebtehaj could not keep all the oil money under Plan Organization control: Millions of dollars and billions of rials were spent on projects that were uncoordinated, disconnected, and frequently subject to budget overruns and graft.[34]

Ebtehaj's personality did not help matters. He was not an easy man to work with, and even his supporters within the Plan Organization regarded him as combative and stubborn.[35] "We fought two wars," recalled 'Abd al-Majid Majidi, a Plan Organization administrator, "one with the Ministry of Finance and, indeed, with the government over the plan's share of the oil revenue ... the second war was within our organization."[36] Despite this, the plan director inspired loyalty from the younger technocrats and he enjoyed the backing of the shah, who supported him even when his bickering reached the upper levels of government.[37]

---

[33] FISDS, *Barnameh rizi-ye*, Interview with Farmanfarmaian.

[34] The "two bridges of Khorramshahr" offered a case in point. Two rival *bongahs* launched separate construction projects in the port city of Khorramshahr, resulting in two bridges constructed at excessive cost where only one was needed. "Construction ... was rationalized on the grounds that all the world's major cities located on rivers have several bridges," reported the embassy. See RG 59 888.00/1-2158, US Embassy Tehran No. 630, January 21, 1958, USNA.

[35] 'Abd al-Majid Majidi, *Khatirat-e 'Abd al-Majid Majidi: vazir-e mushavir va ra'is-e Sazman-e Bar'namah va Budjih, 1351–1356* [Memoirs of 'Abd al-Majid Majidi, Director of the Plan and Budget Organization 1973–1977] Habib Ladjevardi, ed. (Cambridge MA: Iran Oral History Project, Center for Middle Eastern Studies Harvard University, 1998), 82–89; FISDS, *Barnameh rizi-ye*, Interview with Gudarzi, and Farmanfarmaian.

[36] *Barnameh rizi-ye*, Interview with 'Abd al-Majid Majidi.

[37] Ebtehaj, *Khatirat*, 399, 403.

5.2 Modernization Theory, Ebtehaj, and the Second Plan

Preoccupied with military matters, the monarch made time for his technocrats, and men like Farmanfarmaian regarded him as a "liberal" devoted to reform.[38] Yet he did not formally visit the Plan Organization headquarters until 1962 and offered only "general tips" on how the Second Plan should proceed.[39] According to one US profile, even as he pitted various advisors against one another, the Pahlavi monarch showed confidence in Ebtehaj, "the only Iranian he knows with a progressive, Western outlook and the only man with the strength to say no."[40]

Economic growth would presumably presage political development – the shah would not loosen his hold on power until Iran's economic situation had stabilized. Following a pattern set by other governments throughout the Global South, the Second Plan would showcase infrastructural achievements, such as hydroelectric dams and irrigation schemes, which acted as expressions of the state's conquest of nature and mastery of technology.[41] Ebtehaj may have considered himself progressive, but he had no interest in working outside the bounds of Iran's monarchy. The dutiful technocrat, Ebtehaj expended furious energy to execute a large development program quickly, before pressures from Iran's middle-class threatened the shah's hold on power. The plan would boost the prestige of the Pahlavi regime in ways that benefited the shah's authoritarian inclinations.

Financial concerns were overshadowed by a preoccupation with a shortage in skilled personnel. "The lack of experts," noted Hasan Shahmirzadi, a Plan Organization administrator, "was obvious in irrigation, agriculture, electricity, management, accounting, and other disciplines." There were simply not enough people to fill the thousands of roles created by the plan's growing list of projects.[42] Like the foreign developmentalists with whom he was closely identified, Ebtehaj thought his country was backward and underdeveloped. "Private, free-competitive industrial enterprise, as understood in America, does not at present exist, either in Iran or in the Middle East," he declared at a gathering of development advocates in San Francisco in late 1957. "Entrepreneurial activity, industrial management know-how, and technical skills are all in very short supply," and foreign help was welcomed "with open arms."[43] Ebtehaj did not prescribe to the notion of Iranian

---

[38] HIOHP, Farmanfarmaian, Tape 8, 1.
[39] Majidi, *Khatirat-e 'Abd al-Majid Majidi*, 93; HIOHP, Farmanfarmaian, Tape 8, 3.
[40] *FRUS 1955–1957*, XII: 910–920. [41] Mitchell, *Rule of Experts*, 21.
[42] FISDS, *Umran-e khuzistan*, Interview with Hasan Shahmirzadi.
[43] "Public and Private Enterprise in the Development of Iran," International Industrial Development Conference, San Francisco, October 17, 1957, DELP Box 406, SGMML.

incapacity. His eagerness for foreign help stemmed from pragmatism. For the plan to be successful, it would have to be executed with great speed and on a large scale. "I would *never* engage a foreign national if an Iranian was available," he later wrote, "[but] at the time I took over the Plan Organization, there was not a *single* Iranian group with any experience ... in carrying out important building projects."[44]

For this reason, the plan director invited assistance from a multitude of foreign organizations. By the late 1950s the World Bank, Ford Foundation, Rockefeller Foundation, Near East Foundation, Harvard University, and Government Affairs Institute operated alongside the Point Four technical cooperation mission. By 1957 these programs employed nearly 4,000 Americans and constituted one of the largest foreign aid efforts in the world.[45] For foreign observers, Iran's problem went deeper than a mere manpower shortage. In the aftermath of the coup, the US government continued to believe that Iran needed foreign guidance to achieve stability. According to the US embassy's official summary, the First Plan had failed not due to a lack of revenue, but because Iran lacked "competence and a sense of public responsibility in Government," and because it had not surrendered to the "guidance and discipline" provided by foreigners like Max Thornburg, the World Bank, and OCI.[46] "The Iranians," wrote one consular officer, "don't really understand how to use the wealth they have."[47] The view that Iran needed foreign assistance was widespread in the developmentalist community. "Iran is a country ancient in its culture, but young in concepts of modern development and education," according to Ford Foundation officer Kenneth Iverson.[48] Dual integration was too important to leave in Iranian hands. As Hector Prud'homme of the World Bank wrote to the developmentalist David Lilienthal, the Pahlavi regime had little need for more money. "What they need," he said, "is management."[49]

5.3 "A Pioneering Kind of Pattern": Lilienthal, Clapp, and the KDS

Ebtehaj met David Lilienthal at a World Bank event in Istanbul in 1955. Aware that Lilienthal was scouting on behalf of his company,

---

[44] Quoted in Bostock and Jones, *Planning and Power*, 141. Emphasis original.
[45] Bill, *The Eagle and the Lion*, 124–125.
[46] RG 469 RUSFAA Iran Branch, Subject Files 1952-1959, Box 1, Iran Economic Paper No. 1, "Summary of the Current Economic Situation," January 1953, USNA.
[47] RG 59 788.00/7-2057, US Embassy Tehran No. 83, July 20, 1957, USNA.
[48] Iverson to Hill, March 9, 1957 and May 23, 1957, FFR R-0812, RAC.
[49] Lilienthal, *The Road to Change*, 9–10.

5.3 "A Pioneering Kind of Pattern": Lilienthal, Clapp, and the KDS   163

Development and Resources Corporation, Ebtehaj invited the American to visit Iran. The plan director was "intense, cultivated, and utterly sincere ... positively incandescent, full of feeling," wrote Lilienthal, who agreed to a visit in early 1956. Hungry for opportunities, Lilienthal had been sniffing around for potential contracts in Africa and South America. The Plan Organization, he wrote to his business partner Gordon R. Clapp, was offering too much "hard money" to resist.[50]

In the global development movement, Lilienthal was a titanic figure. During the 1930s he spearheaded the Tennessee Valley Authority, a multipurpose dam project that brought electricity and irrigation to the Southeastern United States. The TVA was the most evocative symbol of New Deal-era liberalism, what social scientist James Scott has called the "grand-daddy of all regional development projects."[51] Lilienthal ranked among its most esteemed ambassadors, a man whose international contacts made him well-suited to advertising the benefits of TVA abroad. In the mid-1950s Lilienthal became an outspoken advocate for development, which he considered to be something of a religious calling.[52] Development and Resources Corporation was the chief means by which he spread his gospel.

Headquartered at 50 Broadway, New York City, D&R was a for-profit consulting firm specializing in construction projects outside the English-speaking world. It received financial backing from the investment firm Lazard Freres facilitated through Lilienthal's friend and sponsor, the financier Andre Meyer, and was in its infancy a speculative venture that won contracts largely through Lilienthal's name and international reputation. D&R's mandate was "to provide organizational, technical and financial guidance in the development of natural resources outside the United States."[53] Beneath that altruistic credo was commercial interest: Lazard and Meyer expected D&R and Lilienthal to produce some return on their investment.

---

[50] Lilienthal, *The Road to Change*, 10, 26; Lilienthal to Meyer, September 15, 1955, DELP, Box 398, SGMML.

[51] James Scott, *Seeing Like a State: How Certain Schemes to Improve the Human Condition Have Failed* (New Haven, CT: Yale University Press, 1998), 6; David C. Ekbladh, "'Mr. TVA:' Grass-Roots Development, David Lilienthal and the Rise and Fall of the Tennessee Valley Authority as a Symbol for Overseas Development, 1933–1973," *Diplomatic History* 26, no. 3 (Summer 2002): 335–374; Jason Scott Smith, "The Liberal Intervention of the Multinational Corporation: David Lilienthal and Postwar Capitalism," in Kim Phillips-Fein and Julian E. Zelizer, eds., *What's Good for Business: Business and American Politics since World War II*, (London: Oxford University Press, 2012), 107–122.

[52] David E. Lilienthal, *This I Do Believe* (New York, 1949), and *TVA: Democracy on the March* (New York, 1953); Fisher, "Moral Purpose is the Important Thing," 431–451.

[53] Announcement, September 1, 1955, DELP, Box 456, SGMML.

Expertise was the main export commodity of D&R. "In most of the so-called underdeveloped countries," Lilienthal wrote with his customary flourish, "there is an absence of business imagination, character, and creative financial judgement and experience."[54] The guiding concept for D&R was locked in the DNA of the TVA. Development schemes designed along the lines of the TVA could appeal to developing states, focusing national attention on infrastructural projects utilizing capital and expertise drawn from the free market: "a corporation clothed with the power of government," in President Roosevelt's original formulation, "but possessed of the flexibility and initiative of a private enterprise."[55] Lilienthal preached the gospel of development while quietly advancing the interests of American corporations in the Global South.

A talented promoter with a wide-ranging association that included prominent politicians, publishers, businessmen, and foreign heads of state, Lilienthal spent most of his time touring the world drumming up business for his fledgling firm. He left D&R's day-to-day management in the hands of Gordon R. Clapp, D&R president (Figure 5.3). "That red-headed boy," the quiet and hardworking Clapp joined TVA at twenty-seven and rose through the ranks to become Lilienthal's successor, serving as chairman for eight years. In many ways, Clapp was Lilienthal's polar opposite: "cautious and precise" where Lilienthal was bold, "formal in manner" when Lilienthal burst with energy, "a patient and skillful listener ... as much a teacher as an administrator."[56] Despite his reputation as a dry technocrat, Clapp was in fact a man of deeply held convictions who spoke out on a wide range of issues, from monopoly power in American business to the "tyranny of conformity" that gripped US society at the height of the Red Scare.[57]

Upon leaving TVA, Clapp threw himself into the postwar development mission, taking positions on the Advisory Committee on Voluntary Foreign Aid and leading the United Nations Economic Survey Mission to the Middle East in 1950. Working with George C. McGhee and the officers of the Near East Foundation, Clapp saw a use for the TVA model, "because it stands for water and water means life and everything

---

[54] Lilienthal, *The Road to Change*, 1–3.
[55] "Message to Congress Suggesting the TVA," April 10, 1933, FDRPL, www.docs.fdrlibrary.marist.edu/odtvacon.html; David E. Ekbladh, "Profits of Development: The Development and Resources Corporation and Cold War Modernization," *The Princeton University Library Chronicle* 69, no. 3 (Spring 2008): 487–506.
[56] Neuse, *Lilienthal*, 265–266; Harry L. Case, "Gordon R. Clapp: The Role of Faith, Purposes and People in the Administration," *Public Administration Review* 24, no. 2 (June 1964): 87.
[57] Gordon R. Clapp, "Anti-Intellectualism in Government," *Journal of Social Issues* 11, no. 3 (January 1955): 31–35.

5.3 "A Pioneering Kind of Pattern": Lilienthal, Clapp, and the KDS 165

Figure 5.3 Gordon R. Clapp (first on left) at a build site, 1953.
RG 142, Records of the Tennessee Valley Authority, NARA

in the Middle East."[58] Through exploring ways to harness the region's water, Clapp saw an important role for the Middle East's *other* important resource. "As a source of energy and an export to gain hard currency," he said in 1950, "oil is the outstanding economic link between the West and the Middle East." Yet an oil industry provided little in the way of lasting economic benefits. The companies' public relations material notwithstanding, investment in oil alone would not be enough to raise

---

[58] Advisory Committee on Voluntary Foreign Aid, Meeting of Voluntary Agencies and Interests in the Near East with Mr. Gordon Clapp, Chief of the UN Economic Survey Mission, September 2, 1949, Gordon R. Clapp Papers, Box 1, HSTPL.

standards of living, nor would it inoculate local regimes against communism.[59]

Clapp was keenly aware of the battle waged over access to natural resources, a contest to determine whether the world's bounty "will yield their life-giving wealth for a strong economy or be butchered, bartered, monopolized by a few to exact a higher tribute from the many." The TVA, a model replicated around the world, "evidence of its high export value," was proof of what could be accomplished "when people refuse to be intimidated or enchanted by the greedy or diverted from service to the public interest."[60] Clapp imagined wielding oil and water together into projects that delivered broad benefits beyond the narrow financial rewards of the private oil companies.

Lilienthal and Clapp arrived in Iran in February 1956. Their discussions with Ebtehaj focused on the southwestern Iranian province of Khuzestan, home to the national oil industry, "a salt marsh, [where] the heat is fantastic, and the water brackish," according to engineer and former Point Four translator Abdolreza Ansari. In the town of Dezful, the streets ran with filth while children "bathed their faces amidst the dirt and flies ... [and] waste poured into the street gutters."[61] Despite the obvious wealth of oil, Khuzestan ranked among the poorest and most destitute of Iran's rural provinces. Its wayward state belied a storied history. Khuzestan had boasted one of the world's oldest civilizations and Iran's ancient breadbasket. The historical connection offered the Pahlavi regime a unique opportunity to link former glories to the desires of the new, post-coup government. After a quick tour of the province, Clapp and Lilienthal concluded that Khuzestan offered an "unusually favorable setting" for a major development project.[62]

What D&R envisioned for Khuzestan was a TVA-style endeavor linking oil, water, and soil. Within the scope of the plan were fourteen hydroelectric dams, with the first constructed on the Dez River in a narrow canyon twenty-five kilometers northeast of Dezful (Figure 5.4); an irrigation project delivering water stored by the dam to 125,000 hectares of arable land turned over to sugar cane cultivation; a sugar mill and refinery capable of producing 30,000 tons of sugar each year; a

---

[59] "An Approach to Economic Development: A Summary of the Reports of the United Nations Economic Survey Mission for the Middle East," Gordon R. Clapp, May 14, 1950, Gordon R. Clapp Papers, Box 3, HSTPL. See also Shafiee, "Cost-Benefit Analysis," 95.
[60] Gordon R. Clapp, *The TVA: An Approach to the Development of a Region* (Chicago IL: University of Chicago Press, 1955), x, 2.
[61] Ansari, *The Shah's Iran*, 101; FISDS, *Umran-e khuzistan*, Interview with Ansari.
[62] Report from Lilienthal-Clapp to Ebtehaj, March 5, 1956, DELP, Box 403, SGMML.

5.3 "A Pioneering Kind of Pattern": Lilienthal, Clapp, and the KDS   167

Figure 5.4 Artist's rendition of the Dez Dam, 1958.
DELP, Box 426, SGMML

fertilizer factory fed from the excess natural gas produced in the oil fields; a polyvinyl chloride (PVC) factory, also fed by natural gas; and a transmission line linking Abadan to the city of Ahwaz, one that would draw on electricity in the oil city to power Ahwaz and its new industries until the

Dez Dam was completed. The total cost would be approximately $140 million.[63]

Spurred on by a profound sense of urgency, Ebtehaj offered D&R a contract laying out a "pioneering kind of pattern."[64] The company would have authority over budget disbursements, acting as the sole executive agency charged with managing contract labor and construction schedules. It was autonomy from within the Plan Organization, which was itself independent from the central state: For all intents and purposes, "D&R would *be* the Iranian Plan Organization in the Khuzistan region," boasted Lilienthal in his diaries.[65] Such freedom was immensely useful to D&R, as the company relied on its lucrative Iran contract to expand operations elsewhere. None of the company's other projects came close to the size and scope of the Khuzestan Development Service, which cost $11 million per year and employed 100 foreign staff and 5,000 Iranians by 1961.[66]

While D&R's focus remained fixed on the dam and irrigation project – "to free people from the tyranny of the rivers" was the company's stated goal – an important element of the KDS concerned Iran's fossil fuel resources.[67] "To many people," Lilienthal wrote to Ebtehaj, "oil is but a valuable raw material …. It is much more than that." Properly utilized, oil and gas could form the basis for "a great complex of inter-related chemical manufacturing … [and] a great industrial empire to balance with Iran's agriculture."[68] Cheap to produce though inordinately expensive to transport, natural gas from Iran's oil fields was treated as a byproduct: D&R estimated that 1 billion cubic feet burned off, with only 60 million retained for domestic consumption.[69] Moreover, a single PVC factory in Ahwaz, if suitably managed, could "open the way for private development of a sizeable petrochemical industry," growing the culture of free enterprise inside Iran.[70] Discussing it with oil expert Walter Levy, Lilienthal explained that his goal was to marshal oil and gas "to Iran's

---

[63] Lilienthal-Clapp to Ebtehaj, August 16 and 28, 1957, DELP, Box 406, SGMML; *The Unified Development of the Khuzestan Region*, August 28, 1958, 15–45, DELP, Box 409, SGMML.
[64] Lilienthal to Meyer, December 4, 1956, DELP, Box 403, SGMML.
[65] Lilienthal, *The Road to Change*, 125–129.
[66] DRCR Statement of Administrative Expense, July 1, 1957–June 30, 1958, DELP Box 408, John Allen, "The Khuzestan Development Project of Development and Resource Corporation," May 1962, 23, DRCR Box 559, SGMML.
[67] Lilienthal-Clapp to Ebtehaj, August 28, 1957, DELP Box 406, SGMML.
[68] Report from Lilienthal-Clapp to Ebtehaj, March 5, 1956, FFR R-0811, RAC.
[69] Seymour to Moment, July 27, 1962, DELP, Box 433, SGMML.
[70] Iran, Lilienthal-Clapp to Ebtehaj, August 28, 195, DELP, Box 406, Lilienthal to Black, September 3, 1958, DELP Box 409, SGMML. Summary of the project is in *The Unified Development of the Khuzestan Region*, 28 August 1958, 19, DELP Box 409, SGMML.

benefit ... so they can see the tangible human rewards of technical efforts," rather than simply draw rents from their export by foreign companies.[71] The KDS would act as the foundation of a national petrochemical industry, offering Iran a way to realize economic gains beyond the revenues generated by the consortium.

As D&R looked into Iran's future, to a vista of fracturing towers, gas flares, and plastics manufacturing, Lilienthal and Clapp consciously mined Iran's ancient past to bolster the KDS' propaganda potential. The KDS was a campaign "[to] restore the ancient fertility of the soil ... and build a modern agricultural and industrial nation," Lilienthal wrote to Ebtehaj.[72] A petrochemical industry would act as a demonstration, said Clapp, of how to "break through the inertia" holding back a general national takeoff: "The sooner the conversion of Iran's natural gas, now wasted, can result in new articles of use in Iranian homes and factories, the sooner the Iranian people will realize the significance of the aims and objectives of the Plan Organization's program."[73] Linked together, the oil, water, and soil of Khuzestan would be used to construct a new community of industry and agriculture, centered on the exploitation and utilization of fossil fuels: a petrochemical paradise.

Despite its supposed utility as a propaganda tool for Iran's new government, the KDS was a foreign enterprise. Touring the Dez Dam construction site, Abdolreza Ansari noted that all the managers supervising construction were Westerners, while all the laborers were Iranians.[74] Publicity was a problem: Few inhabitants of Khuzestan knew what the KDS was and those that did considered it "a foreign organization whose activities have little application to the ordinary life of the region."[75] There was very little voluntary mingling of Iranians and foreign staff. While efforts were made to find local housing in Ahwaz, a shortage of suitable apartments forced D&R to construct a cluster of modern homes on an estate just outside Ahwaz: "compound living had taken over" by 1960, much as it had been in the British oil city of Abadan before 1951.[76] Development work was lucrative for the foreign expert. One KDS official working a two-year contract received $21,000 a year, in addition to a pension, and thanks to the low cost of living in Khuzestan could save

---

[71] Lilienthal, *The Road to Change*, 104–107.
[72] Lilienthal-Clapp to Ebtehaj, August 28, 1957, DELP, Box 406, SGMML; Fisher, "Moral Purpose is the Important Thing," 437–443.
[73] Clapp to Ebtehaj, August 28, 1957, DELP, Box 406, SGMML.
[74] Ansari, *The Shah's Iran*, 102.
[75] T. A. Mead to Clapp, May 1, 1958, DELP Box 409, SGMML.
[76] "The Khuzestan Development Project of Development and Resource Corporation," John Allen, May 1962, DRCR, Box 559, SGMML.

$1,500 a month. This compared to an annual salary of $6,400 for high-ranking Iranian economists in the Plan Organization.[77] Coping with demands from the Plan Organization and hot weather put a strain on performance, but according to one American consul, "his skin grows thicker every time he receives a bank statement."[78]

Autonomous, cash-rich, and run entirely by foreigners, KDS was unpopular within the Pahlavi government. Critics lambasted it as a foreign attempt to exploit Iran's natural resources. As Lilienthal toured the world to drum up new business, Clapp fought bitter battles with Pahlavi bureaucrats to maintain D&R's autonomy and preserve its access to oil revenues. Many in the shah's government could not understand how a foreign company operated with such freedom, while others were genuinely disturbed by the stupendous amounts of money directed into an endeavor of dubious short-term benefit. Clapp offered a blunt response to such inquiries, noting that D&R's projects "are not intended to be subject to the ordinary regulations of government transactions."[79] Clapp was successful thanks to timely interventions from the plan director, who could bring his influence to bear and overrule other ministers. Ebtehaj missed few opportunities to boast of the KDS or its administrators. "There is no more competent, no more qualified and more reliable institution," he told *Ettela'at*, "than that of Lilienthal and Clapp."[80]

Ebtehaj's influence mattered because he enjoyed the shah's support. While rivals within the government, particularly the Minister of Mines and Industries Ja'far Sharif Imami, sparred with Ebtehaj over access to oil riches, the shah played favorites, maneuvering his ministers against one another. The shah saw value in KDS as a demonstration of his government's economic vitality, while Lilienthal was a useful ally in Iran's constant battle to secure international financing. In an address to a group of American businessmen in July 1958, the shah emphasized Iran's commitment "to use our vast oil resources wisely ... on the lines of the Tennessee Valley."[81] Bills supporting the plan only passed the Majlis

---

[77] Khodadad Farmanfarmaian, head of the Economic Bureau of the Plan Organization, received a salary of 4,000 tomans (or 40,000 rials) per month, for 480,000 rials or $6,400 a year. He noted later that his salary was second only to Ebtehaj. HIOHP, Farmanmaian, Tape No. 2, 18–19.
[78] RG 59 888.053/4-2460, US Consulate Khorramshahr, No. 65, April 24, 1960, USNA.
[79] Clapp to Asfia, September 29, 1958, DRCR, Box 456, SGMML.
[80] *Ettela'at*, August 28, 1957.
[81] From foreword to *The Unified Development of the Khuzestan Region*, 28 August 1958, DELP Box 409, SGMML.

"due to the shah's intervention," while criticism of KDS never stepped over the line into outright hostility.[82]

While controversial inside Iran, KDS collected plenty of critics from the development community. The Ford Foundation, which mockingly referred to Lilienthal's March 5, 1956, letter to Ebtehaj as the "'Rivers, Land and Sunshine' Report," regarded the TVA ethos as outdated, distracted by large-scale construction when more important work was being done at the village level.[83] In 1958 a team of Harvard University economists and administrators arrived in Iran, funded by the foundation and tasked with assisting Ebtehaj in establishing an economic bureau dedicated to formal analysis of development projects.[84] Team leader Kenneth Hansen was critical of the KDS, which he saw as symptomatic of an undue emphasis on "grandiose" construction projects that burnished the regime's prestige without delivering long-term economic benefits. Along with two other dam projects at Karaj and Sefid Rud, the Dez Dam made up more than 80 percent of total irrigation expenditure in the plan, and little money was left over for rural improvement, education, or sanitation.[85]

By 1958 D&R had burned through roughly $40 million in plan funds.[86] Construction on its major constituent parts had yet to begin. With progress on the Dez Dam, petrochemical plants, and irrigation network still years away, Clapp grew concerned with the project's lack of support. "In all honesty," he concluded, "what [Iranians] have observed thus far of KDS efforts is automobiles running around the countryside and expensive homes being built for occupancy by foreigners." Clapp proposed a further broadening of KDS into the realm of rural development that would immediately improve the lives of peasants living in Khuzestan, illustrating how Iran's government, "our client, is actively concerned with the welfare of its people."[87]

---

[82] Ebtehaj, *Khatirat*, 399.   [83] Egger to Iverson, May 4, 1956, FFR R-0812, RAC.
[84] For Ford Foundation activities in Iran, see Nemchenok, "That So Fair a Thing Should Be So Frail," 261–284; Matthew K. Shannon, "American-Iranian Alliances: International Education, Modernization and Human Rights during the Pahlavi Era," *Diplomatic History* 39, no. 4 (2015): 661–689; Brew, "What They Need is Management," 1–22.
[85] Division of Economic Affairs (Economic Bureau), Plan Organization, Iran, *Review of the Second Seven Year Plan Program in Iran* (Tehran, 10 March 1960), 28.
[86] KDS was classified in the general plan budget as "Regional Development," a subchapter that it shared with projects in the Kerman, Baluchistan, and Sistan provinces, which collectively made up 9 percent of the total and KDS the remaining 91 percent. See World Bank, *The Economic Development Program of Iran: An Appraisal, Part I, Main Report* (April 17, 1963), Report No. AS-93a, Table 25.
[87] Memo from Clapp, "Village Development," August 8, 1958, DRCR, Box 455, SGMML.

The founder of the TVA appeared less concerned. Lilienthal proposed more publicity aimed at a Western audience to increase support for KDS and the Second Plan internationally. Lilienthal worked through his friends Edward Luce of *Time* magazine and Arthur H. Sulzberger, publisher of the *New York Times*, to promote Iran's new program. He approached Edward R. Murrow, the famed American journalist, who flew to Iran in late 1959 to shoot a television program. The result, "Iran: Brittle Ally" was not the propaganda piece Lilienthal had hoped for: Murrow emphasized Iran's oil industry, the struggles of the Second Plan, and the authoritarian nature of the shah's government.[88] Lilienthal, a perpetual optimist, seemed curiously blasé about the risks surrounding his massive undertaking. The shah, he was sure, retained his "sense of social mission and urgency," and would continue in his steadfast support of both the plan and KDS.[89]

5.4 Scapegoat: The Shah Turns on the Second Plan, 1958–1962

Between 1958 and 1962, mounting political and economic crises arose to challenge Ebtehaj, D&R, and the whole idea of oil-based economic development in Iran. These crises, much like the events of 1949–1951 detailed in Chapter 2, undermined Iran's development program and exposed its American allies to pressures from opponents within the Pahlavi government. The shah, formerly the strongest backer of Ebtehaj and the Second Plan, lost faith in the program and turned both the plan and foreign developmentalists into scapegoats for his government's mounting problems. This *volte face* came after a series of major changes to Iran's internal and external circumstances.

In February 1958, SAVAK uncovered a conspiracy of military officers led by General Valiollah Qarani to overthrow the government. The officers, dissatisfied with the shah and the rampant corruption within his regime, hatched a plot to seize control and appoint the technocrat 'Ali Amini as prime minister.[90] In July, the neighboring pro-Western monarchy in Iraq fell to a bloody military coup led by General Abd al-Karim Qassem. Large-scale irrigation projects funded by oil revenues had done little to bolster the Hashemite regime's legitimacy. The events were a

---

[88] Lilienthal to Ebtehaj, June 25, 1958, DELP Box 409, "Iran: Brittle Ally," CBS Reports December 18, 1959, hosted by Edward R. Murrow, DELP Box 413, SGMML.
[89] Lilienthal, *Road to Change*, 278–279.
[90] Mark J. Gasiorowski "The Qarani Affairs and Iranian Politics," *International Journal of Middle East Studies* 25, no. 4 (November 1993): 625–644.

5.4 Scapegoat: The Shah Turns on the Second Plan, 1958–1962

wake-up call, particularly for the shah, who demanded greater support from the Eisenhower administration. Washington relented and increased aid to Iran in 1958. But US officials argued internally that the shah needed to shift away from his army and emphasize economic reforms. Iran's government was run "by a corrupt group of rich landowners," admitted CIA Director Allen Dulles at a meeting of Eisenhower's National Security Council. Without substantive changes, "[the shah's] days will be numbered."[91]

The Second Plan was supposed to have been the shah's tool for expanding his base of support. But three years into its seven-year run, the plan was underperforming. In January 1958, Ebtehaj admitted that the original $1.1 billion budget could not cover all the plan's projects, many of which were now experiencing cost overruns. A progress report completed the following month found that out of 1,023 social improvement projects, only 76 were complete, including schools and street asphalting left over from the First Plan.[92]

The problem went beyond the development program. After several years of frantic spending, Iran's finances were nearing at a breaking point. Hansen and Farmanfarmaian at the Economic Bureau examined Iran's accounts and found that expenditures on development, the military, and general administration far exceeded revenues. While the government was technically solvent by the end of 1958 thanks to larger-than-expected oil revenues and aid from the United States, in terms of total government spending Iran would post a $933 million deficit by September 1962. The World Bank, which had already extended several sizable loans to the Second Plan, suspended additional offers "until Iran's financial house is put in order."[93]

By the end of the year, Ebtehaj's position had grown tenuous. The budget dilemma had created an opening for his enemies, who were legion, to chip away at the Plan Organization's access to oil revenues. The Majlis passed a bill reducing the plan's budget, encountering no opposition from the shah. But Ebtehaj remained defiant. Iran was making "a gigantic effort," he wrote to Lilienthal in January 1959,

---

[91] *FRUS 1958–1960, XII*: 585, 604–615.
[92] RG 59 888.00/1-2058, US Embassy Tehran No. 637, January 20, 1958, 888.00/4-2658, US Embassy Tehran No. 876, April 26, 1958, 888.00 SEVEN YEAR/2-458, US Embassy Tehran No. 693, February 4, 1958, USNA.
[93] RG 59 888.00/10-2158, Economic Review, October 21, 1958, 888.00/1-659, Economic Review, January 6, 1959, 888.00/2-1756, Economic Assessment, February 17, 1959, USNA; Report on Economic Bureau (undated), FFR R-0812, RAC.

demonstrating "that it is possible to bring about rapid and far-reaching progress ... through democratic means and private enterprise."[94]

Though he held his ground on the budget debacle, Ebtehaj was undone by his criticism of Iran's military spending. Ebtehaj had always considered such expense a waste and insisted to one US military advisor that a "strong defense could only be built upon the back of a strong economy."[95] Such talk, made in the open and without consulting the shah, was dangerous given the monarch's "virtually insatiable" desire for new and expensive armaments.[96] During a final audience, the plan director implored Mohammed Reza Pahlavi to set aside military spending and embrace the plan. "If we invested oil revenues honestly, competently, and with dedication," he said, "we would not have to depend on armed forces. The people of Iran would be behind us."[97] Ebtehaj failed to carry the day. As with the First Plan, the shah faced a choice of whether to divert Iran's financial resources into arms or development. He chose the former, and had authority over all plan projects placed in the hands of the prime minister, an office which he effectively controlled. Ebtehaj had lost his independence and resigned shortly thereafter.[98]

The US embassy welcomed his departure. John Bowling, the political counselor, held a dim view of the Iranian developmentalist, whom he regarded as politically divisive and incompetent.[99] The embassy was growing leery of the Second Plan and had moved toward a more avowedly pro-shah position, one that would become much more apparent by the 1960s. Those closer to the development effort were more worried. While he had criticized Ebtehaj and his penchant for grandiose construction projects, economic advisor Kenneth Hansen felt the dismissal was carried out "with very little thought as to the consequences." Proponents of economic development "[have] lost a significant battle in favor of military [spending]," and Hansen feared the shah would choose to rely more heavily on the army.[100]

The fall of Ebtehaj and the shift in priorities away from development in 1959 had major consequences for D&R. As Clapp had feared, the project

---

[94] Ebtehaj to Lilienthal, January 12, 1959, DELP, Box 413, SGMML.
[95] FISDS, *Barnameh rizi-ye*, Interview with Farmanfarmaian.
[96] RG 59 888.00/2-1759, US Embassy Tehran No. 576, February 17, 1959, USNA.
[97] RG 888.00/2-1259, Wailes to State, February 12, 1959, USNA; Bostock and Jones, *Planning and Power*, 156.
[98] Imami, *Khatirat-e Ja'far Sharif Imami*, 185–189; Ebtehaj, *Khatirat*, 445–451.
[99] RG 59 888.00 SEVEN YEAR/2-2159, "Fall of Plan Organization Director Ebtehaj," February 21, 1959, USNA.
[100] FISDS, *Barnameh rizi-ye*, Interview with Majidi.

5.4 Scapegoat: The Shah Turns on the Second Plan, 1958–1962

was soon under attack from Iranian critics and foreign skeptics. The new plan director Khosrow Hedayat suggested a reduction in the KDS budget so that funds could be diverted to other projects of more immediate use. Framing the project in political rather than economic terms, D&R's leaders argued the Dez Dam had to be completed as a demonstration of the shah's desire for change. "The great tangibles," wrote Lilienthal, leaning on his gift for eloquence, "dams, power generators, better crops, and more factories – are as much the product of will and persistence as of money and skill … Khuzestan can once again become the breadbasket for Iran."[101]

As they parried blows from the Plan Organization, Lilienthal and Clapp came under new pressure from the World Bank. With the financial crunch, the Dez Dam needed $40 million in bank funding. Displaying some of the commercial conservatism that had featured so heavily during the First Plan period, the bank noted that the dam would take decades to pay for itself.[102] Lilienthal dismissed cost concerns and instead cited the project's "value as a symbol of progress and as proof of Iran's ability to meet the challenge of a great material achievement."[103] Rather than provide the program's economic bona fides, D&R instead emphasized the political potential of seeing KDS through to completion.

Lilienthal won a partial victory. The World Bank agreed to supply a $42 million loan to fund the Dez Dam in late 1959. But their conditions were strict. The irrigation project would be reduced from 125,000 hectares to a 20,000-hectare pilot project.[104] The showdown with the Pahlavi government also ended in a draw after Lilienthal and Clapp threatened to terminate their contract. The shah was loath to lose Lilienthal, a famous American who had proven useful in drawing international attention to Iran and had a good relationship with the World Bank. KDS would continue, but in a reduced capacity. The PVC plant was turned over to private financing, the fertilizer factory canceled, and total funding for the year reduced from $18.5 to $14.5 million.[105] D&R would also lose its autonomy in 1962 when it agreed to hand operational control over the remaining KDS programs to a new Iranian agency, the Khuzestan Water and Power Authority. The project as a whole would

---

[101] Lilienthal-Clapp to Hedayat, March 10, 1959, DELP, Box 413, SGMML.
[102] "Iran: Appraisal of the Dez River Project," June 30, 1959," DELP, Box 413, SGMML.
[103] Memo to Files, Seymour, July 23, 1959, DELP, Box 413, SGMML.
[104] Clapp to Oliver, September 15, 1959, Chapter IV, "Pilot Irrigation Project, First Phase of Dez Irrigation Scheme," Draft, October 7, 1959, DELP, Box 413, SGMML.
[105] Clapp to Hedayat, March 27, 1959, Status of PVC Program, March 31, 1959, DELP, Box 413, SGMML.

survive but the petrochemical paradise, built up and managed by American capital, receded from view.

Clapp did his best to bolster morale among the KDS staff, pointing out the Dez Dam's significance as a "national aspiration," one that the shah's government would be unwilling to abandon.[106] But confidence among the American developmentalist community in Iran reached a low ebb in 1959 when Iran's runaway economic bonanza finally ended. In 1960 Iran's unsustainable spending collapsed into a fiscal crisis. By early 1961 the economy had slipped into recession, teachers were campaigning for higher pay, and the National Front was calling for free elections after the Majlis vote in 1960 was revealed to be a fraud. Having ruled "through the security forces" for years, the shah now faced a growing wave of popular and political discontent.[107] Lilienthal found the shah "worried, fearful, and defensive," his mind consumed by fears of "internal enemies."[108]

The shah responded to this situation by pivoting away from development. Politically, the Second Plan lost its appeal once it became clear that the project's vast outlays had done little to allay middle-class discontent with the regime. In April 1961 the shah pushed out Hedayat and installed Ahmed Aramesh as plan director. The brother-in-law of the shah's hand-chosen prime minister and Ebtehaj arch-nemesis Ja'far Sharif Imami, Aramesh was a court lackey believed by the US embassy to be "corrupt, venal and highly anti-American."[109] Upon assuming his position, Aramesh went on a highly publicized speaking tour denouncing the Second Plan, Ebtehaj, foreign experts, the World Bank, and the idea of oil-backed development. The plan, he said, was marked by "extravagance and indecision," particularly in the case of the KDS. Lilienthal and Clapp, he railed, had "pillaged Iran's money and had to return it."[110] While the shah remained above the fray, it was clear Aramesh acted on royal instruction and functioned to discredit the plan and its foreign experts in order to steer attention away from the government's mounting political and fiscal challenges.

In the last two full years of KDS operations, the fortunes of Clapp and Lilienthal waxed and waned with those of the Second Plan. Forced by the

---

[106] Notes on Clapp Remarks to KDS Staff, September 4, 1959, DELP, Box 413, SGMML.
[107] John Bowling, "Current Internal Political Situation in Iran," February 11, 1961, NSF Box 115a, JFKPL.
[108] Lilienthal to Clapp, March 8, 1961, DELP, Box 426, SGMML.
[109] RG 59 888.00/2-2861, "Preparation of the Third Economic Development Plan," February 28, 1961, USNA; FISDS, *Barnameh rizi-ye*, Interview with Gudarzi.
[110] Ansari, *The Shah's Iran*, 114–115.

5.4 Scapegoat: The Shah Turns on the Second Plan, 1958–1962

United States to appoint the pro-development 'Ali Amini as prime minister, the shah relieved Aramesh from his post as head of the Plan Organization in May 1961. The new chief of development, the stolid engineer Safi Asfia, extended an olive branch to Clapp and the government publicly expressed its support of KDS.[111] But despite high expectations, the Amini government was incapable of turning the tide of opposition against the Plan Organization. This was made abundantly clear when in November 1961 Ministry of Justice agents arrested Ebtehaj. The charges, which were not announced formerly until January, centered around "illegally spending public funds and concluding agreements against the interests of the nation." Lilienthal and Clapp were directly implicated.[112]

The arrest marked the end of the Second Plan's credibility and the beginning of the end for D&R. The public arrest of such a prominent figure meant that "planning, Plan Organization, development schemes and foreigners are all under suspicion," according to one Harvard economist working in Tehran.[113] Once again, the move originated with the shah, who was trying to undermine Amini and divert more political attention toward foreign development firms and the discredited Second Plan. Iran's monarch, who had rarely concerned himself with the precise details of KDS, now became openly critical of its shortcomings. "We've spent $25 million on 2500 hectares," he argued to Ansari, yet what was there to show for it?[114] Even Asfia, compelled by political pressure, declared an end to "one-sided contracts ... lavish concessions and privileges to foreign experts."[115] Behind closed doors, Ansari and Asfia tried to mollify an increasingly frustrated Clapp, promising to preserve the D&R contract. Clapp and his staff struggled with the cognitive dissonance surrounding them, as both the Plan Organization and D&R "were simultaneously patted on the back and kicked in the teeth."[116]

After the collapse of the Amini government in June 1962 it was unclear how the Pahlavi regime would proceed, either politically or economically, to settle the challenges arrayed against it. The nature of these challenges – examined in greater detail in Chapter 7 – eluded easy

---

[111] Memo, Asfia and Ansari to KDS, May 16, 1961, DRCR, Box 457, SGMML.
[112] Summary of Report read by Alamouti, Minister of Justice, January 21, 1962, DELP, Box 433, SGMML.
[113] McLeod to Mason, December 3, 1961, FFR R-0813, RAC.
[114] Blumberg to Oliver, August 23, 1962, DRCR, Box 458, SGMML.
[115] Hanson, Letter to NYC Office, January 13, 1962, DELP, Box 433, SGMML.
[116] Oliver to Clapp, February 20, 1962, Blumberg to Oliver, July 10, 1962, Blumberg to Oliver, July 18, 1962, Blumberg to Oliver, August 23, 1962, DRCR, Box 458, SGMML.

solutions. But it was obvious that both the Second Plan and the Khuzestan Development Service had been thoroughly disgraced and the reputation of the development effort sullied beyond repair. Lilienthal fretted to George C. McGhee that a "paralysis" had set in at the Plan Organization.[117] In mid-1962, the shah's government faced a dissatisfied populace, an empty treasury, and a defunct economic policy. It was not clear what would fill the void. "We don't have a government," Farmanfarmaian grumbled. "The Shah doesn't control the state. The Prime Minister doesn't. We have about 3000 men, each with places of authority, and nobody can make them work together."[118]

5.5 Conclusion

Gordon R. Clapp died on April 28, 1963, the victim of a heart attack brought on by years of overwork. Clapp's death left Lilienthal and much of the D&R reeling. "It just doesn't seem possible that he is no longer with us," wrote D&R's Tehran representative John Blumberg.[119] His loss was felt just as acutely in Iran, where the community of developmentalists in the Plan Organization held an impromptu memorial service. "A great American," wrote Farmanfarmaian, "he calmly and firmly faced the attacks of the demagogues and the indifference of the ignorant, in his country and ours, without wavering a moment in his convictions."[120]

With Clapp's death, D&R's marginalization inside Iran accelerated. Having slandered D&R in the press, the shah's government was determined to reduce foreign experts "to an absolute minimum." The terms of D&R's new contract greatly restricted its former autonomy.[121] Political opposition was not enough to kill the Dez Dam. Renamed the Mohammed Reza Pahlavi Dam, the massive structure was completed in March 1963 and commemorated by several speeches, none of which mentioned D&R, the World Bank, Clapp, or Lilienthal. The shah kept Lilienthal at a distance and D&R's activities in Iran declined. By 1967 the company was in such dire financial straits that Lilienthal was forced to invest $50,000 of his own money to keep it afloat.[122]

---

[117] Memo of Conversation, Lilienthal and McGhee, April 4, 1962, DELP Box 433, SGMML.
[118] Memo of Conversation, Haldore Hansen and Farmanfarmaian, April 16, 1962, DRCR Box 537, SGMML.
[119] Blumberg to Oliver, May 12, 1963, DRCR, Box 458, SGMML.
[120] *Kayhan*, May 2, 1963.
[121] Oliver to Clapp, February 25, 1963, DRCR, Box 458, SGMML.
[122] Neuse, *Lilienthal*, 273.

5.5 Conclusion

The former TVA chairman remained a friend to the Pahlavi court, writing fawning letters to the shah that the "heroic and historic" endeavor in Khuzestan "is only a beginning."[123] Though it would remain active in Iran until the late 1970s, Lilienthal's enterprise would never again reach the size or scale of the Khuzestan Development Service.[124]

D&R's project was not a total failure. The Pahlavi Dam produced electricity to power the Khuzestan region. The sugar fields at Haft Tapeh provided the basis for an industry that endured into the twenty-first century. Men like Farmanfarmaian, Manuchehr Gudarzi, 'Abd al-Majid Majidi, Hasan Shahmirzadi, and Abdolreza Ansari earned administrative experience working alongside Clapp and his colleagues. For D&R's president, watching a cadre of dedicated patriots emerge from the ashes of KDS "has been one of the most heartening facts of the Iranian scene," and worth the estimated $135 million in oil funds and World Bank loans expended on the project between 1956 and 1963.[125]

Lilienthal and Clapp had come to Iran in the hopes of transplanting the TVA into an Iranian context, uniting agricultural, industrial, and fossil fuel operations into a petrochemical paradise that could kick-start private investment in Iran's economy. They also hoped to run their project as an autonomous entity, free from Pahlavi state interference. A belief in Iranian incapacity motivated American aid to the Second Plan, both from D&R and other developmentalist groups that flocked to Iran in the wake of the coup. Yet Lilienthal and Clapp were dependent upon the support of Iranians, primarily Ebtehaj and the shah, for their autonomy. Once their political support ebbed, the scope of their project shrank from its original, lofty heights, until the shah himself turned on D&R and used the company as a scapegoat for his government's broader failure to secure itself in the face of financial and political crises.

The disappointing results of the KDS reflected the larger problems affecting the Second Plan (Figure 5.5). The plan's major achievements were infrastructural: the national road network expanded, the port at Khorramshahr enlarged, three hydroelectric dams and four smaller irrigation dams erected, and countless smaller projects completed across the

---

[123] Lilienthal to Mohammed Reza Pahlavi, April 15, 1964, DRCR, Box 458, SGMML.
[124] Iran, Memorandum, April 3, 1963, DELP, Box 439, SGMML.
[125] Clapp to Farmanfarmaian, February 27, 1962, DRCR, Box 458, SGMML.

Expenditures	1955–56	1956–57	1957–58	1958–59	1959–60	1960–61	1961–62	1962	Total	%
Agriculture/Dams	5.9	19.5	38.1	40.4	34.2	36.9	30.7	13.2	218.9	21.8
Transportation	14.2	43	53.2	49.4	61.9	72.6	69.7	32.8	396.8	39.5
Industry	5.7	16.2	22.3	19.3	14.4	4.8	3.5	1.1	87.3	8.7
Social Affairs	4.8	15.5	20.2	21.1	16.3	19.8	25.6	18.2	141.5	14.1
Regional (including KDS)	0.6	3.5	12.2	26.4	30.4	32.7	37.8	15.3	158.9	15.8
Totals	31.2	97.7	146	156.6	157.2	166.8	167.3	80.6	1,003	100

Receipts

Oil	23.5	72.6	100.3	103.5	125.9	143.3	155.6	87.2	811.9	64.6
World Bank Loans	–	10	55	10	16.1	25.4	31.4	19.9	167.8	13.2
US Aid	–	–	–	6.5	33.8	12.9	57.3	19.1	129.6	10.2
Non-US Foreign Aid	–	–	–	–	–	–	4.2	3	7.2	.5
Private Capital and Short-Term Credits	8.9	18.1	–	45.6	13.3	36.4	16.3	6.8	145.4	11.5
Total Receipts	32.4	100.7	155.3	165.5	189.1	218	264.8	136	1,261.9	100
Deficit Balance	–	–	+3.8	–	–2.9	–0.9	+14.9	+16.1	+31	

Figure 5.5 Total Second Plan spending (million $)[126]

country.[127] The Second Plan period of 1954–1962 laid the foundation for Iran's transition into a modern industrial state and helped raise living standards in the major cities, accelerating the rise of an educated and upwardly mobile middle class. Yet for countless millions, it was hard to gauge the plan's accomplishments. Critics blamed Iranian incapacity, arguing that the country did not possess the indigenous expertise needed to handle a project on the scale of the Second Plan. While such views reflected cultural prejudice, they nevertheless contained a kernel of truth. Plan spending proceeded in an uncoordinated fashion, disconnected from the equally rapid expansion of the Pahlavi government. The Second Plan's ambition was matched by its disorganization. These problems did not reflect a lack of Iranian skill, but rather the corruption and political imbalances present within the shah's government.

Urgency compelled Ebtehaj to approve projects without the proper preparation. His solution to a lack of skilled manpower was to hire

---

[126] World Bank, *The Economic Development Program of Iran: An Appraisal*, Part I, *Main Report* (April 17, 1963), Report No. AS-93a, Table 22, 23, and 25. "U.S. Aid" includes grants from the Development Loan Fund, PL 480, and the Export-Import Bank. "Private Capital and Short-Term Credits" includes money carried over from the First Plan.

[127] Bostock and Jones, *Planning and Power*, 138–139.

5.5 Conclusion

foreign experts. But this left the plan vulnerable to criticism and fomented a backlash that set in after the shah deprioritized development in 1958. Finally, the plan's shortcomings revealed the inadequacies of Ebtehaj's conception of development. The plan director's enthusiasm for grand construction projects diverted millions of dollars and billions of rials into expensive irrigation schemes like the KDS. These projects would, in time, deliver productivity gains to the rural peasantry, but they were launched first and foremost as propaganda tools to benefit the political needs of the Pahlavi government. The success of the plan was not solely measured in economic terms. Its purpose was to provide a justification for the shah's return to power in August 1953.

The Second Plan was an Iranian enterprise. Yet it also reflected American foreign policy and the aspirations of the global development movement. Support for the Second Plan represented the US belief that dual integration – the idea that oil could fund development and petroleum produce progress – would secure Iran for the West. In the case of the Khuzestan Development Service, oil and natural gas were directly linked to projects designed to boost Iran's agricultural output and improve the living conditions of the peasantry. By the 1960s, however, US policymakers viewed the dual integration of Iranian oil with increasing skepticism. The political results of oil-based development were disappointing. The shah's reign looked as shaky in 1960 as it had been in 1953. Given how the shah's rule after 1953 turned authoritarian and emphasized material improvements over more meaningful political and social reforms (including land reform), the result should not have been surprising. To US diplomats, professional developmentalists, and Iranian bureaucrats the country appeared at yet another point of transition – a moment that coincided with a period of intense change and upheaval in the global oil economy.

6   The Golden Goose
Iran, the Consortium, and the First OPEC Crisis, 1954–1965

In April 1959, six men gathered at the Cairo Yacht Club. They arrived in separate cars and staked out a table under the shade of a single palm tree. It was all very "James Bond," as one participant recalled.[1] The conspiratorial atmosphere was apropos. These men represented the six major oil-producing countries of Latin America and the Middle East, and what they met to discuss was nothing less than the destruction of the oil oligopoly and the transformation of the global oil economy. The most vocal advocates, Venezuela's Juan Pablo Pérez Alfonso and 'Abdullah al-Tariki of Saudi Arabia, pressed their four comrades – including Manuchehr Farmanfarmaian of Iran[2] – to pressure the companies into relinquishing their hold over price and production. The six men signed a "gentleman's agreement," henceforth known as the Maadi Pact, to establish a "consultative assembly" from which to challenge the oligopoly. The group proposed in Cairo would become the Organization of the Petroleum Exporting Countries (OPEC) the following year. For the first time, petro-nationalism had been organized on an international scale.[3]

Where did Iran fit in all this? It was not entirely clear. While Farmanfarmaian was present at the Cairo meeting, he declined to make any kind of commitment on behalf of his government. When Iran joined OPEC in 1960, it did so from a position of ambivalence. Mohammed Reza Pahlavi liked to talk about oil, but he rarely stuck to the same policy for very long. In 1962, the shah dined with Kermit Roosevelt, former CIA agent and now an executive for Gulf Oil. The shah seemed skeptical of OPEC, admitting "with a wry smile" that some of the ideas bandied about by the group's more enthusiastic supporters did not interest him.[4]

---

[1] Quoted in Pierre Terzian, *OPEC: The Inside Story* (London: Zed Books, 1985), 25.
[2] Manuchehr's half brother Khodadad worked with Ebtehaj in the Plan Organization. Their father was Abdolhossein Farmanfarma, a Qajar prince who served as prime minister from 1915 to 1916.
[3] Farmanfarmaian, *Blood and Oil*, 339–342; other accounts of the meeting are Terzian, *OPEC: The Inside Story*, 25–26, Garavini, *The Rise and Fall of OPEC*, 114–115.
[4] FO 371/164606 Rose to Eagers, May 11, 1962, UKNA.

In December 1963 Roosevelt visited Iran yet again. The shah had now changed his tune. Against the advice of some of his closest councilors, Iran's monarch was pushing the companies to the brink, requesting more money and more production while threatening unilateral action if his demands were not met. "Bargaining is what the companies and governments will have to live with for a number of years to come," he told Roosevelt.[5] The dove had turned hawk.

The shah's changing stance reflected a transformative time in the global oil economy. In the late 1950s, the oligopoly's two historic problems – abundance and petro-nationalism – returned to the fore. A persistent supply glut and increasing competition coupled with a growing assertion of national rights over petroleum resources eroded the dominance the major oil companies had demonstrated during the Mosaddeq crisis. Dual integration had been firmly established, but its effects altered the balance between states and companies, as did the conditions of the Cold War. The companies retained the power to cut the price of oil. But doing so would have ramifications for the oil-producing governments that had become financially dependent on the oligopoly's operations. The shah's oil advisor and OPEC general secretary Fu'ad Ruhani argued that national governments deserved sovereign control over changes in price and production. The shah himself felt that Iran deserved more money due to its importance as a US ally in the Cold War. By the early 1960s, the fifty-fifty mechanism for dividing profits between producers and companies had lost its relevance. It was unclear how the companies or the member countries of OPEC would replace it.

The result was the "First OPEC Crisis," an episode in oil's history that has, until now, gone largely untold. The first showdown between OPEC and the oligopoly unfolded across boardrooms and conference halls on three continents between 1960 and 1965. Iran played a central role.[6] The dispute centered on esoteric elements in the payment of royalties. But at its core lay a debate over how to manage the global oil economy and whether there needed to be a new basis of equitability between sovereign governments and oil-producing states. Within Iran's oil consortium, "a hydrocephalic ... sometimes frustrating mechanism," members debated

---

[5] FO 371/172530 Powell to Rose, December 4, 1963, UKNA; *FRUS 1961–1963, XVII*: 826–830.
[6] See Garavini, *The Rise and Fall of OPEC*, 145–153. Other brief accounts can be found in Bamberg, *Vol. III*, and Bennett H. Wall, *Growth in a Changing Environment: A History of Standard Oil Company (New Jersey), Exxon Corporation, 1950–1975* (New York: McGraw-Hill, 1988). Documents from the UK National Archives related to this period of OPEC's early history have been published: see A. L. P. Burdett, *OPEC Origins & Strategy, 1947–1973*, vol. 1 (Slough: Archive Editions, 2004).

how producers' desires should be satisfied.[7] The debate revealed deep fissures among the companies, presaging the divisions that would tear apart the oligopoly a few years later during the oil price revolution of the 1970s. The Pahlavi state was equally divided. Among the shah's ministers, OPEC supporters led by Ruhani battled more conservative ministers who hoped to preserve a close relationship with the consortium.[8] Try as he might to play the petro-nationalist, the shah was hesitant to jeopardize his relationship with the oligopoly.

Traditionally dismissed in histories of global oil, OPEC's first crisis ended in a draw. Yet the showdown resulted in Iran embracing a state of perpetual petroleum dependence, linking the shah more closely to the operations of the companies. It demonstrated OPEC's inability to act collectively, highlighting individual state interests and members' overriding desire to earn more revenue from oil, rather than utilize market power to overturn unequal terms of exchange across the global economy. In that sense, the first OPEC crisis illustrated the group's fundamentally conservative nature, rather than its capacity for revolutionary action. As power shifted away from the oligopoly, the crisis of the early 1960s marked the end of oil's "golden age" and the beginning of the oligopoly's slow decline, a gradual retreat on price and production that presaged the more spectacular events of the 1970s. This process began with a return of oil's perennial problems: overabundance of petroleum and a surge of petro-nationalism in the Global South.

6.1 Golden Age: The Mechanics of the Oligopoly, 1954–1960

Between 1951 and 1961, the growth in the world oil trade was 75 percent greater than the aggregate increase in movements of all other commodities. By a wide margin, oil was the most valuable traded good on earth.[9] The 1950s saw the local integration of oil across the industrialized West, the birth of what Daniel Yergin has called "Hydrocarbon Man," where every facet of daily life revolved around the consumption of fossil fuels.[10] As a source of energy, oil finally surpassed coal, increasing *Fu'ad* from

---

[7] RG 59 888.2553/3-3158, US Embassy Tehran No. 868, March 31, 1958, USNA.
[8] FISDS, Gholamreza Tajbakhsh and Farokh Najmabadi, eds., *Yad'dasht'ha-ye Fu'ad Ruhani, nukhustin Dabir-e Kull-e Sazman-e Kishvar'ha-ye Ṣadir'kunandah-ye Naft (Upik) va Na'guftah'hayi darbarah-ye siyasat-e nafti-e Iran dar dahah-yi pas az milli shudan* [The Diaries of Fu'ad Ruhani, First Secretary General of the Organization of the Petroleum Exporting Countries (OPEC), and Understanding the Oil Policy of Iran in the Age After Nationalization] (Published online by the Foundation for Iranian Studies, 2013).
[9] BP 100334 The Price of Oil, Trade Relations, July 13, 1962.
[10] Yergin, *The Prize*, 523–542.

6.1 The Golden Age: The Mechanics of the Oligopoly

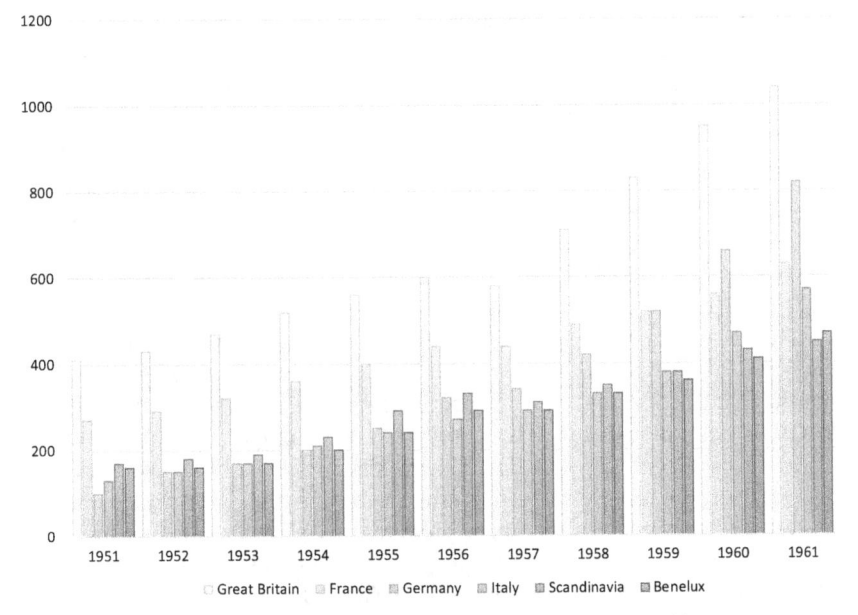

Figure 6.1 European oil consumption (thousand bpd)[11]

24 percent of global energy consumption in 1949 to 43 percent in 1971. It supplied 57 percent of the energy consumed in Western Europe, where consumption grew from 1.4 million bpd to 4.6 million bpd between 1951 and 1961 (see Figure 6.1). Global production in 1948 was 9.4 million bpd, with 25 percent produced for export; by 1959, production had doubled to 20 million bpd with the share for export rising to 40 percent.[12] There was more oil flowing throughout the world and almost all of it passed through the hands of the oligopoly.

The seven majors – BP, Gulf, Texaco, Socal, Jersey Standard, Shell, and Socony-Mobil, or the "Seven Sisters" as Italian oil magnate Enrico Mattei called them – together with the French firm CFP controlled 84 percent of production, 90 percent of reserves, and 65 percent of refining capacity in the Eastern Hemisphere in 1959. There was a constellation of smaller companies, many of them American, that worked around the edges of the oligopoly. But the major companies exerted an irresistible influence over the global oil economy. While sources in

---

[11] F. S. Smithers and Co, *International Oil Industry* (New York: F. S. Smithers and Co, September 1962), 51.
[12] Garavini, *Rise and Fall of OPEC*, 107.

Venezuela and Indonesia remained important to the global oil trade, the center of oil's galaxy was the Middle East. Middle East reserves were conservatively estimated at 78 billion barrels in 1953, 2.5 times greater than those of the United States. Yet the region, which accounted for 26 percent of production capacity, amounted to only 4 percent of production costs. Gross receipts in 1960 equaled $3.6 billion. A report by the consulting firm of Arthur D. Little concluded that the rate of return on Middle East oil between 1956 and 1960 was over 60 percent, with an average in Iran over 70 percent. Operations in the Middle East remained very cheap and extremely profitable.[13]

The bedrock of the oligopoly's energy order was the fifty-fifty concession system. Since 1930, the major companies had invested $4.1 billion in the Middle East, which according to some estimates would supply 80 percent of global demand by 1970.[14] The oligopoly's members managed the region's production through concessions that were split and shared between them. Given its importance to the global oil economy and their own profitability, the companies prioritized extending fifty-fifty profit-sharing agreements with all producing states in the early 1950s. With the regional implementation of fifty-fifty complete after 1954, producers' "take" from the oligopoly's operations increased, rising to over $400 million annually for Kuwait, $350 million for Saudi Arabia, and $280 million for Iran by 1958 (Figure 6.2).[15] The oligopoly had constructed an engine for the production of wealth, and the terms of equitability meant that much (though not most) of the wealth was shared with local governments.

The fifty-fifty division of profits was based on oil's posted price. First published in 1950, the posted price was the result of a calculation adding freight costs to the Gulf of Mexico price, the global benchmark used since the 1930s. The resulting price for Persian Gulf oil was between $1.75 and $2.00 per barrel, compared to $2.65–$3.00 for oil produced in United States and Venezuela. This arbitrary pricing mechanism served an important purpose.[16] For the oligopoly, setting the price for Persian Gulf oil according to the Gulf of Mexico benchmark prevented "unnatural demand for oil coming from the cheapest source," according to one

---

[13] Figures are from Jacoby, *Multinational Oil*, 49–55; Charles Issawi and Mohammed Yeganah, *The Economics of Middle Eastern Oil* (New York: Preager, 1963), 61, 75, 104; Ian Seymour, *OPEC: Instrument of Change* (New York: St. Martin's Press, 1981), 15.

[14] Burdett, *OPEC Origins & Strategy, 1947–1973*, vol. I, "Middle East Oil: Report by a Working Party of Officials," 267–349.

[15] Issawi and Yeganah, *Economics of Middle Eastern Oil*, 129.

[16] For an analysis of the posted price, see Helmut J. Frank, *Crude Oil Prices in the Middle East* (New York: Praeger, 1966), 29–60; Penrose, *The Large International Firm*, 173–197.

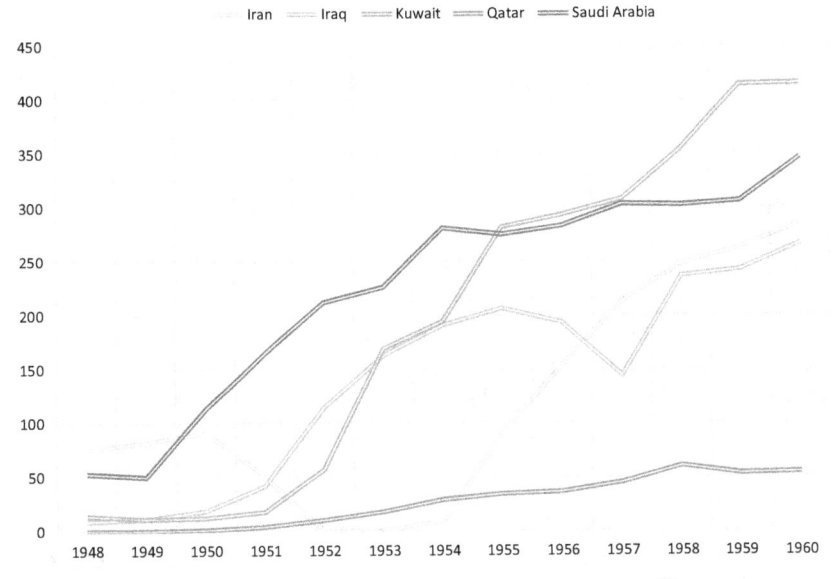

6.1 The Golden Age: The Mechanics of the Oligopoly

Figure 6.2 Revenues from oil (millions $) 1948–1960[17]

BP study.[18] In layman's terms, it meant that Middle East oil was not *too* cheap compared to crude from North America and Venezuela, where the oligopoly retained significant interests.[19]

As a measure of oil's value, the posted price was pure invention. Each oligopoly member was vertically integrated: Crude oil passed from wellhead to market without ever leaving the hands of the firm and produced no real market transactions, as each company was simply selling the oil to itself via subsidiaries.[20] Oil sold between the oligopoly's members or to third parties did not abide by the posted price, but instead went for market rates that fluctuated, usually at a discount below the posted price ranging from $0.10 to $0.35 per barrel. That meant that the posted price was usually more (sometimes much more) than what the oil was actually

---

[17] Issawi and Yeganah, *Economics of Middle Eastern Oil*, 129.
[18] BP 115920 W. D. Brown, "Middle East Crude Oil Prices – Explanatory Note," September 1, 1952.
[19] In 1957, Shell drew 51.8 million tons of oil from its concessions in Venezuela against 10.2 million from the Middle East (including 4.2 million from Iran). Jersey drew 53.6 million from Venezuela and other South American countries, compared to 21.6 million from the Middle East. See Burdett, *OPEC Origins & Strategy, 1947–1973*, vol. I, "British Working Group Report," 317.
[20] Edith Penrose, "Vertical Integration with Joint Control of Raw-Material Production: Crude Oil in the Middle East," *Journal of Development Studies* 1 (April 1965): 251–268.

worth. "Only fools and affiliates pay posted prices," went the saying in industry circles.[21]

The real utility of the posted price was not in market transactions but as a tool to measure the companies' payments to producing governments. According to oil economist Edith Penrose, who studied the oligopoly throughout the 1950s and 1960s, a price mutually agreed to be the "correct" price for a barrel of oil could function as a benchmark for profit-sharing: "[a] bit of economic make-believe" by which the companies could measure their profits and calculate a 50 percent tax for producing governments. The fifty-fifty division could be considered fair, "presumably because equality implies fairness."[22] The fact that the posted price was higher than oil's true market value benefited the producing states, who enjoyed higher revenues as a result; a lower, more competitive price would have benefited consumers but would have hurt both the companies and the producing states equally. Finally, payments made according to the posted price and fifty-fifty were tax deductible according to US and British law.[23] In effect, the system transferred money from taxpayers in the West to producing states in the oil-producing regions – a Western subsidy for propping up the pro-Western governments of Iraq, Saudi Arabia, Iran, Kuwait, and other oil-rich states.

Paying oil-producing states a hefty chunk of profits – regardless of whether they were calculated by an arbitrary metric or deducted from the companies' domestic taxes, as was the case – was an important part of how the oligopoly imagined its security. Robert Siegel, an executive for Socony-Mobil, remarked in September 1958: "Middle Eastern leaders [are aware that] the present system ... is essential to the creation of their revenues." Repeating rhetoric used countless times during the Mosaddeq crisis, Siegel argued that Middle Eastern oil was "valueless until a market is found for it." Nationalizations were unlikely since Middle Eastern leaders "knew a good business deal when they've got one."[24] Dual integration served the companies' interests, for as the producer states became dependent on oil revenues, their need for the companies' market – and the stable profitability captured within that

---

[21] Leeman, *The Price of Middle East Oil*, 3.
[22] Edith Penrose, "Middle East Oil: The International Distribution of Profits and Income Taxes," *Economica* 27, no. 107 (August 1960): 209.
[23] Glenn P. Jenkins and Brian D. Wright, "Taxation of Income of Multinational Corporations: The Case of the United States Petroleum Industry," *The Review of Economist and Statistics* 47, no. 1 (February 1975): 1–11.
[24] Robert Siegel, "Observations on the Current Situation in the Middle East," September 30, 1958, Exxon-Mobil Collection, Box 2.207/E183.

market – grew. By the late 1950s, oil contributed between 57 and 80 percent of major producers' foreign exchange balances, as well as 61 percent of the state budget in Iraq, 87 percent in Kuwait, and 81 percent in Saudi Arabia.[25] Dependence formed the cornerstone of the global oil economy. As Dr. Francisco Parra, future OPEC general secretary, noted years later: If the "carrot" of high revenues based on fifty-fifty agreements served to keep the producers satisfied, "the defeat of Iran was the big stick that threatened anyone who got too far out of line."[26] The companies were confident that "Mosaddeq madness" would not spread to other producers.

Powerful though they were, the oligopoly's members were not impervious to change. Conditions in the global oil economy underwent a shift in the late 1950s, producing effects that undermined the companies' dominance. First was the ever-present specter of petro-nationalism. Though an economic and a political failure, Mosaddeq's nationalization struck a chord in the Global South. After addressing the UN Security Council in October 1951, Mosaddeq made a pit stop in Cairo on his way back to Tehran. Egyptians gave him a rapturous reception.[27] In 1952 the Free Officers overthrew the pro-British monarchy in Egypt and installed a new government led by nationalist leader Gamel Abdul Nasser. Nasser espoused an ideology of pan-Arabism that argued for a united Arab world. Oil was one of three "main elements" upon which a pan-Arab state could be erected, "the blood of civilization and progress." Control over its production and sale had to be wrested from foreign control.[28] Nasser's nationalization of the Suez Canal Company in 1956 illustrated the ability of Arab states to disrupt the flow of the companies' oil, while the spectacular Anglo-French failure to retake the canal demonstrated the waning authority of the imperial powers.[29] Following his triumph, Nasser became a key sponsor for further petro-nationalist action against the companies.

---

[25] Issawi and Yeganah, *The Economics of Middle East Oil*, 145–146, year in question was 1958; Burdett, *OPEC Origins & Strategy, 1947–1973*, vol. I, "British Working Group Report," 335.
[26] Francisco Parra, *Oil Politics: A Modern History of Petroleum* (New York: IB Tauris, 2004), 30.
[27] Lior Sternfeld, "Iran Days in Egypt: Mosaddeq's Visit to Cairo in 1951," *British Journal of Middle Eastern Studies* 3, no. 1 (2015): 1–20.
[28] Gamel Abdul Nasser, *The Philosophy of Revolution* (Washington DC: Public Affairs Press, 1955); quoted in Terzian, *OPEC: The Inside Story*, 87.
[29] For the Suez Crisis, Arab nationalism, international oil, and US foreign policy, see Bamberg, *Vol. III*, 75–99; Citino, *From Arab Nationalism to OPEC*, 87–117; Salim Yaqub, *Containing Arab Nationalism: The Eisenhower Doctrine and the Middle East* (Chapel Hill, NC: University of North Carolina Press, 2004), 1–9, 31–34.

Global developments after Suez further challenged the oligopoly's control over the market. A recession in 1957 created overflowing stocks of oil and oil products, what oil expert Paul Frankel dubbed the "Horrors of Peace."[30] Oil in search of a market had to contend with increased competition. After decades of dormancy, the Soviet Union ramped up production in 1956, using cheap oil to penetrate markets in Western Europe.[31] In the United States, smaller independent oil companies successfully lobbied President Eisenhower for measures designed to prevent the majors from importing cheaper foreign oil. In March 1959 the US government instituted mandatory quotas capping imports at 9 percent of total consumption (later increased to 12 percent).[32] Meanwhile, producer governments eager to earn more revenue and improve their negotiating position against the oligopoly offered new oil concessions to smaller firms. While the amount of oil produced from these concessions was relatively small, the growing number of firms engaged in Middle East oil production added more output to an already glutted market. The result was steadily falling market prices between 1957 and 1959.[33]

Falling prices were not immediately reflected in companies' payments to producer states, due to the artificial nature of the posted price. The posted price had been introduced "precisely because [it] could be regarded as genuinely representative of going market prices," according to an internal BP memo.[34] If that had been true in 1950, it was no longer true nine years later. There was a widening gulf between the posted price (what the companies claimed oil was worth), and the market price (what oil was *actually* worth).[35] The effect was a relative increase in payments to governments – who were paid according to the posted price – and declining profitability for the majors. Penrose calculated that in 1958 BP paid more than half its net income to producing states in taxes or royalties (though it should be noted that such payments were

---

[30] Frankel, "A Turning Point," October 1957, in *Paul Frankel: Common Carrier of Common Sense*, ed. Ian Skeet (Oxford: Oxford University Press, 1989), 90.
[31] Elisabetta Bini, "A Challenge to Cold War Energy Politics? The US and Italy's Relations with the Soviet Union, 1958–1969," in *Cold War Energy: A Transnational History of Soviet Oil and Gas*, ed., Jeronim Perovic (Cham, Switzerland: Palgrave Macmillan, 2017), 201–230.
[32] Moran, "Oligopoly of Would-Be Sovereigns," 590–591.
[33] Yergin, *The Prize*, 482–491.
[34] BP 100334 "Middle East Concession and Tax-Paying Arrangements: Posted Prices," August 13, 1962.
[35] Seymour, *OPEC: Instrument of Change*, 12.

tax deductible, thanks to the terms of the fifty-fifty agreements, so the actual cost to the companies was negligible).[36]

The Seven Sisters dominated global oil. But their commercial success did not insulate them from political shifts in the oil-producing and oil-consuming world. Despite their impressive political power, the companies could not control such shifts – they could only endure them and maneuver for best advantage. By 1959 the oligopoly's carefully constructed system of maximum profitability, limited competition, posted prices, and fifty-fifty concessions was slowly unraveling. The companies could boost their earnings by cutting the posted price, bringing it closer in line with oil's actual value. But a cut to the posted price would lower payments to producing states, effectively transferring more of oil's value from the producer states to the companies and to consumers. Such a move was certain to increase producer antagonism.

It would also annoy the companies' host governments. Both the United States and Great Britain prioritized the economic well-being of pro-Western oil producers like Iran, Kuwait, and Saudi Arabia.[37] While the United States' government and the major companies held parallel interests immediately after World War II, by the late 1950s the relationship between policymakers and the oligopoly was not quite as close. Though they did not wish to see the companies lose their concessions, US officials quietly pushed the majors to maintain the flow of revenues to the producers. Cold War strategic priorities thus worked to constrain the oligopoly.[38] This was true even in Iran, a country ruled by a pro-Western monarch who was dependent on oil revenues generated by the companies.

6.2 Iran, the Consortium, and Performative Petro-Nationalism, 1954–1960

In 1954, a consortium of oil companies that included all seven majors reasserted foreign control over Iran's oil industry three years after

---

[36] Penrose, "Middle East Oil," 212. See also Francesco Petrini, "Public Interest, Private Profits: Multinationals, Governments and the Coming of the First Oil Crisis," *Business and Economic History* 12 (January 2014): 8–9.

[37] Great Britain, for example, depended on Iranian and Kuwaiti oil, which could be produced and sold in sterling within the United Kingdom at a far lower cost than other sources while netting profits for BP and Shell, the two British companies. As a result, London consistently backed a policy of increasing Iranian and Kuwaiti oil production. FO 371/157651 EP 1535/3 Harrison Note of a Conversation, Undated; FO 371/157652 EP 1537/3, Note by Hiller, February 15, 1961, EP 1537/5, Record of Meeting, February 28, 1961, UKNA; Burdett, *OPEC Origins & Strategy, 1947–1973*, vol. I, "British Working Group Report," 281–284.

[38] Wolfe-Hunnicutt, *Paranoid Style*, 4–5.

Mosaddeq's nationalization. The official justification for Iran's "de-nationalization" rested on an argument of Iranian incapacity.[39] When company inspectors arrived in Abadan in February 1954, they found that Iranian engineers had done an "excellent job" maintaining security and warned that reasserting foreign control would pose problems due to the "competence of the Iranian staff."[40] The final terms of the 1954 agreement obscured this reality. The deal confirmed Iran's ownership of the oil in the ground but clarified the seven members of the consortium would manage the industry "on behalf of Iran," confirming that the Iranians "were incapable of running [it] ... and were inviting the consortium to come in and run it for them."[41] According to AIOC's Neville Gass, a new agreement could outwardly reflect the law of nationalization while retaining for the oligopoly complete control over price and production, "to preserve the façade of control of the oil industry by the Persian Government."[42]

While AIOC (renamed British Petroleum, or BP, in 1954) was eager to recover its position in Iran, the rest of the oligopoly participated at the behest of the US government. The 1954 agreement stipulated that Iran's oil production be increased as quickly as possible: The Eisenhower administration wanted the shah to receive high revenues that he could then use to fund the Second Plan. The companies, despite their interests elsewhere in the oil-producing world, complied. Between 1954 and 1960 Iran's exports increased from 330,000 to 1.19 million bpd, while revenues rose from $99 million in 1955 to $285 million in 1960.[43] The annual production level was set through a process of bidding, though the dominance of high bidders within the group meant that Iran's oil production after 1957 grew quickly.[44] The British applied "gentle but

---

[39] Brew, "De-nationalized," 100.
[40] RG 59 888.2553/2-1354, Henderson to State, February 13, 1954, 888.2553/2-2454, Aldrich to State, February 24, 1954, USNA.
[41] BP 126490 Minutes of Principals Meeting June 2, 11 and 15 1954, US Companies: Nationality of the Operating Companies, June 3, 1954, AIOC: Memo on Nationality of Companies, June 31, 1954.
[42] BP 67067 "Management – South Persian Oilfields and Refinery," Abadan Technical Mission, N.A. Gass, February 17, 1954.
[43] Smithers and Co, *International Oil Industry*, 51; Bennett H. Wall, *Growth in a Changing Environment: A History of Standard Oil Company 1952–1975* (New York: McGraw Hill, 1988), 599; Karshenas, *Oil, State, and Industrialization*, 135; Shwadran, *The Middle East, Oil and the Great Powers*, 161.
[44] It is often argued that Iran's production was kept down after the 1954 agreement. See Shafiee, "Cracking Petroleum with Politics," 429–432; Blair, *Control of Oil*, 104–105. In reality, however, the highest bidders were BP, CFP, Socony-Mobil, Shell, and IRICON, a group of smaller US firms allowed into the consortium in 1955. The high bidders commanded 72 percent of the consortium, which gave them enough weight to bring the final figure *up*, rather than down. See RG 59 888.2553/2-2959, US Embassy Tehran

continuous pressure" on BP and Royal Dutch/Shell to treat Iran with a degree of leniency, while the US government was favorably disposed toward any measure that increased Iran's access to oil revenue.[45] As a result of these factors, Iran recovered its pre-1951 position very quickly (Figure 6.2).

Wary of repeating AIOC's mistakes, the consortium took steps to manage its relationship with the Iranians. Rather than rely on foreign experts, the consortium hired a large number of Iranian engineers. The consortium partners held regular meetings with representatives of the National Iranian Oil Company (NIOC), where they discussed issues such as management of Abadan, labor, wages, and problems pertaining to nonbasic operations over which NIOC had authority. The meetings were chiefly designed to ensure good relations and had little impact on production, which the consortium controlled without input from the Iranian government. While Iranians sat on the board of the consortium's operating companies, their role was ceremonial: The boards voted on directives issued from the partners in London, "and had no role in the decision," according to engineer Parviz Mina.[46] Baqer Mostowfi, charged with running nonbasic services in Abadan, recalled that consortium executives held a tight control over production and refining schedules: "We were unable to change the decision-making process."[47]

While comparable to AIOC's pre-nationalization position, the consortium operated in a different environment. Gone was the weak postwar Pahlavi government. In its place was the assertive regime of the shah, who was interested in increasing Iran's oil production, both for economic and political reasons. In 1957, emboldened by his increasing power and driven by the need to secure more revenue for the ever-growing budget, the shah signed new concessionary deals with Italy's ENI, as well as Japanese and American independents, for areas outside the consortium zone. Drafted by NIOC's Fu'ad Ruhani and Fathallah Nafisi, the new deals split profits 75-25 in Iran's favor, with the foreign firm covering the initial investment and providing Iran a cash bonus. Given Iran's fiscal dependence on the consortium's operations, offering Iranian oil to competitors on terms that broke fifty-fifty was a clear

---

No. 781, April 29, 1959, USNA; Text of Participants Agreement, *The International Petroleum Cartel*, 95–117; Brew, "De-nationalized," 102–103.

[45] FO 371/120740 Riches to Stevens, January 16, 1956, UKNA; RG 59 888.2553/3-1358, US Embassy Tehran No. 811, March 13, 1958, Grove to Robert Siegel, March 11, 1958, USNA.

[46] FISDS, *Tahavvul-e san`at-e naft-e Iran*, Interview with Mina.

[47] FISDS, *San`at-e petroshimi-e Iran: az aghaz ta astane-ye enqelab* [The Evolution of Iran's Petrochemical Industry], Interview with Baqer Mostowfi.

provocation. NIOC chairman 'Abdullah Entezam, regarded by the companies as their "friend at court," privately fretted that the shah's actions would "unfavorably affect the Consortium's operations," while the shah's finance minister threatened to resign over the new concessions.[48]

This opposition was not enough to deter the shah. In a speech to the Majlis, he boasted that his new deals would make NIOC "the biggest oil concern in the world."[49] Mohammed Reza Pahlavi took every opportunity to criticize the "oil magnates" and "foreign powers" that controlled Iranian oil and did little to hide his dissatisfaction with Iran's level of oil production and its annual payment.[50] As Iran was a sovereign nation, there was nothing the consortium could do to prevent the shah from offering new concessions to their competitors, exacerbating the global supply glut and depressing prices, all for the sake of Pahlavi prestige.

Attacking the companies was a logical move for the shah. Regardless of their financial importance to the Seven-Year Plan and the postcoup economic recovery, the consortium represented a moment of national humiliation. The Western companies maintained a façade of nationalization but carried on much as AIOC had done. The oil industry remained an inorganic, artificial element, "a foreign-owned enclave," in the words of one British official, and a constant reminder of the defeat of Iran's nationalization effort.[51] With the middle class still dissatisfied and the regime's legitimacy tied to the 1953 coup, the shah was conscious of positioning himself as a petro-nationalist rather than the willing tool of the companies. Signing concessions with companies outside the consortium – accompanied with splashy articles in the state-controlled press and speeches before the tame Majlis – served as a kind of performative petro-nationalism calculated to silence the shah's critics without endangering his government's relationship with the oligopoly, upon which state finances, the shah's military ambitions, and the Second Seven-Year Plan depended.

The shah was also banking on US support. Utilizing a form of blackmail for which he would eventually become famous, Mohammed Reza Pahlavi argued that Iran needed money to fulfill its role in containing the Soviet Union. He noted his economic development programs meant the money would be used more "wisely" than in nearby Arab states, where

---

[48] FO 371/164221 Harrison to FO, October 24, 1962, UKNA; RG 59 888.2553/5-456, Memo of Conversation, May 4, 1956, USNA; *FRUS 1955–1957, XII*: 873.
[49] FO 371/127210 Russell to FO, July 31, 1957, UKNA.
[50] RG 59 888.2553/8-957, US Embassy Tehran No. 154, August 9, 1957, USNA.
[51] FO 371/140857 British Consul, Khorramshahr December 9, 1958, UKNA.

6.2 Iran, the Consortium, & Performative Petro-Nationalism 195

he contended oil money was wasted on lavish palaces.[52] His arguments were not entirely unpersuasive: Saudi Arabia, the largest regional oil producer, struggled with corrupt leadership and a top-heavy administration, while other Arab producers like Iraq flirted with Nasser-style Arab nationalism. Ruled by a pushy yet staunchly pro-Western authoritarian monarch, Iran appeared a safe source of oil, while US policymakers were conscious of the shah's persistent budget problems.

Initial reactions to the shah's concession deals in Washington were nevertheless marked with concern.[53] The US embassy eventually succumbed to a policy of restrained support, with Ambassador Seldon Chapin encouraging the shah to secure more deals "which would possible provide immediate substantial revenue for next year's hard-pressed budget."[54] Faced with a choice of propping up the shah or maintaining the companies' profits, the Eisenhower administration leaned toward the former, though the national security policy document completed in May 1958 admitted the monarch "has become increasingly difficult to deal with."[55] The companies continued to raise Iran's oil production throughout the 1950s, despite the shah's provocations, with the tacit approval of US policymakers.

Performative petro-nationalism was the shah's response to changes in the oil world outside of Iran. The ground shifted after the Suez crisis, as the oligopoly faced a new and rising wave of opposition throughout the oil-producing world.[56] Gatherings like the Arab Petroleum Congress held in Nasser's Egypt in April 1959 offered a platform to critics of the companies like Venezuela's Juan Pablo Pérez Alfonso, who had helped push through Venezuela's original fifty-fifty tax law in 1948, and Saudi Arabia's 'Abdullah al-Tariki. Holding a degree in petroleum engineering from the University of Texas, Tariki dismissed the posted price system as an "irrational device by which big companies pull wool over [our] eyes." The industrialized world, by driving up the prices of manufactured goods and depressing the price of commodities like sugar, cotton, and oil, hoped to keep the postcolonial Global South in a perpetual state of economic slavery, argued Tariki. The current situation could be remedied "through more deliberate production policies," starting with the nationalization of oil industries and the seizure of the companies' control over price.[57] In such an environment, and with the legacy of Mosaddeq

---

[52] RG 59 888.2553/3-1358, US Embassy Tehran No. 811, March 13, 1958, Grove to Robert Siegel, March 11, 1958, USNA.
[53] *FRUS 1955–1957, XII*: 932–933.
[54] RG 59 888.2553/11-1257, Chapin to Dulles, No. 939, November 12, 1957.
[55] *FRUS 1958–1960, XII*: 547–549.   [56] Dietrich, *Oil Revolution*, 61–88.
[57] RG 59 888.2553/8-460, Heath to State, Tariki Comments, August 8, 1960, USNA.

still present in Iran's simmering domestic politics, the shah could not afford to look overly comfortable with the status quo. His aggressive stance against the companies was designed to allay both domestic and foreign criticism.

Such considerations compelled the Pahlavi government to join OPEC in September 1960. Spearheaded by Tariki and Pérez Alfonso, OPEC formed in direct response to the companies' decision to cut the posted price for Persian Gulf oil, a move intended to bring the price closer in line with oil's actual market value, which had been steadily deteriorating amid the market glut after 1957. The cuts brought the posted price from $2.05 per barrel in January 1959 to $1.80 in August 1960, with a total cost to oil producers estimated at $270 million. Executives like Jersey Standard Chairman Monroe J. Rathbone considered it a necessary move to preserve profitability, returning parity between posted and "realized" prices. To Tariki and Pérez Alfonso, it was a callous act of plunder. Cutting the posted price would benefit the companies and Western consumers while depriving producers of money that was needed to sustain economic growth and raise standards of living. OPEC's charter included a call to return oil prices to their pre-August 1960 level, as part of a general push to establish formal relations between producer nations and oil companies based on the principle of collective action.[58] Where the producer states had once acted separately, they would now speak with one voice.

Iran joined OPEC. The shah's attitude remained equivocal, however. Though he railed against the companies' reduction of the posted price – a move that cut Iran's oil revenues by $50 million, though the companies compensated for this by raising its production – he told oil journalist Wanda Jablonski in November 1960 that Iran was categorically opposed to cutting production, as Tariki and Pérez Alfonso were advocating.[59] According to NIOC's Parviz Mina, "the shah did not want to show that he was opposed to the creation and formation of OPEC," a position that would have classed him with the Middle East's reactionaries.[60] The shah's goal was to walk the line between petro-nationalists and the oligopoly, supporting measures that would improve producers' takes without jeopardizing his relationship with the companies. It was to prove

---

[58] Bamberg, *Vol. III*, 147–151; Wall, *Growth in a Changing Environment*, 603–605; Farmanfarmaian, *Blood and Oil*, 341–342.
[59] RG 59 888.2553/12-560, US Embassy Tehran No. 158, December 5, 1960, 888.2553/9-2960, US Embassy Tehran No. 96, September 29, 1950, USNA.
[60] FISDS, *Tahavvul-e san`at-e naft-e Iran*, Interview with Mina.

an awkward dance, one that would draw out divisions within the shah's government, as crisis overcame the oil world in the first half of the 1960s.

6.3 The Scholar and the "Wild Men"

Most of the shah's ministers supported his middle-of-the road approach. Prime ministers 'Ali Amini (1961–1962) and Asadollah 'Alam (1962–1964) were not hostile to the companies and did not wish to see the 1954 agreement altered. "The world … needs our oil," said Amini, "[and] supply can only be maintained if stability in producing countries prevails."[61] There was a strong contingent of ministers within the government and NIOC who supported a close and mutually beneficial relationship with the consortium.

At the same time, rising petro-nationalism gave Iran opportunities to secure better terms. Between 1960 and 1961, NIOC negotiated a series of deals with the consortium meant to mitigate the impact of the price cuts. Discussions were held "on a straight business-like basis," according to one consortium executive, while the shah, properly briefed by his advisors, showed a "detailed knowledge" of the issues.[62] When talks concluded in late 1961, the consortium had agreed to increase Iran's revenue above $300 million for that year, and included a $10 million payment to settle claims on production from the Abadan refinery.[63] The shah and his ministers, reported the British ambassador, sought an absolute increase in Iran's revenues. They were conscious that in the companies, "they have a goose it would be unwise to kill off."[64]

For the shah's more conservative ministers, OPEC offered a potential source of leverage in negotiations with the consortium. But others viewed it as a means to substantively change the status quo forced upon Iran by the oligopoly. The most prominent supporter of OPEC was Fu'ad Ruhani, a lawyer and former translator for AIOC who rose through the ranks of NIOC and became a key oil advisor to the shah in the late 1950s. A "first-rate lawyer" with thirty years of experience in oil affairs, Ruhani climbed to the top of the Pahlavi government through a skillful combination of intellect and political acumen. In 1951, having left AIOC, Ruhani assisted Mosaddeq's government in oil negotiations, though he later said he found the prime minister's approach to the oil question

---

[61] RG 59 888.2553/11-161, US Embassy to State No. 113, November 1, 1961, 888.2553/12-2761, US Embassy to State No. 15, December 27, 1961, USNA.
[62] RG 59 888.2553/3-2862, US Consul Khorramshahr No. 40, March 28, 1962, USNA.
[63] BP 46193 Notes of Discussion with NIOC Representatives, September 25, 1961.
[64] FO 371/164220 Harrison to FO, January 10, 1962, UKNA.

"flawed."[65] Working as Amini's assistant during the 1954 Consortium Agreement negotiations, Ruhani thereafter served as NIOC's legal advisor. A scholar who would later pen lengthy and detailed histories of Iran's oil industry, Ruhani was known for his fiscal honesty – unlike the shah's other advisors, he did not use his office for personal gain.[66] At a time when most of the shah's advisors were against the idea of OPEC, Ruhani emerged as the group's fiercest champion. The shah's decision to join OPEC against the advice of NIOC was in part due to Ruhani's influence.[67] In 1960, the shah nominated Ruhani to be OPEC's first secretary general, a post he held until early 1964.

Despite his enthusiasm for international petro-nationalism, Ruhani was a royalist at heart and viewed OPEC through the lens of Pahlavi priorities. He held a limited view of what the producers could achieve, given the market power of the oligopoly. Discussing matters with Saudi Arabia's oil minister Ahmed Zaki Yamani, who replaced Tariki in 1962, Ruhani acknowledged OPEC's weak bargaining position. The glut had squeezed prices, but it also gave the companies the flexibility to isolate producer states that demanded better terms. This scenario played out in Iraq, where the companies responded to the petro-nationalist actions of the Qassim government by slowing investment, causing Iraqi output to stagnate for most of the 1960s.[68] The Iraqi experience was illustrative: disunity within OPEC would doom it to irrelevance. "Not only would the organization disappear," wrote Ruhani, "but the individual countries would no longer have any ability to pressure the companies." The threat of sanctions could wring concessions from the companies, "but we know we aren't in a position" to make real demands.[69]

Ruhani led OPEC, but he also represented the interests of his government. He would not break with the shah, whom he regularly consulted on OPEC matters. Ruhani's pragmatism reflected his desire to maximize OPEC's utility for Iran's benefit. In meetings with the companies, Ruhani emphasized Iran's role as a moderating influence. Without

---

[65] Milani, *Eminent Persians*, vol. I, 273–275; Ian Skeet, *OPEC: Twenty-Five Years of Prices and Politics* (New York: Cambridge University Press, 1988), 19.

[66] See Ruhani, *Tarikh-e milli shudan-e san'at-e naft-e Iran*, as well as *San'at-e naft-e Iran* and *The History of OPEC*. Ruhani also wrote a biography of Mosaddeq, *Zindagi-ye siyasi-ye Musaddiq: dar matn-e nahzat-e milli-ye Iran* [The Political Life of Musaddiq: In the Context of the National Front] (London: Intisharat-e Nahzat-e Muqavamat-e Milli-ye Iran, 1987).

[67] Skeet, *OPEC: Twenty-Five Years of Prices and Politics*, 19–20.

[68] Samir Saul, "Masterly Inactivity as Brinksmanship: The Iraq Petroleum Company's Route to Nationalization, 1958–1972," *The International History Review* 29, no. 4 (December 2007): 746–792.

[69] Tajbakhsh and Najmabadi, *Yad'dasht'ha-ye Fu'ad Ruhani*, 317–319.

Iran's guidance, OPEC would be lost to the "wild men" from Iraq, Venezuela, and Indonesia, he argued. In May 1962, during discussions with Howard Page of Jersey, Ruhani dismissed Perez Alfonso's call for a 70-30 profit division, which was sure to cause "serious conflict." Instead, he suggested a new scheme. Most oil agreements included both an income tax and a royalty (also called a "stated payment") that was deducted from the tax. Ruhani suggested that the royalty be treated as a separate expense. This would alter existing concessions and end fifty-fifty: Payments would increase by 11c per barrel, with a 58-42 split in Iran's favor. Moreover, it had precedent: In the United States and Venezuela, royalties were expensed rather than deducted. Ruhani considered it a moderate demand, but Page refused to entertain the proposal, arguing that the companies could not afford additional pressures on profitability.[70]

As his proposals with Page fell flat, Ruhani tried pressure tactics. In June 1962, OPEC met for its fourth annual conference. Anti-company rhetoric dominated the proceedings and the group adopted a series of resolutions establishing grounds for negotiations. While mandating that posted prices return to their pre-August 1960 level, the OPEC resolutions made the case for a new price mechanism divorced from the companies' control. "It is no longer possible," OPEC concluded, "to live in peace in a world where the rich are getting richer and the poor poorer ... an equitable balance between the two groups of nations [oil producers and oil consumers] must be established."[71] Prices would be adjusted according to consultations between the companies and OPEC states. Otherwise, the member states would use legislation to raise the posted price unilaterally.[72]

Ruhani couched OPEC's argument in the language of dual integration. Higher oil revenues were needed for "projects of reform" and the "betterment of social conditions." Cutting prices at a time when industrial goods and imports were becoming more expensive was tantamount to economic warfare and a return of coercive imperialism. Discussions with the companies would focus on "fixing oil revenues ... on a stable and guaranteed basis in conformity with the principles of equity and reason."[73] Just as in the days of Reza Shah, Iran wanted

---

[70] BP 100334 Bridgeman to Mitchell, June 5, 1962, Memorandum for the Record, Conversation with Ruhani, March 12, 1962, Mitchell to Bridgeman, Unnumbered, May 29, 1962, Note on Page's Meeting with Ruhani, June 1962.
[71] FO 371/164220 Amuzegar for Velders, July 11, 1962, UKNA.
[72] BP 100334 Memorandum: Government Revenues and the Price of Crude Oil in the Middle East; Tajbakhsh and Najmabadi, *Yad'dasht'ha-ye Fu'ad Ruhani*, 51.
[73] FO 371/164220 Press Communique Issued by F. Ruhani, July 2 1962, UKNA.

security from price drops and assurances that revenues would never decline. The companies had shown they were incapable of providing such security through the existing system – the system, therefore, had to be altered.

Ruhani made plans to meet with the oligopoly's members in October 1962 to discuss the OPEC resolutions. As the companies did not recognize OPEC's legitimacy, Ruhani would be met as a representative of Iran. Whatever terms Iran accepted would then be offered to the rest of OPEC, with similar negotiations held between Saudi Arabia and the Aramco partners. As both Tehran and Riyadh were led by pro-Western governments, the companies had reasons to be optimistic. British Ambassador Geoffrey Harrison was confident that the shah and other "serious oil people" within his government would pursue reasonable negotiations: "[he] remembers the events of 1953-54 all too well." But the companies would also have to show flexibility or risk following AIOC's path in 1951 toward nationalization.[74] To manage OPEC's challenge, the companies would have to strike a balance. They would also have to speak with one voice.

6.4   Conciliation or Conflict: Oil Negotiations, 1962–1963

To call the Seven Sisters an oligopoly, and not a cartel, was to acknowledge a basic truth: They rarely operated as a single entity. While joint ownership of concessions, a mutual acceptance of the fifty-fifty profit-sharing mechanism, and a collective embrace of efforts to suppress production united the major firms, they continued to compete with one another for markets. On a more personal level, the companies differed in outlook, character, and priorities. When it came to OPEC, the oligopoly split into several camps defined by differing geographic and commercial interests.

Royal Dutch/Shell and Jersey Standard, the largest and oldest companies, held major shares in Venezuela. This tended to influence their thinking regarding OPEC, an organization tied to Middle East politics.[75] The two firms agreed that fifty-fifty be modified with the posted price retaining a "flexibility" that would allow payments to producer states to

---

[74] FO 371/164220 Harrison to Reilly, August 20, 1962, Harrison to Reilly, August 23, 1962, UKNA.
[75] In 1957, Shell and Jersey drew 51.8 million and 53.6 million tons from Venezuela, against 10.2 million and 21.6 million tons from the Middle East, respectively. See Burdett, *OPEC Origins & Strategy, 1947–1973*, vol. I, 317.

6.4 Conciliation or Conflict: Oil Negotiations, 1962–1963

match the value of oil on the market.[76] In a memo delivered in late August 1962, Shell declared that fifty-fifty had "worn so thin as to deceive nobody, least of all the host governments."[77] Jersey's Howard Page, regarded as the American executive with the broadest knowledge of the Middle East, argued that the posted price system had failed to function properly: It worked when prices were high, but did not stipulate "what would happen should prices fall."[78] Socony-Mobil, an American firm dependent on crude from its shares in Iraq, Iran, and Saudi oil fields, presented a proposal for a new system based on a guaranteed minimum price fixed to each barrel of oil – an "assured value plan," in Socony's terminology.[79] Socony's proposal would do away with fifty-fifty in favor of a guaranteed annual return per barrel, an arrangement quite similar to what Reza Shah had asked John Cadman thirty years before.

In opposition to these ideas were the remaining American companies – Socal, Gulf, and Texaco – which flatly refused to consider any measure that would increase producer revenues at the expense of company profits. The US companies favored their investments in Kuwait and Saudi Arabia above their holdings in Iran.[80] Suspicious and conservative, the American firms tended to dismiss the producer states' concerns and were set against giving concessions. One Socal executive pointed out that Iran's higher-cost crude was not worth the effort. If the shah or Ruhani proved obstinate, the companies could shift investment and increase production in Kuwait or Saudi Arabia.[81]

In the middle lay BP, the successor to the Anglo-Iranian Oil Company, which held a 40 percent stake in the consortium. BP Chairman Maurice Bridgeman was not prepared to give in to Jersey's flexibility proposal or Socony's assured value plan. Instead, Bridgeman suggested they focus their efforts in a single direction – Iran. A shrewd and calculating businessman in Cadman's mold, Bridgeman had accompanied the former

---

[76] BP 100334 "The Case for 'Flexibility' of Posted Price of Crude in the ME," August 9, 1962, Shell Memo, "Middle East Concession and Tax-Paying Arrangements" August 16, 1962.
[77] BP 100334 Possible Approaches to OPEC Member Countries, August 30, 1962.
[78] Quoted in Terzian, *OPEC: The Inside Story*, 39.
[79] BP 100334 Socony-Mobil, "Assured Value Plan: A Response to Recent OPEC Demands," August 20, 1962.
[80] According to the terms of the Consortium Participants' Agreement, the five US companies were permitted to take 7.5 percent of total output. For 1958, Jersey and Socony-Mobil took 7.4 and 7.35 percent, while Texaco took 7.11 percent, Socal 6.85 percent, and Gulf 4.42 percent. See RG 59 888.2553/2-2959, US Embassy Tehran No. 781, April 29, 1959, USNA.
[81] RG 59 888.2553/6-1962, Memo of Conversation, June 19, 1962, 888.2553/7-2662, Memo of Conversation, July 26, 1962, 888.2553/8-962, Memo of Conversation, August 9, 1962, USNA.

chairman during negotiations with Reza Shah in the 1920s, and his thinking reflected Cadman's conciliatory approach.[82] In his mind, Iran was OPEC's "weak link." The shah would betray the group's united front if he felt he could get a better deal by negotiating with the companies separately. This would obviate the need for a settlement covering all OPEC states. "It may be necessary," wrote one BP executive, "to give the Middle East governments a better take, but [we] are convinced that at this moment we cannot afford it."[83] Rather than negotiate, the companies would use Iran to break OPEC internally, postponing a more serious confrontation.

Bridgeman's push for direct diplomacy with the shah threatened to split the consortium partners. The US firms disliked the idea of rewarding the shah, whom they viewed as a grasping and difficult autocrat. Discussions in September 1962 grew heated. Oil expert Walter Levy sided with Bridgeman, arguing that the consortium reach a "side deal" with Iran, the most "sophisticated" producer, and disrupt OPEC's fragile unity.[84] But Shell, Jersey, and Socony thought Bridgeman's plan inadequate, while the remaining US firms refused point-blank to discuss further concessions for Iran. At one point, Page lost his temper at Bridgeman, declaring that Jersey would make its own arrangements. Though he walked back his inflammatory remarks, Page's outburst did not augur well for the consortium's unity ahead of its October talks with Ruhani.[85]

These talks were a total disaster. While the consortium representatives argued that "market realities" prevented any increase in the producers' take, Ruhani insisted that it was not "equality of profit," but rather "an equitable sharing of profits" that was the goal. He warned them that he was acting in their interests, for if his demands were not met Iran would cease to act as a moderating influence, allowing the "wild men" to take over and pursue production cuts and nationalization. "If the companies realized Iran had cause for anxiety," they must in turn "do something about it," or risk OPEC's wrath.[86]

---

[82] Bamberg, *Vol. III*, 50–62.
[83] BP 100369 Stockwell to Drake, OPEC October 9, 1962, Note for Pattinson, OPEC, October 10, 1962.
[84] BP 100219 Minutes of Meeting with Levy, September 21, 1962.
[85] BP 100219 OPEC, September 3, 1962, Notes of Meeting of the Steering Group, September 12, 1962, Meeting at Finsbury Park, September 25, 1962.
[86] BP 77987 OPEC Subjects, Note from Addison, October 8, 1962; BP 100369 Attachment No. 4, Note by Mr. Ruhani for Meeting of October 4, 1962, Attachment No. 6, Summary and Conclusions, Report on Meetings in Paris, October 8, 1962.

6.4 Conciliation or Conflict: Oil Negotiations, 1962–1963

Despite Ruhani's aggressive stance, his rhetoric hid a weak hand. The Pahlavi government was nearly as divided as the consortium. Technocrats in NIOC were split between supporters of Ruhani and older conservatives like Chairman Abdullah Entezam who hoped to preserve good relations with the consortium.[87] Personalities were important, as Finance Minister Abdolhossein Behnia backed his friend Ruhani over a rival faction led by Prime Minister Asadollah 'Alam, the most cautious member of the cabinet.[88] With popular discontent bubbling up after the failure of the Second Plan, 'Alam feared a resurgence of the "Mosaddeq spirit" among Iran's middle class. While the shah gained politically from opposing the companies in public, 'Alam worried what would happen if he pushed matters too far, potentially triggering another outburst of petro-nationalism that would prove difficult to control. After the failed talks in October 1962, 'Alam assured Ambassador Harrison that Iran was only interested "in gaining more money." If he could secure this, "he would be perfectly prepared to let OPEC and Ruhani go hang."[89]

The shah, with his characteristic indecision, navigated a middle ground between Ruhani and 'Alam. He hoped to retain the goodwill of the consortium while preserving his reputation as a petro-nationalist. He was against cutting Iran's production, both for financial and political reasons. Opposing OPEC's extremists offered him the chance to appear "moderate" while still securing concessions that burnished his nationalist credentials. This was where Ruhani's influence was crucial. The secretary general claimed Iran did not expect the full acceptance of the OPEC resolutions, "just something … that would improve their income per barrel."[90]

In 1962 the shah was set on taking a tough approach against the oligopoly. During his April visit to Washington, the shah raised the point with President John F. Kennedy, suggesting Kennedy use his "influence" and force the companies to increase Iran's output.[91] At a private dinner in San Francisco in May, the shah told Kermit Roosevelt that OPEC's more extreme ideas were not "in the interests of Iran," but he did nothing to hide his hope that Iran would gain more revenues through Ruhani's negotiations.[92] The shah did not wish to endorse OPEC – the group's international ethos placed too much of a constraint on Iran's

---

[87] BP 100369 Page, Talk with Entezam, October 22, 1962.
[88] HIOHP, Behnia, Tape No. 3, 1.
[89] FO 371/164221 Harrison to FO, October 24, 1962, Harrison to FO, October 26, 1962, UKNA.
[90] BP 100369 Conversation with Ruhani and Fallah, October 11, 1962.
[91] RG 59 888.2553/6-762, Memo, McGhee to Rusk, June 7, 1962, USNA.
[92] FO 371/164606 Rose to Eagers, May 11, 1962, UKNA.

independence and some of its more revolutionary ideas could impede Iran's access to oil revenues – but he was clearly interested in using the group to further his own agenda.

After October's stalemate, the consortium fell in behind Bridgeman's conciliation approach. It was to be a two-pronged offensive aimed at the largest and most influential OPEC members. While the Aramco partners swayed Prince Faisal of Saudi Arabia, the consortium would ameliorate the shah of Iran with financial and material concessions. In November 1962, during a visit to Tehran, Bridgeman offered 'Alam a "gentleman's agreement," whereby the consortium promised to increase investment in Iran, funding a new products export terminal at Bandur Mashur and a crude terminal on Kharg Island. Encouraged by these offers, the shah softened his tone. The days of Iranian "ultra-nationalism," he told Bridgeman, were over and Iran could now "behave reasonably."[93] Iran would remain a "moderating force" he told US Ambassador Julius Holmes, in order to balance the "madmen" in the more radical OPEC states.[94] The shah noted with satisfaction that the consortium's investments would make Kharg Island the largest crude export terminal in the world.[95] With these concessions in hand, the shah instructed Ruhani to delay the OPEC vote on punitive action when the group met in July 1963.[96] Conciliation had worked to blunt the shah's militancy while delaying OPEC action on the 1962 resolutions.

But by late 1963, the shah grew restless again. That year the Pahlavi government embarked upon the shah's White Revolution, discussed at greater length in Chapter 7. The new reforms would cost money. The Pahlavi monarch had found pressure effective in late 1962 and a year later he permitted Ruhani to again push the companies to the breaking point. The issue would be royalty expensing, which Ruhani presented as a fait accompli during a meeting with Page in September. By fully expensing the royalty, the consortium would reward Iran an additional 11c per barrel, increasing its take to nearly 60 percent of total profit, "in

---

[93] BP 100369 Details of Bridgeman's Trip to Tehran, November 8, 1962; FO 371/164221 EP 1532/26, Note by Lamb, November 8, 1962, EP 1532/27, Kellas to Cope, October 22, 1962, UKNA; Bamberg, *Vol. III*, 154.
[94] RG 59 PET 3 IRAN US Embassy to State A-501, February 7, 1963, USNA.
[95] BP 100372 Danner Report of Meeting with Behnia, May 15, 1963, "Financial Assistance to Iran Through the Oil Consortium," Undated; BP 100330 Meeting with the Iranian Prime Minister, Audience with the Shah, August 11, 1963; FO 371/170415 Wright to FO, June 5, 1963, UKNA; Bamberg, *Vol. III*, 154.
[96] BP 100383 Briefing Note, August 28, 1963, Note on the June 1963 OPEC Conference, August 30, 1963; Tajbakhsh and Najmabadi, *Yad'dasht'ha-ye Fu'ad Ruhani*, 97–110; Bamberg, *Vol. III*, 155.

6.4 Conciliation or Conflict: Oil Negotiations, 1962–1963

order to meet its well-known and urgent need for additional funds to implement development projects."[97]

While Ruhani delivered his ultimatum, the shah cut a defiant figure in Tehran. During a press conference, the shah explained how Mosaddeq's folly had been believing that a single country "could bring the oil companies' to their knees." If they acted together, "the countries of OPEC were a great power," he said, capable of delivering better terms for all oil producers.[98] During a meeting of his advisors, with Ruhani, Entezam, and 'Alam present, he asked why punitive action was not taken immediately, so that Iran could increase its take unilaterally. Ruhani explained that such action "would not be expedient" without the support of every OPEC member. The shah gave Ruhani authority to push the companies further. When OPEC met again in December, the secretary general would bring a proposal on royalty expensing to all members. If the companies did not agree to full royalty expensing, OPEC would take unilateral action.[99]

The companies had reached the limits of conciliation and were now prepared to call Ruhani's bluff. The stakes of failure were high. Within the shah's circle of advisors Ruhani held sway, shutting down 'Alam and Entezam, who resigned as chairman of NIOC that October. No help came from Washington, where the US government declined calls to pressure the shah, remaining "more of a spectator than a participant" according to one US report.[100] There was little sense of what would happen that December, when OPEC members gathered in Beirut to hear Ruhani's proposal on royalty expensing. In pure financial terms, OPEC was threatening to raise taxes by mere pennies. But should it set the precedent and shift the price of oil through collective action, the oligopoly's hold over the global oil economy would look very shaky indeed. If OPEC succeeded in demanding royalty expensing, nationalization might not be too far behind.

At this point, rhetoric within the consortium shifted decisively against the secretary general. "I had some evidence," Page reported, "that Rouhani had been misled ... he was being badly misinformed," as to what the companies considered acceptable.[101] Ruhani was deceiving the

---

[97] BP 100331 "Memorandum Concerning the Expensing of Royalties" Handed out by Ruhani, September 16, 1963; Tajbakhsh and Najmabadi, *Yad'dasht'ha-ye Fu'ad Ruhani*, 366–367, Pattinson to Behnia, November 5, 1963.
[98] FO 371/170416 Wright to FO, October 17, 1963, UKNA.
[99] Tajbakhsh and Najmabadi, *Yad'dasht'ha-ye Fu'ad Ruhani*, 370–378, 382–384, 385387, 387–388.
[100] RG 59 PET 2 SAUD US Consul Dharan A-278, June 5, 1963, USNA.
[101] BP 100331 Page to Pattinson, November 11, 1963

shah, argued Socony. Neither the Pahlavi monarch nor his ministers "fully appreciate the consequences of unilateral action."[102] The consortium manager in Abadan agreed: Ruhani was "thoroughly untrustworthy," and an effort ought to be made "to discredit him in the eyes of his own people."[103] There were those in the shah's government who were "jealous and resentful" of Ruhani's influence.[104] To get around OPEC, the consortium needed to get rid of Ruhani. The shah's divided government gave them the tools to do so in the final days of 1963.

6.5 Sabotage: Fallah's Intervention

By late 1963, the spark had gone out of OPEC. Tariki was gone. Removed by Prince Faisal during the palace coup of March 1962, the Saudi firebrand retreated to Beirut and launched a new career as a journalist, publishing screeds against the companies and the pro-Western producing governments.[105] While Iraq and Indonesia proposed aggressive actions to pressure the companies, OPEC remained too divided to coalesce behind a coherent strategy. Even Ruhani, despite his hard negotiating style, was in favor of leaving the existing system essentially intact. Dual integration had made Iran, Saudi Arabia, and the other oil producers dependent on the companies' operations. Despite the consortium's fears, Ruhani did not want to take punitive action. Along with Saudi Arabia's Yamani, his hope was to negotiate a slight increase in producers' take, establish the principle of collective negotiation, and move on. His goals were modest, though he failed to take into account OPEC's divided assembly, the determination of the companies to avoid punitive action, or his own monarch's interest in pursuing Iran's interests at the expense of other producers.

Ruhani arrived in Beirut in December 1963 confident the rest of OPEC would rally to his side. Within the assembly, Ruhani pushed for a gradual approach. Instead of fully expensing royalties, he proposed accepting a compromise with the companies, whereby royalties were gradually expensed through an annual discount. OPEC, "a young and fresh organization," could not launch frontal attacks on "huge international companies." Calls to restore the pre-1960 price should be "laid aside," and member states concentrate on securing a higher take through

---

[102] BP 100553 Socony's Suggestion – Considerations Prior to OPEC Riyadh Conference, December 12, 1963.
[103] A. L. P. Burdett, *OPEC Origins & Strategy, 1947–1973: Volume 3, the Middle Period, 1963–1966* (Slough: Archive Editions, 2004), 85–90, 98–100.
[104] Rockwell to Rusk, November 21, 1963, NSF Box 116a, JFKPL.
[105] Garavini, *The Rise and Fall of OPEC*, 131.

6.5 Sabotage: Fallah's Intervention

royalty expensing. Yet the OPEC meeting did not go according to plan. Abdul-Aziz al-Wattari, the Iraqi delegate, accused Ruhani of being "too soft," and called the proposed compromise "shameful." The Kuwaiti delegate argued that the money saved by the companies through the discount would be used to develop production outside of OPEC. Bowing to the group's collective will, Ruhani declared the consortium offer unacceptable "as written." The companies could either offer full royalty expensing or prepare for OPEC sanctions.[106]

OPEC's rejection of Ruhani's compromise caught the companies by surprise. Page guessed that the shah and Saudi Arabia's King Faisal were flying blind, "since all information was being channeled through Rouhani," while executives at Socony argued for a direct approach to the Iranian and Saudi governments.[107] The consortium heads felt the situation could be defused by approaching 'Alam and convincing him of Ruhani's deviousness. "Industry representatives are the only ones who can give him full facts," wrote Page.[108] To avoid a confrontation, Ruhani would have to be removed.

Divisions within the Pahlavi government gave the companies the opening they needed to resolve the crisis in their favor. 'Alam resented Ruhani's influence over the shah. To strengthen his position and undermine his rival, 'Alam began communicating details of the shah's OPEC strategy meetings to the British ambassador, who then passed them along to the consortium. The information gave the British and consortium insight into the divided state of the Pahlavi government. The Iranian prime minister, "more worried than I have ever seen him," was ready to quit OPEC, but the shah remained adamant, wrote British Ambassador Dennis Wright. 'Alam guessed his friend was worried backing away from OPEC would make Iran look "ridiculous," tarnishing the shah's reputation as a champion of Iran's sovereignty. The prime minster felt they could find a way around Ruhani by having an Iranian representative meet the consortium in secret. The consortium partners agreed "with surprising speed" to meet an Iranian representative on December 16.[109]

'Alam's tool in this endeavor would be Reza Fallah, who had replaced Entezam as head of NIOC in November 1963. Like Ruhani, Fallah had a Western education, spoke excellent English, and understood the

---

[106] Tajbakhsh and Najmabadi, *Yad'dasht'ha-ye Fu'ad Ruhani*, 391, 392–395; BP 100553 Account of OPEC Meeting in Beirut, December 9, 1963, Lamb to Stockwell, December 10, 1963.
[107] *FRUS 1961–1963, XVIII*: 826–830; BP 100553 Socony's Suggestions – Considerations Prior to OPEC Riyadh Conference, December 12, 1963.
[108] Burdett, *OPEC Origins & Strategy*, vol. 3, 104–106.
[109] Burdett, *OPEC Origins & Strategy*, vol. 3, 112, 123–125, 126, 158.

structure of the global oil economy thanks to his time as an employee of AIOC in the pre-nationalization days. His most consistent quality was a close, friendly relationship with the Western oil companies, one that he would maintain throughout his career as the shah's personal oil envoy.[110] During a strategy meeting on December 14, Fallah argued that the companies would increase Iran's production if given suitable incentives. He harangued Ruhani, arguing that for "two and a half years, you kept me and NIOC in the dark," conducting negotiations as OPEC's leader rather than a loyal servant of the shah. All Ruhani could do was excuse himself from the London talks, claiming it would undermine OPEC's "integrity" and noting how Fallah's visit would attract less attention. The shah hoped for Ruhani to attend but took his excuse in stride: Fallah would be dispatched alone.[111] Apart from 'Alam, neither the shah nor any of his ministers knew that Fallah was in close contact with Joseph Addison, the chairman of the consortium, and informed Addison of almost all his private meetings with Iranian government officials and OPEC.[112]

Fallah's discussions with the consortium were carefully stage-managed to ensure a satisfactory settlement. Fallah argued that Iran only wanted "more money": The lofty goals of OPEC were window dressing. He freely accepted the consortium offer of 3.5c per barrel achieved through partial royalty expensing and a discount, but suggested it be properly camouflaged to obscure the discounting method, which the shah found disagreeable. His monarch's goals were political, said Fallah, and beyond the need for more money what he desired was the appearance of a victory over the companies. If the shah could demonstrate to the Iranian people "that he can get better returns from the oil industry through his own efforts," explained Fallah, "he was prepared to vote against sanctions." As long as Iran's revenues were maintained, "the Iranian government would be willing to give the Consortium freedom to vary posted prices" according to their commercial needs.[113] It was to be a repeat of Cadman's deal with Reza Shah in 1933: A performative display of Pahlavi petro-nationalism designed to conceal the close cooperation and mutual dependence tying the oligopoly to the Iranian government.[114]

---

[110] Reza Fallah, *Encyclopaedia Iranica* www.iranicaonline.org/articles/fallah [Accessed May 30, 2019].
[111] Tajbakhsh and Najmabadi, *Yad'dasht'ha-ye Fu'ad Ruhani*, 396–401.
[112] BP 100553 Message from FO, December 13, 1963, Warder to Addison, December 15, 1963; Burdett, *OPEC Origins & Strategy*, vol. 3, 149–168.
[113] Burdett *OPEC Origins & Strategy*, vol. 3, 184–189.
[114] BP 100553 Three P's Meeting with Fallah, December 17, 1963, Memo #3 "Effect of Small Increases in Costs on Outlets for Persian Gulf Oil"; Tajbakhsh and Najmabadi, *Yad'dasht'ha-ye Fu'ad Ruhani*, 187–194.

6.5 Sabotage: Fallah's Intervention

The oligopoly prepared an offer calculated to satisfy Iran's fickle monarch. Along with the partial expensing of royalties, the consortium would capitalize their drilling and exploration expenditures, yielding Iran a total increase of 6c per barrel and increasing its profit share to 57–58 percent. This would cost the consortium very little, as such expenditure would have been capitalized at some point between 1963 and 1968, but the immediate increase in revenues gave the shah the chance to claim victory.[115] Fallah returned to Iran with the terms in hand and presented them to the shah at a meeting on December 21. Ruhani was close to reaching a deal with Yamani of Saudi Arabia, but the shah dismissed his effort: "Fallah had already settled this issue," and the companies "will produce more for Iran" in future years, even if the shah opted to leave OPEC.[116]

At the OPEC conference on December 26, Iran's delegates led Kuwait and Saudi Arabia to accept the consortium terms, despite denunciations from Iraq and Venezuela. Matters grew so heated that Yamani, still a relatively junior oil minister, chose to leave the assembly rather than suffer Iraq's accusations "that Saudi Arabia was the agent of the oil companies."[117] At Jakarta in November 1964, OPEC disunity reached its apex, as the meeting dissolved without a resolution and each member was freed to accept the companies' terms on partial royalty expensing with diminishing discounts extended over the next four years (Figure 6.3). Most members did so, accepting the companies' terms rather than pushing for new demands.[118]

For OPEC, the royalty expensing crisis ended in confused and disorganized fashion. Divisions between the pro-Western conservatives and the other members were exposed at the Jakarta meeting, leading to a nadir in OPEC's collective action that would last three years. But within the shah's government, the showdown resolved itself neatly. Ruhani had been outmaneuvered. The shah did not renew his application as a member of Iran's delegation to OPEC and the former secretary general retired to a quiet life in 1964, spending the remainder of his career writing and researching Iran's oil history. Fallah retained a special position as an advisor on the talks and continued to feed information from the OPEC side, communicating with the consortium's Joseph Addison for much of 1964.[119]

---

[115] BP 126538 Note on Capitalizing Drilling, February 11, 1964.
[116] Tajbakhsh and Najmabadi, *Yad'dasht'ha-ye Fu'ad Ruhani*, 407–409.
[117] Jeffrey Robinson, *Yamani: The Inside Story* (New York: Atlantic Monthly Press, 1988), 283–284.
[118] Garavini, *Rise and Fall of OPEC*, 154–155.
[119] POWE 61 297 Minute by Rose, July 17, 1964, UKNA; BP 126538 Sutcliffe to Pattinson, Report of Wright Conversation with Fallah, January 7, 1964, Note on Talk with Dr. Fallah, January 4, 1964.

Posted Price	$1.76
Discount	$0.15 in 1964
	$0.13 in 1965
	$0.11 in 1966
Cost	$0.20
Royalty (Expensed)	$0.22
Price Before Taxes	$1.19
Company Take	$0.595
Producer Take	$0.815

Figure 6.3 Royalty expense compromise, 1964[120]

While Fallah's role was kept secret, the shah's acceptance of the consortium's offer in March 1964 opened up his government to criticism from petro-nationalists like Tariki. "Why is it," Tariki wrote in *Al-Anwar*, "that Iran ... should be the differing partner in OPEC? Imperialism is the real winner from our differences."[121] An answer to these attacks came from Iran's Prime Minister Hasan 'Ali Mansur in May 1964. Oil, he said, had "completely lost its political aspect for us ... [it] is no longer a subject for demagogy and political platform." Arab politicians hoping to sway public opinion away from moderation "should keep their preachings on patriotism for their own people."[122]

The shah's role in the crisis was mostly passive. Matters of greater urgency, including his White Revolution land reform campaign, dominated his attention in 1963. Analysis of the meetings he held with his oil advisors, for which Ruhani kept detailed notes, shows a monarch who could be swayed by courtiers – first Ruhani, and then 'Alam and Fallah – who steered him toward policies they believed would most benefit Iran or themselves. Ultimately, however, the shah made the decision to move Iran away from OPEC and toward a compromise with the consortium in the pivotal final weeks of 1963. His interests remained consistent and prioritized increasing Iran's revenue from oil and burnishing his own

---

[120] BP 44796 Oil Companies New Royalty Reckoner, December 31, 1964.
[121] Quoted in Dietrich, *Oil Revolution*, 113–115; *Al-Anwar*, April 30, 1964, re-printed in BP 44796.
[122] FO 371/178153 Wright to FO, May 6, 1964, UKNA.

6.6 Conclusion

reputation as a petro-nationalist. Though he would push the companies whenever possible, the shah avoided an open break that could produce a messy confrontation *a la* Mosaddeq. Faced with a choice between OPEC and the oligopoly, the shah chose the latter.

6.6 Conclusion

Though Iran's decision to accept the consortium's offer split OPEC down the middle, in reality both the oil producers and the oil companies could claim victory in 1964. OPEC members had won a higher take and the principle of royalty expensing. Iran, Saudi Arabia, and Kuwait earned an additional 3.5–5.5c per barrel through partial royalty expensing in 1964, and more in 1965–1966 as the discount was reduced (Figure 6.3). Government takes gradually increased, from $0.70 per barrel to $0.86 per barrel as company profits per barrel inexorably fell over the course of decade.[123] The companies resisted the more costly demands of the 1962 resolutions and retained, in theory, their control over price. The companies were far from destitute: By their own calculation, while return on assets fell from 14 percent to 8.1 percent between 1955 and 1965, net income had increased from $1.6 billion to $2.2 billion over the same period.[124]

Nevertheless, the terms of equitability had shifted in OPEC's favor. Fifty-fifty was dead, and the discussion after 1965 was not whether the governments would ever enjoy the full profit of their oil industries, but when. The balance between the two sides would now be subject to neverending negotiations. Aramco executives defined it as a "war of attrition."[125] The conclusion of negotiations in 1964 suggested that this would be a gradual shift, one that would depend, in large part, on the interests of the large oil-producing states. Most producers were pro-Western and disinclined to alienate the consumer countries. The persistent glut meant that the companies could isolate troublesome states – a strategy used with great effect in Iraq, a state hostile to the companies, which saw its annual production stagnate between 1961 and 1972 as output from Saudi Arabia, Kuwait, and Iran soared.[126]

---

[123] Petrini, "Public Interest, Private Profits," 9.
[124] "Outline for a Talk by Paul Smith, Jr., General Manager, Middle East and Indonesian Affairs Department, Mobil Oil Corporation," October 24, 1966, Exxon-Mobil Collection, Box 2.207/E183.
[125] *FRUS 1964–1968 XXXIV*: 321–323.   [126] Garavini, *The Rise and Fall of OPEC*, 141.

Most importantly, dual integration made oil revenues critical to the economic well-being of the producer states. As long as OPEC's members were content "to wring financial advantage ... without disturbing the present structure of the industry," the companies could gradually accede to petro-nationalist requests, according to a British report.[127] The fear of isolation and the risk of losing access to the oligopoly's profits remained a major concern for the pro-Western governments that dominated OPEC. It also produced complacency among Western officials who believed OPEC would remain shackled to a market outside of its control. As Geoffrey Harrison, former ambassador to Iran, noted in January 1964, "the Arabs cannot drink their oil and must sell it."[128] Such statements were made during a time of abundance. Few considered how the balance might shift should oil suddenly become more scarce, as it would in the final years of the 1960s.

British officials felt that a crisis had been averted "thanks to the stand taken by Iran."[129] Though the shah was demanding and fickle, he was considered a more reliable source of oil than countries vulnerable to nationalist pressure. "The moderation of Iran's oil policies," concluded one British oil report in July 1964, "offers some comfort against the possibility of actions by Arab states to withhold or restrict oil supplies."[130] Even the recalcitrant US majors had agreed "not to let Iran go down the drain." They were helped toward this conclusion by the Cold War priorities of the US government, which continued to regard the successful dual integration of Iranian oil as a major policy objective. During a meeting with President Lyndon Johnson and Secretary of State Dean Rusk in June 1964, Howard Page of Jersey Standard and George Parkhurst of Socal were reminded that for the sake of the Free World, it would be wise to maintain amicable relations with the shah. "The president," Page admitted, "could be very persuasive."[131]

The result of the first OPEC crisis constituted an important victory for the shah's government. Yet the crisis also served to bind the Pahlavi regime closer to the global oil economy. In 1954, Iran produced no oil for export. By 1965, its annual output exceeded 95 million tons. From $285 million in 1959, the shah's government earned $514 million from oil in 1965. Conservative estimates predicted $1 billion in annual oil

---

[127] FO 371/178149 British Oil Interest in the Context of HMG Policy in the Middle East, October 16, 1964, UKNA.
[128] *FRUS 1964–1968, XXXIV*: 317–320.
[129] POWE 61 297 Minute by Rose, July 17, 1964, UKNA.
[130] FO 371/178149 Oil Aspects of Middle East Defence Policy, July 10, 1964.
[131] Memo of Conversation, June 5, 1964, National Security File, Box 136, LBJPL.

6.6 Conclusion

revenues by 1970 (it would exceed this figure in 1969).[132] This wealth was not the product of the shah's government, but the result of the operations of the oligopoly. Though the shah's importance to the global oil industry had risen dramatically since the dark days of 1954, the monarch's adversarial relationship with the companies masked dependence. Ruhani's arguments and the potential to use OPEC as a means with which to squeeze concessions from the companies influenced the shah for a time, but fear of an open break compelled his advisors, particularly 'Alam and Fallah, to push him toward the companies' side. Iran's calculation mirrored that of other pro-Western governments, who steered OPEC away from the political ideology of resource nationalism in the first half of the 1960s.[133]

The shah's wariness would fade, of course. The late 1960s and the early 1970s saw the monarch embrace the role of petro-nationalist par excellence. Yet all that lay ahead. In the early 1960s, the companies found in the Pahlavi state a willing ally in its campaign to neuter OPEC. The shah did this because he relied upon the company's operations. He could not kill the golden goose. The Pahlavi petro-state that consolidated in the mid-1960s did so thanks to the financial returns of oil produced, shipped, and sold by the Seven Sisters. Yet if the shah succeeded between 1954 and 1965 to secure a financial foundation for his government, he struggled during the same period to apply oil power to resolve the country's internal economic and political instability. Oil flowed, but the failures of the Second Plan period produced an age of uncertainty and upheaval, one that would redefine the shah's relationship with the United States and the global development movement.

---

[132] Amuzegar and Fekrat, *Iran: Economic Development Under Dualistic Conditions*, 138; World Bank, "Current Economic Position and Prospects of Iran," March 30, 1965, Report No. AS-107a, Table 6.

[133] Citino, *From Arab Nationalism to OPEC*, 155.

7 Controlled Revolution
Expertise, Economics, and the American View of Iran, 1960–1965

It was on June 6, 1960, that the shah's ministers shuffled into his office to deliver their bad news. In the lead was Khosrow Hedayat, director of the Plan Organization. Flanking him on either side were Dr. Khodadad Farmanfarmaian and Dr. Ghulam-Reza Muqaddam, chiefs of the Plan Organization's Economic Bureau. The technocrats had met with the World Bank, the US Treasury, and the International Monetary Fund (IMF). Their view was grim: Iran was broke. The general budget, bloated from years of overspending, was wildly out of balance. Corruption and mismanagement had drained away billions in oil revenues and loans. A balance of payments crisis, inflation, and economic calamity loomed. The shah's economists advised they seek an emergency stabilization package from the IMF – an austerity program for which the international agency would become famous in subsequent decades. The move would balance the budget but almost certainly cause a recession. There was no other option.[1]

The financial crisis of 1960 sent shock waves through Iran's economy. In May the following year, with thousands of teachers and students protesting low wages and the National Front reorganizing to demand new elections, Mohammed Reza Pahlavi appointed 'Ali Amini as prime minister and withdrew from directing Iran's government. The very same economists who had brought on the IMF stabilization package would now assist the Amini government with a new economic development program. The United States took this as a positive sign, "the best, and maybe the last, hope of averting political chaos and the possible loss of Iran to the West."[2] The Kennedy administration was ready to throw its support behind Amini and his economists. The shah, it seemed, was finished.

---

[1] HIOHP, Farmanfarmaian, Tape 8, 3.
[2] "Report of the Presidential Task Force on Foreign Economic Assistance," Komer, Memo for the President, May 19, 1961, Wailes to Rusk, May 25, 1961, NSF Box 115, JFKPL.

Four years later, a very different mood prevailed. Instead of economic chaos, Iran was booming. Amini was gone, Kennedy was dead, and US officials urged their government to move away from directly pressuring the shah, "more firmly in [the] saddle ... than ever before."[3] Over the course of the early 1960s, the Pahlavi government underwent a transformation, as the shah consolidated his rule through the White Revolution and Western-trained Iranian technocrats replaced foreign developmentalists. The American perspective of Iran changed from a narrative of collapse to one of revolution, progress, and stability. Once a country wracked with internal problems, governed by an administration seen as incompetent and incapable, Iran became by the late 1960s a poster child for modernization theory and a key US ally in the Middle East.

This chapter examines how these two developments – Iran's internal transformation and its transformation in the eyes of American policymakers – occurred during the tumultuous period from 1960 to 1965. Seven years after the August 1953 coup, American confidence in the shah reached a nadir. A new government headed by the reformer 'Ali Amini arose in 1961 and drew its strongest support from a group of technocrats in the Plan Organization. The "young planners," selected and trained by the Ford Foundation, a major American philanthropic organization, successfully steered Iran through the fiscal crisis and proposed a bold new program, the Third Plan, to bring the entire national economy under the umbrella of coordinated development planning. New Frontiersmen in the Kennedy administration endorsed Amini and the plan, which offered a path to a "controlled revolution" that would stabilize Iran internally. Though this signaled a new strain in American thinking, the goal – maintaining the dual integration of oil and preserving Iran's pro-Western strategic alignment – remained unchanged.[4]

---

[3] *FRUS 1964–1968, XXII*: 195–200.
[4] James F. Goode, "Reforming Iran during the Kennedy Years," *Diplomatic History* 15 (Winter 1991): 13–29; Victor V. Nemchenok, "In Search of Stability Amid Chaos: US Policy Toward Iran 1961–1963," *Cold War History* 10 (2010): 341–369; Roland Popp, "Benign Intervention? The Kennedy Administration's Push for Reform in Iran," in *John F. Kennedy and the 'Thousand Days:' New Perspectives on the Foreign and Domestic Policies of the Kennedy Administration*, eds., Manfred Berg and Andreas Etges (Heidelberg: Universitatsverlag Winter Heidelberg, 2007), 197–219; Popp, "An Application of Modernization Theory during the Cold War? The Case of Pahlavi Iran," *International History Review* 30, no. 1 (March 2008): 76–98; April R. Summitt, "For a White Revolution: John F. Kennedy and the Shah of Iran," *The Middle East Journal* 58, no. 4 (Autumn 2000): 560–575; Collier, *Democracy and the Nature of US Influence in Iran*, 186–228; Andrew Warne, "Psychoanalyzing Iran: Kennedy's Iran Task Force and the Modernization of Orientalism, 1961–1963," *International History Review* 35, no. 2 (2013): 396–422.

Both Amini and the New Frontier failed to achieve their intended objectives. A powerful bloc of conservative Kennedy administration officials doubted any course of action that did not serve to prop up the shah. In the conservatives' view, it was pointless to imagine Iran achieving any greater degree of stability than what the shah could impose through top-down, oil-funded authoritarianism. With the tacit support of the conservative group in Washington, the shah outmaneuvered Amini and launched the White Revolution, a program specially designed to outflank the young technocrats and appeal to American sensibilities. Though it won praise in Washington, the shah's program threatened to further destabilize the economy. The shah's revolution was saved by the timely injection of oil revenues – a reward for his cooperation with the consortium described in Chapter 6 – and the assistance of pro-shah technocrats who managed the Iranian economy after 1963.

The Pahlavi petro-state emerged from the crises of the early 1960s, when the shah crafted the myth of modernization that would inspire the remainder of his reign. The United States and American developmentalists abandoned further efforts to influence the course of Iranian economic development, resigning to a new narrative of the shah as a revolutionary monarch. The shah's "Great Civilization" was born from the first half of the 1960s: A state fueled by oil and economic growth, yet one possessed of internal contradictions that would in time bring about its disintegration.

7.1 "The Harvard Boys": The Economic Bureau and the Financial Crisis of 1960

Between 1954 and 1960, the US government backed Iran with large disbursements of economic and military aid. The administration's policy was designed to bolster the shah's government so that it might broaden its base of support while suppressing communist or revolutionary groups. This would keep Iran in the Western camp, preserving the victory won in August 1953 and retaining Western control of the Middle East's oil fields. The results of the strategy were disappointing. Within several years, it was clear that the shah's regime struggled against corruption, nepotism, inefficiency, and waste.[5]

Officials used the language of incapacity to describe the Iranian effort. Apart from the principle of applying oil money to development and asserting independence from the central government, the Second

---

[5] Milani, *The Shah*, 237–242.

7.1 "The Harvard Boys"

Seven-Year Plan appeared to have no guiding ideology. "Administrative chaos … mismanagement, political rivalries, inertia and lack of skills," plagued the plan effort, according to a National Security Council report from February 1957.[6] Officials noted that many Iranians were "pessimistic" about the plan's prospects, regarding it as a foreign-backed program that chiefly benefited Iran's elite.[7] Despite "oft-repeated and widely publicized promises," the plan delivered few physical benefits while serving as a focal point for discontent among Iran's political classes.[8]

Frustrations with the pace of Iran's development were compounded by growing exasperation with the shah, a "sensitive and mercurial individual," prone to bouts of "uncertainty and petulance" in the view of US officials.[9] "His Majesty likes to think of himself as a reformer," concluded the embassy in 1957, but appeared incapable of proposing structural change to Iran's creaking economic system.[10] His dependence on US assistance did not dissuade the shah from indulging in conspiracy theories, and he remained suspicious of US and British intentions. In the late 1950s he conducted desultory negotiations with Moscow, teasing out a closer relationship with the Soviet Union to demonstrate his strategic independence.[11]

While the United States regarded this activity as a minor concern, new doubts emerged in 1958 regarding Iran's internal stability in the wake of the revolution in Iraq, the Qarani coup plot of February, and the mounting financial problems of the plan. "Dissatisfaction with the Shah's regime appears … widespread," according to a National Security Council report from October 1958, and the monarch's ability to retain power appeared doubtful without "dramatic reforms in the near future." The report noted the increasing problem of US "overidentification" with the shah's government.[12]

Though patience with the shah had been stretched, it had not broken. As in 1953, a narrative of collapse dogged the United States. Fears that Iran was close to some calamity recurred in diplomatic correspondence. John Bowling, a Farsi-speaking political officer at the embassy in 1958, felt Iranian discontent could be offset if the shah offered economic

---

[6] *FRUS 1955–1957, XII*: 900–910.
[7] RG 59 888.00/12-2255, US Consulate Meshed No. 30, Dissatisfaction with Plan Organization, December 22, 1955, USNA.
[8] *FRUS 1955–1957, XII*: 816–819, see also 880–881.
[9] *FRUS 1955–1957, XII*: 747–748, 702.   [10] *FRUS 1955–1957, XII*: 910–920.
[11] Roham Alvandi, "Flirting with Neutrality: The Shah, Khrushchev, and the Failed 1959 Soviet-Iranian Negotiations," *Iranian Studies* 47, no. 3 (2014): 419–440.
[12] National Security Council, Operations Coordinating Board Report on Iran, NSC 5703/ 1, October 8, 1958, National Security Council Staff Papers, Disaster File, Box 66, DDEPL.

opportunities "financed by oil revenues." Bowling believed this eventually would lead to political reform, but only after a transitory period of authoritarian rule.[13] According to Bowling, the freest elections in Iran's history had resulted in "demagogues" like Mosaddeq and Kashani "swaying the city masses."[14] It was safer to leave Iran in the hands of a reasonably friendly autocrat, particularly one who was amenable to accepting assistance and employed foreign experts in large numbers.

At the forefront of that effort was the Ford Foundation and Harvard University's project to develop a cadre of professional economists within the Plan Organization. Plan director Abolhassan Ebtehaj requested Ford Foundation assistance in September 1954. Conscious of the scale of the Second Plan, Ebtehaj desired a team of professional economists who could assist with budgeting and programming. He also believed a team of Western-trained economists would help Iran secure loans from the World Bank. The Ford Foundation was already active in Iran in the fields of rural improvement, health, and sanitation. The evident need for administrative reform, both within the Plan Organization and across the Pahlavi government more broadly, attracted the foundation's attention. According to consultant Paul Parker, Iran's government required "rigorous administrative reorganization," incorporating technical experts throughout the bureaucratic hierarchy.[15] After an initial appraisal, Ford Foundation officer Kenneth Iverson concluded that Iran needed a staff of Western-trained Iranian economists "responsible for preparing a sound economic development program ... of the magnitude possible with oil revenues."[16]

The Ford Foundation was not interested in oil, but knowledge. Modernization theorists had concluded that education, along with urbanization and the consumption of mass media, were crucial to the construction of modern societies built around a thriving middle-class.[17] Economic development, noted political scientist Robert Packenham, could be "orchestrated by a well-educated elite ... dedicated to the

---

[13] RG 59 788.00/3-2656, "Analysis of the Plan Organization and the Political Stability of Iran," March 26, 1956, 788.00/9-458, "Current Political Situation in Iran and Assessment of Future," September 4, 1958, 788.00/10-2158, "Aspects of Current Political Situation in Iran," October 21, 1958, USNA.

[14] *FRUS 1958–1960, XII*: 696–698.

[15] Paul Parker, "Planning for Development in Iran, 1954–1962," November 1954, FFR R-0811, RAC.

[16] Iverson to Hill, March 9, 1957, FFR R-0812, RAC.

[17] Daniel Lerner, *The Passing of Traditional Society: Modernizing the Middle East* (New York: Free Press, 1958), 45–53.

7.1 "The Harvard Boys"

principle of sustained economic growth."[18] The foundation's plan to inculcate economic expertise in Iran mirrored similar efforts launched in the 1950s in Taiwan and South Korea, and in the mid-1960s in Indonesia.[19] Iran had a large community of expatriate students and a long tradition of aristocrats and elites seeking credentials from foreign universities. The foundation worked with Edward Mason, a prominent professor of development economics at Harvard University and a future advisor to the Kennedy administration. In their search to fill out Iran's new Economic Bureau, the foundation and Harvard hunted for Iranians with advanced degrees in administration and economics from American universities.[20]

Mason succeeded in luring Dr. Khodadad Farmanfarmaian, a scion of one of Iran's oldest families and an economist with a PhD from the University of Colorado, with the promise of a large salary and rapid promotion. Farmanfarmaian, or "Joe" to his American colleagues, was a dynamic personality who enjoyed influence within the government thanks to his aristocratic pedigree. The bureau's workhorse was Dr. Ghulam-Reza Muqaddam, a Stanford graduate and one of Iran's few economists "in the Anglo-Saxon sense of the word," as he understood both macroeconomic theory and the practical application of economic ideas.[21] Farmanfarmaian was assisted by his deputy, Hossein Mahdavy, a French-educated economist and "first-class" intellect.[22] Working alongside the bureau was the Harvard Advisory Group (HAG), a team of less

---

[18] Robert A. Packenham, *Liberal America and the Third World: Political Development Ideas in Foreign Aid and Social Science* (Princeton NJ: Princeton University Press, 1973); quoted in Edward H. Berman, *The Ideology of Philanthropy: The Influence of the Carnegie, Ford and Rockefeller Foundations on American Foreign Policy* (Albany NY: State University of New York Press, 1983), 4, 8–9.

[19] Ramin Nassehi, "Domesticating Cold War Economic Ideas: The Rise of Iranian Developmentalism in the 1950s and 1960s," in *The Age of Aryamehr: Late Pahlavi Iran and Its Global Entanglements*, ed. Roham Alvandi (London: Gingko Library, 2018), 45; Gregg Brazinsky, "Korean Modernization: Modernization Theory and South Korean Intellectuals," in *Staging Growth: Modernization, Development and the Global Cold War*, eds. Engerman, et al (Amherst MA: University of Massachusetts Press, 2003), 195–288; Simpson, *Economists with Guns*, 1–37.

[20] Shannon, *Losing Hearts and Minds*, 17–42.

[21] Farmanfarmaian, Report on the Formation and Development of the Economic Bureau 1336–1342, Box 559, 17, 19, RAC. Muqaddam and Farmanfarmaian had studied Iran's oil industry: Both concluded that oil had done little to spur general changes to Iran's economy. Khodadad Farmanfarmaian, "An Analysis of the Role of the Oil Industry in the Economy of Iran" (PhD Diss., University of Colorado, 1956); Reza Muqqadam, "Iran's Foreign Trade Policy and Economic Development in the Interwar Period," (PhD Diss., Stanford University, 1956).

[22] HIOHP, Farmanfarmaian, Tape No. 2, 4–5; FISDS, *Barnameh rizi-ye*, Interviews with Farmanfarmaian, Gudarzi, and Majidi; Majidi, *Khatirat-e 'Abd al-Majid Majidi*, 45–48, 82–89; HIOHP, Muqaddam, Tape No. 1, 7–10.

than a dozen economists and administrators led by Harvard's Kenneth Hansen. An administrator in the mold of Arthur C. Millspaugh, Hansen worked in the oil industry before joining Mason at Harvard. "[An] excellent, hard-working executive, persuasive, able, intelligent and hard-driving," Hansen was also impatient and outspoken, with a habit of talking down to his Iranian colleagues."[23] He spoke no Persian and rarely left Tehran.

Farmanfarmaian remembered his time in the bureau fondly: "We were the Young Turks … it was like a Camelot."[24] Others recalled the punishing hours and Ebtehaj's dictatorial style of management. The Tehran press took to calling the bureau's economists "American chickens," while in government circles they were labeled "Harvard Boys," "Massachusetts' men," or the "Ford Mafia."[25] The bureau and the HAG owed their position to support from Ebtehaj, but that ended when the plan director fell from power in early 1959.[26] Command of plan funds then passed to the Ministry of Finance, led by a pro-shah military commander whose education had not proceeded past elementary school.[27] While the bureau was not an executive body – "[it] advised and argued but it did not make decisions," noted Farmanfarmaian – the group was tasked with drawing up Iran's foreign loan applications, reviewed major project proposals, and set to work drafting a Third Plan to commence upon the Second Plan's conclusion in September 1962.[28]

It would take a financial crisis to bring the economists to the fore of Pahlavi policymaking. For years, Iran's economy had been running hot, racking up substantial trade imbalances funded through foreign loans, oil revenues, and internal credit. Capital inflows, including World Bank loans, financial assistance from the US government, and payments from the consortium, helped Iran manage the burden. But in 1958 trends began to reverse. Input slowed and expenditures mounted, partly due to the growing demands of service payments on the nation's many loans. Hansen and Farmanfarmaian warned that the nation was at risk of draining its foreign exchange reserves if it did not correct its budget and trade deficits. The state would have to contract $450 million in

---

[23] Papanek to Mason, May 22, 1959, FFR R-0812, RAC.
[24] HIOHP, Farmanfarmaian, Tape No. 2, 11–12.
[25] Majidi, *Khatirat-e 'Abd al-Majid Majidi*, 93–96.
[26] George Baldwin, *Planning and Development in Iran* (Baltimore MD: Johns Hopkins Press, 1967), 110–114; Papanek to Mason, May 22, 1959, FFR R-0812, RAC.
[27] Farmanfarmaian, Report on the Formation and Development of the Economic Bureau 1336–1342 (1963), Box 559, 47, RAC; RG 59 888.00/11-3060, US Embassy Tehran No. 303, November 30, 1960, USNA.
[28] Farmanfarmaian, Report on the Formation and Development of the Economic Bureau 1336–1342 (1963), Box 559, 63, RAC.

7.1 "The Harvard Boys"

new loans to meet its ambitious spending goals. Otherwise, "the resulting inflation and balance of payments difficulties" would be significant.[29] In 1959, pressure from the bureau convinced the shah to cut the Second Plan from 113 billion rials to 93 billion rials, or $1.2 billion, with several high-profile projects delayed to the next planning period.[30]

This was too little, too late. By February 1960, the Bank-e Melli reported that stocks of foreign exchange were nearly depleted. The country faced a balance of payments crisis, one that government officials – including the shah – should have anticipated, given the regime's spending habits.[31] If left unresolved, the crisis would have dire effects on the pace of the shah's development program. Plan operations would have to be shut down, leaving thousands of Iranians without work. Trade would freeze, inflation accelerate, and the national economy sputter to a halt. The US embassy wasted little time in assigning blame. The shah's failure to identify the growing danger represented "the irrational Iranian characteristic to ignore unpleasant realities."[32] Eisenhower fretted that economic aid and technical assistance had failed in "properly orienting the Iranian people" around programs of fiscal responsibility: "[T]he situation in Iran sounded rather hopeless."[33] The bureau estimated a $49 million hard currency deficit by the end of 1960.[34]

Rather than manage the crisis himself, the shah deputized the Plan Organization and its economists to address the country's economic problems. Plan Director Khosrow Hedayat, Farmanfarmaian, and Muqaddam traveled to Washington in June 1960 to negotiate a bailout from the IMF. Rather than ask for more loans – a request which they knew would be denied – the economists proposed an economic stabilization package that would accompany reforms to Iran's administration and financial system, including greater budget oversight and a central bank, the Bank-e Markazi, to regulate the currency. Hedayat argued that the country could not simply fall back on its favored tactic of diverting oil revenues. Such resources "exist underground and at present only serve

---

[29] Farmanfarmaian, Report on the Formation and Development of the Economic Bureau 1336–1342 (1963), Box 559, 44, RAC.
[30] RG 59 888.00/3-2660, US Embassy Tehran No. 609, March 26, 1960, USNA.
[31] Farhad Daftary, "The Balance of Payments Deficit and the Problem of Inflation in Iran, 1955–1962," *Iranian Studies* 5, no. 1 (Winter, 1972): 2–24.
[32] RG 59 888.00/7-660, US Embassy Tehran No. 4, July 6, 1960; see also 888.00/9-860, US Embassy Tehran No. 120, September 8, 1960, 888.00/5-2460, US Embassy Tehran No. 757, May 24, 1960, USNA.
[33] *FRUS 1958–1960, XII*: 669–670.
[34] *Review of the Second Seven Year Plan Program of Iran*, March 10, 1960: Division of Economic Affairs (Plan Organization. Tehran, Iran), 13.

as a basis of Iran's ability to repay its debts in the future."[35] It was an impressive presentation.

The IMF agreed to provide $35 million in standby credits, while the US government offered loans to cover the Second Plan funding gap, provided the shah implement the economists' plan, cut the budget, and freeze spending. Despite protests from his ministers, the shah approved the program on June 14, with the first credits delivered that September. Both the government and plan budgets were brought into balance. Efforts to enforce the program drew the ire of the powerful bazaar merchants who continued to dominate Tehran's urban economy. One merchant stormed the bank's offices, brandished a knife in Muqaddam's face and threatened to impale whoever was responsible for rescinding his banana import license.[36] Nevertheless, the financial crisis had been averted. The US embassy praised the efforts of Iran's young professionals who had struggled "[against] the backwardness and indiscipline of a whole society," yet had emerged triumphant.[37]

Though the Second Plan had produced disappointing results, the efforts of the Economic Bureau had borne fruit. Iran's government, noted Harvard's Edward Mason, "is learning how economists can and should be used."[38] The activities of the young economists inspired genuine enthusiasm in Washington and in the embassy at a time when exasperation with the shah was reaching a peak. Where there had once appeared no viable alternative to the shah's brand of authoritarianism, the crisis of 1960 suggested a new way forward, one that officials in the administration of President John F. Kennedy would embrace during the brief, eventful ascendance of the bureau's young economists under Prime Minister 'Ali Amini.

7.2 The Kennedy Administration and the Amini Experiment

The administration of President John F. Kennedy (Figure 7.1) took office at a time when Iran appeared to be teetering on the brink of a

---

[35] RG 59 888.00/6-1160, US Embassy Tehran No. 799, June 11, 1960, Enclosure to No. 799, Memo of Conversation, May 3, 1960, USNA. For memos of the June meetings, see RG 59 888.00 SEVEN YEAR/6-2260, Memo of Conversation, June 22, 1960, 888.00 SEVEN YEAR/6-2460, Memo of Conversation, June 24, 1960, 888.00 SEVEN YEAR/6-2960, Memo of Conversation, June 29, 1960, USNA; *FRUS 1958–1960, Near East Region, Vol. XII*, No. 292, Herter to Wailes, No. 24, July 1, 1960.

[36] HIOHP, Muqaddam, Tape No. 1, 15–17. The license, he explained, had been his reward for organizing crowds to support the shah on August 19, 1953.

[37] RG 59 888.00/11-3060, US Embassy Tehran No. 303, November 30, 1960.

[38] Mason to Ward, June 23, 1960, FFR R-0813, RAC.

7.2 The Kennedy Administration and the Amini Experiment

Figure 7.1 The Shah with President John F. Kennedy (middle) and Secretary of Defense Robert S. McNamara (right), 1962.
Photo ID AR7165-M, JFKPL

new disaster. While a foreign exchange crisis had been avoided thanks to the Economic Bureau and the IMF stabilization package, the economy slumped into recession in the second half of 1960. Majlis elections fell apart amid obvious signs of vote rigging, forcing the shah to take the embarrassing step of holding new elections later in the year. The National Front reformed and began demonstrating for the first time in nearly a decade.[39] The shah responded in haphazard fashion and displayed a growing paranoid suspicion that foreign agents – including the Americans and British – were working with internal actors to topple him, as they had Mosaddeq.[40] NIOC Chairman 'Abdullah Entezam privately felt the shah "could not build real political stability purely on his own," and would soon have to relax his personal rule.[41] Assessments from the United States were decidedly gloomy. Eisenhower himself admitted in

---

[39] *FRUS 1958–1960, XII*: 692–693.   [40] Cottam, *Iran and the United States*, 124.
[41] RG 59 788.00/9-360, Memo of Conversation, September 3, 1960, USNA.

June 1960 that the situation looked as bad "as it had been during the time of Mossadegh," and wondered whether Iranian liberals might depose the shah.[42] Soviet Premier Nikita Khrushchev declared that Iran would soon fall "like a ripe plum" into the Soviet sphere of influence, an idle boast that US officials nevertheless took seriously.[43]

Dissatisfied with the Eisenhower-era policies that focused on propping up right wing dictatorships, the New Frontiersmen of the Kennedy administration who came to power in early 1961 hoped to use American political and financial power to sponsor political reform abroad.[44] Modernization theory inspired the administration's policies, with Kennedy surrounding himself with academics like Walt Rostow and Edward Mason, the sponsor for the Harvard Advisory Group to Iran's Economic Bureau. Despite the new administration's vigor, changes in personnel and rhetoric concealed strong elements of continuity. Development, police training, and internal security assistance were all tools that could, according to Kennedy aide Robert Komer, "prevent revolutionary situations" from arising in countries threatened by communism.[45] A hyperactive man close to Kennedy and National Security Advisor McGeorge Bundy, Komer advocated for policies that would push the shah toward substantive reforms, using economic and military aid as leverage. Komer's allies included the president's brother Robert Kennedy and Supreme Court Justice William O. Douglas; experts like Princeton University's T. Cuyler Young, William K. Polk of the Policy Planning staff, and Richard Cottam in the State Department; and the new Deputy Director of the Bureau of Budget, Kenneth Hansen.[46]

While acting as head of the Harvard Advisory Group, Hansen had seen the disorder within the shah's government firsthand. Unlike most American developmentalists, Hansen made no effort to kowtow to the shah, whom he regarded as myopic and militaristic. During a final audience with Iran's ruler in January 1961, Hansen explained that the shah's preoccupation with military affairs was misplaced. What Iran needed was better management and a firmer commitment to executing the terms of the stabilization package. Inflation and the "unsettling effect of price increases" were much more dangerous than having "5,000

---

[42] *FRUS 1958–1960, XII*: 676–678.
[43] Cottam, *Iran and the United States*, 142; Goode, "Reforming Iran," 16.
[44] Westad, *Global Cold War*, 27.
[45] Komer to "Bill," March 24, 1962, NSF Box 116, JFKPL. See Michael E. Latham, *Modernization as Ideology: American Social Science and 'Nation Building' in the Kennedy Era* (Chapel Hill NC: University of North Carolina Press, 2000).
[46] Popp, "'Benign Intervention?'," 204; Goode, "Reforming Iran," 18.

7.2 The Kennedy Administration and the Amini Experiment

disgruntled officers on the streets of Tehran." The shah did not dispute any of Hansen's points.[47] Once in Washington, Hansen was the most vocal advocate for "prompting and prodding" the shah's government toward major reform, while his knowledge of Iran gave him influence with Komer.[48] Komer and Hansen joined a special Iran Task Force formed in May 1961 to reconsider US policy, joining representatives from State, Treasury, the Agency for International Development (AID, the successor to Point Four), and the CIA.[49]

The timing for the new task force was significant. In Iran, the National Front organized teachers, students, and government workers to demonstrate against the stabilization package, which had frozen wages and caused a business depression, and call for fair elections. On May 2, a crowd of 50,000 teachers and students gathered in Baharestan Square. The military opened fire, killing one teacher. To avoid further violence, the shah removed his loyalist prime minister and appointed Dr. 'Ali Amini to serve as premier.[50] An aristocrat and a landowner with a long career in politics, Amini held progressive bona fides, having served in Mosaddeq's first cabinet. After appointing Amini, the shah withdrew from public life. The new prime minister announced a raft of reform measures, including an accelerated land reform program and anti-corruption drive, designed to mollify the protesting National Front and head off a general political crisis. Inside Iran, it was assumed that pressure from the United States had played a role in Amini's appointment.[51]

The shah, to put it mildly, was uncomfortable with Amini. Since his ascension in 1941, Mohammed Reza Pahlavi had contended with a string of powerful prime ministers – Ahmed Qavam, 'Ali Razmara, Mohammed Mosaddeq – and had outlasted or outmaneuvered each one. Amini appeared particularly dangerous. An old associate of Qavam and a member of the Qajar family (the dynasty which the shah's father had overthrown in the 1920s), Amini was well-regarded in Washington and widely considered to be "America's man" in Iranian politics.

The shah appointed Amini for several reasons. The first was his suspicion of the Kennedy administration, which he feared intended to

---

[47] Hansen to Mason, Interview with the Shah, February 15, 1961, FFR R-0813, RAC.
[48] Hansen, "Some Notes on the Situation in Iran," March 20, 1961, NSF Box 115a, Memo by Komer, October 28, 1961, NSF Box 116, JFKPL.
[49] Goode, "Reforming Iran," 18–19.   [50] Milani, *The Shah*, 251–253.
[51] Milani, *The Shah*, 255–258. David Collier argues that the shah would not have selected Amini without pressure from the United States. James Goode and Victor Nemchenok argue that the United States supported Amini, but do not imply the United States forced his hand. See Collier, *Democracy and the Nature of US Influence in Iran*, 198–200; Nemchenok, "In Search of Stability," 349; Goode, "Reforming Iran," 19–20.

pressure him into passing reforms or possibly even force him to abdicate the throne. Amini's appointment was meant to relieve such pressures. Amini was also very popular with the young technocrats of the Economic Bureau and was personal friends with Abolhassan Ebtehaj, the father of Iran's development program. "He believed in economic and financial discipline," recalled Muqaddam, and supported the stabilization program, without which Iran would return "to the brink of bankruptcy."[52] This lent Amini an air of technocratic competence and a connection to the foreign developmentalist community that was close to the Kennedy administration. Fearful of Kennedy's agenda and alarmed at the rising tide of middle-class opposition, the shah publicly stepped aside in favor of a figure who appeared suitable both to Washington officials and the protesting National Front.[53] As he had with Razmara and Mosaddeq, the shah calculated that a tactical retreat would mollify the United States and allow him to reassert his authority once the situation had improved.

The shah's calculation proved correct. While there is no evidence suggesting the United States directly imposed Amini on the shah, US officials in Tehran and Washington welcomed his appointment, which seemed to be Iran's "last chance" of maintaining a stable pro-Western trajectory.[54] Amini's platform was a bold one. His most high-profile promise was to implement land reform and he brought on Hasan Arsanjani, the country's most articulate proponent for rural improvement, to serve as his minister of agriculture. The key to the new government's vitality would be its dependence on "able and reasonably reliable new men rising in Iranian society," wrote Kennedy's advisor Walt Rostow.[55] The Iran Task Force concluded that the United States must take "vigorous action" to back Amini and his reformers.[56] Part of that action would be to support the Economic Bureau, arguably Amini's most important base of support within the Pahlavi government, and the country's new development strategy, the Third Plan, which Farmanfarmaian's team was finishing in 1961.

Budgeted at 190 billion rials or $2.4 billion, the Third Plan was a response to the failures of the Second Plan. Rather than assemble a laundry list of infrastructural projects, the Third Plan targeted Iran's entire economy in a coordinated fashion. The goal was an annual expansion of Iran's gross national product (GNP) at a rate of 6 percent for five-

---

[52] HIOHP, Muqaddam, Tape No. 2, 11–12. [53] Milani, *The Shah*, 257.
[54] Komer, Memo for the President, May 19, 1961, NSF Box 115, JFKPL.
[55] Rostow to McGhee, March 28, 1961, NSF Box 115a, JFKPL.
[56] "A Review of the Problems in Iran and the Recommendations for the NSC," from the Iran Task Force, May 15, 1961, NSF, Box 115a, JFKPL.

7.2 The Kennedy Administration and the Amini Experiment

	Second Plan		Third Plan
	Planned	Estimated	Planned
Multi-Purpose Dams	13.21	12.4	12.3
Training, Extension, Direct Aid to Production	2.61	1.7	10.1
Credit and Cooperatives	1.81	1.19	11
Roads and Railroads	23.83	24.37	18.8
Telecommunications	1.13	0.99	4.9
Public Sector Industrial Investment	5.83	5.74	24.87
Private Sector Industrial Investment	0.91	0.93	6.13
Regional Development (Khuzestan Development Service)	11.39	11.6	–
Manpower Training	–	–	6.2
Health & Education	4.52	4.8	23.5

Figure 7.2 Comparison of Second and Third Plans (billion rials)[57]

and-a-half years. Investment would be directed toward projects increasing agricultural productivity, with a particular focus on training and cooperatives to improve practices.[58] More than 24 billion rials would be pumped into industrialization projects to spur economic growth. An equally large investment into education and health would improve living standards (Figure 7.2).

Funded with Iran's oil revenues, the Third Plan would need around $900 million in foreign assistance, primarily from the World Bank. The bureau wanted foreign involvement because they believed it would instill a greater degree of fiscal discipline within the Pahlavi state. "Our society ... were not sufficiently versed in the benefits of planning," recalled Farmanfarmaian. "Unless the Plan was given an enforcement instrument, there was little chance of its success."[59] Constraints imposed by

---

[57] Figures for Third and Second Plan disbursements from *IBRD, The Economic Development Program of Iran: An Appraisal, Part I, Main Report* (April 17, 1963), Report No. AS-93a, Table 26. Figures supplied by Economic Bureau.
[58] RG 59 888.00/1-1460, US Embassy Tehran No. 432, January 27, 1960, USNA.
[59] Farmanfarmaian, Report on the Formation and Development of the Economic Bureau 1336–1342 (1963), Box 559, 60.

the bank would provide the planners an instrument for assuring government compliance.

The New Frontiersmen in Washington latched on to the Third Plan as a vehicle to reform the entire Pahlavi regime. It was an instrument, wrote Komer, for "end-running revolutionaries," and carrying out the controlled revolution he felt was needed in Iran.[60] Komer's enthusiasm was enough to get Kennedy's attention. The president asked whether the United States could do more to help Amini "glamorize" the Third Plan "as a bold new effort to modernize Iran," and use it as a tool for the prime minister to outmaneuver the National Front and assemble a pro-Western middle-class coalition.[61] For Hansen, the ultimate goal was political, rather than economic. "We are looking to the present regime of Prime Minister Amini rather more than to the Shah ... to provide the impetus toward faster economic progress," he wrote to the president.[62] By assisting the Third Plan, the United States would obtain leverage it could then use to push the shah toward major institutional reforms, including cutting military spending, permitting greater political expression, and withdrawing permanently from major decision-making.

While the New Frontiersmen initially held sway within the administration, Komer and Hansen's drive to pressure the shah encountered stiff resistance. John Bowling, now the State Department's Iran expert, doubted whether a regime detached from the shah could succeed at practical reform. He continued to push the policy he had advocated while at the embassy in the 1950s. The shah, despite his many faults, was "the sine qua non ... without [him], moderation and sensible reform will disappear from the Persian scene."[63] Supporting Amini made tactical sense, "but it is only with [the shah's] support" that the reform program was possible in the first place, according to Ambassador Julius C. Holmes in Tehran, who was personally close to the shah. "The character of the Persian people," wrote Holmes in an extraordinary message to the State Department's Armin Meyer, lead him to believe that the country required leadership from a "central authority not subject to the daily whims ... of the disunited, highly individualistic and uncooperative people."[64] The United States had to remain unwavering in its support of the shah. The alternative, as Holmes liked to note, was

---

[60] Memo for Rostow, November 24, 1961 NSF Box 116, JFKPL.
[61] Bundy to Rusk, Iran, August 7, 1961, NSF Box 116, JFKPL.
[62] *FRUS 1961–1963 XVII*: 580–582.
[63] RG 59 788.00/1-2362, Bowling to Talbot/Miner, January 23, 1962, USNA.
[64] RG 59 788.00/9-961, Holmes to Meyer, August 27, 1961, USNA.

7.2 The Kennedy Administration and the Amini Experiment

surrendering to the National Front, "demagoguery [and] hysterical xenophobia."[65]

Most of the policymaking bureaucracy sided with the conservatives like Bowling and Holmes. Gesturing at the expensive failures of the Second Plan era, Meyer was "extremely dubious" that any "political mileage" could be gotten out of the Third Plan. "The Persian people," wrote Meyer, "have become almost bored with economic planning" and would reject more "castles in the sky" as empty promises "associated with hated foreign contractors and with high-level corruption."[66] While there was skepticism of the plan's potential as a political tool, the Iran Task Force report to Kennedy in October concluded that the "risks to the maintenance of a pro-Western regime" prohibited more intensive actions, including the conditional aid that Komer and Hansen were pushing.[67]

This do-nothing approach inspired a reaction from the frustrated deputy budget director. "I am uneasy about the heavy emphasis ... on the primacy of the Shah," Hansen wrote.[68] The Iran Task Force continued to argue that support should be offered to Amini. But such measures were to be limited and would not threaten Iran's military budget, which both Komer and Hansen believed needed to be cut to ensure success of the plan and sustain the influence of Amini and his technocrats.[69]

That influence had begun to wane by early 1962. While Amini and the bureau had made some progress implementing a round of administrative reforms, the government lacked a broad base of support. Amini's efforts to launch a land reform program had stalled, as had his negotiations with the National Front. The arrest of his friend Ebtehaj in late 1961 was a blow to his credibility, as justice ministry agents had acted without his knowledge.[70] The shah, meanwhile, steadily worked to undermine Amini from behind the scenes even as he feigned support of the Third Plan. Visiting Plan Organization headquarters on January 3, 1962, the shah viewed presentations by Manuchehr Gudarzi, who emphasized the coordinated and comprehensive nature of the plan strategy.[71] The shah

---

[65] Holmes to Rusk, February 19, 1962, NSF Box 116, JFKPL.
[66] RG 59 Records of the Iranian Affairs Desk, 1958–1963, Box 3, NEA Study of Possible US Actions Re: The Long-Term Political Situation in Iran, August 10, 1961, USNA; Meyer to Holmes, August 11, 1961, NSF Box 116, JFKPL.
[67] *FRUS 1961–1963, XVII*: 293–300.   [68] *FRUS 1961–1963, XVII*: 307–311.
[69] *FRUS 1961–1963, XVII*: 416–427.
[70] RG 59 788.00/2-1462, Minor to Acheson, February 14, 1962, 788.00/3-2062, Holmes to State, No. 743, March 20, 1962, 788.00/4-162, Holmes to State, No. 787, April 1, 1962, USNA.
[71] Farmanfarmaian, Report on the Formation and Development of the Economic Bureau, 58; FISDS, *Barnameh rizi-ye*, Interview with Gudarzi.

publicly endorsed the Third Plan, which Thomas MacLeod, Hansen's successor at HAG, praised as the "best drafted piece of legislation I have seen since coming here."[72] His support came even as the Tehran press attacked the bureau and other ministers in Amini's government denounced the Third Plan, dismissing the "inept young men interminably repeating their foreign textbooks," and foreign advisors, "an invasion of locusts."[73]

As Amini's position came under greater pressure in Tehran, the shah received an important morale boost during a trip to Washington, DC. His meetings with Kennedy and Secretary of State Dean Rusk were frosty and featured considerable pressure on Iran to focus on economic development. Despite the tension, the administration promised additional military aid, though a report from the joint chiefs indicated the shah's army was "corrupt, wasteful, and inefficient."[74] More importantly, the visit proved the Kennedy administration was no longer seriously considering any policy that sidelined the shah. Confident of support from Washington, the shah returned to Tehran just as his prime minister's position began to deteriorate.[75]

Collapsing under the strain of his many responsibilities, Amini's strength began to leave him in May 1962. He failed to confirm the Plan Organization's authority over the budget due to the resistance of the shah's allies in the Ministry of Finance. A furious Farmanfarmaian confronted the exhausted prime minister in his office, demanding an explanation: "You are the Prime Minister of the country, what power do you have?"[76] Farmanfarmaian opted to resign rather than continue the struggle. Edward Mason visited Tehran from Harvard and found the government in "disarray."[77] The Economic Bureau and Third Plan "[have] been under continuous political attack," with the shah offering only "sporadic assistance."[78]

The final blow to Amini came during the budget deliberations of June 1962. Try as he might, Amini found the budget gap of $30 million could not be filled without financial aid or cuts to the military budget. Kennedy sent a note to Tehran, reminding the shah of their conversations in April, "where he had been told that accelerated economic development was the

---

[72] MacLeod to Mason, No. 7, February 17, 1962, FFR R-0813, RAC.
[73] FO 248/1588 Record of Conversation, March 17, 1962, UKNA.
[74] *FRUS 1961–1963, XVII*: 557–563.   [75] Nemchenok, "In Search of Stability," 356.
[76] FISDS, *Barnameh rizi-ye*, Interview with Farmanfarmaian.
[77] Rusk to Rockwell, June 16, 1962, NSF Box 116, JFKPL.
[78] Mason to Ward, June 8, 1962, FFR R-0813, RAC.

7.2 The Kennedy Administration and the Amini Experiment

best road toward a bright future."[79] But the shah, no doubt confident that his support in Washington trumped that of his prime minister, held firm and refused to consider a cut to the military budget. Amini would not cut plan spending or divert oil revenues and resigned on July 19, after one last failed attempt to secure US assistance.[80] The shah, having outmaneuvered yet another rival, reasserted his control over the government and appointed his friend Asadollah 'Alam as prime minister.

The Amini experiment was over. With their chief sponsor gone, the influence of the Economic Bureau vanished overnight. 'Alam had the plan budget slashed by 30 percent, using the spare cash to plug the budget deficit.[81] A report from Lilienthal's D&R noted that while the plan would technically begin in September, it would have "no teeth [and] no money behind it."[82] Farmanfarmaian was gone. Muqaddam resigned. His choice was, as he recalls, a personal one: "I had come to the conclusion that a person like me ... could absolutely not be a minister in the shah's regime."[83]

Western developmentalists found themselves without institutional support. HAG leader Thomas MacLeod delivered an informal address to his staff in August. His speech dripped with invocations of Iranian incapacity. Iran has "learned nothing," and did not have the administrative skills to handle the Third Plan, "something alien, prepared by foreigners, for foreigners in the interest of foreigners."[84] American developmentalists, frustrated by yet another failure, blamed Iran's corrupt political culture and the incompetence of its leadership for their lack of progress. MacLeod's speech also served to acknowledge the new political realities. The days of foreign developmentalists guiding Iran's economic program were fast coming to an end.

In Washington, the pro-shah faction was in ascendance. As the shah announced a new program centered on land reform, Holmes declared Iran "the most stable" country in the Middle East and insisted military aid be expanded to ensure the shah's disposition remained favorable.[85]

---

[79] Komer to Bundy, June 20, 1962, Attached: Personal Message for Shah from JFK, NSF Box 116, JFKPL.
[80] Holmes to Rusk, June 24, 1962, Holmes to Rusk, July 1, 1962, Holmes to Rusk, July 2, 1962, Holmes to Rusk, July 4, 1962, Rusk to Holmes, July 13, 1962, NSF Box 116, JFKPL.
[81] RG 59 888.008-2162, Holmes to Rusk, No. 250, August 21, 1962, USNA.
[82] Blumberg to Oliver, July 7, 1962, DELP Box 433, SGMML.
[83] HIOHP, Muqaddam, Tape No. 2, 14, Tape No. 3, 3.
[84] The address was recounted by John Blumberg of KDS in a message to D&R headquarters in New York. See Blumberg to Oliver, August 2, 1962, DELP Box 433, SGMML.
[85] *FRUS 1961–1963, XVIII*: 202, ft. 2.

Komer was irate. "I find such euphoria hard to believe," he wrote. "The Alam government is a nonentity, and the new development plan a shadow." The situation seemed just as bad as it had been a year before – worse, perhaps, than in 1953. Komer remained convinced the United States needed a controlled revolution in Iran, but he was at a loss for how to produce one, now that Amini was gone and the shah firmly ensconced in a position of power.[86] The Iranians appeared incapable of managing their own progress. "They lack ... the capacity for sustained, dynamic effort," he concluded. "They don't have what it takes to run a country themselves."[87]

The Economic Bureau had attempted to bring Iran's government under technocratic management during the fourteen months of the Amini government. The New Frontiersmen, together with the Ford Foundation and the HAG, revived the old missionary spirit of World War II in their efforts to assist Iran's young economists. It was a view informed by Cold War strategic priorities and Iranian incapacity. Komer and Hansen felt that Iran needed foreign assistance and outside guidance. The bureau had concluded the Third Plan needed foreign supervision to protect it from Pahlavi politics. But just as the wartime idealism had fallen afoul of a more conservative attitude – dismissed as "messianic globaloney" and ultimately abandoned – the push for a vigorous policy in Iran failed due to resistance from a conservative bloc within the Kennedy administration. With the tacit approval of allies in Washington, the shah overthrew his competitor and launched his own reform campaign – a revolution that would reshape US-Iranian relations and change the course of Pahlavi governance for the remainder of his reign.

7.3 "A Revolutionary Monarch"

The White Revolution (*Engelab-e Sefid*), also known as the "Revolution of the Shah and the People," was in full swing by late 1962. The shah, supported by 'Alam and agricultural minister Hasan Arsanjani, accelerated Amini's land reform effort with a vigor that surprised Iranian and foreign observers alike. In the first phase, about 500 of Iran's largest landowning families had their estates forcibly broken up. Though some landlords resisted the distribution efforts, by November 1962 the aristocracy's power in the countryside "[had] been substantially broken," according to the US embassy, as agricultural ministry agents moved in to

---

[86] Komer to Bundy, November 5, 1962, NSF Box 116a, JFKPL.
[87] *FRUS 1961–1963*, XVIII: 189–194.

7.3 "A Revolutionary Monarch"

supplant the landlords.[88] The shah tied the land reform effort to a broader reform program that included women's suffrage, extended benefits for industrial workers, privatizing the state-owned factories, and expanded efforts to improve literacy in rural areas. In early 1963 the shah and Arsanjani organized a popular referendum that indicated 99 percent support for the White Revolution. The result was "artificially stimulated," yet gave the shah the legitimacy he needed and even garnered a congratulatory note from President Kennedy.[89]

The White Revolution, at first glance, offered a dazzling package of reforms that would dramatically alter Iran's political structure and social life. It seemed that the shah, after rejecting the idea of political reform in favor of the politics of promise symbolized by the Second Plan, had made a sudden and dramatic change in course. Land reform – or rather, land distribution – lay at the center of the new agenda. For years, Mohammed Reza Pahlavi had moved warily on the subject, for fear of upsetting his support among the country's aristocracy and Shi'a clergy, the two major landowning groups and critical bases of support for his regime following the coup of August 1953. This political calculus underwent a shift by the late 1950s. 'Alam explained it all to a British diplomat in 1958: The shah could not rely on conservative support as the country modernized and the middle-class grew larger. He had to lead a "popular and national crusade" that 'Alam termed a White Revolution, in order to broaden his base of support.[90]

While the White Revolution symbolized a shift in the shah's tactics, it was designed with careful political calculations in mind. The shah worried about the National Front – which he felt was "100 percent more dangerous than the Tudeh" – and sought to mollify middle-class frustrations.[91] The goal was the controlled revolution Komer had been pining for in Washington, a demonstration of the shah's desire for reform to silence critics in Iran and abroad. Politically, the White Revolution was effective. Rural landlords had little time to react, and the shah took measures to ensure most were well compensated. The National Front also failed to register a swift response. The most meaningful resistance came from Iran's Shi'a religious leadership. Led by the charismatic

---

[88] RG 59 888.16/11-1062, US Embassy Tehran, November 10, 1962, USNA.
[89] RG 59 POL IRAN Tehran to Paris, February 5, 1963, USNA. For the White Revolution, see Abrahamian, *Iran between Two Revolutions*, 423–424; Ann Lambton, *Persian Land Reform, 1962–1966* (Oxford: Clarendon Press, 1969), 60–69. For an analysis of land reform, see Afsaneh Najmabadi, *Land Reform and Social Change in Iran* (Salt Lake City UT: University of Utah Press, 1987).
[90] Quoted in Ansari, *Modern Iran*, 189–190.
[91] RG 59 888.00/1-2663, Holmes to State, January 26, 1963, USNA.

Ayatollah Ruhollah Khomeini, a body of clerics condemned the program, particularly the extension of women's suffrage, as contrary to the laws of Islam. Anywhere from 300 to several thousand people died on June 6 as security forces put down clerical demonstrations with fearsome efficiency. The shah, showing uncharacteristic confidence, also dispersed the National Front, whom he regarded as "an ill-assorted mixture of malcontents," with another round of arrests.[92] Further demonstrations were banned and a meek Majlis returned in late 1963 dominated by a mix of deputies handpicked through rigged ballots.

The shah and 'Alam, eager to implement the political provision of the White Revolution, neglected the economic repercussions of forcefully breaking apart the country's largest landed estates. The distribution campaign was rushed and poorly funded. Arsanjani allocated only 10 million rials, or roughly 250 rials for each of Iran's 40,000 villages, to sponsor local village councils and put aside very little to fund extension programs or agricultural credit.[93] By late 1963, land distribution had depressed business activity, while the demoralized and defunded Plan Organization slowed public investment, deepening the recession.[94] The shah shifted the focus "from long-term, centralized planning" to a new policy "designed to build up mass political support," according to one US analysis.[95] The result was that Iran's economy, after three years of recession, was in a state of chaos. "Land reform ... is failing," wrote the US consulate in Khorramshahr.[96]

The White Revolution did not co-opt the New Frontier. While the American response to the shah's reforms was positive, it was not rapturous. "I have never seen the shah quite so confident," wrote Ambassador Holmes, praising the land reform program to officials in Washington as "truly revolutionary."[97] Others less personally attached to the monarch were more critical. The CIA concluded that the political situation in Iran would remain "extremely fragile" for the foreseeable future.[98] Robert Komer, who still had Kennedy's ear despite the failure of the Amini policy, admitted the United States would have to "ride this tiger" after the shah's rigged referendum in January 1963. He remained eager to

---

[92] Holmes to State, February 5, 1963, NSF Box 116a, JFKPL; Bakhtiyar, *Khatirat*, 60, 70; Abrahamian, *Iran between Two Revolutions*, 425–426.
[93] Blumberg to Oliver, May 13, 1963, DRCR, Box 458, SGMML.
[94] RG 59 E 12 IRAN, US Embassy Tehran, September 30, 1963, USNA.
[95] SNIE 34-63, "The Iranian Situation" April 10, 1963, NSF, Box 116a, JFKPL.
[96] RG 59 E 12 IRAN US Consulate Khorramshahr, October 19, 1963, USNA.
[97] Holmes to Rusk, November 26, 1962, NSF Box 116a, JFKPL; *FRUS 1961–1963*, XVIII: 201–202.
[98] *FRUS 1961–1963*, XVIII: 84–88.

7.3 "A Revolutionary Monarch"

apply pressure as a means of maintaining US influence over the program.[99] John Bowling, while positive on the shah's overall reform effort, thought the White Revolution was proceeding "under growing signs of inept planning and administration."[100] Eventually, Holmes acknowledged that the shah's program suffered from an "incredible dearth of managerial competence ... from the shah on down."[101] A move to apply economic pressure or offer expert advice would fail, "[as] there is literally no one in real authority we can talk to on major economic problems," according to the embassy's economic staff.[102] Powerful voices near the president, including his brother Robert and Supreme Court Justice William O. Douglas, called for dumping the shah in favor of a "white-collar groups around the National Front."[103] The question of what to do in Iran remained an open one.

In an important memo written for Kennedy in April 1963, Secretary Rusk argued against any further efforts to intervene in Iran's development program. Enthusiasm for the Amini government in Washington had been based on the belief that a "local force" was emerging, one that would "[implement] a rapid modernization of Iranian institutions along lines long recommended by foreign advisors." But the shah was undertaking a reform program based on "self-help" over and above what Amini and Farmanfarmaian had hoped to achieve. Expecting the technocrats to triumph had been unrealistic, in part due to Iranian incapacity. "Sophisticated central planning institutions and procedures," noted Rusk, "have always faced an uncomprehending and suspicious environment in Iran ... the bazaar mentality of most Iranian businessmen is not, for example, well suited to the management of modern financial institutions."[104]

Rusk's memo clarified the US position. Both the secretary and Ambassador Holmes regarded the White Revolution as "extremely important for the progress and political stability of Iran."[105] They were equally sure that there was little the United States could do to interfere. "Revolutions can't be controlled by foreigners," wrote Holmes, "[and] we could endanger all we have gained" by intervening.[106] Foreign

---

[99] Komer to Bundy, January 29, 1963, NSF Box 116a, JFKPL.
[100] Memo for Bundy, January 21, 1963, NSF Box 116a, JFKPL.
[101] RG 59 E 12 IRAN, Holmes to Rusk, May 15, 1963, USNA.
[102] RG 59 E 12 IRAN, US Embassy Tehran, A-723, June 13, 1963, USNA.
[103] Milani, *The Shah*, 304.
[104] Dean Rusk, Memo for President, "Report on the US Strategy for Iran" April 20, 1963, NSF Box 116a, JFKPL.
[105] RG 59 E 12 IRAN, Rusk to Holmes, May 8, 1963, USNA.
[106] RG 59 E 12 IRAN, Holmes to Rusk, May 15, 1963, USNA.

involvement might discredit the shah's effort and blunt its political significance, "even if it were to contribute to its more technically perfect execution" according to Bowling.[107]

By September 1963 this was the accepted view within the administration. Continuing efforts at fostering economic development must be "carefully tailored to the desires of the Iranian government," and must not intrude into the land reform program, "as to create the impression ... among the peasantry that it is an American and not their program."[108] That still left the problem of incapacity. Iran's economy remained in recession, and without a return to growth the Kennedy administration worried that Iran would suffer another round of internal crises. It was clear from Holmes' reports that "the incompetence of the present Iranian government" presented a problem, wrote Komer. "There must be ways of getting across to [the shah] how much he needs a higher level of economic competence in his cabinet," Komer concluded. That meant bringing technocrats back into government.[109]

The changes desired by the United States began to occur in early 1964. In March, just as the shah secured his new arrangement with the consortium on royalty expensing, 'Alam stepped down in favor of Hasan 'Ali Mansur. Young, educated, and ambitious, Mansur was a tame Amini. He had US connections – he counted John J. McCloy, former president of the World Bank, among his friends – and had formed a "Progressive Circle" of educated Iranians, in partnership with his friend Amir Abbas Hoveyda, to discuss economic and intellectual concepts. The group focused on industrialization and economic productivity – issues that were non-threatening to the existing political status quo.[110] Mansur filled his cabinet with members of his "New Iran Party," including middle-class economists trained in Western universities. It was *rushvah dadan bi-rawshanfikran*, "the Bribery of the Intellectuals," evidence of the shah's interest in outflanking the National Front, which he continued to regard as his most dangerous opposition, and forming a new state over which he could exercise total dominance.[111]

The new government prioritized restarting the economy after the chaotic land distribution and the years-long recession. The pace of land reform slowed, as attention and resources moved back to the Third Plan and public investment in the economy. Cut to the bone in late 1962, the

---

[107] Memo for Bundy, Drafted by Bowling and Miklos, January 21, 1963, NSF Box 116a, JFKPL.
[108] RG 59 E 12 Iran, "Land Reform in Iran: A Status Report," September 30, 1963, USNA; SNIE 34-63, "The Iranian Situation" April 10, 1963, NSF, Box 116a, JFKPL.
[109] Memo for Harriman, June 20, 1963, Robert W. Komer Papers, Box 424, JFKPL.
[110] Milani, *Eminent Persians*, 231–235. [111] Bill, *The Eagle and the Lion*, 164–167.

7.3 "A Revolutionary Monarch"

plan grew from 140 billion rials to 200 billion rials, or $2.6 billion, in 1964. The Plan Organization, renamed the "Plan and Budget Organization" (PBO), operated in the mid-1960s as a planning office for the entire government with authority over the general administrative and development budgets, though the military budget (which grew from $577 million in 1964 to $1.19 billion in 1970) remained the sole province of the shah.[112]

The biggest changes were in industrial policy. 'Alinaqi 'Alikhani, the thirty-four-year old minister of commerce, drew from the hypothesis of American economist Simon Kuznets and argued that Iran should rapidly industrialize, using oil revenues to construct an industrial base that could feed internal demand and cut down on imports.[113] The shah pushed for projects in petrochemicals and mechanized farming, two sectors that could attract foreign interest. "The shah was very interested in this," 'Alikhani recalled.[114]

Apart from a new cadre of technocrats, the key to Iran's economic growth after the White Revolution was oil. Thanks to the shah's deal with the consortium, revenues in 1964 exceeded $500 million and the shah eagerly anticipated $1.2 billion by 1970.[115] This wealth spurred rapid growth in key sectors. According to the World Bank, manufacturing grew at an annualized rate of 11.4 percent between 1960 and 1970. The money provided Iran the means to attract foreign investment. The old dream of OCI and Max Thornburg came true by the mid-1960s – from $24.3 million in 1964, medium and long-range foreign capital investment reached $694 million by 1970. While imports had drained the country's foreign exchange reserves in 1960, by 1970 the bank estimated Iran possessed $1.8 billion for import financing.[116]

For the United States, Iran's improving economic picture, the elimination of major political opposition to the shah, and the rise of technocratic government in 1964 helped smooth over the concerns of the previous year. US policy toward Iran changed for other reasons as well. Kennedy's death in November 1963 brought important personnel shifts.

---

[112] Brew, "'What They Need is Management'," 16.
[113] Simon Kuznets, "Economic Growth and Income Inequality," *American Economic Review* 45, no. 1 (1955): 1–28.
[114] FISDS, *Siyasat va siyasatguzari-ye eqtesadi dar Iran, 1340–1350* [Ideology, Politics, and Process in Iran's Economic Development, 1960–1970], Part 2. For 'Alikhani and economic policy in the late 1960s, see Vali Nasr, "Politics within the Late-Pahlavi State: The Ministry of Economy and Industrial Policy, 1963–1969" *International Journal of Middle East Studies* 32, no. 1 (February 2000): 97–122.
[115] *FRUS 1964–1968, XXII*: 28–29.
[116] World Bank, "Current Economic Position and Prospects of Iran, Vol. I: The Main Report," May 18, 1971, Report No. SA-23a, 4, v.

238   Controlled Revolution: Expertise, Economics, & American View

The president's brother Robert, an advocate for political reform who was hostile toward the shah, resigned as attorney general in September 1964. President Lyndon B. Johnson enjoyed an amicable relationship with the shah, whom he viewed as a true agrarian reformer.[117] As incentives to pressure the shah declined, the drive to keep him happy grew stronger. One reason was financial. Beginning in 1964, the United States began to experience mounting balance of payments pressures, stemming from the escalating costs related to the war in Southeast Asia and Johnson's welfare programs.[118] Rather than sending dollars into Iran, after 1964 the United States started looking for ways to reverse the flow – the origins of the petrodollar recycling that would become a hallmark of US-Iranian relations in the 1970s.[119] "Iran has made such progress in financial management," wrote one USAID report, "that we are able gradually to shift ... from aid projects to market development." Trade with Iran offered "potential commercial advantages," particularly in arms.[120]

Secretary of Defense Robert McNamara grumbled that the shah seemed determined to buy more weaponry than Iran could ever need. But it was difficult to resist the monarch, particularly when Iran's orders contributed to the US balance of payments.[121] In 1964 the Majlis voted on a $200 military arms credit, which would produce "a major gold flow," noted Komer.[122] Recognizing that foreign developmentalists were no longer welcome in the shah's new Iran, Johnson decided to end US technical assistance to Iran by 1967. In return for the arms credit, the United States received the shah's promise that military advisors sent to Iran would be exempt from prosecution under Iranian law. The Status of Forces Agreement (SOFA) caused an uproar in the shah's normally quiescent Majlis and provoked a firm response from Ayatollah Khomeini, who compared it to the D'Arcy Concession and other capitulations forced upon Iran by imperial powers decades earlier. The shah

[117] Claudia Costiglioni, "No Longer a Client, Not Yet a Partner: the US-Iranian Alliance in the Johnson Years," *Cold War History* 15, no. 4 (2015): 491–509.
[118] Daniel Sargent, "Lyndon Johnson and the Challenges of Economic Globalization," in *Beyond the Cold War: Lyndon Johnson and the New Global Challenges of the 1960s*, eds. Francis J. Gavin and Mark Atwood Lawrence (New York: Oxford University Press, 2014): 17–43.
[119] David M. Wight, *Oil Money: Middle East Petrodollars and the Transformation of US Empire, 1967–1988* (Ithaca NY: Cornell University Press, 2021).
[120] *FRUS 1964–1968, XXII*: 105–107.
[121] Stephen McGlinchey, "Lyndon B. Johnson and Arms Credit Sales to Iran 1964–1968," *The Middle East Journal* 67, no. 2 (Spring 2013): 229–247.
[122] Robert W. Komer Oral History Interview, JFK #4 10/31/1964, Papers of John F. Kennedy, Presidential Papers, JFKPL.

7.3 "A Revolutionary Monarch"

exiled Khomeini and the SOFA passed.[123] Several months later, Prime Minister Mansur was assassinated by members of a religious terrorist group.[124]

The skepticism that greeted the White Revolution never fully vanished. The CIA concluded in April 1965 that while the shah's government was more competent thanks to the influx of new technocratic expertise, it was unclear "whether a bureaucracy ... noted for its inefficiency and corruption can maintain sufficient momentum" to meet rising expectations.[125] In meetings with Johnson and Averell Harriman, the shah was nudged toward further economic reforms, with Harriman maintaining that the nation's rising oil income should be spent on development projects rather than on weaponry.[126] These were suggestions, not instructions. As Rusk noted, so long as Iran enjoyed rising oil revenues and a booming economy, "there is probably little we can do directly ... to curtail his military spending" without angering the monarch "and thereby jeopardizing what influence we have."[127]

Some analysts continued to warn of imminent calamity. These predictions would recur until 1977, when they began to come true. But in the immediate aftermath of the White Revolution, the United States abandoned efforts to push the shah toward reform or influence the scope or direction of Iran's national economic development program. It did so for a variety of reasons, including the persistent pro-shah prodding of the conservatives in the State Department, the decline in influence of reform advocates like Robert Kennedy and Kenneth Hansen, the shah's adroit decision to push forward a reform program calculated to appeal to American sensitivities, and shifting priorities tied to a new US economic position.

The most important reasons were the legacy of Operation TPAJAX, the lingering specter of Iranian incapacity, and the overriding importance of maintaining Iran's pro-Western strategic alignment. Having helped put the shah on his throne, the US government saw no suitable alternative to replace him and doubted the ability of Iranians to stave off Soviet influence without a pro-Western strongman to lead them. The Amini experiment seemed to justify the skepticism of the conservative bloc. Foreigners could not support a controlled revolution in Iran, and the best the United States could do was back a friendly autocrat like the shah and hope for the best. Iran's oil windfall in 1964, a product of the shah's mutually beneficial relationship with the consortium, made surrendering

---

[123] Bill, *The Eagle and the Lion*, 156–161. [124] *FRUS 1964–1968, XXII*: 127–128.
[125] *FRUS 1964–1968, XXII*: 141–142. [126] *FRUS 1964–1968, XXII*: 326–330.
[127] *FRUS 1964–1968, XXII*: 156–159.

to the shah's dominance all the easier. The political coup in 1963 and the success of Mansur's cabinet to set the nation's economic course toward growth in 1964 allowed the United States to disentangle itself from Iran's decades-long process of dual integration.

7.4 The End of Development?

Throughout the postwar period, American policymakers and their allies in the development community wrestled with an apparent contradiction in their approach to Iran. While the country's need for assistance was evident, direct interventions provoked a backlash and often proved self-defeating. Modernization theory suggested democracy was inevitable, provided development occurred along the proper lines, but accomplishing development encouraged authoritarianism while Cold War strategic imperatives emphasized military modernization over democratic initiatives.

The paradox was not lost on policymakers or their developmentalist allies. In late 1961, at the height of the Amini experiment, Kenneth Hansen and T. Cuyler Young convened a group of academics at Princeton University for a conference on US-Iranian relations. Experts discussed the need to "ease the shah out of government operations" so as to make room for a new, modern, and middle-class political order. But as talk wore on, the panel grew convinced that when it came to development policy, "our economics are ahead of our politics." Unlike the Soviet Union, the United States lacked a theory of political change "to match our theory of economic development ... we have only an ad hoc approach to revolution." The gathering dispersed without determining whether economic change or an increase in productivity would lead to political progress.[128]

While Komer and Hansen believed the United States could push Iran toward a modernizing path that empowered elements outside the monarchy, more conservative members of the administration thought such intervention risky and ultimately futile. The conservatives leaned toward the historic norm in US policy toward Pahlavi Iran, one that reflected a general view of an undemocratic Global South: From the point of view of US Cold War strategic interests, backing the shah's brand of top-down modernist authoritarianism was the safest option. They held a narrow view of US capabilities and were skeptical of what the United States could accomplish inside other countries. Twenty years

---

[128] Memo for Komer, "Near East Conferences: 'Iran and the US' December 20, 1961," NSF Box 116, JFKPL.

7.4 The End of Development?

of scattershot development assistance periodically punctuated by displays of Iranian nationalist resistance tended to bolster this view. From Millspaugh and the World Bank through Point Four, Lilienthal and Clapp, and the Ford Foundation and HAG, projects to support administrative reform and economic development in Iran had ended in frustration. The White Revolution and the shah's shift on economic policy between 1962 and 1964 offered a way for policymakers to resolve this debate by surrendering to the shah and trusting that he could guide his country toward stability, protect Western interests, and ensure continued access to Iranian oil.

That meant the end of developmentalist influence inside Iran. The Ford Foundation completed its withdrawal in 1964, acknowledging that the political conditions had made it impossible to operate. "Under present leadership," the foundation could no longer propose "a truly constructive effort" in the fields of rural development or education. The Harvard Advisory Group's mission to the now-defunct Economic Bureau was terminated.[129] The United States' technical assistance mission remained until 1967 as the emphasis shifted toward the Peace Corps and small-scale education, health, and sanitation efforts overseen by the shah's government.[130] The age of foreigners guiding or influencing Iran's economic development ended with the White Revolution.

The economist and former Finance Minister Jahangir Amuzegar concluded in his 1966 study that the US technical assistance mission was ineffective at fostering economic growth. But in terms of broader policy, the American effort had been a success: "Ideologically, the United States wished to keep Iran in the Western camp ... Economically, the goal was to keep Iranian oil flowing to Western markets."[131] Conservatives like Bowling and Holmes would have agreed. While reform had eluded them, the United States' government had accomplished the short-term objective of Operation TPAJAX. The shah had not fallen from power. Iran had not collapsed – at least, not by the mid-1960s.

Social scientist Leonard Binder noted in 1962, just before the launch of the White Revolution, that the shah's approach had no evolutionary goals in mind, simply a situation "in which he can keep his place ... it is not surprising that many remain unconvinced that development is being

---

[129] Hill to Foundation, on the "Final Report on Iran: A Possible Basis for Re-Entry," July 11, 1964, FFR R-0814, RAC
[130] Jasamin Rostam-Kolayi, "The New Frontier Meets the White Revolution: The Peace Corps in Iran, 1962–1976," *Iranian Studies* 51, no. 4 (2018): 587–612.
[131] Jahangir Amuzegar, *Technical Assistance in Theory and Practice: The Case of Iran* (1966), 46–47.

seriously pursued."[132] William R. Polk of the Policy Planning Staff visited Iran in late 1963 and returned "disturbed by almost everything that I saw." All hopes for a government like Amini's, one that could bridge the divide between the regime and the middle class, had evaporated. Should the shah die, Iran would "disintegrate."[133] Kenneth Hansen departed government service in late 1963. He had little confidence in the White Revolution. "Instead of accelerating development activity, the Shah virtually scuttled the approach we had fostered."[134]

While Hansen had advocated for a greater degree of American involvement in Iran's development effort, his successor at the HAG departed Iran disenchanted by the idea of foreign assistance. "The traditional society," wrote HAG chief Thomas MacLeod, "must follow its own unique and probably tortuous path to development and progress ... there are few, if any, universal forces at work on which the development planner can readily or effectively capitalize." MacLeod was equally critical of Iran's new technocratic leadership, the successors to the Economic Bureau. The new Pahlavi state, dominated by men and women who adopted Western methods and Western ideologies, was a "schizoid state ... an unusual combination of oriental and western mental processes," organized not by merit but by "political arrangements and accommodations."[135]

It was a scathing critique of modernization theory, one that would presage the general decline of the ethos in the late 1960s. Yet it also repeated the well-worn tropes of Iranian incapacity. Even Western-educated Iranians, argued MacLeod, could not save their country. Through their otherness, they would alienate and repel their countrymen, leaving political confusion and instability rather than the orderly society the HAG's sponsors at the Ford Foundation had once envisioned. Asked to offer his views on the legacy of the Economic Bureau, Khodadad Farmanfarmaian chose more diplomatic language to convey essentially the same assessment. The bureau had used American development strategies, "because they subconsciously wished their society and people to enjoy what 'Americanism' had made possible for the Americans .... The Bureau should have understood a little better that a society can only rise as high, or go as far forward, as the progressive forces

---

[132] Leonard H. Binder, *Iran: Political Development in a Changing Society* (Berkeley, CA: University of California Press, 1962), 313.
[133] *FRUS 1961–1963, XVIII*: 843–845.
[134] Memo for Komer, May 7, 1963, Robert W. Komer Papers, Box 424, JFKPL.
[135] MacLeod, National Planning in Iran: A Report Based on the Experiences of the Harvard Advisory Group in Iran, December 31, 1964, Vol. I, 59–61, 74–75, 76–80, FFR Box 287, RAC.

7.4 The End of Development?

within it permit it to."[136] It was an argument the shah's supporters would later adopt: The regime, in a sincere effort to improve the lives of all Iranians, had attempted to do too much, too fast.

For while Iran did experience a profound economic boom – GDP grew by 9.5 percent annually between 1965 and 1970 – the gains of oil-driven and technocrat-led prosperity were distributed unevenly. According to the World Bank, growth was skewed toward the nation's top earners, while those at the bottom saw "little or none at all." Less than half of all Iranians received any education in 1970, while two-thirds of the country went without access to medical facilities.[137] Land reform, ostensibly designed to create a new class of prosperous landholding peasants, diverted sharply in 1964 as the government pushed corporatized agriculture to accelerate mechanization and attract foreign investment.[138] In the Dez region, fifty-eight villages were compelled to sell 67,000 hectares to eleven new corporations which evicted the inhabitants, razed the remaining villages, and leveled the ground for cultivation. This policy improved Iran's crop yields – though not appreciably, as growth barely exceeded 2 percent – and drove millions of farmers off the land and into the cities in search of work.[139]

Farmanfarmaian, speaking after the shah's fall from power, argued that the program "could have been far more modern."[140] Reza Muqaddam was more blunt: "[L]and reform ... was turned into a political tool of the shah," used first to consolidate his position and later to reward his friends and supporters, both within Iran and abroad.[141] The political program that accompanied land reform contained ersatz progress, including a women's rights campaign, while continuing to sideline moderate nationalists. This, in turn, raised the profile of other dissidents, most notably Ayatollah Khomeini, who after 1964 became the shah's most prominent opponent. With hindsight, it is possible to see the seeds of future revolution planted in the heady days of 1963–1965.

A small group of developmentalists foresaw the potential risks of the shah's controlled revolution. Among them was Hossein Mahdavy, Farmanfarmaian's former deputy at the bureau. Like thousands of other

---

[136] Farmanfarmain, Report on the Formation and Development of the Economic Bureau 1336–1342 (1963), Box 559, 63, 76–80, RAC.
[137] World Bank, "Current Economic Position and Prospects of Iran, Vol. I: The Main Report," May 18, 1971, Report No. SA-23a, i.
[138] Hooglund, *Land and Revolution in Iran*, 62–63; CIA Special Report, "Reform in Iran: Progress and Prospects," December 11, 1964, National Security File Box 136, LBJPL.
[139] Hooglund, *Land and Revolution in Iran*, 84–85; Karshenas, *Oil, State, and Industrialization*, 146–147.
[140] HIOHP, Farmanfarmaian, Tape No. 2, 9–10.
[141] HIOHP, Muqaddam, Tape No. 3, 1–2.

young Iranians, Mahdavy found the shah's brand of authoritarianism repugnant. His assessment of the land reform program, written for the Ford Foundation, was damning. Rather than develop the countryside or improve the lives of peasants, the White Revolution had upended rural life solely to impose the will of the state in place of the aristocracy. "The government has succeeded in moving into the village ... no genuine democratic force was allowed to fill the vacuum."[142] The Ford Foundation agreed. "It seems certain that the pressures from the rural element will ultimately compel a recognition of the economic and social rightness of their cause," concluded the foundation, "or force a basic change in government."[143] The most likely outcome, argued Mahdavy, was a violent confrontation between the winners and losers of Iran's economic growth, "as the only way to bring about a solution to Iran's ills."[144] His prediction would take fourteen years to come true.

Cassandra-esque gloominess from obscure Iranian intellectuals made few waves in either Washington or Tehran. President Lyndon B. Johnson wrote to the shah in glowing terms, noting how the White Revolution "demonstrated your wisdom and compassion."[145] American views of Iran under the shah after 1963 emphasized the country's rapid economic growth, relative stability, and cultural and social modernization. The shah's reforms had ended "2,500 years of feudalism," reported the *New York Times*.[146] Criticism continued, while human rights' activists and Iran's expatriate student community spent the remainder of the decade protesting the shah's repressive policies. Within mainstream US policymaking, however, these protests were peripheral.

By the late 1960s the shah had attracted an interest group of "Pahlavists" in American media, government, and private industry who were ready and willing to support him and his regime.[147] The revolutionary narrative that emerged from the 1960–1965 period, like the collapse narrative that preceded it, proved resilient, bolstered by the shah's own personal propaganda.[148] The shah's label of revolutionary monarch would stick, in one form or another, until the contradictions underlying

---

[142] Hossein Mahdavy, "Iran's Land Reform: Its Problems and Prospects," FFR R-0814, RAC.
[143] Hill to Foundation, on the "Final Report on Iran: A Possible Basis for Re-Entry," July 11, 1964, FFR R-0814, RAC.
[144] Hossein Mahdavy, "The Coming Crisis in Iran," *Foreign Affairs* 44, no. 1 (October 1965): 146.
[145] LBJ to Shah, September 16, 1965, National Security File, Box 136, LBJPL.
[146] "Iran's Shah Leads a 'White Revolution'," *New York Times*, October 27, 1963.
[147] Bill, *The Eagle and the Lion*, 319–378.
[148] Mohammed Reza Pahlavi, Shah of Iran, *The White Revolution of Iran* (Tehran: Imperial Pahlavi Library, 1967).

7.4 The End of Development?

his hold on power – the same contradictions noted by Iranian and American developmentalists as far back as the 1940s – became too great to contain. Underneath it all was a foundation of oil wealth stemming from the monarch's alliance with the consortium and the world's continued need for cheap Iranian crude, together with the petroleum of other pro-Western Middle Eastern states.

The White Revolution was a resolution to twenty years of conflict inside the Iranian state over the future of the national economy. It resolved the ambivalence within the US effort to assist oil-based development. The persistent issue of Iranian incapacity was never fully addressed. Instead, the United States told itself that the shah was now responsible and could not be swayed from the course he had charted. "To understand Iran, one must understand [the] Shah," wrote Armin Meyer, the new US ambassador, in November 1965. The legitimating myth of the Pahlavi regime was born from the experience of the early 1960s, defined by top-down modernization carried out by a clique of technocrats and a ruler "convinced that he has mastered the job of pulling his listless and backward people forward." Mohammed Reza Pahlavi's personality would dominate Washington's relationship with Iran as never before. Yet this was not an admission of defeat. Rather, as Meyer saw it, the United States had achieved its objective. Iran's economic future looked bright, particularly now that the shah had drawn in support from "skilled Western-trained civil servants." The oil was safe and flowing as never before. This to Meyer constituted a victory: "Our help has assisted Iran to stand on its own feet."[149]

---

[149] *FRUS 1964–1968, XXII*: 195–200.

Epilogue

E.1 Unthinkable

In February 1973, representatives from the consortium gathered in the ski resort town of St. Moritz, Switzerland. They were met by Iranian negotiators, led by the shah, Mohammed Reza Pahlavi, who was fresh off the slopes. Since 1954, the major oil companies had exercised control over Iran's oil industry. Now, their era had come to an end. At the height of his power, a key US ally and a monarch in absolute control over his government, the shah could afford to make demands. Even a personal letter from President Richard M. Nixon, the shah's ally in Washington, imploring him to avoid "any unilateral action" that might upset the regional status quo was not enough to deter him.[1] He got what he wanted. The consortium announced the termination of the 1954 agreement and agreed to a new contract, one that identified the National Iranian Oil Company (NIOC) as the "owners and operators of assets and activities in the oil concession area." The shah hailed it as a triumph. "Seventy-two years of foreign control," he declared, "was ended."[2]

The dominance of the oligopoly over price and production disappeared in the 1970s. The United States, which produced 60 percent of the world's oil in 1938, saw its share shrink to only 21 percent in 1970.[3] A series of developments, beginning with the Libyan Revolution of 1969 and continuing through the Tehran and Tripoli Agreements of 1971, shifted the balance of power toward the oil-producing states. What consortium Chairman Joseph Addison had called a "rear-guard action" in 1961 turned into a full-blown retreat when the shah helped orchestrate a quadrupling of posted prices between October 1973 and January 1974.[4] From $1 billion per year in 1970, Iran earned $20 billion

---

[1] Asadollah Alam, *The Shah and I: The Confidential Diary of Iran's Royal Court, 1969–1977*, ed. 'Alinaghi 'Alikhani (IB Tauris: London, 2007), 276–277.
[2] Quoted in Daniel Yergin, *The Prize*, 567.
[3] Degolyer and Macnaughton, *Twentieth Century Petroleum Statistics*, 3.
[4] Quote from FO 371/157652 Note by Hiller, February 15, 1961, UKNA.

in 1974: "one of the world's outstanding success stories," according to economist and former Minister of Finance Jahangir Amuzegar.[5]

Tamaddon-e Bozorg, "Great Civilization," was how the shah chose to characterize his kingdom. The monarch demonstrated his personal prestige and the country's wealth with displays of raw power, from annexing a series of small Persian Gulf islands to gathering hundreds of the world's elite to Persepolis for a ceremony celebrating the 2,500th anniversary of the monarchy in 1971.[6] Iran's military power and importance as a US ally were recognized in 1972 when President Nixon extended the shah a blank check for whatever nonnuclear weapons systems he wanted, in return for a guarantee to protect Western access to Persian Gulf oil. Far from needing US assistance, the Pahlavi state had now supplanted Great Britain as the most important American ally in the Middle East.[7]

Warnings of rapid inflation and investment bottlenecks fell on deaf ears as the shah's Iran became ever more "petrolic." Where it had once served mainly as a prop to Iran's trade deficit, contributing no more than 10 percent to state revenue and dwarfed by agriculture as a share of the national GNP, oil mushroomed into Iran's principal economic sector. Petroleum constituted 38 percent of GNP, 77 percent of government revenue, and 87 percent of foreign exchange earnings in 1977.[8] While he continued to address Iran's need for more reliable sources of energy – including nuclear power – the shah never relented in his drive to maximize Iranian oil production. "Iran needs money," he told journalist Oriana Fallaci in December 1973. "One can make a lot of money with oil."[9] Oil power was the key to economic growth and Iran's burgenonig regional dominance.

Despite the impressive statistics, the shah's Iran was defined by inequality and uneven growth. Social scientists Grace Goodell and Farhad Kazemi presented exhaustive research illustrating the results of decades of oil-driven development. "Considering the vast oil wealth," wrote Kazemi, "the official performance in low-income housing has been abysmal," as development funds went toward luxury high-rises in

---

[5] Jahangir Amuzegar, *Iran: An Economic Profile* (Washington DC: The Middle East Institute, 1977), ix.
[6] Alvandi, *Nixon, Kissinger, and the Shah*, 59–60; Robert Steele, "Pahlavi Iran on the Global Stage: The Shah's 1971 Persepolis Celebrations," in *Iran and the Age of the Aryamehr*, ed. Roham Alvandi (London: Gingko Press, 2018), 110–146.
[7] Stephen McGlinchey, "Richard Nixon's Road to Tehran," *Diplomatic History* 37, no. 4 (September 2013): 841–860.
[8] Halliday, *Iran: Dictatorship and Development*, 138; Suzanne Maloney, *Iran's Political Economy Since the Revolution* (New York: Cambridge University Press, 2015), 70–72.
[9] Quote from Oriana Fallaci, "The Shah of Iran: An Interview with Mohammad Reza Pahlevi," *The New Republic*, December 1, 1973.

248 Epilogue

Tehran.[10] Goodell noted that in the Dez region, which Lilienthal's KDS had tried to transform a decade earlier, peasants had been herded into "model villages" and placed under rigorous state surveillance. Landless locals left behind by the White Revolution worked for agribusinesses in conditions similar to those which had prevailed in the 1940s. "Economic development" had not rationalized life in the countryside. Instead, the expanding power of the state, centered on the "shining Mecca of all bureaucracies, the Plan Organization," had brought "murkiness and uncertainty" to life in the Dez region.[11]

Iran's growing middle-class benefited from the country's rapid urbanization, industrialization, and the expansion of a state bureaucracy that provided education and jobs. But despite the shah's infatuation with Western-trained technocrats, the military dominated his attention. When Plan Director and former Economic Bureau alumnus Abd al-Majid Majidi tried to allocate $30 million for upgrades to Tehran University, he received barely a third of what he had requested as the shah showered billions on the army, navy, and air force.[12]

The shah's push to turn Iran into a petro-state did not go unopposed. Abolhassan Banisadr, an Iranian economist living in exile in Paris, wrote a number of articles decrying the shah's oil policies. Oil had become "the curse of Iran's soul." Local authoritarian rule and global imperialism had worked hand in hand: "[O]il became a factor for sabotaging and destroying the foundations of Iran's independent economy," by keeping a corrupt elite in power and subordinating Iran to an unjust exploitative international economic system.[13] Economist Hossein Mahdavy coined a new term to describe the shah's perilous, oil-based authoritarian model: the rentier state.[14] Critics of the shah felt this situation was untenable: "If the flow of oil is cut off ... this regime will have no choice but to disappear," went one bulletin printed by the National Front in 1972.[15]

Doubts surrounding the viability of the shah's rule circulated internationally. American academics like T. Cuyler Young, James Bill, and Richard Cottam warned that without reforms to correct the widening

---

[10] Farhad Kazemi, *Poverty and Revolution in Iran: The Migrant Poor, Urban Marginality and Politics* (New York: New York University Press, 1985), 52.

[11] Grace Goodell, *The Elementary Structures of Political Life: Rural Development in Pahlavi Iran* (New York: Oxford University Press, 1986), 4–5.

[12] Alam, *The Shah and I*, 283.

[13] Abolhassan Banisadr, *Naft va Solteh* [Oil and Domination] (Tehran: Intisharat Mossadiq, 1977), 4–5, 13, 21.

[14] Mahdavy, "The Patterns and Problems of Economic Development in Rentier States," 428–429.

[15] News Bulletin of the National Front, No. 28, August 1972, "Naft va Khun," [Oil and Blood], in *Naft va Solteh*, 13.

economic inequality, the Pahlavi regime would return to its former instability. Yet these warnings were drowned out by the regime's advocates.[16] The shah's outward strength and support from a powerful coterie of "Pahlavists" inside the United States, including Richard M. Nixon, Henry Kissinger, David Rockefeller, and David E. Lilienthal, encouraged an acceptance of his authoritarianism, as did his status as a staunch anti-communist.[17] While criticism of the shah's human rights record was common in the international press, so too were glowing reports extolling Iran's rapid modernization and economic growth, "second only to Japan" in the words of the *Economist* in 1970.[18]

The shah was a reliable US ally. He maintained Iran's pro-Western strategic alignment, had close ties with Israel (an excellent customer for Iranian oil), and offered diplomatic support to the United States during the Vietnam War. Though he scolded the West for its "wastefulness" as his own regime dumped billions into vanity projects and military hardware, the shah never turned away from his alliance with the United States. Before popular demonstrations began in 1977, triggered in part by spiraling inflation and invigorated by the charged rhetoric of Ayatollah Khomeini, few in the United States felt the days of the monarchy were numbered. The revolutionary narrative that grew after 1963 stuck. When the collapse narrative returned in the waning days of 1978, it came as a shock. To imagine the disintegration of Pahlavi Iran was truly to think the unthinkable.[19]

E.2 Tragedy

The phenomenon of oil-based development and the consolidation of an authoritarian US-backed regime in Iran were closely linked to the formation and evolution of a global oil economy dominated by an oligopoly of vertically integrated oil companies. The process of dual integration, whereby Iran's oil moved through the companies' operations, producing wealth that could then be funneled into projects of economic development, was fraught with conflict and subject to the ideas and

---

[16] Matthew K. Shannon, "Reading Iran: American Academics and the Last Shah," *Iranian Studies* 51, no. 2 (2018): 294–295.
[17] Claudia Castiglioni, "No Longer a Client, Not Yet a Partner: The US-Iranian Alliance in the Johnson Years," *Cold War History* 15, no. 4 (October 2015): 18–19; Bill, *The Eagle and the Lion*, 319–379.
[18] "Another Persia: A Survey of Iran," *The Economist* October 31, 1970, recovered from DELP Box 546, SGMML.
[19] William Sullivan, Cable to State Department, November 9, 1978, National Security Archive.

intentions of disparate actors. The shah depended on the companies, just as the companies depended on his support to hold back petro-nationalism. Local integration was the site of bitter battles between rival developmentalists, where grandiose visions clashed with economic realities or entrenched fiscal conservatism. Efforts by Iranian technocrats to bring economic changes had to contend with the bureaucratic divisions of the Pahlavi state and the shah's political priorities. Dual integration served as the foundation upon which the modern US-Iranian relationship was built: The assumption that there could be no progress without petroleum, and that without the global integration of Iranian oil through the oligopoly, a stable Iran could not be realized. Given its position straddling both the Soviet Union and the major oil fields of the Middle East, Iran's apparent instability was too dangerous to be left untreated. American developmentalists and US officials wrestled with the politics of the Pahlavi state and their own perceptions of Iranian incapacity, eventually surrendering to the idea that an autocratic regime was better than the chaos presumed to result from Iranian democracy.

Such attitudes endured into the 1970s. Jack Miklos, a former embassy official and colleague of John Bowling, argued the Iranian "national character" and rejection of modernity had caused the revolution: "the Persians resemble the pre-Hobbesian man."[20] These comments mirrored prior criticisms from Arthur Millspaugh, Max Thornburg, Robert M. Carr, Loy W. Henderson, John Bowling, and Julius Holmes. They reflected the consistent critique of Iranian administrative competence that colored the views of countless foreign developmentalists, US officials, and oil executives. Pahlavism encouraged an acceptance of what became US policy: Only the shah and his immediate supporters could cure Iran of its socio-economic sickness, a view reflecting the shift from modernization theory toward "military modernization" in the Global South.[21]

The tragedy of US-Iranian relations, as historian James Bill describes, reflects the idea that the United States made the wrong decisions in navigating its encounter with Pahlavi Iran. David Collier, in his study of US influence in Iran, contends that "American interference" stymied

---

[20] Jack C. Miklos, *The Iranian Revolution and Modernization: Way Stations to Anarchy* (Washington DC: National Defense University Press, 1983), 47.

[21] Bill, *Eagle and the Lion*, 349–355. Military modernization was most closely associated with Manfred Halpern and Samuel P. Huntington. See Halpern, *The Politics of Social Change in the Middle East and North Africa* (Princeton NJ: Princeton University Press, 1963); Samuel P. Huntington, *Political Order in Changing Societies* (New Haven CT: Yale University Press, 1968); for military modernization, see Simpson, *Economists with Guns*, 67–73.

Iran's democratic development. Without US meddling, Collier contends, progressive forces in Iran might have countered the authoritarian tendencies of the shah, sending Iran on a different trajectory and avoiding the rupture of 1979.[22] This interpretation is tempting, particularly as the events of August 1953 or June 1963 offer clues as to how the Pahlavi monarchy would collapse years later. Collier argues that the United States possessed leverage and linkages within Iranian society that allowed it to support the growth of Iranian democracy. The tragedy, therefore, is that US power was used to pursue the wrong ends.

The decisions made by the US government to back the shah over rival political formations were the result of conscious calculation. Postwar concerns were bound up in a preoccupation with Iranian incapacity and concern over the country's possible collapse. American policymakers did not believe Iran capable of stability without oil revenues and backed authoritarianism as the safest option. After the White Revolution, the United States relaxed pressure on the shah, both because it served US interests and, in a somewhat more indulgent sense, confirmed the belief that regimes in the Global South could achieve stability by surrendering to pro-Western autocrats. It helped that the shah's new Iran was a much more welcoming place for American capital. Max Thornburg and David Lilienthal acted as forerunners for commercial interests like Northrop Grumman, which sold $16.2 billion in weaponry to Iran between 1972 and 1977.[23]

Conceptualizing the Pahlavi period as a tragedy of American policy conceals the importance of Iranian agency. The petro-state of the late 1960s was a product of Pahlavi ambitions. Oil offered a means to an end. In the era of Reza Shah, leaders leaned on petro-nationalism to squeeze more revenue from the oligopoly. During the war, they found it convenient to attract the support of the United States, first through an oil concession and then by embracing planned development. The First and Second Plans, masterminded by Abolhassan Ebtehaj, were designed to systematically apply Iran's oil revenues to the economy. Yet they were also meant to burnish the legitimacy of Iran's monarchy and functioned as tools for attracting the support of the United States' government, lending institutions like the World Bank, and development groups like the Ford Foundation and Development and Resources. Foreign developmentalists entered Iran by invitation, and their influence over the course of Iranian development were bound by the political constraints of the Pahlavi state. Ebtehaj and other technocrats were subject

---

[22] Collier, *Democracy*, 299.   [23] Bill, *The Eagle and the Lion*, 202.

to the whims of the shah, by far the dominant personality in the country. Efforts to produce progress from petroleum constantly bumped against the shah's interest in consolidating his rule over Iran's state and society.

The Pahlavi petro-state that emerged in the mid-1960s resulted from decisions made and actions undertaken by a host of different parties. Some succeeded in achieving their ends. Others failed, yet a majority found it necessary or expedient to back a model of oil-based authoritarianism that empowered the person of Mohammed Reza Pahlavi. Conflating this with tragedy ignores the objections of those who, like Hossein Mahdavy, could see how the shah's particular brand of modernization was ultimately unsustainable.

Mahdavy's prediction was proven true by the events of the 1978–1979 Islamic Revolution. The new government quickly asserted its own brand of petro-nationalism. "The word 'consortium' will, with Allah's help, be eliminated from Iran's oil vocabulary," one revolutionary official proclaimed. The companies' assets were expropriated and the economic policies pursued by the shah changed to "revolutionary economics" focused on self-sufficiency. It was to be de-integration, writ large.[24] But the Islamic Republic could not shake itself free of oil. It remains both a crucial ingredient of Iran's national economy and a factor in the Islamic Republic's foreign policy. In the wake of the 2015 nuclear deal between Iran and the international community, increasing oil production took on new significance. "The progress of our oil industry in just a few months," declared President Hasan Rouhani, "has surprised the world .... The residents of oil-rich regions should profit from this industry by creating employment opportunities and developing education and health care systems."[25] Iran's status as a major oil producer remains linked to promises of economic opportunity and an equitable society. The local and the global have remained intertwined, a consequence of the Pahlavi period. Oil is a contradictory element in Iran, as it is throughout the world: A blessing and a curse, a source of freedom and of dependence, of tremendous potential and slow, inevitable environmental degradation, both the life blood of the nation and "a calamity and plague" that afflicts Iran forty years after the shah's departure.[26]

---

[24] *The Washington Post*, "Western Oil Consortium is Cut Loose by Tehran," March 1, 1979; CIA Intelligence Memo, "Banisadr's Foreign Policy Views," February 5, 1980, CIA Crest Computer [Accessed February 9, 2018].
[25] *Al Monitor*, "Rouhani Inaugurates Production at New Oil Fields," November 14, 2016.
[26] Banisadr, *Naft va Solteh*, 3.

Bibliography

State Archives

CIA Records Search Tool (CREST) Digital Reading Room
Dwight D. Eisenhower Presidential Library, Abilene, Kansas
    National Security Council Staff Papers
Franklin Delano Roosevelt Library, Hyde Park, New York
    President's Official File
Harry S. Truman Library, Independence, Missouri
    White House Confidential File
    Henry F. Grady Papers
    Dean Acheson Papers
    Oscar L. Chapman Papers
    Gordon R. Clapp Papers
John F. Kennedy Library, Boston, Massachusetts
    National Security File
    Robert W. Komer Papers
Library of Congress, Washington, DC
    Papers of Averell Harriman
Lyndon Baines Johnson Presidential Library, Austin, Texas
    National Security File
The National Archives of the United Kingdom, Kew Gardens, UK
    CAB 128 Minutes of Cabinet Meetings
    FO 371 Foreign Office: Political Departments: General Correspondence from 1906–1966
    FO 248 Foreign Office: Embassy and Consulates, Iran (Formerly Persia): General Correspondence
    POWE 33 Ministry of Technology: Petroleum Division
    POWE 61 Ministry of Fuel and Power: Petroleum Division
    T 273 Treasury: Papers of Lord Bridges
    T 236 Treasury: Overseas Finance Division, Subseries – Iran
United States National Archives and Records Administration, College Park, Maryland
    Record Group 59: General Records of the Department of State
    Record Group 84: Records of the Foreign Service Posts of the Department of State

254 Bibliography

>   Record Group 312: Records of the Petroleum Administration for Defense
>   Record Group 469: Records of US Foreign Assistance Agencies, 1948–1961

Non-state Archives and Personal Papers

BP Archive, University of Warwick, Coventry, UK
Briscoe Center for American History, Austin, Texas
> Exxon-Mobil Collection

Booth Family Center for Special Collections, Georgetown University
> Papers of George C. McGhee

DeGolyer Library, Southern Methodist University
> Papers of Lon Tinkle

Rockefeller Archive Center, Tarry Town, New York
> Records of the Ford Foundation

Seeley G. Mudd Manuscript Library, Princeton University, New Jersey
> David E. Lilienthal Papers
> Development and Resources Corporation Records

Published Document Collections and Official Publications

Burdett, A.L.P. *OPEC Origins & Strategy, 1947–1973: Volume 1, Developments and Events Leading to the Creation of OPEC.* Slough: Archive Editions, 2004.

OPEC Origins & Strategy, 1947–1973: Volume 3, the Middle Period, 1963–1966. Slough: Archive Editions, 2004.

Federal Trade Commission. *The International Petroleum Cartel: Staff Report Submitted to the Subcommittee on Monopoly of the Select Committee on Small Business, United States Senate.* Washington DC: US Government Printing Office, 1952.

Foreign Relations of the United States 1942: Volume IV, Near East and Africa. US Government Printing Office: Washington DC, 1963.

Foreign Relations of the United States 1943: Volume IV, Near East and Africa. US Government Printing Office: Washington DC, 1964.

Foreign Relations of the United States 1945: Volume VIII, The Near East and Africa. US Government Printing Office: Washington DC, 1969.

Foreign Relations of the United States 1946: Volume VII, Near East and Africa. US Government Printing Office: Washington DC, 1969.

Foreign Relations of the United States 1947: Volume V, the Near East and Africa. US Government Printing Office: Washington DC, 1971.

Foreign Relations of the United States 1948: Volume V, The Near East, South Asia, and Africa. Part 1. US Government Printing Office: Washington DC, 1975.

Foreign Relations of the United States, 1948: Volume IX, The Western Hemisphere. US Government Printing Office: Washington DC, 1972.

Bibliography

Foreign Relations of the United States, 1950: Volume V, The Near East, South Asia and Africa. US Government Printing Office: Washington DC, 1978.
Foreign Relations of the United States, 1951: The Near East and Africa, Volume V. US Government Printing Office: Washington DC, 1982.
Foreign Relations of the United States, 1952–1954: Volume X, Iran, 1951–1954. US Government Printing Office: Washington DC, 1989.
Foreign Relations of the United States, 1952–1954: General: Economic and Political Matters, Vol. I Part 2. US Government Printing Office: Washington DC, 1983.
Foreign Relations of the United States, 1952–1954: The Near and Middle East, Vol. IX, Part 1. Government Printing Office: Washington DC, 1986.
Foreign Relations of the United States, 1952–1954: Retrospective, Iran, 1951–1954. US Government Printing Office: Washington DC, 2017.
Foreign Relations of the United States, 1955–1957: Volume XII, Near East Region, Iran, Iraq. US Government Printing Office: Washington DC, 1991.
Foreign Relations of the United States, 1958–1960: Volume XII, Near East Region, Iraq, Iran, Arabian Peninsula. US Government Printing Office: Washington DC, 1993.
Foreign Relations of the United States, 1961–1963: Volume XVIII, Near East, 1962–1963. US Government Printing Office: Washington DC, 1995.
Foreign Relations of the United States, 1964–1968: Volume XXXIV, Energy Diplomacy and Global Issues. US Government Printing Office: Washington DC, 1999.
Foreign Relations of the United States, 1964–1968: Volume XXII, Iran. US Government Printing Office: Washington DC, 1999.
Multinational Corporations and United States Foreign Policy: Report Together with Individual Views to the Committee on Foreign Relations, United States Senate, Part 7. Washington DC: US Government Printing Office, 1975.
Overseas Consultants Inc. *Report on the Seven Year Development Plan for the Plan Organization of the Imperial Government of Iran.* New York: Overseas Consultants, 1949.

Online Collections

Foundation for Iranian Studies Development Series (FISDS)

> *Barnameh rizi-ye `omrani va taṣmim giri-e siasi*. Interview with Manuchehr Gudarzi, Khodadad Farmanfarmaian, and 'Abd al-Majid Majidi. www.fis-iran.org/fa/resources/development-series/planning
> *Tahavvul-e san`at-e naft-e Iran: negahi az darun*. Interview with Parviz Mina. www.fis-iran.org/fa/resources/development-series/oil
> *San`at-e petroshimi-e Iran: az aghaz ta astane-ye enqelab*. Interview with Baqer Mostowfi. www.fis-iran.org/fa/resources/development-series/petrochemical
> *Siyasat va siyasatguzari-ye eqtesadi dar Iran, 1340-1350*. Interview with 'Alinaqi 'Alikhani. www.fis-iran.org/fa/resources/development-series/financialpolicy

256 Bibliography

Umran-e khuzistan. Interview with Abdolreza Ansari, Ḥasan Shahmirzadi and Ahmed Ahmadi. www.fis-iran.org/fa/resources/development-series/omrankhuzestan

Tajbakhsh, Gholamreẓa and, Najmabadi, Farrokh eds. *Yad'dasht'ha-ye Fu'ad Ruhani, nukhustin Dabir-e Kull-e Sazman-e Kishvar'ha-ye Ṣadir'kunandah-ye Naft (Upik) va Na'guftah'hayi darbarah-ye siyasat-e nafti-e Iran dar dahah-yi pas az milli shudan.* Published on-line Foundation for Iranian Studies, 2013. www.fis-iran.org/fa/resources/development-series/Rouhani

Harvard Iranian Oral History Project (HIOHP): Interviews

Abolhossein Behnia
Mahdi Aẓar
Gholam Reza Muqaddam
Karim Sanjabi
Khodadad Farmanfarmaian

National Security Archive

The Battle for Iran. Published on-line by National Security Archive, June 27, 2014. www.nsarchive2.gwu.edu/NSAEBB/NSAEBB476/

Koch, Scott A. *"Zendebad Shah!": The Central Intelligence Agency and the Fall of Iranian Prime Minister Mohammed Mossadeq, August 1953.* Washington DC: CIA, June 1998. Published on-line November 2017. www.nsarchive2.gwu.edu//dc.html?doc=4375470-Document-2-Zendebad-Shah

Wilber, Donald. *CIA Clandestine Service History: "Overthrow of Premier Mossadeq of Iran, November 1952–August 1953."* Published on-line November 29, 2000. www.nsarchive2.gwu.edu/NSAEBB/NSAEBB28/

World Bank Group Archives

Records of the Middle East and North Africa Regional Vice Presidency, Iran Oil Nationalization Inventory List www.pubdocs.worldbank.org/en/458211475595816522/Archives-mediation-exhibit-Iran-oil-folder-list-2.pdf

Published Persian Sources

Amini, 'Ali. *Khatirat-e 'Ali Amini: nukhust vazir-e Iran, 1340–1342.* Edited by Habib Ladjevardi. Cambridge MA: Center for Middle Eastern Studies of Harvard University and Distributed by Ibex Books, 1995.

Asnad va mukatibat-e Taymurtash, vazir-e darbar-e Riza Shah. Tehran: Sazman-e Chap va Entesharat-e Vezarat-e Farhang va Ershad-e Eslami, 2005

Asrar-e khanah-e Siddan. Tehran: Mu'assasah-'e Intisharat-e Amir Kabir, 1979.

Bakhtiyar, Shapur. *Khaṭirat-e Shapur Bakhtiyar: nukhust-e vazir-e Iran, 1357.* Edited by Habib Ladjevardi. Cambridge MA: Center for Middle Eastern Studies of Harvard University and Distributed by Ibex Books, 1996.

Bani Ṣadr, Abu al-Ḥasan. *Naft va Solteh.* Tehran: Intisharat Mossadiq, 1977.

Ebtehaj, Abolhassan. *Khatirat-e Abu'l-Hasan Ebtehaj.* Vol. I-II. London: Alireza Arouzi, 1991.
Fateh, Mostafa. *Panjah sal naft-e Iran.* Tehran: Entesharat-e Payam, 1979.
Imami, Ja'far Sharif. *Khaṭirat-e Jaʻfar Sharif Imami: nukhust-e vazir 1339-1340 va 1357.* Edited by Habib Ladjevardi. Cambridge MA: Center for Middle Eastern Studies of Harvard University and Distributed by Ibex Books, 1999.
Muhammed Ibrahim Amir Taymur Kalili, *Khatirat-e Muhammed Ibrahim Amir Taymur Kalali.* Edited by Habib Ladjevardi. Cambridge MA: Center for Middle Eastern Studies of Harvard University and Distributed by Ibex Books, 1997.
Kay-Ustavan, Hussein. *Siyasat-e muvazanah-e manfi dar Majlis-i Chahardahum,* Vol I and II. Tehran: 1949.
Majidi, 'Abd al-Majid. *Khaṭirat-e ʻAbd al-Majid Majidi: vazir-e mushavir va ra☒is-e Sazman-e Bar'namah va Budjih, 1351-1356.* Edited by Habib Ladjevardi. Cambridge MA: Iran Oral History Project, Center for Middle Eastern Studies Harvard University, 1998.
Makki, Hossein. *Duktur Muṣaddiq va nuṭq'hā-ye tarikhi-ye.* Tehran: Sazman-e Intisharat-e Javidan, 1985.
Kitab-e Siyah. Vol. I. Tehran: Sazman-e Intisharat-e Na, 1970.
Naft va nuṭq-e Makki: jarayan-e muzakirat-e naft dar Majlis-e Panzdahum dar barah-e qarardad-e naft-e Iran va Ingilis. Tehran: Intisharat-e Amir Kabir, 1978.
Makki, Husayn. *Vaqayi'-e 30 Tir 1331.* Tehran: Bungah-i Tarjumah va Nashr-i Kitab, 1982.
Ruhani, Fu'ad. *Ṣanʻat-e naft-e Iran: 20 sal pas az millī shudan.* Tehran: Kitabha-yi Jibi, 1977.
Tarikh-e milli shudan-e ṣanʻat-e naft-e Iran. Tehran: Kitabhaye Jibi, 1973.
Zindagi-ye siyasi-ye Musaddiq: dar matn-e nahẓat-e milli-ye Iran. London: Intisharat-e Nahzat-e Muqavamat-e Milli-ye Iran, 1987.
Sanjabi, Karim. *Omidha va Namidha: Khatirat-e Siyasi.* London: Nashr-e Kitab, 1989.
Shayegan, 'Ali. *Sayyed ʻAli Shayegan: Zendagi-nama-ye siasi.* Vol. I. Tehran: 2006.
Taqizadeh, Sayyed Ḥasan. *Zendegi-ye Tufani: khaṭerat-e Sayyed Ḥasan Taqizadeh.* 2nd ed. Edited by Iraj Afshar. Tehran: 'Elmi, 1993.
Tavanayan-Fard, Hasan. *Duktur Mosaddeq va iqtisad.* Tehran: Sazman-e Intishrat-e 'Alavi, 1983.
Tayarani, Amir. *Namah'ha va yaddasht'ha-ye Muhandis Kazim Hasibi, mushavir-e arshad-e duktur Muṣaddiq dar umur-e naft.* Tehran: Gam-e Naw, 2011.
Yamagani, Parsa. *Karnamah-e Musaddiq.* Tehran: Ravaq, 1978.

Secondary Sources

Abrahamian, Ervand. *The Coup: 1953, the CIA and the Roots of Modern U.S.-Iranian Relations.* New York: New Press, 2013.
Iran between Two Revolutions. Princeton: Princeton University Press, 1982.
Acemoglu, Daron and Robinson, James A. *Why Nations Fail: The Origins of Power, Prosperity, and Poverty.* New York: Crown Publishers, 2012.

Acheson, Dean. *Present at the Creation: My Years at the State Department.* New York: Norton, 1969.

Adams, Walter, Brock, James W., and Blair, John M. "Retarding the Development of Iraq's Oil Resources: An Episode in Oleaginous Diplomacy, 1927–1939." *Journal of Economic Issues* 27, no. 1 (March 1993): 69–93.

Adkin, Laurie E., ed. *First World Petro-Politics: The Political Ecology and Governance of Alberta.* Toronto: University of Toronto Press, 2016.

Afary, Janet. *The Iranian Constitutional Revolution, 1906–1911: Grassroots Democracy, Social Democracy and the Origins of Feminism.* New York: Columbia University Press, 1996.

Afkhami, Gholam R. *The Life and Times of the Shah.* Berkeley: University of California Press, 2009.

Alacevich, Michele. *The Political Economy of the World Bank: The Early Years.* Stanford: Stanford University Press, 2009.

"The World Bank and the Politics of Productivity: The Debate on Economic Growth, Poverty, and Living Standards in the 1950s." *Journal of Global History* 6, no. 1 (2011): 53–74.

Alvandi, Roham. *Nixon, Kissinger and the Shah: The United States and Iran in the Cold War.* New York: Oxford University Press, 2014.

Amuzegar, Jahangir. *Iran: An Economic Profile.* Washington, DC: Middle East Institute, 1977.

"Point Four: Performance and Prospect." *Political Science Quarterly* 73, no. 4 (December 1958): 530–546.

Technical Assistance in Theory and Practice: The Case of Iran. New York: Praeger, 1966.

Amuzegar, Jahangir and Fekrat, M. Ali. *Iran: Economic Development under Dualistic Conditions.* Chicago: University of Chicago Press, 1971.

Anderson, Irvine. *Aramco, the United States and Saudi Arabia: A Study of the Dynamics of Foreign Oil Policy, 1933–1950.* Princeton: Princeton University Press, 1981.

Ansari, Abdolreza. *The Shah's Iran, Rise and Fall: Conversations with an Insider.* Translated by Katayoon Ansari-Biglari. London: I. B. Tauris, 2017.

Ansari, Ali M. *Modern Iran: The Pahlavis and After,* 2nd ed. New York: Pearson Education, 2007.

"The Myth of the White Revolution: Mohammed Rezā Shah, 'Modernization' and the Consolidation of Power." *Middle Eastern Studies* 37, no. 3 (July 2001): 1–24.

The Politics of Nationalism in Modern Iran. New York: Cambridge University Press, 2012.

Askari, Hossein. *Middle East Oil Exporters: What Happened to Economic Development?* Cheltenham: Edward Elgar, 2006.

Atabaki, Touraj and Zürcher, Erik, eds. *Men of Order: Authoritarian Modernization under Ataturk and Rezā Shah.* London: I. B. Tauris, 2004.

Azimi, Fakhreddin. *Iran: The Crisis of Democracy: From the Exile of Rezā Shah to the Fall of Moṣaddeq.* London: I. B. Tauris, 2009.

"The Overthrow of the Government of Mosaddeq Reconsidered." *Iranian Studies* 45, no. 5 (2012): 693–712.
Bakhash, Shaul. "Britain and the Abdication of Rezā Shah," *Middle Eastern Studies* 52, no. 2 (2016): 318–334.
Baldwin, George. *Planning and Development in Iran*. Baltimore: Johns Hopkins Press, 1967.
Bamberg, J. H. *The History of the British Petroleum Company, Vol. II*. Cambridge: Cambridge University Press, 1994.
The History of the British Petroleum Company, Vol. III. Cambridge: Cambridge University Press, 2000.
Bayne, Edward A. "Crisis of Confidence in Iran." *Foreign Affairs* 29, no. 4 (July 1951): 578–590.
Beblawi, Hazem and Luciani, Giacomo, eds. *The Rentier State*. New York: Croon Helm, 1987.
Beck, Peter J. "The Anglo-Persian Oil Dispute 1932–1933." *Journal of Contemporary History* 9, no. 4 (October 1974): 123–151.
Behrooz, Maziar. "Tudeh Factionalism and the 1953 Coup in Iran." *International Journal of Middle East Studies* 33, no. 3 (August 2001): 363–382.
Berman, Edward H. *The Ideology of Philanthropy: The Influence of the Carnegie, Ford and Rockefeller Foundations on American Foreign Policy*. Albany: State University of New York Press, 1983.
Bet-Shlimon, Arbella. *City of Black Gold: Oil, Ethnicity and the Making of Modern Kirkuk*. Stanford: Stanford University Press, 2019.
"The Politics and Ideology of Urban Development in Iraq's Oil City: Kirkuk, 1946–1958." *Comparative Studies of South Asia, Africa, and the Middle East* 33, no. 1 (2013): 75–88.
Bharier, Julian. *Economic Development in Iran, 1900–1970*. New York: Oxford University Press, 1971.
Bill, James A. *The Eagle and the Lion: The Tragedy of American-Iranian Relations*. New Haven: Yale University Press, 1988.
Binder, Leonard. *Iran: Political Development in a Changing Society*. Berkeley: University of California Press, 1962.
Black, Megan. *The Global Interior: Mineral Frontiers and American Power*. Cambridge: Harvard University Press, 2018.
Blair, John. *The Control of Oil*. New York: Pantheon Books, 1976.
Bostock, Frances and Jones, Geoffrey. *Planning and Power in Iran: Ebtehāj and Economic Development Under the Shah*. London: F. Cass, 1989.
Brew, Gregory. "In Search of 'Equitability': Sir John Cadman, Rezā Shah and the Cancellation of the D'Arcy Concession, 1928–1933." *Iranian Studies* 50, no. 1 (2017): 115–148.
"'What They Need Is Management': American NGOs, the Second Seven Year Plan and Economic Development in Iran, 1954–1963." *The International History Review* 44, no. 1 (2019): 1–22.
Brown, Jonathan C. "Why Foreign Companies Shifted Their Production from Mexico to Venezuela During the 1920s." *The American Historical Review* 90, no. 2 (April 1985): 362–385.

Byrne, Malcolm and Gasiorowski, Mark J., eds. *Mohammad Mosaddeq and the 1953 Coup in Iran.* Syracuse: Syracuse University Press, 2004.

Castiglioni, Claudia. "No Longer a Client, Not Yet a Partner: The US-Iranian Alliance in the Johnson Years." *Cold War History* 15, no. 4 (October 2015): 491–509.

Chaudhry, Kiren Aziz. "Economic Liberalization and the Lineages of the Rentier State." *Comparative Politics* 27, no. 1 (October 1994): 1–25.

Chehabi, Houchang E. "Staging the Emperor's New Clothes: Dress Codes and Nation-Building Under Rezā Shah." *Iranian Studies* 26, no. 3–4 (1993): 209–233.

Citino, Nathan J. *Envisioning the Arab Future: Modernization in US-Arab Relations, 1945–1967.* Cambridge: Cambridge University Press, 2017.

Citino, Nathan J. *From Arab Nationalism to OPEC: Eisenhower, King Saud and the Making of US-Saudi Relations,* 2nd ed. Bloomington: Indiana University Press, 2005.

Clawson, Patrick and Sassanpour, Cyrus. "Adjustment to a Foreign Exchange Shock: Iran, 1951–1953." *International Journal of Middle Eastern Studies* 19, no. 1 (February 1987): 1–22.

Collier, David. *Democracy and the Nature of American Influence in Iran, 1941–1979.* Syracuse: Syracuse University Press, 2017.

Connelly, Matthew. *Fatal Misconception: The Struggle to Control World Population.* Cambridge: Belknap Press of Harvard University Press, 2008.

Coronil, Fernando. *The Magical State: Nature, Money and Modernity in Venezuela.* Chicago: University of Chicago Press, 1997.

Cottam, Richard. *Iran and the United States: A Cold War Case Study.* Pittsburgh: University of Pittsburgh Press, 1989.

Nationalism in Iran. Pittsburgh: University of Pittsburgh Press, 1964.

Cowhey, Peter F. *The Problems of Plenty: Energy Policy and International Politics.* Berkeley: University of California Press, 1985.

Cronin, Stephanie. "Conscription and Popular Resistance in Iran, 1925–1941." *International Review of Social History* 43, no. 3 (1998): 451–471.

ed. *The Making of Modern Iran: State and Society Under Riza Shah, 1921–1941.* New York: Routledge, 2003.

"The Politics of Debt: The Anglo-Persian Oil Company and the Bakhtiyāri Khans." *Middle Eastern Studies* 40, no. 4 (July 2004): 1–31.

Cullather, Nick. *The Hungry World: America's Cold War Battle against Poverty in Asia.* Cambridge: Harvard University Press, 2011.

Daftary, Farhad. "The Balance of Payments Deficit and the Problem of Inflation in Iran, 1955–1962." *Iranian Studies* 5, no. 1 (Winter 1972): 2–24.

Davis, Simon. "'A Projected New Trusteeship?' American Internationalism, British Imperialism, and the Reconstruction of Iran, 1938–1947." *Diplomacy & Statecraft* 17, no. 1 (2006): 31–72.

Dietrich, Christopher. "Mossadegh Madness: Oil and Anti-Colonialism, 1951 to 1970." *Humanity: An International Journal of Human Rights, Humanitarianism, and Development* 6, no. 1 (Spring 2015): 63–78.

Oil Revolution: Anticolonial Elites, Sovereign Rights and the Economic Culture of Decolonization. Cambridge: Cambridge University Press, 2017.

Dochuk, Darren. *Anointed with Oil: How Christianity and Crude Made Modern America*. New York: Basic Books, 2019.

Ehsani, Kaveh. "Social Engineering and the Contradictions of Modernization in Khuzestan's Company Towns: A Look at Abadan and Masjed-Soleyman." *International Review of Social History* 48, no. 3 (2003): 361–399.

"The Social History of Labor in the Iranian Oil Industry: The Built Environment and the Making of the Industrial Working Class (1908–1941)." PhD Thesis, Leiden University, 2014.

Ekbladh, David C. *The Great American Mission: Modernization and the Construction of an American World Order*. Princeton: Princeton University Press, 2010.

Ekbladh, David C. "'Mr. TVA': Grass-Roots Development, David Lilienthal and the Rise and Fall of the Tennessee Valley Authority as a Symbol for Overseas Development, 1933–1973." *Diplomatic History* 26, no. 3 (Summer 2002): 335–374.

Elm, Mostafa. *Oil, Power, and Principle: Iran's Oil Nationalization and Its Aftermath*. Syracuse: Syracuse University Press, 1992.

Elwell-Sutton, L. P. *Persian Oil: A Study in Power Politics*. London: Lawrence and Wishart, 1955.

Engerman David C., Gilman, Nils, Haefele, Mark H. and Latham, Michael E., eds. *Staging Growth: Modernization, Development and the Global Cold War*. Amherst: University of Massachusetts Press, 2003.

Fagre, Nathan and Wells, Jr. Louis T. "Bargaining Power of Multinationals and Host Governments." *Journal of International Business Studies* 13, no. 2 (Autumn 1982): 9–23.

Farmanfarmaian, Manuchehr. *Blood and Oil: Memoirs of a Persian Prince*. New York: Random House, 1997.

Fawcett, Louise L'Estrange. *Iran and the Cold War: The Azerbaijan Crisis of 1946*. Cambridge: Cambridge University Press, 1992.

Ferrier, Ronald. *The History of the British Petroleum Company, Vol. I*. Cambridge: Cambridge University Press, 1982.

Fisher, Christopher T. "'Moral Purpose is the Important Thing': David Lilienthal, Iran and the Meaning of Development in the US, 1956–1963." *The International History Review* 33, no. 3 (2011): 431–451.

Frank, Alison Fleig. *Oil Empire: Visions of Prosperity in Austrian Galicia*. Cambridge: Harvard University Press, 2005.

Freitag, Ulrike, Fuccaro, Nelida, Ghrawi, Claudia and Lafi, Nora, eds. *Urban Violence in the Middle East: Changing Cityscapes in the Transformation from Empire to Nation-State*. New York: Berghahn Books, 2015.

Galpern, Stephen S. *Money, Oil and Empire in the Middle East: Sterling and Postwar Imperialism, 1944–1971*. Cambridge: Cambridge University Press, 2013.

Garavini, Giuliano. *The Rise and Fall of OPEC: In the Twentieth Century*. Oxford: Oxford University Press, 2019.

Garlitz, Richard. *A Mission for Development: Utah Universities and the Point Four Program in Iran*. Logan: Utah State University Press, 2018.

Gasiorowski, Mark J. "The 1953 Coup D'etat in Iran." *International Journal of Middle East Studies* 19, no. 3 (August 1987): 261–286.
"The CIA's TPBEDAMN Operation and the 1953 Coup in Iran." *Journal of Cold War Studies* 15, no. 4 (Fall 2013): 4–24.
"The Qarani Affairs and Iranian Politics." *International Journal of Middle East Studies* 25, no. 4 (November 1993): 625–644.
US Foreign Policy and the Shah: Building a Client State in Iran. Ithaca: Cornell University Press, 1991.
"US Perceptions of the Communist Threat in Iran during the Mossadegh Era." *Journal of Cold War Studies* 21, no. 3 (Summer 2019): 1–37.
Gavin, Francis J. and Lawrence, Mark Atwood, eds. *Beyond the Cold War: Lyndon Johnson and the New Global Challenges of the 1960s.* New York: Oxford University Press, 2014.
Gelb, Alan. *Oil Windfalls: Blessing or Curse?* New York: Oxford University Press, 1989.
Gendzier, Irene. *Managing Political Change: Social Scientists and the Third World.* Boulder: Westview Press, 1985.
Gilman, Nils. *Mandarins of the Future: Modernization Theory in Cold War America.* Baltimore: Johns Hopkins University Press, 2003.
Goode, James F. "Reforming Iran during the Kennedy Years." *Diplomatic History* 15, no. 1 (Winter 1991): 13–29.
The United States and Iran, 1946–1951: The Diplomacy of Neglect. New York: St. Martin's Press, 1989.
The United States and Iran: In the Shadow of Musaddiq. New York: St. Martin's Press, 1997.
Gunder Frank, Andre. *Capitalism and the Underdevelopment of Latin America: Historical Studies of Chile and Brazil.* New York: Monthly Review Press, 1969.
Hadary, Gideon. "The Agrarian Reform Problem in Iran." *Middle East Journal* 5, no. 2 (Spring 1951): 181–196.
Halliday, Fred. *Iran: Dictatorship and Development.* New York: Penguin Books, 1979.
Halpern, Manfred. *The Politics of Social Change in the Middle East and North Africa.* Princeton: Princeton University Press, 1963.
Heiss, Mary Ann. *Empire and Nationhood: The United States, Great Britain, and Iranian Oil, 1950–1954.* New York: Columbia University Press, 1997.
Hogan, Michael J. "Informal Entente: Public Policy and Private Management in Anglo-American Petroleum Affairs, 1918–1924." *The Business History Review* 48, no. 2 (Summer 1974): 187–205.
Hooglund, Eric. *Land and Revolution in Iran, 1960–1980.* Austin: University of Texas, Austin Press, 1982.
Huber, Matthew. "Enforcing Scarcity: Oil, Violence, and the Making of the Market." *Annals of the Association of American Geographers* 101, no. 4 (2011): 816–826.
Lifeblood: Oil, Freedom, and the Forces of Capital. Minneapolis: Minnesota University Press, 2013.

Hunt, Michael H. *Ideology and US Foreign Policy*. New Haven: Yale University Press, 1987.
Huntington, Samuel P. *Political Order in Changing Societies*. New Haven: Yale University Press, 1968.
The Third Wave: Democratisation in the Late Twentieth Century. Norman: University of Oklahoma Press, 1991.
Issawi, Charles P. and Yeganeh, Mohammed. *The Economics of Middle East Oil*. New York: Praeger, 1963.
Jacobs, Matthew. *Imagining the Middle East: The Building of an American Foreign Policy, 1918–1967*. Chapel Hill: University of North Carolina Press, 2011.
Jacoby, Neil H. *Multinational Oil: A Study in Industrial Dynamics*. New York: Macmillan, 1974.
Johnson, V. Webster. "Agriculture in the Economic Development of Iran." *Land Economics* 36, no. 4 (November 1960): 313–321.
Jones, Gareth G. "The British Government and the Oil Companies 1912–1924: The Search for an Oil Policy." *The Historical Journal* 20, no. 3 (September 1977): 647–672.
Jones, Toby. "America, Oil and War in the Middle East." *Journal of American History* 99, no. 1 (June 2012): 208–218.
Desert Kingdom: How Oil and Water Forged Modern Saudi Arabia. Cambridge: Harvard University Press, 2010.
Karl, Terry Lynn. *Paradox of Plenty: Oil Booms and Petro States*. Berkeley: University of California Press, 1997.
Karshenas, Massoud. *Oil, State and Industrialization in Iran*. New York: Cambridge University Press, 1990.
Katouzian, Homa. *Musaddiq and the Struggle for Power in Iran*. London: Tauris, 1990.
The Political Economy of Modern Iran: Despotism and Pseudo-Modernism, 1926–1979. New York: New York University, 1981.
Kazemi, Farhad. *Poverty and Revolution in Iran: The Migrant Poor, Urban Marginality, and Politics*. New York: New York University Press, 1985.
Keddie, Nikki. *Modern Iran: Roots and Results of Revolution*. New Haven: Yale University Press, 2006.
Kent, Marian. *Oil and Empire: British Policy and Mesopotamian Oil, 1900–1920*. London: Macmillan, 1976.
Kuniholm, Bruce R. *The Origins of the Cold War in the Near East: Great Power Conflict and Diplomacy in Iran, Turkey, and Greece*. Princeton: Princeton University Press, 1980.
Ladjevardi, Habib. *Labor Unions and Autocracy in Iran*. Syracuse: Syracuse University Press, 1985.
"The Origins of US Support for an Autocratic Iran." *International Journal of Middle Eastern Studies* 15, no. 2 (May 1983): 225–239.
Lambton, Ann. *Landlord and Peasant in Persia*. Oxford: Oxford University Press, 1953.
Persian Land Reform, 1962–1966. Oxford: Clarendon Press, 1969.

Latham, Michael E. *Modernization as Ideology: American Social Science and "Nation Building" in the Kennedy Era*. Chapel Hill: University of North Carolina Press, 2000.

The Right Kind of Revolution: Modernization, Development, and US Foreign Policy from the Cold War to the Present. Ithaca: Cornell University Press, 2011.

Leeman, Wayne A. *The Price of Middle East Oil: An Essay in Political Economy*. Ithaca: Cornell University Press, 1962.

Leffler, Melvyn. *A Preponderance of Power: National Security, the Truman Administration and the Cold War*. Stanford: Stanford University Press, 1992.

Safeguarding Democratic Capitalism: US Foreign Policy and National Security, 1920–2015. Princeton: Princeton University Press, 2017.

Lerner, Daniel. *The Passing of Traditional Society: Modernizing the Middle East*. New York: Free Press, 1958.

Lilienthal, David E. *The Journals of David E. Lilienthal: The Harvest Years, 1959–1963*. New York: Harper & Row, 1969.

The Journals of David E. Lilienthal: The Road to Change, 1955–1959. New York: Harper & Row, 1969.

This I Do Believe. New York: Harper & Row, 1949.

TVA: Democracy on the March. New York: Harper & Row, 1953.

Lockman, Zachary. *Contending Visions of the Middle East: The History and Politics of Orientalism*. New York: Cambridge University Press, 2004.

Lorenzini, Sarah. *Global Development: A Cold War History*. Princeton: Princeton University Press, 2019.

Lovell, Bryan. *Challenged by Carbon: The Oil Industry and Climate Change*. Cambridge: Cambridge University Press, 2011.

Louis, W. Roger. *The British Empire in the Middle East, 1945–1951: Arab Nationalism, the United States, and Postwar Imperialism*. Oxford: Oxford University Press, 1984.

Louis, W. Roger and Bill, James, eds. *Musaddiq, Iranian Nationalism and Oil*. London: Tauris, 1988.

Luthi, Lorenz. *Cold Wars: Asia, the Middle East, Europe*. New York: Cambridge University Press, 2020.

Lytle, Mark H. *The Origins of the Iranian-American Alliance, 1941–1953*. New York: Holmes & Meier, 1987.

Macekura, Stephen J. and Manela, Erez, eds. *The Development Century: A Global History*. New York: Cambridge University Press, 2018.

Mahdavy, Hossein. "The Coming Crisis in Iran." *Foreign Affairs* 44, no. 1 (October 1965): 134–146.

"The Patterns and Problems of Economic Development in Rentier States: The Case of Iran." In *Studies in the Economic History of the Middle East: From the Rise of Islam to the Present Day*. Edited by M. A. Cook. London: U.P., 1970.

Majd, Mohammad Gholi. *Great Britain and Rezā Shah: The Plunder of Iran, 1921–1941*. Gainesville: University of Florida Press, 2001.

Maloney, Suzanne. *Iran's Political Economy Since the Revolution*. New York: Cambridge University Press, 2015.

Marsh, Steve. *Anglo-American Relations and Cold War Oil: Crisis in Iran*. New York: Palgrave Macmillan, 2003.

Matin-Asgari, Afshin. *Both Eastern and Western: An Intellectual History of Iranian Modernity.* New York: Cambridge University Press, 2018.

McAlister, Melani. *Epic Encounters: Culture, Media, and US Interests in the Middle East,* 2nd ed. Berkeley: University of California Press, 2005.

McFarland, Stephen L. "Anatomy of an Iranian Political Crowd: The Tehran Bread Riot of December 1942." *International Journal of Middle East Studies* 17, no. 1 (February 1985): 51–65.

"A Peripheral View of the Origins of the Cold War: The Crises in Iran, 1941–1947." *Diplomatic History* 4, no. 4 (October 1980): 333–351.

McFarland, Victor. *Oil Powers: A History of the US-Saudi Alliance.* New York: Columbia University Press, 2020.

McGlinchey, Stephen. "Lyndon B. Johnson and Arms Credit Sales to Iran 1964–1968." *The Middle East Journal* 67, no. 2 (Spring 2013): 229–247.

US Arms Policies towards the Shah's Iran. New York: Routledge, 2014.

Melosi, Martin and Pratt, Joseph A. *Energy Metropolis: An Environmental History of Houston and the Gulf Coast.* Pittsburgh: University of Pittsburgh Press, 2007.

Mikdashi, Zuhayr M. *A Financial Analysis of Middle Eastern Oil Concessions, 1901–1965.* New York: Praeger, 1966.

Miklos, Jack C. *The Iranian Revolution and Modernization: Way Stations to Anarchy.* Washington: National Defense University Press, 1983.

Milani, Abbas. *Eminent Persians: The Men and Women Who Made Modern Iran, 1941–1979, Vol. I and II.* Syracuse: Syracuse University Press, 2008.

The Shah. New York: Palgrave Macmillan, 2011.

Miller, Aaron David. *Search for Security: Saudi Arabian Oil and American Foreign Policy, 1939–1949.* Chapel Hill: University of North Carolina Press, 1980.

Millspaugh, Arthur C. *Americans in Persia.* Washington: Brookings Institute, 1948.

The Financial and Economic Situation of Persia. New York: The Persia Society, 1926.

Mirsepassi, Ali. *Intellectual Discourse and the Politics of Modernization: Negotiating Modernity in Iran.* New York: Cambridge University Press, 2000.

Mitchell, Timothy. *Carbon Democracy: Political Power in the Age of Oil.* New York: Verso, 2011.

Mofid, Kamran. *Development Planning in Iran: From Monarchy to Islamic Republic.* Outwell: Middle East & North African Studies Press, 1987.

Mommer, Bernard. *Global Oil and the Nation State.* Oxford: Oxford University Press, 2002.

Moran, Theodore H. "Managing an Oligopoly of Would-Be Sovereigns: The Dynamics of Joint Control and Self-Control in the International Oil Industry Past, Present, and Future." *International Organization* 41, no. 4 (Autumn 1987): 575–607.

Mosaddeq, Mohammad. *Musaddiq's Memoirs.* Translated by Homa Katouzian and S. H. Amin. London: National Movement of Iran, 1988.

Motamen, H. "Development Planning in Iran." *Middle East Economic Papers* 3 (1956): 98–111.

Motter, T. H. Vail. *The Persian Corridor and Aid to Russia*. Washington: Office of the Chief of Military History, Dept. of the Army, 1952.

Najmabadi, Afsaneh. *Land Reform and Social Change in Iran*. Salt Lake City: University of Utah Press, 1987.

Nash, Gerald D. *United States Oil Policy, 1890–1964*. Pittsburgh: University of Pittsburgh Press, 1968.

Nasr, Vali. "Politics within the Late-Pahlavi State: The Ministry of Economy and Industrial Policy, 1963–1969." *International Journal of Middle East Studies* 32, no. 1 (February 2000): 97–122.

Nemchenok, Victor. "'That So Fair a Thing Should Be So Frail': The Ford Foundation and the Failure of Rural Development in Iran, 1953–1964." *Middle East Journal* 63, no. 2 (Spring 2009): 261–284.

Nemchenok, Victor V. "In Search of Stability Amid Chaos: US Policy toward Iran 1961–1963." *Cold War History* 10, no. 3 (August 2010): 341–369.

Neuse, Steven M. *David E. Lilienthal: The Journey of an American Liberal*. Knoxville: University of Tennessee Press, 1996.

Nunan, Timothy. *Humanitarian Invasion: Global Development in Cold War Afghanistan*. New York: Cambridge University Press, 2015.

Nye, David E. *Consuming Power: A Social History of American Energy*. Cambridge: Harvard University Press, 1998.

Offner, Amy. *Sorting Out the Mixed Economy: The Rise and Fall of Welfare and Developmental States in the Americas*. Princeton: Princeton University Press, 2019.

Pahlavi, Mohammed Reza, Shah of Iran. *Mission for My Country*. New York: McGraw Hill, 1960.

The White Revolution of Iran. Tehran: Imperial Pahlavi Library, 1967.

Painter, David S. *Oil and the American Century: The Political Economy of US Foreign Oil Policy, 1941–1954*. Baltimore: Johns Hopkins University Press, 1986.

Painter, David S. and Brew, Gregory. *The Struggle for Iran: Oil, Autocracy, and the Cold War, 1951–1954*. Chapel Hill: University of North Carolina Press, 2023.

Parra, Francisco. *Oil Politics: A Modern History of Petroleum*. London: I. B. Tauris, 2004.

Penrose, Edith. *The Large International Firm in Developing Countries: The International Petroleum Industry*. London: Allen and Unwin, 1968.

"Middle East Oil: The International Distribution of Profits and Income Taxes." *Economica* 27, no. 107 (August 1960): 203–213.

Perovic, Jeronim, ed. *Cold War Energy: A Transnational History of Soviet Oil and Gas*. Cham, Switzerland: Palgrave Macmillan, 2017: 79–97.

Petrini, Francesco. "Public Interest, Private Profits: Multinationals, Governments, and the Coming of the First Oil Crisis." *Business and Economic History* 12 (January 2014): 1–18.

Pfau, Richard. "Containment in Iran, 1946: The Shift to an Active Policy." *Diplomatic History* 1, no. 4 (Fall 1977): 359–372.

Philip, George. *Oil and Politics in Latin America: Nationalist Movements and State Companies*. London: Cambridge University Press, 1982.
Popp, Roland. "An Application of Modernization Theory during the Cold War? The Case of Pahlavi Iran." *International History Review* 30, no. 1 (March 2008): 76–98.
"Benign Intervention? The Kennedy Administration's Push for Reform in Iran." In *John F. Kennedy and the "Thousand Days": New Perspectives on the Foreign and Domestic Policies of the Kennedy Administration*. Edited by Manfred Berg and Andreas Etges. Heidelberg: Universitatsverlag Winter Heidelberg, 2007: 197–219.
Qaimmaqami, Linda W. "The Catalyst of Nationalization: Max Thornburg and the Failure of Private Sector Developmentalism in Iran, 1946–1951." *Diplomatic History* 19, no. 1 (January 1995): 1–31.
Rabe, Stephen G. *The Road to OPEC: United States Relations with Venezuela, 1919–1976*. Austin: University of Texas Press, 1982.
Rahnema, Ali. *Behind the 1953 Coup in Iran: Thugs, Turncoats, Soldiers, Spooks*. New York: Cambridge University Press, 2015.
Randjbar-Daemi, Siavush. "'Down with the Monarchy': Iran's Republican Moment of August 1953." *Iranian Studies* (December 2016): 1–21.
Razavi, Hossein and Vakil, Firouz. *The Political Environment of Economic Planning in Iran, 1971–1983: From Monarchy to Islamic Republic*. London: Westview Press, 1984.
Ricks, Thomas M. "US Military Missions to Iran, 1943–1978: The Political Economy of Military Assistance." *Iranian Studies* 12, no. 3/4 (Summer–Autumn 1979): 163–193.
Roosevelt, Kermit. *Countercoup: The Struggle for the Control of Iran*. New York: McGraw-Hill, 1979.
Rosenstein-Rodan, Paul. "Problems of Industrialisation of Eastern and South-Eastern Europe." *The Economic Journal* 53, no. 210/211 (June–September 1943): 202–211.
Ross, Michael. *The Oil Curse: How Petroleum Shapes the Development of Nations*. Princeton: Princeton University Press, 2013.
Rostow, W. W. *The Stages of Economic Growth: A Non-Communist Manifesto*. New York: Cambridge University Press, 1960.
Ruhani, Fu'ad. *A History of OPEC*. New York: Praeger, 1971.
Saikal, Amin. *The Rise and Fall of the Shah: Iran from Autocracy to Religious Rule*. Princeton: Princeton University Press, 1980.
Sampson, Anthony. *The Seven Sisters: The Great Oil Companies and the World They Shaped*. New York: Viking Press, 1975.
Santiago, Myrna. *The Ecology of Oil: Environment, Labor, and the Mexican Revolution, 1900–1938*. New York: Cambridge University Press, 2006.
Sargent, Daniel J. *A Superpower Transformed: The Remaking of American Foreign Relations in the 1970s*. Oxford: Oxford University Press, 2015.
Schayegh, Cyrus. "Iran's Karaj Dam Affair: Emerging Mass Consumerism, the Politics of Promise and the Cold War in the Third World." *Comparative Studies in Society and History* 54 (July 2012): 612–643.

"Mohammed Rezā Shah Pahlavi's Autocracy: Governmental Constraints, 1960s–1970s." *Iranian Studies* 51, no. 6 (2018): 889–904.

Scheid Raine, Fernand. "The Iranian Crisis of 1946 and the Origins of the Cold War." In *The Origins of the Cold War: An International History*, 2nd ed. Edited by Melvyn P. Leffler and David S. Painter. New York: Routledge, 2005: 93–111.

Schneider, Steven A. *The Oil Price Revolution*. Baltimore: Johns Hopkins University Press, 1983.

Scott, James. *Seeing Like a State: How Certain Schemes to Improve the Human Condition Have Failed*. New Haven: Yale University Press, 1998.

Seddon, Mark. "Incorporating Corporations: Anglo-US Oil Diplomacy and Conflict Over Venezuela, 1941–1943." *Journal of Transatlantic Studies* 10, no. 2 (June 2012): 134–149.

Seymour, Ian. *OPEC: An Instrument of Change*. New York: St. Martin's Press, 1981.

Shafiee, Katayoun. "Cost-Benefit Analysis at the Floodgates: Governing Democratic Futures Through the Reassembly of Iran's Waterways." *Social Studies of Science* 50, no. 1 (2020): 94–120.

Machineries of Oil: An Infrastructural History of BP in Iran. Boston: MIT Press, 2018.

Shannon, Matthew K. "American-Iranian Alliances: International Education, Modernization and Human Rights during the Pahlavi Era." *Diplomatic History* 39, no. 4 (2015): 661–689.

ed. *American-Iranian Dialogues: From Constitution to White Revolution, c. 1890s–1960s*, ed. Matthew Shannon. New York: Bloomsbury Academic, 2022.

Losing Hearts and Minds: American-Iranian Relations and International Education during the Cold War. Ithaca: Cornell University Press, 2017.

"Reading Iran: American Academics and the Last Shah." *Iranian Studies* 51, no. 2 (2018): 289–316.

Sharifi, Majid. "*Imagining Iran: Contending Political Discourses in Modern Iran.*" PhD Thesis, University of Florida, 2008.

Shaw, Alexander Nicholas. "'Strong, United and Independent': The British Foreign Office, Anglo-Iranian Oil Company and the Internationalization of Iranian Politics at the Dawn of the Cold War, 1945–1946." *Middle Eastern Studies* 52, no. 3 (2016): 505–524.

Shuster, Morgan W. *The Strangling of Persia: A Record of European Diplomacy and Oriental Intrigue*. London: TF Unwin, 1912.

Shwadran, Benjamin. *The Middle East, Oil and the Great Powers*. New York: Wiley, 1974.

Simpson, Bradley R. *Economists with Guns: Authoritarian Development and US-Indonesian Relations, 1960–1968*. Stanford: Stanford University Press, 2008.

Skeet, Ian. *OPEC: Twenty-Five Years of Prices and Politics*. New York: Cambridge University Press, 1988.

ed. *Paul Frankel: Common Carrier of Common Sense. A Selection of His Writings, 1946–1988*. Oxford: Oxford University Press, 1989.

F. S. Smithers and Co. *International Oil Industry*. New York: F. S. Smithers and Co, September 1962.

Staples, Amy L. S. *The Birth of Development: How the World Bank, Food and Agriculture Organization and World Health Organization Changed the World, 1945–1965*. Kent: Kent State University Press, 2006.

Staples, Amy L. S. "Seeing Diplomacy through Bankers' Eyes: The World Bank, the Anglo-Iranian Oil Crisis, and the Aswan High Dam." *Diplomatic History* 26, no. 3 (Summer 2002): 397–418.

Stern, Roger. "Oil Scarcity Ideology in US Foreign Policy, 1908–1997." *Security Studies* 25, no. 2 (May 2016): 214–257.

Stivers, William. "A Note on the Red Line Agreement." *Diplomatic History* 7, no. 1 (1983): 23–34.

Stoff, Michael B. *Oil, War, and American Security: The Search for a National Policy on Foreign Oil, 1941–1947*. New Haven: Yale University Press, 1980.

Tanzer, Michael. *The Political Economy of International Oil and the Underdeveloped Countries*. Boston: Beacon Press, 1969.

Tinker Salas, Miguel. *The Enduring Legacy: Oil, Culture, and Society in Venezuela*. Durham: Duke University Press, 2009.

Toprani, Anand. *Oil and the Great Powers: Britain and Germany, 1914–1945*. New York: Oxford University Press, 2019.

Truman, Harry S. *Memoirs, Vol 1: Year of Decisions*. London: Hodder and Stoughton, 1955.

Vieille, Paule and Bani Ṣadr, Abu al-Ḥasan. *Pétrole et violence; terreur blanche et résistance en Iran*. Paris: Editions Anthropos, 1974.

Vitalis, Robert. *America's Kingdom: Mythmaking on the Saudi Oil Frontier*. New York: Verso, 2009.

Wall, Bennett H. *Growth in a Changing Environment: A History of Standard Oil Company (New Jersey), Exxon Corporation, 1950–1975*. New York: McGraw-Hill, 1988.

Warne, Andrew. "Psychoanalyzing Iran: Kennedy's Iran Task Force and the Modernization of Orientalism, 1961–1963." *The International History Review* 35, no. 2 (April 2013), 396–422.

Warne, William E. *Mission for Peace: Point 4 in Iran*. New York: Bobbs-Merrill company, Inc., 1956.

Westad, Odd Arne. *The Global Cold War: Third World Interventions and the Making of Our Times*. New York: Cambridge University Press, 2005.

Wolfe-Hunnicutt, Brandon. *The Paranoid Style in American Diplomacy: Oil and Arab Nationalism in Iraq*. Stanford: Stanford University Press, 2021.

Yaqub, Selim. *Containing Arab Nationalism: The Eisenhower Doctrine and the Middle East*. Chapel Hill: University of North Carolina Press, 2004.

Yergin, Daniel. *The Prize: The Epic Quest for Oil, Money, and Power*. New York: Simon and Schuster, 1991.

Zirinsky, Michael. "Imperial Power and Dictatorship: Britain and the Rise of Rezā Shah, 1921–1926." *International Journal of Middle East Studies* 24, no. 4 (November 1992): 639–663.

"A Panacea for the Ills of the Country: American Presbyterian Education in Interwar Iran." *American Presbyterians* 72, no. 3 (Fall 1994): 187–201.

Zubok, Vladislav M. "Stalin, Soviet Intelligence, and the Struggle for Iran, 1945–1953." *Diplomatic History* (2019): 1–25.

Index

'Ala, Husayn, 46, 62
'Alam, Asadollah, 197, 203, 231
'Alikhani, 'Alinaqi, 57, 237
Acheson, Dean, 40, 47, 93, 96, 105, 122, 134, 138
Achnacarry Castle (Scotland), 28
Adams, Robert M., 151
Addison, Joseph, 208–209, 246
Africa, 163, 252
agriculture, 53, 64, 79, 159, 161, 168–169, 227, 243, 247
Alfonso, Perez, 182, 199
Allen, George V., 45–46, 58, 137
al-Tariki, 'Abdullah, 182, 195–196, 198, 206, 210
alternative modernity, 11
American missionaries, 12, 36, 40
American oil, 23, 27–28, 43, 47, 94, 109
American oil companies, 24, 94
American Petroleum Institute, 27
American petroleum market, 24
Amini, Ali, 145, 172, 177, 197–198, 214–216, 222, 225–226, 228–232, 234–236, 239–240, 242
Amuzegar, Jahangir, 241, 247
Anglo-American alliance, 42
Anglo-Iranian Oil Company (AIOC), 24, 33–34, 41, 44, 48, 50–51, 54–55, 62, 67–68, 70–77, 79–82, 90, 92–111, 113–116, 129–130, 138, 146, 192–194, 197, 200, 208
Anglo-Persian Oil Company (APOC), 21–22, 26, 28–33
Ansari, Abdolreza, 125, 166, 169, 177, 179
Arab nationalism, 195
Aramco, 48, 81, 109, 115, 200, 204, 211
Aramesh, Ahmed, 176
aristocracy, 14, 38–39, 56, 155, 232–233, 244
Arsanjānī, Hasan, 226, 232, 234
Asfia, Safi, 177
Aswan High Dam, 161

Atlantic Charter, 37, 52
Australia, 114
authoritarianism, 1, 5–6, 10, 12–14, 16, 52, 120, 139, 148, 154, 156–157, 161, 172, 181, 195, 216, 218, 222, 240, 244, 248–249, 251–252
autocracy, 86, 88
Azerbaijan, 45, 47, 49–50, 54, 57, 62, 65, 122, 133

Baha'i, 155
Baharestan Square, 225
balance of payments, 61, 68, 126, 129–130, 214, 221, 238
Banisadr, Abolhassan, 248
Bank-e Markazi, 221
Bayne, Edward A., 79, 82, 84, 135
Beirut (Lebanon), 205–206
Bevin, Ernest, 68, 72–73
Bill, James, 248, 250
Black, Eugene, 157
Black, Megan, 12, 108
Blumberg, John, 178, 231
Bonn (Germany), 2
Bowling, John, 174, 217, 228–229, 235–236, 241, 250
Bretton-Woods, 38, 58, 62
Bridgeman, Maurice, 201–202, 204
British oil, 22–23, 30, 50–52, 88, 169, 212
British Petroleum (BP), 24–25, 69, 185, 187, 190, 192–193, 201

Cadman, John, 28–33, 52, 68, 71, 75, 92, 97, 201, 208
Cairo (Egypt), 43, 182, 189
Cairo Yacht Club, 182
Carr, Robert M., 128–133, 135–136, 140, 143, 147–148, 250
Central Intelligence Agency (CIA), 2, 95, 99, 118–119, 128, 135–142, 153, 173, 182, 225, 234, 239
Chapin, Seldon, 195

270

Index

Churchill, Winston, 5, 25
Clapp, Gordon R., 16, 152–153, 163–166, 169–171, 174–179, 241
Coca-Cola, 5
Cold War, 5, 7, 9–11, 13, 16, 22, 41, 47, 54–55, 57, 61, 67, 79, 91, 95–96, 112, 116, 118, 125, 147, 152, 157, 183, 191, 212, 232, 240
Collado, Emilio G., 62
Collier, David, 225, 250
colonialism, 22, 24, 28, 36, 40, 50, 124–125, 199, 248
  tools of empire, 28
communism, 10, 13, 41, 44, 47, 49, 52–54, 57, 62, 70, 79, 87, 93–96, 99, 111, 116, 118–120, 129–131, 133, 135–137, 139, 141–142, 144, 147, 157, 166, 216, 224, 249
Compagnie Française des Pétroles (CFP), 185, 192
Company of California (Socal, later Chevron), 24, 48, 64, 185, 201, 212
Company of New York (Socony, later Mobil), 24, 41–42, 48–49, 185, 188, 201–202, 206–207
conservatism, 84, 159, 175, 250
consortium, 145–146, 148, 155, 169, 183, 191–194, 197, 201–211, 216, 220, 236–237, 239, 245–246, 252
corruption, 6, 214
Cottam, Richard, 224, 248
Cullather, Nick, 11
customs duties, 56, 62, 129

D'Arcy Concession, 21, 31
D'Arcy, William Knox, 21, 31–32, 238
Davar, Ali-Akbar, 29, 58
Declaration for Iran, 37
deficit spending, 123, 127, 132
DeGolyer, Everette, 27
democracy, 4, 6, 13, 148, 155, 157, 240, 250–251
destructive competition, 24, 27, 48
Deterding, Henry, 28
development, 1, 4–7, 9–14, 16, 22, 40–42, 46, 49–59, 61–64, 66–68, 75, 77–78, 80–81, 83–84, 116, 120, 124, 127–130, 132, 136, 145–146, 148, 151–152, 156–158, 160–164, 166, 168, 171–174, 176–178, 181, 194, 205, 213–216, 218, 221, 226, 230, 232, 235–242, 245, 247, 249, 251
  American development mission, 11
  definition of, 17
  developmentalism, 64

developmentalists, 1, 10–13, 16, 22–23, 54–55, 67, 119, 125, 148, 151, 156, 158, 161, 172, 174, 178, 181, 215–216, 224, 231, 238, 243, 245, 250–251
development economics, 219
Development and Resources Corporation, 16, 151–152, 163–164, 166, 168–172, 174–175, 177–179, 231, 251
Dez Dam, 167–168, 171, 175–176, 178
Dez Region, 243, 248
Dez River, 166, 175
Dochuk, Darren, 8
dual integration, 5, 9–10, 14–16, 22, 52, 54–55, 80–81, 84, 87, 95–96, 103, 107, 112, 117, 120, 136, 144, 152, 181, 199, 212, 215, 240, 249
Duce, James Terry, 109, 115
Dulles, Allen, 64, 66, 95, 99, 135–136, 138–146, 148, 173

Eastern Bloc, 112
Ebtehaj, Abolhassan, 38–39, 46, 53–54, 58–60, 62–64, 66, 68, 74, 78, 81, 83–84, 124, 151–153, 157–158, 160–162, 166, 168–174, 176–177, 179–181, 218, 220, 226, 229, 251
economic crisis, 5, 77–78, 92
economic development, 4, 9, 23, 52, 54–55, 67–68, 81, 117, 132, 146, 153, 174, 240–241, 248–249
economic growth, 6, 15, 53, 151, 157, 196, 216, 219, 227, 237, 241, 244, 247, 249
economic inequality, 249
Eden, Anthony, 106, 138
Eisenhower, Dwight D., 120, 134, 138–144, 146–147, 153, 173, 190, 192, 195, 221, 223
elite corruption, 22, 36, 40
embargo, 82, 104, 107, 110–112, 115, 117, 119–121, 123, 129, 138, 142
Engineers' Association, 34
Entezamm, 'Abdullah, 194, 203, 205, 207, 223
environmental degradation, 252
exploitation, 13

Fallaci, Oriana, 247
Fallah, Reza, 206–210, 213
Farmanfarmaian, Khodadad, 59, 156, 160–161, 170, 173, 178–179, 182, 214, 219–221, 226–227, 230–231, 235, 242–243
Farmanfarmaian, Manuchehr, 182
Fateh, Mustafa, 21

Index

Fawcett, Louise, 45
feudal landlord, 4
fiscal independence, 30
food shortage, 34
Ford Foundation, 4, 157, 162, 171, 215, 218, 222, 232, 241–242, 244, 251
foreign exchange crisis, 223
Foreign Petroleum Supply Committee (FPSC), 113, 115
fossil fuel capital, 8
fossil fuels, 6, 152, 169, 184
Fraser, William J., 33, 75–76, 81, 97, 99
Freres, Lazard, 163

Garner, Robert L., 62, 86, 104–106
Gass, Neville, 71–72, 74–76, 192
Germany, 33
Gilman, Nils, 157
global development movement. *See* development
global energy economy, 13
Global North, 8
global oil economy, 9, 16, 22, 48, 107, 109, 115, 120, 144–145, 148, 181–183, 185–186, 189, 205, 208, 212, 249
global oil industry, 7, 24, 26, 28, 116, 144, 213
global oil production, 41
Global South, 7, 9, 11, 22, 56, 62, 88, 91, 108, 117, 124, 147, 157–158, 161, 164, 184, 189, 195, 240, 250–251
Golshayan, Abbasqoli, 67, 72, 74, 76–77
Goodell, Grace, 247
Government Affairs Institute, 162
Grady, Henry F., 80, 84, 89, 93, 96–97, 99, 104, 133
Great Britain, 7, 17, 21–23, 25–26, 29–37, 40–47, 50–52, 66, 68–69, 71–72, 76, 81–82, 86–91, 93–112, 114, 116–118, 120–123, 128–129, 131, 135–138, 141–144, 147–148, 156, 169, 188–189, 191–192, 194, 197, 200, 207, 212, 217, 223, 233, 247
British Empire, 25
Foreign Office, 32, 50, 70, 73–74
Labour Party, 88
London, 27, 72, 74, 76, 81, 105, 193, 208
Ministry of Defense, 97
Royal Navy, 24
Treasury, 74
Great Powers, 13, 22, 24, 33, 43
gross domestic product (GDP), 2, 6, 243
Gross National Product (GNP), 59, 226, 247

Gudarzi, Manuchehr, 179, 229
Gulf Oil, 24, 48, 182

Hansen, Kenneth, 4, 171, 174, 220, 224, 239–240, 242
Harden, Orville, 146
Harriman, Averell, 100–103, 116, 134, 239
Harvard Advisory Group (HAG), 218–220, 230–232, 241–242
Harvard University, 162, 171, 218–219
Hasibi, Kazim, 86, 93, 98, 100, 109, 121, 132
Hedayat, Khosrow, 175–176, 214, 221
Henderson, Loy, 40, 44, 47, 106, 117, 121–122, 127–128, 130, 132–134, 136, 138–141, 145–147, 154, 250
Holman, Eugene, 108
Holmes, Julius, 204, 228, 231, 234–235, 241, 250
Hoover Jr., Herbert, 44, 145–146
horizontal integration, 24
Hoskins, Harold, 40
Hoveyda, Amir Abbas, 236
Hull, Cordell, 42–43
human rights, 2, 244, 249
Humble Oil, 28
Huntington, Samuel, 6
Hurley, Patrick J., 36–37, 40
hydroelectric dams, 53, 151, 166, 179

Imami, Ja'far Sharif, 170, 176
Imperial Bank of Persia, 30
imperial order, 11
imperialism. *See* colonialism
India, 26, 68–69, 71, 114, 143
Indonesia, 26, 28, 143, 186, 199, 206, 219
industrialization, 15, 58, 78, 227, 236, 248
inequality, 37, 53, 247
inflation, 34, 39, 56, 132, 214, 221, 247, 249
International Bank of Reconstruction and Development (IBRD). *See* World Bank
international community, 92, 252
International Monetary Fund (IMF), 58, 214, 223
international relations, 8
Iran
'ulama, 34
Abadan, 25–26, 33, 50, 62, 69, 71, 75, 93–94, 97–98, 100–101, 104–105, 108–111, 114–115, 156, 167, 169, 192–193, 197, 206
administrative state, 37
Ahwaz, 167–169
Anglo-Soviet occupation, 21, 33

Index

Bank-e Melli, 30, 34, 38, 58–59, 78, 123–124, 127–128, 132, 143, 221
bourgeoisie, 29
Chia Sorkh, 21
Constitutional Revolution (1906-1911), 14
coup d'etat (1953), 2, 16, 45, 122
coup d'etat (1921), 29
Economic Bureau, 1, 3–4, 170, 173, 214, 216, 218–222, 224, 226–227, 229–232, 241–243, 248
economic reform, 3, 46
economy, 30, 37, 51, 66, 85, 96, 128, 133, 135, 153, 179, 214, 216, 219–220, 226, 234, 236
First Plan, 16, 54, 60, 82–84, 123–124, 156, 158, 160, 162, 173–175
fiscal crisis, 29, 176, 215
Hizb-e Tudeh, 34, 46, 56, 70, 95, 119, 122, 125, 129, 131, 133–142, 145–147, 153, 155, 233
Iranian economists, 170, 218
Iran–Soviet border, 10, 43, 125, 153
Islamic Revolution (1978-79), 15, 252
Kermanshah, 21, 109
Khuzestan, 21–22, 25, 34, 44–45, 51, 83, 151–152, 166, 168–169, 171, 175, 178–179, 181
Majlis, 29, 34–35, 38–39, 43, 46, 50, 54–55, 57, 59, 65–68, 70–71, 74–75, 77–78, 81–84, 88, 90, 98, 101, 120–124, 136, 141, 145–146, 154, 170, 173, 176, 194, 223, 234, 238
military power, 247
military spending, 38, 174, 228, 239
Ministry of Finance, 37, 160, 220, 230
Mohammerah (Khorramshahr), 26, 36, 179, 234
monarchy, 10, 14, 34, 140, 161, 189, 240, 247, 249, 251
national debt, 156
National Front, 77, 81, 90–93, 95, 98–99, 118–119, 121–122, 126, 128–129, 132, 134–137, 141–143, 147–148, 155, 176, 214, 223, 225–226, 228–229, 233, 235–236, 248
oil deposits, 16
oil production, 3, 5, 16, 22–23, 32–33, 44–45, 48, 51–53, 61, 68, 82, 87, 93, 95, 97–98, 102, 104–105, 109–112, 115–116, 120, 138, 143–145, 147, 181, 193, 212, 241, 247, 249–250
Organization of National Intelligence and Security (SAVAK), 153, 155, 172
Pahlavism, 250

Peacock Throne, 29
Plan Organization, 14
Qajar shah, 21, 29
rials, 34, 38, 59, 62, 75, 78–79, 83, 121, 123–124, 126–127, 129, 132, 143, 154, 156, 158–160, 170, 181, 221, 226–227, 234, 237
Second Plan, 16, 151–152, 157–158, 161, 172–174, 176–181, 192, 203, 213, 217–218, 220, 222, 226, 229, 233
Seven Year Plan, 50, 53, 55, 57, 60, 63, 65–66, 74–75, 77, 79–80, 82, 92, 103, 125, 129, 147, 194, 221
state budget, 30, 41, 53, 59, 79, 121, 130, 189
Tabriz, 45
Tamaddon-e Bozorg ("Great Civilization"), 16, 247
Tehran, 21, 26, 29, 36–37, 39, 42, 44–46, 57, 64, 67, 72, 79–82, 86, 89, 97–100, 103, 105, 118, 122, 128, 132, 137, 154, 177–178, 189, 200, 204–205, 220, 222, 225–226, 228, 230, 244, 246, 248
Tehran University, 248
Third Plan, 1, 3, 215, 220, 226–232, 236
Trans-Iranian Railroad, 29, 56
treasury, 31
U.S. consulate, 234
Iraq, 25, 42, 45, 48, 94, 98, 110, 113, 172, 188–189, 195, 198, 201, 206–207, 209, 211, 217
irrigation dams, 179
irrigation network, 171
Islam, 234
Islamic Republic, 252
Istanbul (Turkey), 162
Iverson, Kenneth, 162, 218

Jackson, Basil, 97–101, 103, 110–111, 116
Japan, 51, 62, 65, 109, 249
Jennings, Brewster, 95, 111
Jernegan, John, 36, 40, 52
Jersey Standard, 24, 28, 35, 41–42, 48, 63, 95, 108, 111, 113, 146, 185, 187, 196, 199, 201–202, 212
Jim Crow, 26
Johnson, Lyndon Baines, 212, 238–239, 244
Joint Comprehensive Plan of Action (JCPOA), 252
Jones, Toby Craig, 8
July Uprising (1952), 122, 137

274   Index

Karl, Terry Lynn, 6
Kashani, Ayatollah, 100, 139
Kashani, Ayatollah Abolqassem, 90–93, 137, 139–140, 218
Kashf al-Asrar, 34
Kazemi, Farhad, 247
Kennedy, John F., 1–2, 4, 203, 214–216, 219, 222–226, 228–230, 232–237, 239
Khan, Reza, 29, 34, 37, 88
Khomeini, Ayatollah, 238, 243, 249
Khomeini, Ruhollah, 34, 234, 239
Khuzestan Development Service (KDS), 151–152, 162, 169–172, 175–177, 179, 181, 248
Kissinger, Henry, 5, 249
Komer, Robert, 2, 224–225, 228–229, 232–234, 236, 238, 240
Kuwait, 48, 94, 110, 113, 186, 188–189, 191, 201, 209, 211

League of Nations, 25
Leavall, John, 43
Levy, Walter A., 100–101, 116–117, 168, 202
Levy, Walter J., 100
liberal secular democracy, 1
Libyan Revolution (1969), 246
Lilienthal, David E., 16, 151–152, 162–164, 166, 168, 170–173, 175–179, 231, 241, 248–249, 251
literacy, 2, 233
Little, Arthur D., 186
living standards, 16, 125, 180, 227

MacLeod, Thomas, 230–231, 242
Mahdavy, Hossein, 1, 4, 6, 16, 219, 243–244, 248, 252
Majidi, Abd al-Majid, 160, 248
Mansur, Hasan 'Ali, 210, 236, 239–240
market power, 14, 111, 198
Marshall Plan, 51, 54, 100
Marxist-Leninism, 34
Mattei, Enrico, 112, 185
Mayer, Eugene, 62
McAlister, Melani, 12
McCloy, John, 62, 64, 66–67, 236
McGhee, George C., 80–81, 93, 96, 99, 111, 158, 164, 178
McNamara, Robert, 223, 238
Mexico, 26–28, 88, 96, 107, 186
  constitution, 30
Meyer, Andre, 163, 228, 245
middle class, 2, 14, 123, 156, 176, 180, 203

Middle East, 4, 11, 23, 25, 28, 36, 42–43, 45, 47–48, 50–51, 70, 93, 95, 106, 111, 113, 120, 140, 144, 146–147, 157–158, 161, 164, 182, 186–187, 190, 196, 200, 202, 215–216, 231, 247, 250
Miklos, Jack, 250
military intervention, 31
military modernization, 250
Millspaugh, Arthur C., 21, 30, 37–40, 52, 63, 83, 89, 220, 232, 241, 250
Mina, Parviz, 108–109, 193, 196
Mīnā, Parviz, 92
mines, 53
Ministry of Fuel and Power, 108, 116
Mitchell, Timothy, 7
modernity, 8, 56, 250
modernization, 2, 17, 33, 55–56, 90, 152, 156–157, 215–216, 235, 240, 242, 244–245, 249, 252
modernization theory, 156–157, 215, 242, 250
monopoly, 22, 36, 42, 164
Mordad Coup, 118
Morris, Leland, 39
Morrison-Knudsen, 63–64
Mosaddeq, Mohammed, 16, 29, 34, 39, 43, 70, 77, 81–82, 86–107, 109–112, 114, 116–128, 131–145, 147–148, 154–156, 183, 188–189, 192, 195, 197, 203, 205, 211, 218, 223, 225–226
Moscow (Russia), 11, 43–44, 46–47, 91, 119, 142, 144, 147, 217
Mostowfi, Baqer, 109, 193
multilateral funding networks, 11
multinational capitalism, 8
Muqaddam, Ghulam-Reza, 214, 219
Muqaddam, Reza, 221–222, 226, 231, 243
Murray, Wallace, 36, 44
muvazanah-e manfi, 34

Naficy, Musharaf, 59, 78
Nasr, Taqi, 58, 67, 78, 81
Nasser, Abdel, 189, 195
national economy, 8, 215, 221, 245, 252
National Iranian Oil Company (NIOC), 92, 103, 108–109, 121, 145, 193–194, 196–198, 203, 205, 207–208, 223, 246
national security, 40, 137, 144, 173, 195, 217
nationalization, 14, 16, 31, 54, 77, 81–83, 85–88, 90–104, 106–107, 109, 111, 113, 116, 120, 127, 129–130, 138, 143, 145–147, 155, 188–189, 192–195, 200, 202, 205

Index

natural gas, 5, 167–169, 181
Near East Foundation, 162, 164
negative equilibrium, 34, 89, 91, 125
net exporter, 23
New Deal-era liberalism, 163
New Frontiersmen, 215, 224, 228, 232
New York City (United States), 163
New Yorker Magazine, 36
Nitze, Paul, 137
Nixon, Richard M., 246–247, 249
nongovernmental organization, (NGO), 9, 11
nonnuclear weapons systems, 247
Northrop Grumman, 251
nuclear device, 79
nuclear power, 247

Office of Strategic Services, 44
Oil and Gas Journal, 24
oil deposits, 7, 21, 23
oil diplomacy, 8
oil exports, 16, 123, 126
oil fields, 22, 26–28, 30, 33, 35, 40, 45, 48, 101, 167–168, 201, 216, 250
oil power, 247
oil production, 43, 51, 108, 113, 190, 192–195, 247, 252
oil scarcity ideology, 23
oil wealth, 4–5, 7, 9, 12–13, 52–54, 64, 151–152, 160, 245, 247
Oklahoma (U.S.), 28
oligopoly, 9–10, 13–16, 28, 47, 49, 51, 70, 75, 87–88, 93–94, 101–102, 108–109, 111, 115–117, 119–120, 138, 143–145, 182–186, 188–192, 194–197, 200, 203, 205, 208, 211–213, 246, 249, 251
Operation TPAJAX, 119, 128, 140–142, 144, 147, 151, 154, 239, 241
Organization of the Petroleum Exporting Countries (OPEC), 182–184, 189, 196–200, 202–203, 205–213
  First Crisis, 183–184
  Iran's joining, 182
  rise of, 16
Orient, 12, 36
Oriental Institute, 151
over-production, 22, 48
Overseas Consultants Inc. (OCI), 65–67, 74, 83–84, 135, 162, 237

Page, Howard, 199, 201, 212
Pahlavi, Mohammed Reza, 1–2, 4–5, 9–10, 13–16, 21–23, 29, 31–32, 34–35, 38, 41, 46–47, 49, 51, 53–54, 57–59, 68, 71–72, 75–77, 83–84, 88, 108, 118, 146, 148, 151–156, 158, 161–162, 166, 170, 172, 174–175, 177–182, 184, 193–194, 196–198, 203–204, 206–208, 212–214, 216, 218, 220, 225–228, 232–233, 240, 242, 245–247, 249–252
Pahlavism, 244, 249
paradox of plenty, 6
Parra, Francisco, 189
passive balance. *See muvazanah-e manfi*
peasant population, 4
Penrose, Edith, 188, 190, 252
Persia. *See* Iran
Persian Corridor, 35
Persian Gulf, 10, 31, 33, 42–45, 92, 186, 196, 247
petrochemical plants, 171
Petroleum Administration for Defense (PAD), 113–116
petro-nationalism, 9, 14, 16–17, 27–28, 32, 50–51, 71, 76, 86, 88, 108, 116, 182–184, 189, 194–198, 203, 208, 210–213, 250–252
petro-state, 5, 10, 15, 129, 213, 216, 248, 251
Pirnia, Husayn, 68
Plan Organization, 57, 59, 65–67, 74, 78–79, 82, 123, 132, 156, 158–161, 163, 168–170, 173, 175, 177–178, 214–215, 218, 221, 229–230, 234, 237, 248
Point Four, 119, 124–128, 139, 143, 162, 166, 225, 241
Polk, William R., 242
postwar international order, 13, 44
postwar petroleum order, 14, 51, 88, 95, 144
Potsdam (1945), 45
Prebisch, Raul, 195
price wars, 27
propaganda, 61, 98, 125, 141, 155, 169, 172, 181, 244
public health, 53
public–private cooperation, 24

Qarani, Valiollah, 172, 217
Qavam, Ahmed, 46, 49–50, 53, 57, 61, 119, 122, 137, 225

raw materials, 62
Razmara, Ali, 67, 80–82, 84, 90, 95, 107, 124, 158, 225–226
Red-Line Agreement, 28
rentier state, 4–6, 14, 248

rentier state thesis, 6
repression, 2, 6, 153
resource nationalism, 22, 27, 213
resource primitivism, 12, 108
Rhodesia, 114
Rieber, Torkild, 86, 105–106, 108–109
road construction, 80
Rockefeller, John D., 24, 64–65, 162, 249
  Standard Oil, 24, 41
Roosevelt, Franklin D., 35–38, 40, 42, 135, 141, 164, 183
Roosevelt, Kermit, 95, 128, 141–142, 182, 203
Rostow, Walt W., 40, 157, 224, 226
Rouhani, Hasan, 252
Ruhani, Fu'ad, 86, 183–184, 193, 197–199, 201–210, 213
rural poverty, 4, 128
Rusk, Dean, 212, 230–231, 235, 239
Russia, 29, 35

San Francisco, 151, 161, 203
sanitation, 80, 124, 171, 218, 241
Sanjabi, Karim, 61, 66, 91
Saudi Arabia, 42, 45, 48, 81, 97, 113, 182, 186, 188–189, 191, 195, 198, 200–201, 204, 206–207, 209, 211
Sayre, Joel, 36
Sazman-e Barnameh, 57
Schayegh, Cyrus, 155
Schwarzkopf. Colonel H. Norman, 35
Scott, James, 163
Seven Sisters, 7, 185, 191, 200, 213
Seymour, Ian, 186
Shah of Iran. *See* Pahlavi, Mohammed Reza
Shah, Reza, 15, 29–34, 56–59, 68, 71, 97, 154, 199, 201–202, 208, 251
Shahmirzadi, Hasan, 161, 179
Shell Corporation, 25, 28, 43, 48, 113, 185, 193, 201–202
Shi'a clergy, 56, 155, 233
Shinwell, Emanuel, 45
Sinclair Oil, 43
Snodgrass, C. Stribling, 115
social revolution, 9, 16
South America, 112, 163
sovereign independence, 30
sovereignty, 8, 15, 26–27, 44, 89, 207
Soviet Union, 9–11, 34–35, 41, 43–47, 49, 55, 91, 112, 121, 131, 142, 153, 190, 194, 217, 240, 250
  nuclear tests, 153
Stalin, Joseph, 37, 45–46, 142
Standard-Vacuum Oil Company (StanVac), 41–43

Status of Forces Agreement (SOFA), 238
Stokes, Sir Richard, 101–103, 116
Suez (Egypt), 94, 114, 189, 195
sugar cane, 166
Sulzberger, Arthur H., 172
Supplemental Agreement, 60, 75, 77–78, 81–82, 90, 130
Switzerland, 57
  St. Moritz, 246

Tanzer, Michael, 8
Taqizadeh, Sayyed Hasan, 29, 33, 71
taxes, 56, 59, 72, 76, 129, 188, 190, 205
Teagle, Walter, 28
Technical Cooperation Administration (TCA), 124, 126–127
technocracy, 10, 13–14, 17, 23, 54, 58–59, 66, 83, 90, 133, 151, 158, 160–161, 164, 172, 214–216, 226, 229, 232, 235–237, 239, 242–243, 245, 248, 250–251
technology, 56, 116, 158, 161
Tennessee Valley Authority (TVA), 55, 151, 164, 166, 171–172, 179
Texas (U.S.), 24, 26, 28, 195
Texas Oil Company (Texaco), 24, 48, 86, 185, 201
Teymurtash, Abdolhossein, 30–31, 92
The Economist, 249
Third World, 147
Thornburg, Max, 54, 61, 64–66, 73–74, 79–84, 99, 124, 135–137, 139–141, 144, 147–148, 162, 237, 250–251
tobacco, 29
Tokyo (Japan), 2
trade deficit, 62, 129, 247
Trans-Iranian Railroad, 33
Truman, Harry S., 45, 47, 49, 54, 62, 79, 87, 93, 95–97, 99, 105, 121, 124, 129, 134, 136–137
Turkey, 45, 49, 54, 56, 252

U.S.–Iranian relations, 10, 54, 232, 238, 240, 250
United Nations, 45–47, 62, 104, 164
  Security Council, 99, 104, 134, 139–140, 189, 217
United States, 24, 115
  American model, 56
  Army, 35
  energy security, 41
  expertise, 12, 52, 56, 67
  financial aid, 54, 56, 61, 230
  foreign advisors, 1, 35, 37, 39, 51, 152

Index

foreign assistance, 12, 40, 52, 55, 156, 162, 227, 232, 242
Iran policy, 36, 41–42, 93, 127
Joint Chiefs, 230
military aid, 47, 61, 148, 216, 224, 230–231
National Guard, 28
Office of Petroleum Affairs, 27
petroleum reserves, 23
Policy Planning Staff, 242
policymakers, 3, 9, 11–12, 39, 47, 50, 67, 96, 105, 143, 181, 195
postwar America, 157
State Department, 27, 36–39, 42, 44, 47, 49, 51, 64, 112, 133, 137, 158, 224, 228, 239
technical assistance, 238, 241
urbanization, 218, 248
USAID, 238

Venezuela, 27–28, 72, 76, 182, 186–187, 195, 199–200, 209
vertical integration, 24
Vietnam War, 249
Vitalis, Robert, 7

wartime oil policy, 41
Washington, D.C., 11–12, 24, 27, 41, 47, 51, 81, 104, 112–113, 122, 127–128, 130, 134, 140, 173, 195, 203, 205, 216, 221–222, 225–226, 228, 230–235, 244–246

weaponry, 34, 137, 140, 161, 174, 238–239, 251
well-digging, 80, 124
Western capital, 9, 14–15
Western Europe, 51, 54, 62, 113, 185, 190
White Revolution, 1, 4–5, 17, 204, 210, 215–216, 232–235, 237, 239, 241–242, 244–245, 248, 251
Whitehall (Great Britain), 31
women's suffrage, 233–234
World Bank, 46, 49, 54, 58–59, 61–64, 66, 75, 79, 81, 83–84, 86, 104, 108–110, 115–116, 120, 124, 131, 135, 151, 157, 159, 162, 171, 173, 175–176, 178–179, 214, 218, 220, 227, 236–237, 241, 243, 251
world oil consumption, 24
World War I, 24–25
World War II, 10, 13, 41, 55, 61, 64, 86, 91, 191, 232
    Eastern Front, 35

Yamani, Ahmed Zaki, 198, 206, 209
Young, T. Cuyler, 224, 240, 248

Zahedi, Fazlollah, 118, 136, 141, 145, 154
Zendebad shah!, 118